The Manhattan Project

A Documentary Introduction to the Atomic Age

The Manhattan Project

A Documentary Introduction to the Atomic Age

Edited by

MICHAEL B. STOFF
The University of Texas at Austin

JONATHAN F. FANTON
New School For Social Research

R. HAL WILLIAMS
Southern Methodist University

McGRAW-HILL, INC.
New York   St. Louis   San Francisco   Auckland   Bogotá
Caracas   Hamburg   Lisbon   London   Madrid   Mexico
Milan   Montreal   New Delhi   Paris   San Juan
São Paulo   Singapore   Sydney   Tokyo   Toronto

For our students, past and present

THE MANHATTAN PROJECT
A Documentary Introduction to the Atomic Age

1 2 3 4 5 6 7 8 9 0 MAL MAL 9 5 4 3 2 1 0

ISBN 0-07-557209-5

The editors were David Follmer, Christopher J. Rogers, Niels Aaboe, and Edwin Hanson;
the design was done by Caliber/Phoenix Color Corp.;
the production supervisor was Phil Galea;
Malloy Lithographing, Inc., was printer and binder.

Library of Congress Cataloging-in-Publication Data

The Manhattan project: a documentary introduction to the atomic age
    / edited by Michael B. Stoff, Jonathan F. Fanton, R. Hal Williams.
        p.   cm.
    Includes bibliographical references.
    ISBN 0-07-557209-5
    1. Manhattan Project (U.S.)–History. 2. Atomic bomb–United
States–History.   I. Stoff, Michael B.
QC773.3. U5M26   1991
355.8' 25119–dc20   90-43752

About the Editors

MICHAEL B. STOFF is Associate Professor of History at the University of Texas at Austin, where he directs the honors program in history. The recipient of a Ph.D. from Yale University, he wrote *Oil, War, and American Security: The Search for a National Policy on Foreign Oil, 1941–1947* and is coauthor of *Nation of Nations: A Narrative History of the American Republic.* He recently received the President's Associates Teaching Excellence Award at the University of Texas at Austin.

JONATHAN F. FANTON received his Ph.D. from Yale University and is Professor of History at the New School for Social Research.

R. HAL WILLIAMS, Professor of History At Southern Methodist University, received his Ph.D. from Yale University in 1968. His books include *The Democratic Party and California Politics, 1880-1896* (1973); *Years of Decision: American Politics in the 1890s* (1975); and *America: Past and Present* (1984). In addition to receiving awards for outstanding teaching at both Yale and SMU, Williams has received grants from the American Philosophical Society and the National Endowment for the Humanities. He is currently working on a biography of James G. Blaine, the late nineteenth century presidential candidate, Speaker of the House and Secretary of State.

Document Sources and Credits

1. Roosevelt Papers. President's Secretary's File (PSF), Safe File, Alexander Sachs Folder, Franklin D. Roosevelt Library (FDRL), Hyde Park, N.Y.
2. Roosevelt Papers. PSF, Safe File, Sachs Folder, FDRL, Hyde Park, N.Y.
3. Vannevar Bush-James B. Conant Files. Office of Scientific Research and Development, Section-1 File (Record Group 227) [hereafter cited as Bush-Conant Files, OSRD, S-1 Historical File], National Archives.
4. Roosevelt Papers. PSF, Vannevar Bush File, FDRL, Hyde Park, N.Y.
5. U. S. Department of State, *Foreign Relations of the United States: Conference at Washington, 1941-1942* (Washington, D.C.: Government Printing Office, 1968), p. 432.
6. Henry L. Stimson Papers. Yale University Library, New Haven, Conn.
7. Atomic Energy Commission, Hearing before the Personnel Security Board,"In the Matter of J. Robert Oppenheimer," 12 April through 6 May 1954.
8. Harry Hopkins Papers. FDRL, Hyde Park, N.Y.
9. U.S. Department of State, *Foreign Relations of the United States: Conferences at Washington and Quebec, 1943* (Washington, D.C.: Government Printing Office, 1970), p. 630.
10. Elting Morison, *Turmoil and Tradition*. Copyright © 1960 by Elting E. Morison. Copyright renewed © 1988 by Elting E. Morison. Reprinted by permission of Houghton Mifflin Company.
11. Roosevelt Papers. PSF, Safe File, Sachs Folder, FDRL, Hyde Park, N.Y.
12. U.S. Department of State: *Foreign Relations of the United States: Conferences at Washington and Quebec, 1943* (Washington, D.C.: Government Printing Office, 1970).
13. Roosevelt Papers. Map Room, FDRL, Hyde Park, N.Y.
14. Margaret M. Gowing, *Britain and Atomic Energy, 1939-1945* (New York: St. Martin's, 1964), Appendix.
15. Henry L. Stimson Papers. Yale University Library, New Haven, Conn.
16. Roosevelt Papers. PSF, Safe File, Sachs Folder, FDRL, Hyde Park, N.Y.
17. Henry L. Stimson Papers. Yale University Library, New Haven, Conn.
18. Harrison-Bundy File, Folder 62. Records of the Office of the Chief of Engineers, Manhattan Engineer District (Record Group 77) [hereafter cited as Manhattan Engineer District Records], National Archives.
19. Henry L. Stimson Papers. Yale University Library, New Haven, Conn.
20. Henry L. Stimson Papers. Yale University Library, New Haven, Conn.
21. Harrison-Bundy File. Manhattan Engineer District Records, National Archives.
22. Henry L. Stimson Papers. Yale University Library, New Haven, Conn.
23. *Diplomatic History of the Manhattan Project*. Manhattan Engineer District Records, National Archives.
24. Roosevelt Papers. PSF, Frankfurter Folder, FDRL, Hyde Park, N.Y.
25. J. Robert Oppenheimer Papers. Library of Congress, Washington, D.C.
26. President's Map Room Papers. Naval Aid's File, Box 172, General Folder, FDRL, Hyde Park, N.Y.
27. Atomic Energy Commission (A.E.C.) Files, Doc. 185. OSRD, S-1 Historical File, National Archives.
28. Doc 186, OSRD, S-1 Historical File, A.E.C. Files,National Archives.
29. Doc 187, OSRD, S-1 Historical File, A.E.C. Files,National Archives.
30. Harrison-Bundy File, Folder 69. Manhattan Engineer District Records, National Archives.
31. Henry L. Stimson Papers. Yale University Library, New Haven, Conn.
32. Henry L. Stimson Papers. Yale University Library, New Haven, Conn.
33. Harrison-Bundy File, Folder 2. Manhattan Engineer District Records, National Archives.
34. Henry L. Stimson Papers. Yale University Library, New Haven, Conn.
35. Prem 3/139/6, British Crown copyright material in the Public Record Office, London, reproduced by permission of the Controller of HM Stationery Office.
36. Front page of the *New York Times*, 13 April, 1945. Copyright © 1945 by The New York Times Company. Reprinted by permission.
37. Henry L. Stimson Papers. Yale University Library, New Haven, Conn.
38. Harrison-Bundy File, Folder 60. Manhattan Engineer District Records, National Archives.
39. Top Secret, Box 3, Committee Meetings, Manhattan District Records, National Archives.
40. Henry L. Stimson Papers. Yale University Library, New Haven, Conn.
41. Harrison-Bundy File, Folder 100. Manhattan Engineer District Records, National Archives.
42. Henry L. Stimson Papers. Yale University Library, New Haven, Conn.

43. Arthur H. Compton, *Atomic Quest* (New York: Oxford, 1956), pp. 219, 2236-244.

44. Harrison-Bundy File, Folder 100. Manhattan Engineer District Records, National Archives.

45. Henry L. Stimson Papers. Yale University Library, New Haven, Conn.

46. Harrison-Bundy File. Manhattan Engineer District Records, National Archives.

47. Secretary of War's Safe File. Records of the Office of the Secretary of War (Record Group 107), National Archives.

48. Harrison-Bundy File. Manhattan Engineer District Records, National Archives.

49. Barton J. Bernstein, ed., *The Atomic Bomb: The Critical Issues* (Boston: Little, Brown, 1976), pp.25-28.

50. Harrison-Bundy File. Manhattan Engineer District Records, National Archives.

51. Harrison-Bundy File. Folder 76, Manhattan Engineer District Records, National Archives.

52. Records of the War Department, General and Specific Staffs (Record Group 165), National Archives.

53. Henry L. Stimson Papers. Yale University Library, New Haven, Conn.

54. Harrison-Bundy File, Folder 100. Manhattan Engineer District Records, National Archives.

55. Harrison-Bundy File, Folder 77. Manhattan Engineer District Records, National Archives.

56. Harrison-Bundy File, Folder 77. Manhattan Engineer District Records, National Archives.

57. Henry L. Stimson Papers. Yale University Library, New Haven, Conn.

58. U.S. Department of State, *Foreign Relations of the United States: Conference at Berlin, 1945* (Washington, D.C.: Government Printing Office, 1960)vol.1, pp. 888-892

59. Henry L. Stimson Papers, Yale University Library, New Haven, Conn.

60. Harrison-Bundy File, Folder 71. Manhattan Engineer District Records, National Archives.

61. Harrison-Bundy File, Folder 76. Manhattan Engineer District Records, National Archives. See also: Farrington Daniel and A. Compton, "Poll of Scientists at Chicago, July 1945, "Bulletin of Atomic Scientists, February 1948

62. Harrison-Bundy File, Folder 71. Manhattan Engineer District Records, National Archives.

63. (Record Group 218), Records of the U.S. Joint Chiefs of Staff, p. 10. C.C.S. 643/3 *Estimate of Enemy Situation* (as of 6 July 1945) C.C.S. 381 (6-4-43).

64. Harrison-Bundy File. Manhattan Engineer District Records, National Archives.

65. Harrison-Bundy File. Manhattan Engineer District Records, National Archives.

66. Henry L. Stimson Papers, Yale University Library, New Haven, Conn.

67. Henry L. Stimson Papers, Yale University Library, New Haven, Conn.

68. Top Secret. Manhattan Engineer District Records, National Archives.

69. Henry L. Stimson Papers. Yale University Library, New Haven, Conn.

70. Harrison-Bundy File, Folder 100. Manhattan Engineer District Records, National Archives.

71. Henry L. Stimson Papers. Yale University Library, New Haven, Conn.

72. Henry L. Stimson Papers. Yale University Library, New Haven, Conn.

73. Henry L. Stimson Papers. Yale University Library, New Haven, Conn.

74. U.S. Department of State, *Foreign Relations of the United States: Conference at Berlin* (Washington, D.C.: Government Printing Office,1960) vol. 2, pp. 1474-76.

75. James Forrestal, *The Forrestal Diaries*, Walter Mills and E. S. Duffield, eds (New York: Viking, 1951), p. 78

76. Harry S. Truman Memoirs, (New York: Doubleday, 1955), vol. 1, pp. 415-421.

77. Front page of the *New York Times*, 7 August 1945. Copyright © 1945 by The New York Times Company. Reprinted by permission.

78. M. Hachiya: *Hiroshima Diary, The Journal of a Japanese Physician,* August 6-September 30, 1945. Translated by Dr. Warner Lee Wells. Copyright © 1955, Chapel Hill: The University of North Carolina Press. Reprinted by permission.

79. Top Secret. Manhattan Engineer District Records, National Archives.

80. Front page of the *New York Times,* 9 August 1945. Copyright © 1945 by The New York Times Company. Reprinted by permission.

81. Top Secret. Manhattan Engineer District Records, National Archives.

82. Henry L. Stimson Papers. Yale University Library, New Haven, Conn.

83. Records of Defense Atomic Support Agency (Record Group 374), National Archives.

84. U.S. Strategic Bombing Survey, *The Effects of Atomic Bombs on Hiroshima and Nagasaki,* Summary Report (Pacific War) (Washington, D.C.: Government Printing Office, 1946), pp. 22-25.

85. U.S. Department of State: *Foreign Relations of the United States: vol. 6, The British Commonwealth: The Far East,* 1945 (Washington, D.C. Government Printing Office) pp. 472-473

86. John M. Blum, ed, *The Price of Vision: The Diary of Henry A. Wallace 1942-1946.* Copyright © 1973 by the Estate of Henry A. Wallace and John Martin Blum. Reprinted by permission of Houghton Mifflin Company.

87. U.S. Department of State, *Foreign Relations of the United States: vol. 6, The British Commonwealth: The Far East, 1945* (Washington, D.C. Government Printing Office)p. 627, pp. 631-632.

88. U.S. Department of State, *Foreign Relations of the United States: vol. 6, The British Commonwealth: The Far East, 1945* (Washington, D.C. Government Printing Office) pp. 662-663.

89. Harrison-Bundy File. Manhattan Engineer District Records, National Archives.

90. Harrison-Bundy File. Manhattan Engineer District Records, National Archives.

91. Henry L. Stimson Papers. Yale University Library, New Haven, Conn.

92. Groves, 201 File. Manhattan Engineer District Records, National Archives.

93. George H. Gallup, *The Gallup Poll, Public Opinion, 1933-1971* (New York: Random House, 1972), vol. 1. pp. 521-522.

94. U.S. Strategic Bombing Survey, *Japan's Struggle to End the War* (Washington, D.C.Government Printing Office, 1946), p. 13.

95. Paul Fussell, "Hiroshima: A Soldier's View," *The New Republic*, 22 and 29 August 1981. Copyright © 1981 by the publisher. Reprinted by permission. Appendix. Manhattan Engineer District Records, National Archives.

Contents

Part 1

CREATION, ORGANIZATION, AND SECURITY   15

Part 2

QUEST FOR POSTWAR PLANNING   61

Part 3

PLANNING THE DROP   89

Part 4

THE SCIENTISTS' DEBATE   135

Part 5

SUCCESSFUL TEST, THE POTSDAM SUMMIT, AND PREPARATIONS FOR USE   179

Part 6

THE DROPS AND THE SURRENDER OF JAPAN   219

Part 7

AFTERMATH   251

Chronology, 1938-1945

Atomic Developments	War Developments

1938

December	Nuclear fission discovered in Germany.	September 29	Munich Pact, ceding Sudetenland of Czechoslovakia to Germany, signed.

1939

August 2	Albert Einstein writes President Roosevelt of need for an American atomic bomb project.	August 23	German-Russian nonaggresion pact signed.
October 21	First meeting of President's advisory committee on uranium.	August 24	British-Polish mutual assistance pact signed.
		September 1	Germany invades Poland, setting off Second World War.

1940

		June 22	France surrenders to Germany.
		Summer-Fall	Battle of Britain.
		September 2	American destroyers exchanged for British bases.
		September 27	Germany, Italy, and Japan sign Tripartite Pact, creating Triple Alliance.

1941

		March 11	Congress approves lend-lease assistance to aid Allies.

Atomic Developments	War Developments

1941 cont'd

April 13	Russian-Japanes five-year neutrality pact signed.
June 22	Germany invades Russia.
December 7	Japanese attack American base at Pearl Harbor.
December 8	United States declares war on Japan.
December 11	Germany declares war on United States.
May 6	Fall of the Philippines to Japanese.

1942

September 17	Leslie R. Groves appointed military chief of newly created Manhattan Engineer District (MED).
December 2	Scientists under Enrico Fermi produce first self-sustaining chain reaction.

1943

January 14-23	Casablanca conference: Roosevelt and Churchill announce policy of "unconditional surrender."
May 13	Surrender of Axis forces in North Africa.
August 14-24	Quebec Conference: Roosevelt and Churchill negotiate Quebec Agreement.
September 8	Surrender of Italy.
September 18	Roosevelt and Churchill meet at Hyde Park and agree on atomic policy.
November 22-26	Cairo conference: Roosevelt, Churchill, and Chiang Kai-shek meet to discuss postwar far eastern policy.

Atomic Developments	War Developments

1943 cont'd

| | | November 28-December 7 | Teheran conference: First wartime meeting of "BigThree" (Roosevelt, Churchill, and Stalin), who agree on Anglo-American invasion of western Europe and on postwar international security organization. |

1944

| | | June 6 | Allied invasion of Normandy, France (D day). |

| | | December 16-26 | Battle of the Bulge. |

1945

| | | February 4-9 | Yalta conference: Roosevelt, Churchill, and Stalin meet for extensive planning for postwar Europe and Asia; Stalin promises Russian entry into war against Japan two or three months after defeat of Germany. |

| | | April 7 | Japanese Prime Minister Suzuki forms new cabinetto bring war to end. |

| April 25 | Secretary of War Stimson informs Truman of Manhattan Project. | April 12 | Roosevelt dies; Truman becomes President. |

| May 9 | Interim Committee to advise President on atomic weapons holds first meeting. | May 7 | Surrender of Germany. |

| June 12 | Franck Report is delivered to office of secretary of war, and its substance is communicated to Scientific Advisory Panel. | | |

| | | June 22 | Japanese Supreme War Council approves effort to negotiate peace and to seek Russian mediation. |

<u>**Atomic Developments**</u>

<u>**1945 cont'd**</u>

<u>**War Developments**</u>

	July 12 — Japanese Foreign Minister Togo instructs Ambassador Sato in Moscow to implore Russians to mediate end to war.
July 16 — Successful test of atomic bomb at Alamogordo, New Mexico.	
	July 17–August 2 — Potsdam Conference: First wartime meeting of Truman, Stalin, and Churchill (replaced by Attlee); inconclusive talks about postwar settlements; on July 24, Truman informs Stalin that United States has developed a "new weapon of unusual destructive force."
July 25 — General Carl Spaatz, commander of U.S. Strategic Air Force, receives directive from Truman ordering 509 Composite Group to "deliver its first special bomb as soon as weather will permit visual bombing after about 3 August 1945."	July 26 — Potsdam Declaration is issued.
	July 28 — Japanese Prime Minister Suzuki calls Potsdam Declaration "unworthy of notice."
August 6 — Uranium bomb (Little Boy) is dropped on Hiroshima.	
	August 8 — Russia declares war on Japan and invades Manchuria the next day.
August 9 — Plutonium bomb (Fat Man) is dropped on Nagasaki.	
	August 10 — Japan offers to surrender.
	August 14 — Japan accepts Allied terms of surrender.
	August 30 — U.S. occupation forces land in Japan.
	September 2 — Formal surrender of Japan.

Major Characters

Anderson, John — Chemist by training, director of the Imperial Chemical Company and Lord President of the British Council.

Arneson, R. Gordon — Lieutenant in U.S. Army and recording secretary of Interim Committee.

Arnold, Henry H. (Hap) — General in the U.S. Army and commander of the U.S. Army Air Corps.

Attlee, Clement — British prime minister elected during the Potsdam conference in the summer of 1945.

Bard, Ralph A. — Under secretary of the Navy and member of the S-1 Interim Committee.

Barkley, Alben — Democratic senator from Kentucky and Senate majority leader (1937-1946); later became Vice President.

Bohr, Niels — Danish physicist.

Bundy, Harvey H. — Special assistant to Secretary of War Henry L. Stimson.

Bush, Vannevar — Director of the OSRD (1941-1946) and president of the Carnegie Institution.

Byrnes, James F. — Director of the Office of War Mobilization (1943-1945), adviser to Presidents Roosevelt and Truman, and secretary of state (1945-1947).

Cherwell, Lord (Frederick Lindemann) — Personal science adviser to Churchill.

Chiang Kai-shek — Leader of the Chinese Nationalists.

Churchill, Sir Winston — Prime minister of Great Britain (1940-1945; 1951-1955).

Clayton, William L. — Assistant secretary of state and member of the Interim Committee.

Compton, Arthur H. — Nobel prize-winning physicist (1927), professor of physics at the University of Chicago, and, during the war, director of the "Metallurgical Laboratory" at the University of Chicago and a member of the Scientific Advisory Panel to the Interim Committee.

Compton, Karl T. — President of the Massachusetts Institute of Technology and chief of field service in the OSRD.

Conant, James B. — Assistant to Vannevar Bush, president of Harvard University, and chairman of the National Defense Research Committee (1941-1946), later known as OSRD.

de Gaulle, Charles — Leader of the Free French.

Einstein, Albert — Nobel prize-winning physicist (1921) driven from Germany and stripped of his citizenship in 1933. Became an American citizen in 1940.

Engel, Albert J.	Republican congressman from Michigan (1935-1951) and member of House Subcommittee on Military Appropriations.
Farrell, Thomas F.	Brigadier general in the U.S. Army, deputy of General Leslie Groves, and director, along with Groves, of the Target Committee.
Fermi, Enrico	Italian-born physicist, Nobel prize winner (1938), professor of physics at Columbia University (1935-1945), the first to achieve a sustained chain reaction (1942), and director of research at the "Metallurgical Laboratory."
Forrestal, James V.	Secretary of the Navy (1944-1947) and member of the "Committee of Three."
Franck, James:	German chemist and Nobel laureate (1925); during the war associate director of the chemistry division of Metlab.
Frankfurter, Felix	Supreme Court justice (1939-1962) and confidant of President Franklin Roosevelt.
Grew, Joseph	Under secretary of state (1944-1945) and member, along with Secretary of the Navy James Forrestal and Secretary of War Henry Stimson, of the "Committee of Three".
Groves, Leslie R.	Brigadier general in the U.S. Army in charge of the Manhattan Project.
Hachiya, Michihiko	Physician and victim of Hiroshima bombing.
Halifax, Earl of (Edward Frederick Lindley Wood)	British ambassador to the United States.
Harriman, William Averill	American ambassador to Russia (1943-1946).
Harrison, George L.	President of New York Life Insurance Company serving during the war as special assistant to Secretary of War Henry Stimson.
Hirohito	Emperor of Japan.
Hopkins, Harry	Special assistant to President Roosevelt.
Joliot-Curie, Frederic	French physicist whose seminal work on fission contributed to the creation of the Manhattan Project.
King, Ernest J.	Fleet admiral in the U.S. Navy, first commander-in-chief of the U.S. fleet (1941), chief of naval operations (1942-1945), and a vital member of the joint chiefs of staff during the war.
Konoye, Prince Fumimaro	Special envoy for the Emperor of Japan.
Lawrence, Ernest Orlando	Nobel prize-winning physicist (1939), director of the Radiation Laboratory at the University of California at Berkeley (1936-1958), and member of the Scientific Advisory Panel to the Interim Committee.
Leahy, William D.	Admiral serving as chief liaison officer to the joint chiefs of staff.
Lovett, Robert A.	Assistant secretary of war for air (1941-1945).
Lowe, Frank	Brigadier general assigned as executive officer to the Senate's Special Committee Investigating the National Defense Program.
MacArthur, Douglas	General of the U.S. Army, supreme commander of forces in the southwestern Pacific and later of the Allied forces during the occupation of Japan (1945-1951).
McCormack, John	Democratic congressman from Massachusetts (1928-1971) and, during the war, House majority leader.

Marshall, George C.	Army chief of staff (1939-1945).
Martin, Joseph	Republican congressman from Massachusetts (1925-1967) and leader of the Republican minority in the House of Representatives.
May, Andrew Jackson	Democratic congressman from Kentucky (1931-1947) and chairman of the House Committee on Military Affairs.
Murray, Philip	Successor to John L. Lewis as president of Congress of Industrial Organizations (1940) and, two years later, militant president of the United Steel Workers of America (1942-1952).
Nimitz, Chester	Fleet admiral of the U.S. Navy and head of naval fighting forces in the Pacific.
Oppenheimer, J. Robert	American physicist and director of the atomic energy research project at Los Alamos, New Mexico (1942-1945). Later chairman of the General Advisory Committee of the A.E.C. (1947-1953).
Patterson, Robert P.	Under secretary of war (1940-1945); later secretary of war.
Purnell, William R.	Rear admiral in the U.S. Navy and member of the Military Policy Committee.
Ramsey, Norman F.	Physicist from Columbia University and member of the Target Committee.
Rayburn, Sam	Democratic congressman from Texas and speaker of the House of Representatives (1940-1946, 1949-1961).
Roosevelt, Franklin D.	President of the United States (1933-1945).
Sachs, Alexander	Russian-born Lehman Corporation economist instrumental in the creation of the advisory committee on uranium.
Smith, Harold	Director of the Bureau of the Budget.
Spaatz, Carl	Commanding general of the United States Strategic Air Forces.
Stalin, Joseph	Premier of Russia.
Stimson, Henry L.	Secretary of war (1940-1945).
Suzuki, Kantaro	Japanese prime minister who came to power in April 1945.
Szilard, Leo	Hungarian-born physicist, developer (along with Enrico Fermi) of the chain reaction system, and during the war, a member of Metlab.
Taber, John	Republican congressman from New York (1923-1963) and member of the House Committee on Military Appropriations.
Thomas, Elbert	Democratic senator from Utah (1933-1951) and chairman of the Senate Subcommittee on Military Appropriations.
Togo, Shigenori	Foreign minister of the Suzuki government in Japan.
Truman, Harry S.	Democratic senator from Missouri (1934-1944) and, for most of the war, chairman of the Senate's Special Committee Investigating the National Defense Program. Elected Vice President in 1944 and elevated to the presidency upon the death of Franklin Roosevelt on April 12, 1944.
Urey, Harold C.	Nobel prize-winning (1934) professor of chemistry at Columbia (1934-1945) and research director of the Manhattan Project (1942-1945).
Wallace, Henry W.	Vice President of the United States (1941-1945); secretary of commerce (1945).
White, Wallace	Republican senator from Maine (1931-1949) and leader of the Republican minority in the Senate.

Preface

Good history begins with a good story, and there is none better than the story of the Manhattan Project. It contains all the elements of high drama: an earth-shaking discovery; a desperate race for life or death; a climax that changed human affairs—all played out on a global stage in the most fearsome war ever waged.

No novelist could have created a more exciting plot or, for that matter, more memorable characters. There are the scientists, who stand at the very center of the Manhattan Project, seeking to penetrate the inner structure of the atom. In it, they find a bewitching beauty, but when its energy is unleashed, when its eager inventors confront the bomb's incredible destructiveness, they recoil. Albert Einstein gropes for the right English words to urge the President to make a Uranium bomb, then, years afterward, disowns the creation in disgust. Danish physicist Niels Bohr travels across the Atlantic to enlist the aid of scientists, only later to repeat the journey with dark prophecies of an arms race. J. Robert Oppenheimer drives himself to exhaustion to solve the puzzle of how to sustain an explosive nuclear reaction. Yet as he watches the first atomic fireball rise from the New Mexican desert, he thinks only of death and destruction.

One step removed, possessing a different kind of power, are the bureaucrats. They, too, must readjust their calculations as the atomic bomb changes the hand they hold. At first they imagine the weapon as nothing more than a big bomb. But soon they realize that the quantitative jump they can imagine so easily is, in fact, a frightening qualitative leap. Leslie Groves—soldier, super organizer, master of the Manhattan Project—literally sees as much. He lies near the test site, burying his face in the sand, awe-struck at the blast. It is brighter than anything he has ever beheld, brighter than the sun, like "several suns at midday." Secretary of War Henry Stimson, eighty years old and ill, sees a new danger in the weapon on which he has hung so many hopes. It is a double-edged sword, he warns, "a Frankenstein which would eat us up or . . . a project 'by which the peace of the world would be helped in becoming secure.' "

Farthest from the sunburst at ground zero but at the center of political power are the Presidents. They control a weapon whose astonishing force they have never seen but whose use, they slowly realize, will change everything. Franklin Roosevelt decides to build the bomb but refuses to say whether he will use it. With the project near completion, he dies unexpectedly, before the device can be tested. Four months later, as the war with Japan draws to a close, Harry Truman faces a terrible choice—to drop a bomb that may vaporize a city or to rely on a conventional invasion that may cost millions of lives. Still a novice President, he nevertheless appreciates the stakes implied by the "possession of a weapon that would not only revolutionize war but could alter the course of history and civilization."

Such a story and such characters have long fascinated historians. They have told the tale scores of times and analyzed it over and over again. In their hands, the Manhattan Project has served as a lens through which to examine the triumphs and tensions of the Grand Alliance, the seeds of the cold war, and the emergence of a powerful new trinity—government, industry, and science.

This version is different. It covers many of the same themes but relies on raw documents to do it. The story unfolds in the words of those who were there. They speak with their own voices and from their own points of view. Sometimes their message is discreet and personal, conveyed in a diary entry or a letter. Sometimes it is broad and corporate, communicated through a position paper, the minutes of a committee meeting, or the results of a survey. Thus, this collection serves a dual purpose: to tell the story of an important wartime episode, the Manhattan Project, from as many perspectives and in as much detail as space permits; and to give readers the chance to do some history on their own, using the evidence in its most original form.

By piecing together the story and puzzling out its meaning, readers can begin to understand not just the Manhattan Project but history itself. They can be their own historians as they confront the sources and try to make sense of them. In the process, they may gain some valuable insights: that history is not a static record of past things but a creative act; that historians are not mere "messengers from the past," shuttling back to the future with news of what happened long ago, but detectives and analysts, ferreting out information, making assessments, and searching for meaning.

Some explanation of strategies, organization, and the division of labors is in order. The present book originated in a collection of documents assembled by Jonathan F. Fanton and R. Hal Williams for a history course at Yale University. Source books often cover several events, presenting only a few documents for each. This book contains a large number of documents that follow a single episode from start to finish. The documents lead to no particular conclusion but leave room for readers to arrive at conclusions of their own.

It took Fanton and Williams countless hours to track down the original group of documents. Encyclopedic coverage was never the goal. The Manhattan Project has generated enough material to fill a library, and to cover it in detail would require more space than was available. Instead, adequacy, balance, and variety governed the search. There are enough documents here to tell the story, at least in its rough outlines and from several points of view.

Over the years, succeeding generations of instructors inherited the collection and added documents to it. When Michael Stoff received it, the manuscript had grown to nearly 400 pages. He added still more documents and spent the next several years shaping them into a book. That entailed removing about half of the documents, dividing them into seven sections, writing a general introduction and seven historiographical essays, and creating a timeline, cast of characters, bibliography, and set of maps. (In the college edition, he also prepared groups of study questions to guide students through the documents.)

For the sake of clarity, the documents are arranged in chronological order and not in order of their discovery. Arranging the documents, like selecting them, risks the charge of cutting the historical record to suit interpretive tastes. The hope is that the wieldiness of the collection and the coherence it achieves outweigh any risk. Great care, moreover, has been taken to avoid emphasizing any single interpretation.

To distinguish the collection still further, the intention was to have the documents photographed so readers could encounter them just as historians do. Unfortunately, that process took far too long. Worse still, many of the photographs turned out to be illegible. To preserve the look of the originals, the collection instead relies on meticulously reproduced facsimiles. Whenever possible, these reproductions duplicate the originals, including even typographical and spelling errors. A few of the documents are typeset, but most are near-exact reproductions. In many cases the documents have been tinted to achieve the look of age. Four typewriters from the 1940s, keyed to the original typefaces, were used to recreate diary entries, letters, memoranda, reports, cables, and minutes of committee meetings. The letterheads, classification stamps, even the marginal notations and signatures have been reproduced.

The result is a unique collection that presents a representative sample of the evidence as historians themselves encounter it. The facsimiles even offer a taste of the illicit pleasures available in the course of the historian's working day. Who, after all, can turn away from a letter or memorandum, worn brown with time, bearing a "Top Secret" stamp or the initials of a high-ranking official? There is a seductiveness in watching fallible men and women come into possession of immense power, all under the cloak of secrecy. That seductiveness—even of watching the drama, to say nothing of acting in it—should perhaps give us all pause.

Grants from the University Research Institute and the Vice President's Fund at the University of Texas at Austin furnished Michael Stoff with valuable time for turning a pile of documents into a book. Additional thanks to Gary Clifford, James Davidson, Jim Holmes, Mark Lytle, Michael Sherry, Allan Winkler, and the legions of students who offered their suggestions over the years. In one way or another, all helped to make this a better book. Thanks also to Niels Aaboe, Larry Goldberg, Ed Hanson, and David Follmer at McGraw-Hill for sheparding the project through the last crucial stages. Finally, a special word of appreciation for Christopher Rogers, former history editor at McGraw-Hill. He placed the book under contract, had patient faith in it, and offered nothing but support along the way.

Michael B. Stoff

Introduction: Trinity

Two hundred fifty miles south of the county of Los Alamos, New Mexico—just beyond Stallion Gate at the foot of the Oscura Mountains—lies a bleak stretch of scrub and cactus country. The mesquite there grows low, stunted from a lack of water Rattlesnakes and scorpions make their homes in the buffalo grass and gray sage. In the summer, temperatures soar to 100° or more, and the earth cracks. Spanish travelers called the region *Jornada del Muerto* ("journey of death") because many had died of thirst trying to get across.

In an isolated spot named Alamogordo, moments before first light on July 16, 1945, night exploded noiselessly into day. Searing colors—gold, purple, blue, violet, gray—illuminated everything in sight. From the floor of the desert, a ball of fire rose like the sun (only brighter, one report read, "equal to several suns in midday"). And hotter than the sun—10,000 times hotter. Thirty seconds later came a blast of burning air, followed almost instantaneously by an awesome roar. A cloud the shape of an immense mushroom ascended nearly eight miles, was caught by the desert winds, and curled into a giant question mark.

Dawn had been preempted by the test of a new weapon that scientists called the "gadget." The experimental model of the weapon looked crude and ungainly—a black globe five feet in diameter, bolted to the floor of a metal shed on top of a one-hundred-foot tower known as Ground Zero. The globe had two rims and patches where the detonator ports were taped. Inside, two identical spheres, coated in nickel to prevent corrosion, were surrounded by molded lenses and explosives.

The spheres contained $13\frac{1}{2}$ pounds of plutonium. This toxic, temperamental substance was new to the world, like the weapon itself. A special plant at Hanford Village, Washington, had only recently synthesized it. Almost none of its properties were known, not even its density. The theory was that compressing the plutonium to critical mass would set off a chain reaction. The energy of the universe would be released, predicted one physicist, with a "very big bang." According to the theorists, only an *implosion*—a perfectly symmetrical, converging shock wave—could start the process. Until the fireball lit the New Mexico sky on July 16, no one knew whether a detonating implosion, let alone the hoped-for explosion, would occur.

The force of the blast equaled 20,000 tons of TNT. It was 2000 times more powerful than the British "Grand Slam," the largest conventional bomb used in the Second World War. The steel tower on which the gadget had rested was no more. In its place yawned a 1200-foot crater, sloping gently into a shallow bowl 130 feet wide and 6 feet deep. Within the depression, only pulverized dirt—greenish around the outer rim—could be found. Not a trace of plant life remained. One-half mile from the epicenter, the twisted remains of a two-hundred-twenty-ton test cylinder, ripped from its concrete moorings, lay flattened on the ground. After seeing the rubble, one general concluded: "I no longer consider the Pentagon a safe shelter from such a bomb."

In a command bunker six miles from Ground Zero, a group of scientists, soldiers, and businessmen-turned-bureaucrats watched with mixed emotions. At once stunned and relieved, most fell into uneasy silence. Some felt a profound disquiet. For three years they had been engaged in the most ambitious scientific effort in history, the Manhattan Project. It dwarfed anything previously undertaken: a crew of over 100,000; 37 installations in 13 states (some, like the Hanford complex, the size of small towns); more than a dozen university laboratories from New York to Berkeley; and, finally, a secret compound on a breathtaking desert mesa had been involved. The staff had pursued a single objective—the production of an atomic bomb. The few who first saw its power were not quite sure what to do.

The Scientists

J. Robert Oppenheimer, for one, could finally draw a long breath. As director of the Los Alamos laboratory, the nerve center and staging ground of the Manhattan Project, Oppie had had responsibility for turning scientific theory into military reality. The challenge had been irresistible, but the burden of meeting it had weighed heavily on his gaunt frame. Never robust, the six-footer had withered to one hundred sixteen pounds under the strain of command. With his closely cropped hair, hollowed cheeks, and drooping shoulders, he looked strangely like a victim of the Holocaust.

Oppenheimer's anxiety reached a new peak on the eve of the test. He was still uncertain whether the bomb would actually work. Even if it did, physicist Edward Teller calculated that there was a 3-in-1-million chance that the explosion would ignite the hydrogen in the atmosphere and burn the earth to a cinder. Enrico Fermi, an Italian émigré who had created the first controlled chain reaction in 1942, urged postponement. "There could be a catastrophe," he warned Oppenheimer. Wind and rain might catch the powdery debris and shower the whole region with deadly radioactive dust.

To Oppenheimer, the risks seemed worth taking. After all, one atomic bomb might end the war in the Pacific. Four years of bloody battle against Japan had, so far, cost tens of thousands of American lives, and the end was still barely in sight. Operation Downfall, the invasion of the Japanese home islands, was planned as a lengthy, two-stage affair: Operation Olympic, the assault on Kyushu (the southern-most island of Japan) was scheduled for the autumn of 1945; Coronet, the attack on the main island of Honshu, would not begin until the following spring. Conservative estimates put the number of American casualties from these invasions at over half a million. Such a prospect made postponement of the test, except out of sheer technical necessity, unthinkable. At the last minute, especially, Oppenheimer could not afford another delay. An almost apocalyptic thunderstorm, blowing through at thirty miles an hour, had already forced him to reschedule the firing twice. The test, then, was set for July 16 at 5:30 a.m., the last instant before morning light would spoil the chance to take good photographs of Trinity.

Trinity was the code name Oppenheimer had chosen for the test and the test site. As usual, he was showing off. J. Robert Oppenheimer was an intellectual exhibitionist who never missed an opportunity to impress with an obscure reference. He had cultivated this habit all his life. The son of a wealthy German-Jewish importer who had settled in New York, he was a child prodigy who had mastered Greek and delivered a paper before the New York Mineralogical Club before he turned twelve. His tastes were refined, his talents prodigious. An expert sailor, he also spoke fluent French and German. He graduated summa cum laude from Harvard in three years, then studied physics at the Cavendish Laboratory at Cambridge and at Göttingen, from which he obtained his Ph.D. In his spare moments he taught himself Sanskrit—for fun. Wherever he went, he astonished all who met him.

But the accolades brought young Oppenheimer little peace. His moods were vagrant and mercurial. The more he accomplished, the more his mind and body rebelled. He endured bouts of colitis and near-suicidal depressions. He spent five months convalescing from tuberculosis, and at one point a psychiatrist concluded that he was hopelessly unbalanced. He overcame the illnesses of his youth, but he carried their scars into adulthood. An anorectic physique and persistent cough betrayed the anguish and frailty on which his brilliance rested.

At first, physics and high ideas alone consumed him. For the most part, Oppenheimer ignored the world around him. As a student and young professor, he read neither newspapers nor magazines. He did not own a radio or telephone. He learned of the great stock-market crash of 1929 months after it happened. He cast his first ballot in the presidential election of 1936, when he was thirty-two years old. "I was deeply interested in my science," he explained later, "but I had no understanding of the relations of man to his society."

By the mid-nineteen-thirties, those relations had become badly strained. The great depression and the triumph of fascism in Europe hit Oppenheimer as if he were their target. Massive unemployment at home left his graduate students without jobs; the Nazi persecution of Jews in Germany forced his relatives to flee from their homeland. Oppenheimer could no longer ignore the world of human affairs. Suddenly, as if divinely enlightened, he began to "understand how deeply political and economic events could affect men's lives."

Oppenheimer joined humanity. He even joined the local teachers' union in Berkeley. Soon he was serving as its secretary, up night after night addressing envelopes for one cause or another. He helped rescue Jews from Germany and, to the amazement of friends, began voting. At a time when many intellectuals were attracted to the rhetoric and crusades of the Communist party, Oppenheimer drifted leftward. He donated 100 dollars a month to the Communist-supported anti-Fascists in the Spanish civil war and advertised meetings to raise money for them. His personal and political lives inevitably became entwined. He courted one woman who had belonged to the Communist party and married another.

He was to pay heavily for some of these connections. In 1954, after he had been decorated for wartime service, his earlier activities helped to convince authorities that the man who had once known all the secrets of the bomb was not to be trusted any more. The one-time head of the Los Alamos laboratory and adviser to the Atomic Energy Commission (AEC) was judged a risk to the safety of his nation. In what amounted to a professional execution, the Personnel Security Board stripped J. Robert Oppenheimer of his clearance. It was, some said, the price he paid for opposing development of the "super"—a hydrogen bomb a thousand times more powerful than the atomic bomb.

As arrogant as he was charming, Oppenheimer did not suffer fools. Instead, he made them suffer with his clever, cruel tongue. He was a gifted teacher—part genius, part actor, wholly entrancing. When he took simultaneous appointments at Berkeley and Caltech, his students followed him back and forth for six-month stints at each university. Then and later, he could not resist showing off, inside or outside of a classroom. For all his considerable gifts, as one Army investigator recognized, Oppenheimer always had "a need to dazzle."

Oppenheimer was never more dazzling than during his wartime administration of the Los Alamos laboratory. He had begun pressing for a new laboratory in 1942. Urgent problems—of ordnance, chemistry, and assemblage—had so far been ignored. As he saw it, the project required a central facility where these problems could be solved so a bomb might be built quickly. Oppenheimer had another reason. He hoped to break down the security system that was keeping his colleagues apart. *Compartmentalization*, as its military designers called it, had been imposed to prevent leaks and to stifle internal debate. The various parts of the project and those who worked on them were separated into functional units, each isolated from the rest. Even members of the same staff could communicate only on a "need-to-know" basis.

By and large, the strategy succeeded. Most scientists and engineers worked in ignorance of their overall assignment. Few discussed its larger implications, and only near the end did reservations surface. But there was a hidden cost implicit in the system—a scientific diaspora that produced duplication, waste, and frustration. The mainspring of progress in science is the free interplay of creative minds. If American scientists were to succeed at their task, Oppenheimer knew they had to be brought together and allowed to talk to each other. Only through unrestricted exchange could they make speedy headway.

Speed was vital because the United States had entered into a deadly race with Germany. In 1938, the German physicist Otto Hahn had found that the atom could be split, a process that would release vast amounts of energy. Soon scientific journals all over the world carried news of the discovery of fission. By the end of 1939, nearly one hundred articles on the subject had been published. As war approached, interest naturally turned to the military implications of the find. Could the energy of fission be harnessed in a bomb? It was, Oppenheimer said later, a "technically sweet problem."

In 1939, German scientists had begun to solve the problem, and by the summer, Hungarian-born physicist Leo Szilard was worried. More than anyone else, Szilard was the father of the atomic bomb. He had conceived of such a super weapon in 1933, years before Hahn's breakthrough made it possible. A refugee from the Nazis, Szilard understood only too well what they would do with an atomic bomb. He was determined that the United States develop one first. After learning of Germany's decision to embargo uranium from Czechoslovakia in 1939, he traveled to Albert Einstein's home on Long Island to enlist the support of the Nobel laureate for an American counterproject.

Szilard was unknown in America outside of scientific circles and, like many émigrés during the war, regarded as a potential spy. He hoped that Einstein, the most famous scientist in the world, would help him penetrate the magic circle of government officials. Together, the two physicists composed a letter urging President Roosevelt to build a bomb. It was not for almost another three years, however—after the United States had entered the war and British scientists had taken critical first steps toward demonstrating the feasibility of the weapon—that Roosevelt set up the Manhattan Project. Ultimately, the Germans lost the atomic race, but not until the spring of 1945 did the United States learn for certain that they had failed.

Although he had described it merely as a "technically sweet problem," at Los Alamos Oppenheimer, like Szilard, was driven by nightmares of an atomic bomb in the hands of the Nazis. Chain-smoking, entertaining with meticulously prepared martinis, buying time to construct the impossible (and, a colleague ventured, selling his soul to do it), he performed an exquisite balancing act between disciplined soldiers and scientists without discipline. All the while, he strung together a running commentary on the Manhattan Project, plucking from memory lines of Sanskrit verse, Eastern scripture, and Western prose. The code name Trinity was an allusion to a sonnet by the English poet John Donne. "Batter my heart, three person'd God, for you as yet but knock, breathe, shine, and seek to mend," Donne had written. Oppenheimer, perhaps feeling that his own heart needed mending, dubbed the test and the site Trinity.

For Oppenheimer, Trinity was the culmination of over two years of labor. In 1943, he began work on the bomb at the Los Alamos laboratory, 7400 feet above sea level on the Pajarito Plateau in New Mexico. Oppenheimer had chosen the setting with the deftness of a seasoned angler baiting his hook. Its isolation and majestic view of the Jemez and the Sangre de Cristo Mountains made the mesa a perfect lure—remote enough to satisfy security-conscious generals, beautiful enough to attract even cosmopolitan scientists. For Oppenheimer, it was literally a dream come true. "My two great loves," he had said years earlier, "are physics and desert country. It's a pity they can't be combined."

The Army Corps of Engineers did combine them by building the secret laboratory on the grounds of the old Los Alamos Ranch School. In mid-November 1942, when Army administrators finally agreed to the site, Los Alamos was still a rustic school for toughening up boys from wealthy families. It consisted of little more than a large, ramshackle main house and a group of log cabins set among the poplars just below the timberline. The school was in financial trouble because of the war, so its owners were happy to sell out to the government. Before the end of the year, construction of the new laboratory was under way.

By July 1945, on the eve of the test, more than 4000 people—mostly scientists, engineers, and their families—were living there. Their mission was to enlist the power of the atom in the war. Military police guarded them, Army doctors ministered to their ills (even delivered their babies), a closed-circuit radio station entertained them, and the resources of the largest industrial firms in America were at their disposal. For the most part, the scientific ideal of free discussion prevailed inside the protected community; but outside, no one was supposed to talk. To make sure the residents kept their secret, government agents monitored their telephones, censored their mail, and tailed them on furlough. Los Alamos—desert sanctuary of the new Trinity—stood high above the fray, supported by a nation that did not know it existed.

In the control bunker near the test site, Oppenheimer had trouble standing at all. Nervousness, lack of sleep, and the strain of years of anxious effort threatened to overwhelm him at this climactic moment. Barely breathing, he grabbed hold of a post to steady himself. In the background, a radio tuned to a military frequency was picking up Tchaikovsky's *Nutcracker Suite* from a station on the same band. "I must remain conscious," Oppenheimer remembered saying seconds before the blast. When the explosion occurred, he could think only of a line of Hindu scripture from the Bhagavad Gita: "Now I have become death, the destroyer of worlds." Moments later, he was strutting with pride.

Feelings of pride and fear, of wonderment and foreboding—mainly of being relieved of a dreadful burden—raised the flesh of another scientist. "At first I was thrilled," Isidor Rabi said later. "It was a vision. Then, a few minutes afterward, I had gooseflesh all over me when I realized what this meant for the future of humanity." Rabi's colleague, Kenneth Bainbridge, shared no sense of relief, only foreboding. Bainbridge, the physicist in charge of the test, saw the mark of Cain in the mushroom cloud. As the glow of the first atomic bomb faded, he turned to Oppenheimer and said remorsefully: "Well, Oppie, now we're all sons of bitches!"

The Soldiers

Alongside the scientists stood the soldiers, perhaps less learned but no less impressed or eloquent. One officer said he could find no words to describe what he witnessed, but what he wrote belied his claim. In the burning light, reported Brigadier General Thomas F. Farrell, he saw the "beauty that the great poets dream about but describe most poorly." The explosion inspired in Farrell not only awe but reverence. As he listened to the growing roar of the bomb, he thought of doomsday: ". . . we puny things were blasphemous to dare tamper with the forces heretofore reserved to The Almighty."

Farrell's chief and military commander of the project, Brigadier General Leslie Groves, felt delighted with a job done well. A shade under six feet tall, with piercing blue eyes, curly brown hair, and the hint of a mustache, Groves had overseen the project from the start, barking orders and getting results like a drill sergeant at boot camp. Though he weighed nearly three hundred pounds, his energy, like his confidence, never flagged. He was a "go-getter," said his own chief, with neither the time nor the temperament for niceties. His father had been an Army chaplain, but Groves, recalled one old subordinate, was "the biggest son of a bitch" he had ever known.

Before taking over the Manhattan Project in 1942, Groves was the Army's master builder. An engineer twenty-four years out of West Point (he ranked fourth in his class), he was in charge of all military construction. His last construction assignment was the Pentagon, the largest office building in the world. He completed it in 1942, but Groves was still in a hurry. At forty-six, he was one of the oldest colonels in the Army, and he hoped finally to win promotion through combat. Just when his orders for an overseas tour arrived, however, the Army reassigned him to yet another construction job—building an atomic bomb. "On the day I learned that I was to direct the project which ultimately produced the atomic bomb, I was probably the angriest officer in the United States Army," Groves later wrote. And as if that weren't enough, he found himself with a paltry budget. The development of an atomic weapon, it was estimated in 1942, would cost a total of 100 million dollars, less than Groves had spent on the Pentagon in a single week. His promotion to brigadier general seemed a poor consolation prize.

Groves nonetheless threw himself into the project with typical single-mindedness. When he took command of what was called the "Manhattan Engineer District" or MED (because Groves's predecessor had worked out of an office in Manhattan), Groves instituted a ruthless policy of secrecy. He made compartmentalization his governing administrative principle to insure that few would know enough to compromise the undertaking. He imposed a rigid hierarchy and near-military discipline to control the far-flung operation. Groves also appointed Oppenheimer to take charge of the scientists at Los Alamos despite specious rumors that the physicist might be disloyal.

Groves spared no expense because he knew that the success of the project, however chancy, could mean victory in the war. "If there is a choice between two methods, one of which is good and the other looks promising," one scientist remembered him saying, "then build both." Under such a formula, American scientists could follow several paths at once in their quest to build an atomic bomb. All the major powers—including Germany, Great Britain, the Soviet Union, and Japan—were trying to build such a weapon, but none had the luxury of Groves's formula. It was probably the most important one devised during the Manhattan Project.

No other nation had the resources of the United States, either. They included money, to be sure, but also raw materials (with the exception of uranium), scientific and technical expertise, petroleum and other fuels, and a continent untouched by war. These resources gave the United States an unparalleled edge, and Groves marshalled them with the virtuosity of a seasoned commander arraying his troops for battle. His genius lay in his attention to detail and in his relentless pursuit of his goal. In the middle of his first meeting with his superiors, he abruptly excused himself to catch a train to Tennessee so he could personally inspect the site of a new plant. He allowed no obstacle to block his way. Days after his appointment, he drafted a letter to be sent under the name of the civilian head of the War Production Board (WPB), the agency responsible for allocating resources, giving MED a first-priority rating. WPB chief Donald Nelson balked at first, but within minutes, Groves had steamrolled him into signing the letter. "We had no major priority difficulties for nearly a year," the general noted with satisfaction.

Three years and 2 billion dollars later, Groves lay in the sand at Trinity, 17,000 yards from the point of explosion, facedown, feet toward Ground Zero. Next to him was the director of the Office of Scientific Research and Development (OSRD), Vannevar Bush. As Groves turned to view the flash through dark glasses, he thought of "Blondin crossing Niagara Falls on his tight rope, only to me this tight rope had lasted for almost three years." When Bush remarked that the burst of light had been brighter than a star, an ambitious Groves reportedly pointed to the brigadier general's star on each of his shoulders and shot back, "Brighter than two stars!" Eager to employ his new invention in the war he had been forced to fight from a desk, Groves hurried back to Washington with the good news.

The Bureaucrat and the President

His boss was not even there. Henry Stimson, the seventy-eight-year-old secretary of war, had just arrived in Potsdam, Germany, for a summit conference of Allied leaders. Like an anxious nursemaid, Stimson had insisted on accompanying Harry Truman, the new President, to this final wartime meeting with Winston Churchill and Joseph Stalin ("Mr. Great Britain" and "Mr. Russia," Truman called them). Truman had been in office barely three months. A compromise vice-presidential candidate in 1944, the former senator from Missouri had been chosen because he had been one of the few New Dealers conservative enough to satisfy Democratic party bosses. He was a courthouse politician whose lack of executive experience bothered no one so long as Franklin Roosevelt was in charge.

No one fretted much about Truman's executive education, either. For Truman, the vice presidency turned out to be an even poorer apprenticeship than usual. Roosevelt's staff knew more about the conduct of the war and the plans for peace than did Truman. He was told little about Roosevelt's wartime agreements and nothing about the atomic bomb. During the last year of his life, Roosevelt had met with his Vice President only eight times.

Like the nation, Harry Truman felt that Roosevelt's death on April 12, 1945, had cast him adrift in the critical closing months of the war. He was thrust unprepared—and almost unknown—into the White House. "Who the hell is Harry Truman?" asked Admiral William Leahy, chief liaison officer to the joint chiefs of staff. His military and civilian colleagues shared the dismay, if not the brassiness, that prompted the famous remark. This President, it was clear, would need all the help he could get.

And Truman knew it. "I feel as though the moon and all the stars and all the planets have fallen on me," he told reporters when he heard of Roosevelt's death. "Please, boys, give me your prayers. I need them very much." What he needed more was information, but nearly two weeks passed before he got any details about the Manhattan Project. After the first cabinet meeting on the day of Roosevelt's death, Stimson briefly outlined an "immense project" that would give the United States "a new explosive of almost unbelievable power." Truman was understandably "puzzled" until the next day, when James Byrnes, an old friend from the Senate and Roosevelt's assistant since 1943, dropped by to tell him about a bomb that could "destroy the world."

Then, for two weeks, Truman learned nothing more. The delay was not part of a premeditated plan to keep him ignorant of atomic developments. The technicalities of an unfinished project and an untested weapon simply assumed a lower priority than the management of a grief-stricken nation still at war. Finally, on April 25, 1945, Stimson and Groves sneaked into the White House for a forty-five-minute meeting with the President. The atomic overseers sketched the secret research and the timetable for its completion. Truman asked not a single question. His sole initiative was to appoint an ad hoc Interim Committee to advise him on temporary wartime controls, public announcements, legislation, and postwar organization.

Truman needed advice not only because he was inexperienced and uninformed but because his predecessor had left such an ambiguous legacy. Roosevelt himself had not fully thought out his own atomic policy. For the most part, he had cooperated with the British on the research but had left the Russians completely in the dark. Although he mentioned the possibility of dropping the bomb on Japan, he had made no decisions about using it. In an agreement with Winston Churchill at the President's home in Hyde Park in 1944 (not revealed until after his death, even to Secretary of War Stimson), Roosevelt accepted only the equivocal notion that "when a 'bomb' is finally available, it might perhaps, after mature consideration, be used against the Japanese." Under any circumstances, the meaning of such directions would have been hard to decipher. For Truman, never close to the President and barely acquainted with the conduct of the war, Roosevelt's unexpressed intentions could be interpreted only by the staff he had just inherited and hardly knew. Later legendary for snap decisions and single-handed action, Harry Truman began his presidency as a prisoner of his advisers.

Henry Stimson had been around long enough to appreciate the limitations of his new, untried commander. Truman was the fourth President Stimson had served during a distinguished cabinet career that began under William Howard Taft. His first appointment, like his last, was as secretary of war. In between, he had been Herbert Hoover's secretary of state. In 1940, when Franklin Roosevelt needed a sturdy Republican in the cabinet to lend balance to his program of war preparedness, he selected Henry Stimson. As secretary of war, Stimson had been the natural choice for handling the new Manhattan Project in 1942.

Stimson soon crossed swords with Truman, in mid-1943, when Truman was chairman of a Senate committee investigating the expenditures of the War Department. The feisty senator was determined to guard against waste and dishonesty in the military. He wondered why so much money was being spent on a remote factory in Pasco, Washington. Hiding behind a veil of secrecy, Stimson gave no answers about the plutonium plant. A frustrated Truman continued without success to seek them out. The encounters left Stimson unimpressed. "Truman is a nuisance and a pretty untrustworthy man," he confided in his diary in March 1944. "He talks smoothly but he acts meanly."

Henry Stimson acted smoothly, too, but he could always be trusted. He was born to be in charge, in or out of the cabinet. Sober, sage, well bred and well connected, an attorney by vocation and a public servant by calling, Stimson spent his time away from government building one of the most prestigious and successful corporate law practices in the country. If Oppenheimer represented the fresh breed of government-sponsored scientist and Groves the soldier-as-technocratic-administrator, Stimson was a twentieth-century American mandarin—the bureaucrat who shuttled quietly between the worlds of private enterprise and public service.

Stimson, of course, had been eager to accompany the President in July 1945 to the Potsdam conference. The postwar world could be shaped by what happened there. To keep the globe secure, Truman would have to win the consent of a Russian dictator and a British prima donna, neither of whom he had ever bargained with before. The wartime alliance was already showing signs of strain. British prime minister Churchill, for his part, had never trusted his Russian allies and had successfully convinced Roosevelt to keep the atomic bomb a secret from them. And in May 1945, only a few weeks after Germany capitulated, Truman abruptly canceled further shipments of lend-lease supplies to the Soviet Union. The Russians took it as a signal of new American toughness, and, at Potsdam, they were prepared to take a hard line of their own. They were going to demand bases in Turkey, greater influence in Austria and eastern Europe, and a share of Italy's Mediterranean colonies as part of the peace settlement.

Truman had more to worry about than winning the peace; he still had to win the war. Although the Germans had given up early in May, the Japanese had yet to surrender. Truman's advisers had told him that an invasion of Japan's home islands would cost dearly in human lives. By some estimates, the United States stood to lose between half a million and a million men, and Japan several times that. Though Stalin had informed him of peace feelers from the newly organized Japanese government, Truman suspected (as American intelligence officers predicted) that the Japanese might seek to divide the Allies with offers of surrender on the condition that the sacred institution of the Emperor be retained. Such a provisional peace threatened to violate the Allied policy of "unconditional surrender," which ruled out any negotiations with the enemy. The policy had been established in 1943 to placate a war-drained Stalin and to prevent the kind of separate settlement that had split Russia from the Allies during the First World War.

Stimson and Truman knew that the American people would tolerate no violation of this policy where the Japanese were concerned. The war in the Pacific, largely an American effort, had become more and more ferocious as island-hopping forces closed in on Japan itself. In recent fighting on Okinawa alone, 48,000 American soldiers and sailors had been killed or wounded. Truman's fellow citizens also could not forget the Japanese sneak attack on the American naval base at Pearl Harbor in 1941 or the "death march" in the Philippines in 1942 that had cost the lives of perhaps 10,000 American prisoners of war. Victory against Japan also would have to satisfy the nonnegotiable American need for retribution.

The Test and the Summit

At Potsdam, Stimson received the first reports of the successful atomic test from his assistant George L. Harrison, an insurance executive transformed into yet another warlord. On Monday evening, July 16, after the conference had begun, Harrison wired the following message to his superior in Germany: "Operated on this morning. Diagnosis not yet complete but results seem satisfactory and already exceed expectations." The next evening he sent a second telegram: "Doctor has just returned most enthusiastic and confident that the little boy is as husky as his big brother. The light in his eyes is discernible from here to Highhold [Stimson's one-hundred-acre estate near Huntington, Long Island, two hundred fifty miles from Washington] and I could have heard his screams from here to my farm [in Upperville, Virginia, fifty miles from the capital]."

An exultant Stimson carried word personally to the President. By then, his earlier judgment of Truman had softened. Sympathy had replaced suspicion as he watched Truman "trying hard to keep his balance." At first unaware of the magnitude of the blast or of any details of the test, Truman received the news about Trinity with casual satisfaction, not grasping its full significance. When he learned, on July 21, exactly what had happened in New Mexico, however, he became elated. He found a thorough report from Groves "startling—to put it mildly." In Truman's view, nothing less than a Biblical prophesy had been fulfilled. "It may be the fire destruction," he wrote in his diary, "prophesied in the Euphrates Valley Era after Noah and his fabulous ark."

The effect of the news on the conference was palpable. Truman seemed to develop new resolve and flatly refused Russian demands for greater influence in eastern Europe and Turkey. Churchill was puzzled by this new mood until Stimson handed him Groves's report at which time he "said he now understood how this pepping up had taken place and that he felt the same way." "When he got to the meeting after having read this report he was a changed man," Churchill said of Truman. "He told the Russians just where they got on and off and generally bossed the whole meeting." It seemed that the war-winning weapon might help to win the peace, too, not through overt threats, but through the firmness that would grow from possessing an atomic monopoly. In addition, at least as Stimson saw it, atomic technology could be used as a bargaining chip for concessions elsewhere.

The dangers of relying on atomic diplomacy were already worrying some scientists, however. As early as 1943, the Danish physicist Niels Bohr, long an advocate of the Manhattan Project, had begun to urge both Roosevelt and Churchill to tell the Russians about it. For one thing, Bohr argued, the atomic secret could not practicably be kept. As Albert Einstein later put it, "There is no secret, and there is no defense." Sufficient knowledge already existed to allow the Russians to construct their own bomb. The only disagreement was over how long it would take. Scientists generally predicted four to five years; soldiers estimated twenty.

The Russians, Bohr also pointed out, had "excellent scientists" of their own, and once they had captured German physicists, they would undoubtedly learn enough to make substantial progress without any help from Great Britain or the United States. Not all leaks, moreover, could be prevented in an endeavor as large as the Manhattan Project. Sooner or later, said Bohr, the Russians would find out what their Anglo-American allies were constructing. If they were not told of the existence of the project, the resulting mistrust could produce a fatal arms race.

Bohr's entreaties earned him nothing but suspicion, and by the opening of the Potsdam summit, no official word had been passed to the Russians. Finally, at the end of the formal conference session on July 24, Truman "casually mentioned" to Stalin that the United States "had a new weapon of unusual destructive force." The sly reference seemed to make no impression. Churchill, watching the exchange from across the room, recalled that Stalin's "face remained gay and genial." According to Truman, the Russian premier turned laconic, saying only that he was "glad to hear it and hoped we would make 'good use of it against the Japanese.'"

Truman and Churchill were convinced that Stalin did not realize what he had been told, but it seems certain that he knew exactly what Truman was talking about. The Russians had begun work on their own atomic bomb in 1942. Lack of technical expertise, the absence of a safe haven for conducting their research, and a paucity of critical resources (the British and Americans had virtually cornered the market on fissionable material) had slowed the Russians but had hardly stopped them. Just as important, Russian espionage had been attempting to breach Groves's system of security since 1942, and Groves was as concerned about Russian spies as he was about German ones. He had no illusions, he said later, "but that Russia was our enemy." In fact, since 1943, Klaus Fuchs, a German physicist who fled to Great Britain in 1933, had been surreptiously reporting to the Russians from Los Alamos itself.

Still, Stalin gave no indication that he knew the secret Churchill, Roosevelt, and now Truman had tried to keep from him. Instead, he reaffirmed his earlier pledge to end a 1941 nonaggression pact with Japan and enter the Asian war in early August, three months after the end of hostilities in Europe. In private, he and his advisers agreed to "speed things up" on their own atomic project. Meanwhile, at the close of the summit, the other Allies issued an ultimatum—the Potsdam Declaration—threatening "prompt and utter destruction" of Japan's home islands if an unconditional surrender did not come. Nowhere in the document was the atomic bomb mentioned by name.

Even so, the "nameless thing" was assuming greater and greater importance. Three days before the issuance of the Potsdam Declaration, Stimson, forced to bed every afternoon by migraine headaches and intestinal problems, wrote in his diary: "I am finding myself crippled by not knowing what happens in the meetings in the late afternoon and evening. This is particularly so now that the program for S-1 [the code-name for the bomb] is tying in what we are doing in all fields."

Stimson was right: The bomb had become a linchpin, holding together a host of problems and offering a host of solutions. The test at Trinity gave the Allies, first and foremost, a powerful new weapon, perhaps even the winning weapon, if it were successful in combat. James Byrnes was also worried, as early as the spring of 1945, that there might be criticism in Congress unless the bomb worked—and worked in combat. The unprecedented appropriations for the Manhattan Project could become the subject of hostile investigations if the bomb were a dud, whereas a combat-tested weapon would quell any political revolt at home.

But legitimizing vast expenditures of money and manpower was a fringe benefit, not a rationale for using the weapon. Byrnes believed a more direct benefit would be a quick victory that might make Russian entry into the war against Japan unnecessary. If the Russians became firmly entrenched in Manchuria, Port Arthur, and Darien on the Asian mainland, Byrnes warned that "it would not be easy to get them out."

Finally, an atomic monopoly could make the United States a formidable bargainer in postwar affairs. During the war, Stimson had mused fancifully about such prospects. The technology of the bomb, he speculated, might be used as a *quid pro quo* for Russian territorial concessions in eastern Europe or as a lever to induce the liberalization of Soviet society. Stimson eventually abandoned such dreams, and by the end of the war his thinking had undergone a remarkable evolution. Having seen the power of the bomb, he now echoed the sentiments of some scientists. An impending arms race was so serious a threat that he advocated turning over atomic technology to the Russians free of diplomatic or political charges. ". . . the only way you can make a man trustworthy," Stimson wrote in mid-September 1945, "is to trust him; and the surest way to make him untrustworthy is to distrust him and show your distrust."

Aftermath: The New Trinity

By then, Stimson's star had fallen, and his physical strength had waned as well, so his warning went unheeded. Increasingly, Truman relied on James Byrnes, the no-nonsense negotiator he appointed secretary of state in 1945. Byrnes, much more than Stimson, expected to use the American atomic monopoly as a master card in postwar diplomacy, especially against the Russians. At a meeting in London less than a month after the war, he told Russian foreign minister Vyacheslav Molotov, in a transparent joke, that "if you don't cut out all this stalling and let us get down to work, I'm going to pull an atomic bomb out of my hip pocket and let you have it."

As it turned out, the atomic bomb neither cowed the Russians nor remained for long an American monopoly. Molotov laughed at Byrnes's threat and, later that evening, whispered in his ear: "You know we have the atomic bomb." They did not, but they were working on one. And as it turned out, conventional diplomacy, east-west hostility, and the wartime positioning of Allied troops did more to shape the peace after 1945 than did the "winning weapon." By the end of the decade, Japan, against whom mostly American troops had fought, lay under the stewardship of the United States, while eastern Europe, where Russian soldiers had waged war, was in Soviet hands.

And so was the atomic bomb. In mid-September 1949, as the cold war deepened, American scientists detected traces of radiation drifting westward from Asia. Analysts concluded only that the radioactivity came from a blast "probably younger than one month." Almost four years to the day after the incineration of Hiroshima, the Soviet Union detonated its first atomic bomb (nicknamed "Joe I") in Asiatic Russia. The atomic monopoly of the United States had been transformed into a dangerous atomic stalemate. The first truly global war was brought to an end by an atomic explosion, but the vast power it had unleashed now threatened the world with a nuclear war that would leave no place on earth, however remote, unscathed.

From the vantage points of Los Alamos and Potsdam in the summer of 1945, the ability of the atomic bomb to end war and enforce peace seemed incontrovertible. Ironically, a destiny that appeared so manifest in 1945 soon became the subject of intense debate. For the next four decades, participants in the development of the bomb and historians who wrote about it argued over its utility as a war-winning or peace-shaping weapon.

What turned out to be undeniable—and less manifest at the start—was the power of atomic weaponry to sustain the forces that created it. When J. Robert Oppenheimer labeled the atomic test and its site Trinity, he named more than he knew. During the Second World War, a new trinity emerged. Science, industry, and government (both its civilian and military branches) joined together to win the war. Orchestrated by the Office of Scientific Research and Development (OSRD), the new trinity worked marvels of creation. Radar, penicillin, proximity fuses, flamethrowers, rockets, antisubmarine gear, and even insecticides were but a few of the miraculous results. The Manhattan Project was the most impressive miracle of all. The first "crash" program in the history of science, it served as the precedent for later programs. Intense secrecy, hierarchical bureaucracy, and cooperation among scientists, industrial leaders, and military and civilian officials—the basic mode and structure of the Manhattan Project—characterized later efforts to achieve nuclear superiority and control atomic energy. As the postwar years unfolded into the cold war, the model increasingly typified weapons research and more ordinary scientific research, as well. Born of the Second World War and sustained by the cold war, the new trinity of science, industry, and government remained joined in the pursuit of national advantage. The Manhattan Project was a beginning, not an end.

M.B.S.
Austin, Texas

P A R T 1

Initial planning of the project.
Organizing the public and private
sectors. Problems of the British-
American alliance and their
resolution in the Quebec Agreement
and the Declaration of Trust.
Relations with Congress. Labor
policies. Antitrust policy.

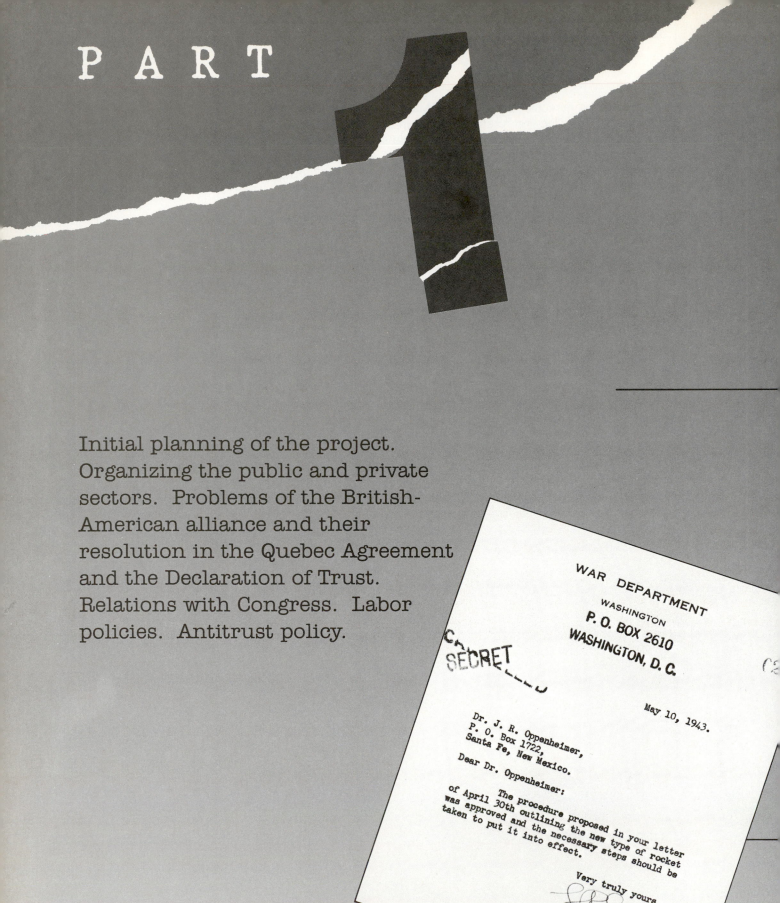

WAR DEPARTMENT
WASHINGTON
P. O. BOX 2610
WASHINGTON, D. C.

SECRET

May 10, 1943.

Dr. J. R. Oppenheimer,
P. O. Box 1722,
Santa Fe, New Mexico.

Dear Dr. Oppenheimer:

The procedure proposed in your letter
of April 30th outlining the new type of rocket
was approved and the necessary steps should be
taken to put it into effect.

Very truly yours,

L. R. GROVES,
Brigadier General, C. E.

Creation, Organization, and Security

Albert Einstein

Franklin D. Roosevelt and Winston Churchill

Quebec Conference - Winston Churchill,
Brendan Braeken, and Harry Hopkins

On August 2, 1939, a simple two-page letter to President Franklin Roosevelt set in motion a complex sequence of events that led to the creation of the Manhattan Project almost three years later. The letter was, on the surface, a plea from Albert Einstein, the Nobel Prize-winning physicist, for the development of a fantastic new explosive from uranium. But it also anticipated key themes in the development of what came to be called the *atomic bomb*: the remoteness and insulation of the presidency; the emphasis on speed and secrecy; the mortal rivalry with a hostile power; the tensions between the Allies and the emergence of an Anglo-American atomic partnership; the rapid deterioration of the scientific ideal of freely flowing information; and, perhaps most important, the entwining of government, industry, and science.

In 1939, word reached Einstein through Hungarian-born physicist Leo Szilard that the Nazis had banned the export of uranium from Germany and German-occupied territory, including the rich Joachimsthal mines in Czechoslovakia. Einstein and Szilard concluded that the Germans were making a weapon of unprecedented force. At the urging of the President's science adviser, Alexander Sachs, the two composed a letter to Roosevelt, though only Einstein signed the letter because he alone had sufficient status to attract presidential attention. "It is conceivable," the physicists warned the President, ". . . that extremely powerful bombs of a new type may thus be constructed" (see Document 1). They beseeched Roosevelt to counter the German threat with an American atomic-bomb project.

Their advice served as an early blueprint for the Manhattan Project. They suggested that "permanent contact" be established between the administration and scientists exploring chain reactions in the United States. The President might even wish to select someone to serve as an "inofficial" atomic liaison. Such a person could keep the government informed of ongoing research and recommend ways of obtaining fissionable material and speeding up experimental work. Through his outside contacts, he might obtain private funds to supplement the limited budgets of university researchers. He also might seek the cooperation of industrial laboratories that had the equipment necessary to pursue the project. The thought of an atomic weapon in the hands of Adolf Hitler gave the prosaic language of the letter an ominous and urgent tone.

The atomic bomb thus began as a deadly competition between two nations not yet at war. During the Second World War, all the major powers, including Great Britain, Japan, and the Soviet Union, embarked on their own atomic quests, but for the most part, the race was between Germany and the United States. And at the start, it was something less than a sprint. The German effort gained momentum slowly, made no real headway in solving the technical problems of building a bomb, and largely petered out by the end of 1943.

In the United States, nearly two years passed before the Manhattan Project was begun in earnest. The sluggish pace stemmed from several sources: an endemic suspicion of émigré scientists such as Szilard; a two-year hiatus between the outbreak of war in 1939 and American entry in 1941; and the speculative nature of such a high-priced undertaking.

Roosevelt's only action in 1939 was the creation of an ad hoc committee on uranium to study the military implications of nuclear physics. Meanwhile, the British began their own atomic project, code-named MAUD. By early 1941, British scientists had come to the conclusion that a uranium weapon was feasible, perhaps within two years. Based on this favorable report—and reports from his own committee—Roosevelt ordered an all-out research effort in early summer 1941 under the direction of Vannevar Bush, head of the Office of Scientific Research and Development (OSRD). In 1942, the program was reorganized, given over to the War Department, and code-named the Manhattan Engineer District. Leslie R. Groves, the Army's chief engineer, was put in charge.

By 1942, then, the outline sketched by Szilard and Einstein in 1939 had taken palpable, though altered, shape. As it turned out, the government played a more prominent role than the two scientists envisioned. The "inofficial" liaison they had suggested became an official one—Brigadier General Leslie R. Groves. And funding came not from the private sector but from the government alone. In other respects, though, Einstein and Szilard anticipated the defining features of the Manhattan Project. The university researchers they had seen as the backbone of the effort remained central to it. Of the thirty-three physicists classified by the government as leaders in the field, twenty worked directly on the bomb. The government relied on industrial laboratories, just as the 1939 letter had suggested, and new laboratories were built for such unprecedented tasks as producing uranium isotopes and plutonium. Previously, those atomic fuels had been available only in microscopic quantities. Because cooperation between the public and private sectors was essential, federal authorities suspended all antitrust actions, even against companies uninvolved with the bomb. To those in urgent pursuit of victory, reform was a luxury affordable only in peacetime.

Surrounding the operation was a shroud of secrecy, unmentioned in the 1939 letter but implicit in the convert race Einstein and Szilard said had already begun. Obviously, the primary aim was to keep any discoveries secret from the Germans and the Japanese, both with atomic projects of their own. But there were other targets as well, and here tensions among the Allies became most manifest. The Russians were excluded entirely from the Manhattan Project, a decision that only aggravated existing Soviet suspicion of the west. Despite their early contributions to the research, the British won access to the project only after vigorous protest. Their success, formalized in the Quebec Agreement of 1943 (see Document 14), was the result of a geologic fact and a diplomatic pledge. The British Empire contained the largest natural reserves of fissionable material in the world, so their cooperation was essential. On top of that, they pledged not to use atomic secrets for commercial advantage after the war.

Even inside the United States, the Manhattan Project was pursued behind closed doors. Congressmen knew nothing about it, except for seven leaders of both parties who were informed in 1944 (see Documents 17 and 22). Most of the scientists and engineers recruited for the project were not told the precise nature of their research. They were kept in the dark, partly to ensure that no one else would learn about their work and partly to keep them from questioning its larger implications.

Little historical controversy has developed over this early phase of the project. Richard G. Hewlett and Oscar E. Anderson's *The New World: A History of the Atomic Energy Commission, 1939/1946* (1962), remains the classic study of the Manhattan Project and offers a richly detailed account of its creation and early organization. The best single-volume study of the atomic bomb and the science that produced it is Richard Rhodes's *The Making of the Atomic Bomb* (1987). The contributions of Great Britain are well covered in Margaret Gowing's *Britain and Atomic Energy, 1939–1945* (1964). Spying on the Manhattan Project is examined in detail in Ronald Radosh and Joyce Milton's *The Rosenberg File: A Search for the Truth* (1984).

Albert Einstein
Old Grove Rd.
Nassau Point
Peconic, Long Island

August 2nd, 1939

F.D. Roosevelt,
President of the United States,
White House
Washington, D.C.

Sir:

Some recent work by E.Fermi and L. Szilard, which has been communicated to me in manuscript, leads me to expect that the element uranium may be turned into a new and important source of energy in the immediate future. Certain aspects of the situation which has arisen seem
to call for watchfulness and, if necessary, quick action on the part
of the Administration. I believe therefore that it is my duty to bring
to your attention the following facts and recommendations:

In the course of the last four months it has been made probable -
through the work of Joliot in France as well as Fermi and Szilard in
America - that it may become possible to set up a nuclear chain reaction
in a large mass of uranium,by which vast amounts of power and large quantities of new radium-like elements would be generated. Now it appears
almost certain that this could be achieved in the immediate future.

This new phenomenon would also lead to the construction of bombs,
and it is conceivable - though much less certain - that extremely powerful bombs of a new type may thus be constructed. A single bomb of this
type, carried by boat and exploded in a port, might very well destroy
the whole port together with some of the surrounding territory. However,
such bombs might very well prove to be too heavy for transportation by
air.

-2-

The United States has only very poor ores of uranium in moderate quantities. There is some good ore in Canada and the former Czechoslovakia, while the most important source of uranium is Belgian Congo.

In view of this situation you may think it desirable to have some permanent contact maintained between the Administration and the group of physicists working on chain reactions in America. One possible way of achieving this might be for you to entrust with this task a person who has your confidence and who could perhaps serve in an inofficial capacity. His task might comprise the following:

a) to approach Government Departments, keep them informed of the further development, and put forward recommendations for Government action, giving particular attention to the problem of securing a supply of uranium ore for the United States;

b) to speed up the experimental work,which is at present being carried on within the limits of the budgets of University laboratories, by providing funds, if such funds be required, through his contacts with private persons who are willing to make contributions for this cause, and perhaps also by obtaining the co-operation of industrial laboratories which have the necessary equipment.

I understand that Germany has actually stopped the sale of uranium from the Czechoslovakian mines which she has taken over. That she should have taken such early action might perhaps be understood on the ground that the son of the German Under-Secretary of State, von Weizäcker, is attached to the Kaiser-Wilhelm-Institut in Berlin where some of the American work on uranium is now being repeated.

Yours very truly,

A. Einstein

(Albert Einstein)

C O P Y

October 19, 1939

My dear Professor:

       I want to thank you for your recent letter and
and the most interesting and important enclosure.[1]

       I found this data of such import that I have
convened a Board[2] consisting of the head of the Bureau
of Standards and a chosen representative of the Army
and Navy to thoroughly investigate the possibilities
of your suggestion regarding the element of uranium.

       I am glad to say that Dr. Sachs[3] will cooperate
and work with this Committee and I feel this is the
most practical and effective method of dealing with
the subject.

       Please accept my sincere thanks.

          Very sincerely yours,

      (signed)   Franklin D. Roosevelt

Dr. Albert Einstein,
Old Grove Road,
Nassau Point,
Peconic, Long Island,
New York.

C O P Y

[1] The enclosure, a memorandum written by Hungarian-born physicist Leo Szilard (who collaborated with Einstein on his letter), is not included.
[2] Advisory committee on uranium.
[3] Alexander Sachs, an economist and adviser to Roosevelt, acted as an intermediary between the President and the two physicists.

SECRET

OFFICE FOR EMERGENCY MANAGEMENT

OFFICE OF SCIENTIFIC RESEARCH AND DEVELOPMENT

1530 P STREET NW.
WASHINGTON, D.C.

VANNEVAR BUSH
Director

March 9, 1942.

The President,
    The White House,
        Washington, D.C.

Dear Mr. President:

On October 9, 1941, Mr. Wallace and I presented to you the status of research in this country and Great Britain on a possible powerful explosive.

In accordance with your instructions, I have since expedited this work in every way possible. I now attach a brief summary report of the status of the matter.[1]

Considerations of general policy and of international relations have been limited for the present to a group consisting of Mr. Wallace, Secretary Stimson, General Marshall, Dr. Conant, and myself. Mr. Wallace called a conference of this group, to which he invited also Mr. Harold D. Smith as the matter of funds was there considered.

The technical aspects are in the hands of a group of notable physicists, chemists, and engineers, as noted in the report. The corresponding British organization is also indicated. The work is under way at full speed.

Recent developments indicate, briefly, that the subject is more important than I believed when I last spoke to you about it. The stuff will apparently be more powerful than we then thought, the amount necessary appears to be less, the possibilities of actual production appear more certain. The way to full accomplishment is still exceedingly difficult, and the time schedule on this remains unchanged. We may be engaged in a race toward realization; but, if so, I have no indication of the status of the enemy program, and have taken no definite steps toward finding out.

[1]The report has not been included.

SECRET

-2-

The subject is rapidly approaching the pilot plant stage. I believe that, by next summer, the most promising methods can be selected, and production plants started. At that time I believe the whole matter should be turned over to the War Department.

You returned to me the previous reports, in order that I might hold them subject to you call. I shall be glad to guard this report also if you wish.

Respectfully yours,

V. Bush,
Director.

SECRET

APPENDIX A
Tubealloy Organization

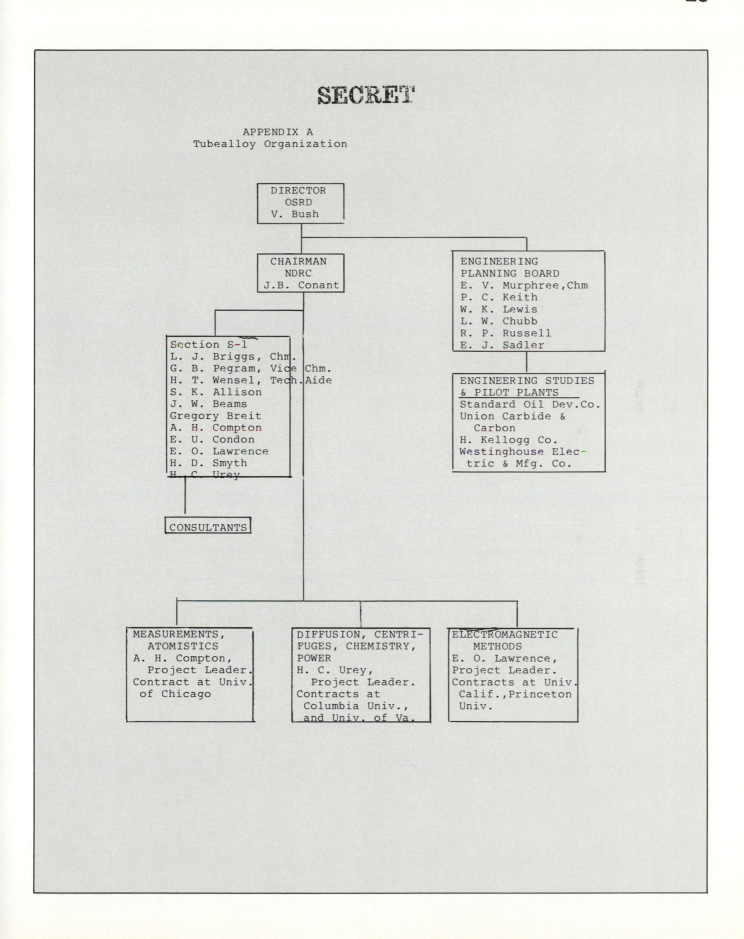

```
                        ┌──────────────┐
                        │ DIRECTOR     │
                        │ OSRD         │
                        │ V. Bush      │
                        └──────┬───────┘
                 ┌─────────────┴──────────────┐
          ┌──────┴────────┐          ┌─────────┴──────────────┐
          │ CHAIRMAN      │          │ ENGINEERING            │
          │ NDRC          │          │ PLANNING BOARD         │
          │ J.B. Conant   │          │ E. V. Murphree,Chm     │
          └──────┬────────┘          │ P. C. Keith            │
                 │                   │ W. K. Lewis            │
     ┌───────────┴──────────┐        │ L. W. Chubb            │
     │ Section S-1          │        │ R. P. Russell          │
     │ L. J. Briggs, Chm.   │        │ E. J. Sadler           │
     │ G. B. Pegram, Vice Chm.│      └─────────┬──────────────┘
     │ H. T. Wensel, Tech.Aide│                │
     │ S. K. Allison        │        ┌─────────┴──────────────┐
     │ J. W. Beams          │        │ ENGINEERING STUDIES    │
     │ Gregory Breit        │        │ & PILOT PLANTS         │
     │ A. H. Compton        │        │ Standard Oil Dev.Co.   │
     │ E. U. Condon         │        │ Union Carbide &        │
     │ E. O. Lawrence       │        │   Carbon               │
     │ H. D. Smyth          │        │ H. Kellogg Co.         │
     │ H. C. Urey           │        │ Westinghouse Elec-     │
     └──────┬───────────────┘        │   tric & Mfg. Co.      │
            │                        └────────────────────────┘
     ┌──────┴───────┐
     │ CONSULTANTS  │
     └──────────────┘
```

MEASUREMENTS, ATOMISTICS	DIFFUSION, CENTRI-FUGES, CHEMISTRY, POWER	ELECTROMAGNETIC METHODS
A. H. Compton, Project Leader. Contract at Univ. of Chicago	H. C. Urey, Project Leader. Contracts at Columbia Univ., and Univ. of Va.	E. O. Lawrence, Project Leader. Contracts at Univ. Calif.,Princeton Univ.

SECRET

APPENDIX B

LIST OF CONTRACTS

Contractor	Subject	Amount
Westinghouse Electric & Manufacturing Company	Experimental centrifuge.	$ 12,000.00
Standard Oil Development Co.	Centrifuge method of separation leading to design of pilot plant.	100,000.00
M. W. Kellogg Company	Diffusion process of separating leading to design of a pilot plant.	50,000.00
Metal Hydrides, Inc.	Purchase of 30 tons of metal.	400,000.00
Consolidated Mining & Smelting Company of Canada	Water electrolysis.	5,000.00
Westinghouse Elevator Co.	Preliminary engineering in connection with a pilot plant.	10,000.00
Westinghouse Electric & Manufacturing Company	Four meter gas separator.	30,000.00
Westinghouse Elevator Co.	Twenty-four gas separators.	193,000.00
Westinghouse Electric & Manufacturing Company	Electric power units.	37,890.75
Standard Oil Development Co.	Studies of exchange reaction.	75,000.00
Westinghouse Electric & Manufacturing Company	Production of 6 tons of metal.	250,000.00
Standard Oil Development Co.	Pilot plant building.	250,000.00

SECRET

-2-

APPENDIX B

LIST OF CONTRACTS

Contractor	Subject	Amount
University of California	Relation between electromagnetic methods and chemical processes.	$305,000.00
Columbia University	Preparation of certain pure chemical substances by physical means.	212,250.00
University of Virginia	Chemical Research.	23,500.00
University of Chicago	Physics aspects of the tube alloy program.	274,500.00
Princeton University	Separation project.	140,925.00
Brown University	Research on separation.	35,000.00
Rockefeller Inst. for Medical Research	Separation of isotopes by mobility method.	10,850.00
Yale University	Methods of electrolytic separation.	49,000.00
Ethyl Gasoline Corporation	Study of possibility of producing volatile "X" compounds.	18,000.00
Iowa State College	Study of possibility of producing volatile "X" compounds.	17,750.00
University of Chicago	Study of possibility of producing volatile "X" compounds.	15,000.00
Standard Oil Development Co.	Search for suitable catalysts.	75,000.00
University of Wisconsin	Rapid rupture in metals.	8,900.00
University of Minnesota	Construction of 3 mass spectrographs, etc.	23,000.00

THE WHITE HOUSE
WASHINGTON

March 11, 1942.

MEMORANDUM FOR DR. VANNEVAR BUSH:

I am greatly interested in your
report of March ninth and I am returning it
herewith for your confidential file. I
think the whole thing should be pushed
not only in regard to development, but also
with due regard to time. This is very much
of the essence. I have no objection to turning over future progress to the War Department on condition that you yourself are
certain that the War Department has made
all adequate provision for absolute secrecy.

F.D.R.

Afternoon, Hyde Park

PRESENT

UNITED STATES	UNITED KINGDOM
President Roosevelt	Prime Minister Churchill
Mr. Hopkins[1]	

Editorial Note

No official record of the substance of the discussion at this meeting has been found. According to Churchill's account in *Hinge of Fate*, pp. 379–381, the meeting was given over to consideration of the problem of sharing American and British information on the development of atomic weapons. In a telegram of February 27, 1943, to Hopkins, Churchill summarized the history of American-British relations on the atomic-bomb project and recalled this particular meeting at Hyde Park in the following terms:

> "The President and the Prime Minister discussed the question generally at Hyde Park in June 1942, and it is the Prime Minister's clear recollection that the whole basis of the conversation was that there was to be complete cooperation and sharing of results." (Hopkins Papers)

In another telegram to Hopkins, also on February 27, 1943, Churchill described the Hyde Park meeting as follows:

> "When the President and I talked of this matter at Hyde Park in June 1942, my whole understanding was that everything was on the basis of fully sharing the results of equal partners. I have no record, but I shall be very much surprised if the President's recollection does not square with this." (Hopkins Papers)

In *The Memoirs of General the Lord Ismay* (London: Heinemann, 1960), p. 254, Ismay remembers that when he reported to the Prime Minister at the White House on the morning of June 21, 1942, Churchill told him that he had reached a satisfactory agreement with Roosevelt on the atomic bomb project. Ismay also was told by Churchill that he had briefly discussed with Roosevelt the question of possible operations in Northwest Africa. It was probably at this meeting that Churchill gave Roosevelt the memorandum printed *post*, p. 461, outlining the strategic decisions facing the Allies. According to the account in Margaret Gowing, *Britain and Atomic Energy 1939–1945* (New York: St. Martin's Press Inc., 1964), p. 145, there was no British written record of this conversation and Churchill did not report upon it when he returned to London.

[1]Harry Hopkins, special assistant to the President.

<u>Thursday, September 10, 1942.</u>

● ● ●

Bundy brought me a report from Bush in reference to S-1[1] recommending that the time had come for a tactical and strategic study under a small group
of officers. I talked it over with Marshall. He was inclined to think that
it would be a little premature and the danger of a leak would be great.

● ● ●

<u>Wednesday, September 23, 1942.</u>

In the afternoon we held a very important meeting on S-1 and arranged
for the organization and immediate prosecution of the work in regard to it. A
policy committee of three consisting of Conant, Bush, and Groves was created and
Groves was chosen for the executive head of the development of the enterprise
from now on.

● ● ●

[1]S-1, the administration's code name for the atomic bomb project.

I was born in New York in 1904. My father had come to this country at the age of 17 from Germany. He was a successful businessman and quite active in community affairs. My mother was born in Baltimore and before her marriage was an artist and teacher of art. I attended Ethical Culture School and Harvard College, which I entered in 1922. I completed the work for my degree in the spring of 1925. I then left Harvard to study at Cambridge University and in Goettingen, where in the spring of 1927 I took my doctor's degree. The following year I was national research fellow at Harvard and at the California Institute of Technology. In the following year I was fellow of the international education board at the University of Leiden and at the Technical High School in Zurich.

In the spring of 1929, I returned to the United States. I was homesick for this country, and in fact I did not leave it again for 19 years. I had learned a great deal in my student days about the new physics; I wanted to pursue this myself, to explain it and to foster its cultivation. I had had many invitations to university positions, 1 or 2 in Europe, and perhaps 10 in the United States. I accepted concurrent appointments as assistant professor at the California Institute of Technology in Pasadena and at the University of California in Berkeley. For the coming 12 years, I was to devote my time to these 2 faculties.

Starting with a single graduate student in my first year in Berkely, we gradually began to build up what was to become the largest school in the country of graduate and postdoctoral study in theoretical physics, so that as time went on, we came to have between a dozen and 20 people learning and adding to quantum theory, nuclear physics, relativity and other modern physics.

My friends, both in Pasadena and in Berkeley, were mostly faculty people, scientists, classicists, and artists. I studied and read Sanskrit with Arthur Rider. I read very widely, mostly classics, novels, plays, and poetry; and I read something of other parts of science. I was not interested in and did not read about economics or politics. I was almost wholly divorced from the contemporary scene in this country. I never read a newspaper or a current magazine like Time or Harper's; I had no radio, no telephone; I learned of the stock-market crash in the fall of 1929 only long after the event; the first time I ever voted was in the presidential election of 1936. To many of my friends, my indifference to contemporary affairs seemed bizarre, and they often chided me with being too much of a highbrow. I was interested in man and his experience; I was deeply interested in my science; but I had no understanding of the relations of man to his society.

Beginning in late 1936, my interests began to change. These changes did not alter my earlier friendships, my relations to my students, or my devotion to physics; but they added something new. I can discern in retrospect more than one reason for these changes. I had had a continuing, smoldering fury about the treatment of Jews in Germany. I had relatives there, and was later to help in extricating them and bringing them to this country. I saw what the depression was doing to my students. Often they could get no jobs, or jobs which were wholly inadequate. And through them, I began to understand how deeply political and economic events could affect men's lives. I began to feel the need to participate more fully in the life of the community. But I had no framework of political conviction or experience to give me perspective in these matters. . . .

Ever since the discovery of nuclear fission, the possibility of powerful explosives based on it had been very much in my mind, as it had in that of many other physicists. We had some understanding of what this might do for us in the war, and how much it might change the course of history. In the autumn of 1941, a special committee was set up by the National Academy of Sciences under the chairmanship of Arthur Compton to review the prospects and feasibility of the different uses of atomic energy for military purposes. I attended a meeting of this committee; this was my first official connection with the atomic-energy program.

After the academy meeting, I spent some time in preliminary calculations about the consumption and performance of atomic bombs, and became increasingly excited at the prospects. At the same time I still had a quite heavy burden of academic work with courses and graduate students. I also began to consult, more or less regularly, with the staff of the Radiation Laboratory in Berkeley on their program for the electromagnetic separation of uranium isotopes. I was never a member or employee of the laboratory; but I attended many of its staff and policy meetings. With the help of two of my graduate students, I developed an invention which was embodied in the production plants at Oak Ridge. I attended the conference in Chicago at which the Metallurgical Laboratory (to produce plutonium) was established and its initial program projected.

In the spring of 1942, Compton called me to Chicago to discuss the state of work on the bomb itself. During this meeting Compton asked me to take the responsibility for this work, which at that time consisted of numerous scattered experimental projects. Although I had no administrative experience and was not an experimental physicist, I felt sufficiently informed and challenged by the problem to be glad to accept. At this time I became an employee of the Metallurgical Laboratory.

After this conference I called together a theoretical study group in Berkeley, in which Bethe, Konopinski, Serber, Teller, Van Fleck, and I participated. We had an adventurous time. We spent much of the summer of 1942 in Berkeley in a joint study that for the first time really came to grips with the physical problems of atomic bombs, atomic explosions, and the possibility of using fission explosions to initiate thermonuclear reactions. I called this possibility to the attention of Dr. Bush during the late summer; the technical views on this subject were to develop and change from them until the present day.

After these studies there was little doubt that a potentially world-shattering undertaking lay ahead. We began to see the great explosion at Alamogordo and the greater explosions at Eniwetok with a surer foreknowledge. We also began to see how rough, difficult, challenging, and unpredictable this job might turn out to be. . . .

In later summer, after a review of the experimental work, I became convinced, as did others, that a major change was called for in the work on the bomb itself. We needed a central laboratory devoted wholly to this purpose, where people could talk freely with each other, where theoretical ideas and experimental findings could affect each other, where the waste and frustration and error of the many compartmentalized experimental studies could be eliminated, where we could begin to come to grips with chemical, metallurgical, engineering, and ordnance problems that had so far received no consideration. We therefore sought to establish this laboratory for a direct attack on all the problems inherent in the most rapid possible development and production of atomic bombs.

In the autumn of 1942 General Groves assumed charge of the Manhattan Engineer District. I discussed with him the need for an atomic bomb laboratory. There had been some thought of making this laboratory a part of Oak Ridge. For a time there was support for making it a Military Establishment in which key personnel would be commissioned as officers; and in preparation for this course I once went to the Presidio to take the initial steps toward obtaining a commission. After a good deal of discussion with the personnel who would be needed at Los Alamos and with General Groves and his advisers, it was decided that the laboratory should, at least initially, be a civilian establishment in a military post. While this consideration was going on, I had showed General Groves Los Alamos; and he almost immediately took steps to acquire the site.

In early 1943, I received a letter signed by General Groves and Dr. Conant, appointing me director of the laboratory, and outlining their conception of how it was to be organized and administered. The necessary construction and assembling of the needed facilities were begun. All of us worked in close colloboration with the engineers of the Manhattan District.

The site of Los Alamos was selected in part at least because it enabled those responsible to balance the obvious need for security with the equally important need of free communication among those engaged in the work. Security, it was hoped, would be achieved by removing the laboratory to a remote area, fenced and patrolled, where communication with the outside was extremely limited. Telephone calls were monitored, mail was censored, and personnel who left the area—something permitted only for the clearest of causes—knew that their movements might be under surveillance. On the other hand, for those within the community, fullest exposition and discussion among those competent to use the information was encouraged.

The last months of 1942 and early 1943 had hardly hours enough to get Los Alamos established. The real problem had to do with getting to Los Alamos the men who would make a success of the undertaking. For this we needed to understand as clearly as we then could what our technical program would be, what men we would need, what facilities, what organization, what plan.

The program of recruitment was massive. Even though we then underestimated the ultimate size of the laboratory, which was to have almost 4,000 members by the spring of 1945, and even though we did not at that time see clearly some of the difficulties which were to bedevil and threaten the enterprise, we knew that it was a big, complex and diverse job. Even the initial plan of the laboratory called for a start with more than 100 highly qualified and trained scientists, to say nothing of the technicians, staff, and mechanics who would be required for their support, and of the equipment that we would have to beg and borrow since there would be no time to build it from scratch. We had to recruit at a time when the country was fully engaged in war and almost every competent scientist was already involved in the military effort.

The primary burden of this fell on me. To recruit staff I traveled all over the country talking with people who had been working on one or another aspect of the atomic-energy enterprise, and people in radar work, for example, and underwater sound, telling them about the job, the place that we were going to, and enlisting their enthusiasm.

In order to bring responsible scientists to Los Alamos, I had to rely on their sense of the interest, urgency, and feasibility of the Los Alamos mission. I had to tell them enough of what the job was, and give strong enough assurance that it might be successfully accomplished in time to affect the outcome of the war, to make it clear that they were justified in their leaving other work to come to this job.

The prospect of coming to Los Alamos aroused great misgivings. It was to be a military post; men were asked to sign up more or less for the duration; restrictions on travel and on the freedom of families to move about to be severe; and no one could be sure of the extent to which the necessary technical freedom of action could actually be maintained by the laboratory. The notion of disappearing into the New Mexico desert for an indeterminate period and under quasi military auspices disturbed a good many scientists, and the families of many more. But there was another side to it. Almost everyone realized that this was a great undertaking. Almost everyone knew that if it were completed successfully and rapidly enough, it might determine the outcome of the war. Almost everyone knew that it was an unparalleled opportunity to bring to bear the basic knowledge and art of science for the benefit of his country. Almost everyone knew that this job, if it were achieved, would be a part of history. This sense of excitement, of devotion and of patriotism in the end prevailed. Most of those with whom I talked came to Los Alamos. Once they came, confidence in the enterprise grew as men learned more of the technical status of the work; and though the laboratory was to double and redouble its size many times before the end, once it had started it was on the road to success.

We had information in those days of German activity in the field of nuclear fission. We were aware of what it might mean if they beat us to the draw in the development of atomic bombs. The consensus of all our opinions, and every directive that I had, stressed the extreme urgency of our work, as well as the need for guarding all knowledge of it from our enemies. . . .

The story of Los Alamos is long and complex. Part of it is public history. For me it was a time so filled with work, with the need for decision and action and consultation, that there was room for little else. I lived with my family in the community which was Los Alamos. It was a remarkable community, inspired by a high sense of mission, of duty and of destiny, coherent, dedicated, and remarkably selfless. There was plenty in the life of Los Alamos to cause irritation; the security restrictions, many of my own devising, the inadequacies and inevitable fumblings of a military post unlike any that had ever existed before, shortages, inequities and in the laboratory itself the shifting emphasis on different aspects of the technical work as the program moved forward; but I have never known a group more understanding and more devoted to a common purpose, more willing to lay aside personal convenience and prestige, more understanding of the role that they were playing in their country's history. Time and again we had in the technical work almost paralyzing crises. Time and again the laboratory drew itself together and faced the new problems and got on with the work. We worked by night and by day; and in the end the many jobs were done. . . .

Secret

OFFICE FOR EMERGENCY MANAGEMENT
OFFICE OF SCIENTIFIC RESEARCH AND DEVELOPMENT
1530 P STREET NW.
WASHINGTON, D.C.

VANNEVAR BUSH
Director

March 31, 1943.

M E M O R A N D U M

TO: Mr. Harry Hopkins

FROM: V. Bush

RE: Interchange on S-1.

    On March twenty-fourth the President passed me
the accompanying file on interchange with the British
on S-1, and instructed me to prepare a reply, undoubtedly by suggesting material for a reply to you,
since the attached cables are marked for your attention.

    There is no longer any assertion of breach of
agreement. The objection of the British must hence be
either to the adopted policy or to the way in which it
is being applied. I have discussed this matter again
with the Military Policy Committee on the subject, and
briefly with Secretary Stimson. None of us can see that
the present policy, which was approved by the President
after it had had the careful review and approval of
General Marshall, Secretary Stimson, and Vice President
Wallace, is in any way unreasonable, or such as to impede the war effort on this matter. Neither can we see
that the application is at present unwise. I believe,
therefore, that it will be necessary to determine more
explicitly why the British object, before any modification
could be recommended. It is true, as indicated in the
last paragraph of CCWD 1744, that a prompt resolution of
this matter is desirable. However, the present unwill-
ingness of the British to conduct certain scientific interchange, to which we have invited them, merely means
that our scientists do not have for the moment the benefit of their collaboration in the studies constantly being conducted. This is of much less importance than a
clear understanding on a matter of the unique significance of this. I will therefore review the policy and
its application, and I suggest that you request the
British for explicit criticism.

-2-

The adopted policy is that information on this subject will be furnished to individuals, either in this country or Great Britain, who need it and can use it now in the furtherance of the war effort, but that, in the interests of security, information interchanged will be restricted to this definite objective.

There is nothing new or unusual in such a policy. It is applied generally to military matters in this country and elsewhere. To step beyond it would mean to furnish information on secret military matters to individuals who wish it either because of general interest or because of its application to non-war or post-war matters. To do so would decrease security without advancing the war effort.

The application of this principle is in no way unilateral. In applying the policy in this instance full over-all information has been withheld, for example, from our own Naval Research Laboratory. This has been done with the concurrence of appropriate Naval authority, and in spite of the fact that the Naval Research Laboratory would like to have full information. That laboratory, like other laboratories engaged on the subject, is furnished with all the technical information necessary for full progress on the part of the program which it is carrying forward. To go further would decrease security, and security on this subject is important. In this connection it should be remembered that the Naval Research Laboratory was engaged on aspects of this research very early, in fact I believe as early as any group anywhere, under the guidance of a special committee appointed by the President. This committee was recognized under NDRC when the latter was formed.

This same policy is applied throughout the OSRD organization. The principle is that no individual receives secret information except as it is necessary for his proper functioning in connection with his assigned duties. It is used by the British themselves, and they occasionally ask us to apply special restrictions on information they furnish us, beyond current practice, when especially secret matters are involved.

-3-

        I find it hard to believe, therefore, that the
present British objection is to the policy. However,
the last two paragraphs of CCWD 1807 Z are very pertinent in this connection. The first of these states the
principle, and the second states that the application
made is a logical result of the principle. It then goes
on to say that this "destroys the original conception of
'a coordinated or even jointly conducted effort between
the two countries'." If the application is logical,
then the objection must be to the principle itself. To
step beyond this principle would, however, involve giving information to those who could use it, not for the
best prosecution of the war effort, but rather for other
purposes, such as after-the-war commercial advantages.

        I have to conclude, therefore, that the British
objection arises because of our withholding information
which they consider might be of value in connection with
their post-war situation. If that is really their position, then presumably it should be duly considered in
connection with the entire post-war relationship between
the two countries. It should be considered on its merits,
and in due perspective to other relations. To transmit
such information for such a purpose would involve our
giving to Great Britain information obtained by this
country as a result of great expense and effort, and,
while we freely transmit for the purpose of furthering
our joint war effort, we can hardly give away the fruits
of our development as a part of post-war planning except
on the basis of some over-all agreement on that subject,
which agreement does not now exist. The proper conduct
of the secure development of a potentially important
weapon should not be modified to produce this further result simply as an incident. In this connection I draw
your attention to the enclosed memorandum by Dr. Conant.[1]

        My recommendation, therefore, is that the reply
to the appended telegrams should attempt to fix the issue
upon this point, if this is indeed, as I am inclined to
believe, the point which is primarily in the mind of the
British, in order that it may be considered in due time
in connection with the broad problem of post-war relationships.

[1]The enclosure has not been included.

-4-

Specific points of application of the principle
other than this are not, I believe, prominently in the
British mind. However, it will be well to review them
briefly; for they are consistent with the policy, appli-
cable without distinction to UK and US groups, and, I
believe, reasonable, and adapted to best progress with
due regard to security.

There has been, from the beginning, full scientific interchange wherever scientific groups are working,
in the two countries, on the same aspect of the subject.
This it is proposed to continue. Recent failure to do
so has been due entirely to British refusal thus to col-
laborate, while a policy to which they object stands.

Thus, there is a group in Chicago working on one
part of the program, and a group on the same phase is being formed in Canada. We proposed complete scientific
interchange between these groups as far as scientific research is concerned, but not on the details of the manufacturing process which we alone are prepared to carry on.
Similarly there are groups on the scientific aspects of
diffusion, and we proposed continued interchange here on
a similar basis.

On the other hand, we have long worked at California on an electromagnetic process, and the British have
not worked along these lines. We see no need for fur-
nishing them information on our scientific results on
this phase. They do not, I feel, object. They could not
use such information, and our scientific group on this
phase is fully adequate, and now includes as many scientific men as should work on this phase, at the expense
of other scientific phases of the war effort.

We propose shortly to gather a special scientific
group at an isolated site to work on some of the phases
involved in actual bomb construction. It is essential
that this be kept from the enemy at all costs. It is exceedingly difficult in this field, where the general background was known to all sorts of scientists all over the
world before the work was brought under control, to secure adequate secrecy. Hence we propose to isolate this

-5-

group, by special measures, from the rest of the world, including the bulk of our own scientists and of British scientists. However, we are quite willing to invite a British scientist or two to join the group, and have so indicated, provided they will render themselves subject to the same rigid control, for a period which may be several years, as apply to the American scientists that we invite.

We are now erecting manufacturing plants. The information gathered in reducing the manufacture to practice will be extensive, and many inventions will result in patent applications assigned to the United States Government. This is being handled through American companies in which we have confidence. We do not propose to make these manufacturing plans available to any group, British or American, unless it is fully necessary thus to extend information in order to maintain full speed. British commercial interests would like to have these plans, and an account of the operations of plants. So would, undoubtedly, various American companies that are not bound under contract to extend patent rights to the U.S. Government on any invention made by them in this connection.

Finally, there is the matter of military use. This will not come into question for some time. If the war is not of long duration, if there is no danger that the method may be used against us with disastrous results, it may never come into question. When it does, there will undoubtedly be set up special military channels for appropriate consideration of strategy, tactics, and use. I feel sure there is no concern in the minds of the British on this point.

In conclusion, before making a final reply, it is my recommendation that you again state the case briefly, and inquire where the specific objection now rests.

G. Cooperation with the United Kingdom in Research on Atomic Energy

HOPKINS PAPERS: TELEGRAM

Prime Minister Churchill to the President's Special Assistant (Hopkins)[1]

SECRET   LONDON, June 10, 1943.

374. From the Prime Minister to Mr. Harry Hopkins personal.

As you will remember, the President agreed that the exchange of information on TUBE ALLOYS should be resumed and that the enterprise should be considered a joint one to which both countries would contribute their best endeavours.[2] I understood that his ruling would be based upon the fact that this weapon may be developed in time for the present war and that it thus falls within the general agreement covering the inter-change of research and invention secrets.

I am very grateful for all your help in getting this question settled so satisfactorily. I am sure that the President's decision will be to the best advantage of both our countries. We must lose no time in implementing it.

I have asked the Lord President[3] to make sure that the right people are on the spot and ready to resume active collaboration as soon as the President has given the necessary instructions. I should be grateful if you would telegraph me as soon as this has been done so that our people can be instructed to proceed to Washington and be at your disposal.

PRIME

HOPKINS PAPERS: TELEGRAM

The President's Special Assistant (Hopkins) to Prime Minister Churchill[4]

SECRET   [WASHINGTON,] June 17, 1943.

●   ●   ●

The matter of TUBE ALLOYS is in hand and I think will be disposed of completely the first of the week.

●   ●   ●

[1]Channel of transmission not indicated.
[2]The reference is to discussions during the TRIDENT Conference held at Washington in May 1943.
[3]Sir John Anderson.
[4]Channel of transmission not indicated.

TELEPHONE CONVERSATION BETWEEN THE SECRETARY

OF WAR AND SENATOR TRUMAN, JUNE 17, 1943.

Sec.   Hello.

Truman   Hello.

Sec.   Hello, is this Senator Truman?

Truman   Yes, this is Senator Truman.

Sec.   Senator, I have been trying to get at you for two purposes.

Truman   I noticed the call and I meant to have returned it right
          away, but I couldn't get you yesterday, and I've been up
          to see Jim Byrnes this morning and that's the reason you
          didn't get me the first time.

Sec.   I see. Well, the first was merely to tell you that I had
          received your letter about the Moral Rearmament Group, and
          I've been taking a good deal of pains to try to see -- to
          use them, to try to carry out their work without putting me
          in an indefensible position toward other people.

Truman   I think you are exactly right on that and I don't want to - -

Sec.   They've got to become soldiers and they've got to go through
          that and then we'll try to see what we can do after they have
          had that experience by assembling them again with much greater
          power than they would have had before they had had that ex-
          perience.

Truman   I think you are exactly right, Mr. Secretary, and that's
          always been my idea on the subject, and I hesitated a long
          time before sending you that letter, but I really think the
          outfit has done some good among the labor people.

Sec.   I have been very glad to hear that and I have very great - -
          well, I try not to forget the various spiritual influences in
          life which these fellows are appealing to, so I wouldn't try
          to lose sight of that.

Truman   Well I appreciate that.

Sec.   The other matter is a very different matter. It's connected
          with - - I think I've had a letter from Mr. Hally, I think,
          who is an assistant of Mr. Fulton of your office.

Truman   That's right.

- 2 -

Sec.   In connection with the plant at Pasco, Washington.[1]

Truman   That's right.

Sec.   Now that's a matter which I know all about personally, and I am one of the group of two or three men in the whole world who know about it.

Truman   I see.

Sec.   It's part of a very important secret development.

Truman   Well, all right then - - -

Sec.   And I - -

Truman   I herewith see the situation, Mr. Secretary, and you won't have to say another word to me. Whenever you say that to me, that's all I want to hear.

Sec.   All right.

Truman   Here is what caused that letter. There is a plant in Minneapolis that was constructed for a similar purpose and it had not been used, and we had been informed that they were taking the machinery out of that plant and using it at this other one for the same purpose, and we just couldn't understand that and that's the reason for that letter.

Sec.   No, No, something - - -

Truman   You assure that this is for a specific purpose and you think it's all right; that's all I need to know.

Sec.   Not only for a specific purpose, but a unique purpose.

Truman   All right, then.

Sec.   Thank you very much.

Truman   You don't need to tell me anything else.

Sec.   Well, I'm very much obliged.

Truman   Thank you very much.

Sec.   Goodby.

Truman   Goodby.

[1]The Hanford Engineer Works for producing plutonium.

Secret

June 29, 1943

My dear General Groves:

I have recently reviewed with Dr. Bush the highly
important and secret program of research, development and
manufacture with which you are familiar. I was very glad to
hear of the excellent work which is being dome in a number
of places in this country under your immediate supervision
and the general direction of the Committee of which Dr. Bush
is Chairman. The successful solution of the problem is of
the utmost importance to the national safety, and I am
confident that the work will be completed in as short a time
as possible as the result of the wholehearted cooperation
of all concerned.

I am writing to you as the one who has charge of
all the development and manufacturing aspects of this work.
I know that there are several groups of scientists working
under your direction on various phases of the program. The
fact that the outcome of their labors is of such great
significance to the nation requires that this project be
even more drastically guarded than other highly secret war
developments. As you know, I have therefore given directions
that every precaution be taken to insure the security of
your project. I am sure the scientists are fully aware of
the reasons why their endeavors must be circumscribed by
very special restrictions. Nevertheless, I wish you would
express to them my deep appreciation of their willingness
to undetake the tasks which lie before them in spite of
the possible dangers and the personal sacrifices involved.
In particular, I should be glad to have you communicate the
contents of this letter to the leaders of each important
group. I am sure we can rely on the continued wholehearted
and unselfish labors of those now engaged. Whatever the
enemy may be planning, American Science will be equal to
the challenge. With this thought in mind, I send this note
of confidence and appreciation.

Very sincerely yours,

Franklin D Roosevelt

Brigadier General L. R. Groves,
Room 5120, New War Department Building,
21st and Virginia Avenue, N.W.,
Washington, D. C.

Memorandum by the Secretary of War's Special Assistant (Bundy)

SECRET

MEMORANDUM OF MEETING AT 10 DOWNING STREET ON JULY 22, 1943

PRESENT

GREAT BRITAIN	U.S.
The Prime Minister,	Secretary of War,[1]
Sir John Anderson,	Dr. Vannevar Bush,
Lord Cherwell.	H. H. Bundy

The Prime Minister opened the question of exchange of information on S-1 and stated that the President had agreed with him several times that the matter would be a joint enterprise, these agreements not having been reduced to writing but having been verbally expressed in June, 1942, and again at Casablanca and in U.S.[2] The British, therefore, were very much concerned when they received on June [*January*] 7, 1943, a memorandum from Dr. Conant rigidly limiting the exchange of information. This appeared to be about the time that the War Department took over the project in the U.S.A.[3] The British have been urging a reexamination of the question in order to carry out what the Prime Minister considers the President's agreement but no satisfactory assurances have been received.

The Prime Minister took the position that this particular matter was so important that it might affect seriously British American relationships; that it would not be satisfactory for the United States to claim the right to sole knowledge in this matter. The Prime Minister further said that Britain was not interested in the commercial aspects but was vitally interested in the possession of all information because this will be necessary for Britain's independence in the future as well as for success during the war; that it would never do to have Germany or Russia win the race for something which might be used for international blackmail; and that Russia might be in a position to accomplish this result unless we worked together. The Prime Minister further said that at the Peace Conference the United States could never take the position that it alone should have control of this matter, and that if the United States took the position that it would not interchange fully it would be necessary for Great Britain immediately to start a parallel development even though this was a most unwise use of energies during the war. Therefore, the Prime Minister stated that he thought it vital that the matter be reexamined and a free exchange brought about.

Dr. Bush stated that the U.S. had always been ready to exchange scientific information but there had been a limitation on exchange of manufacturing information unless it would help the recipient in the task of winning *this* war; that this limitation followed general security principles in war time. He further doubted that

---

[1]Henry L. Stimson.
[2]Note by General Groves:We have been unable to secure any confirmations of this. [Footnote in the source text. See *Foreign Relations*, The Conferences at Washington, 1941–1942, and Casablanca, 1943, pp. 132,S03]
[3]Note by General Groves: The War Department (MANHATTAN Engineer District) started to take over the project in the summer of 1942 and to control the interchange of information in the fall of 1942. [Footnote in the source text.]

the Conant memorandum had been delivered to the British as the final American position; that the wording of this memorandum placed the matter in a negative light; and that the formula for exchange actually offered by the U.S.A.[4] was completely adequate to the best interests of both parties to winning this war; that post war problems were separate, and that the difficulties of complete exchange lay in respect to post war matters, both political and commercial. The Prime Minister placed no importance or emphasis on any hope of commercial advantage and Sir John Anderson stated that the commercial aspect had confused the issue and probably the United States received the idea of the British emphasis on commercial advantage because they had used the commercial possibilities as a camouflage for the real purposes in the effort.[5]

The Secretary then stated his views of the present situation as follows, reading from a memorandum:

1. Two Governments in possession of an unfinished scientific hypothetical formula on which they are working.
2. Both Governments continue working on the development of that formula and are ready to interchange reports of their respective developments.
3. U.S. at large expenditure of public monies sets on foot construction out of which these formulae may be transformed into practical products; on the understanding that U.K. may share these products for the joint object of winning the war.
4. U.K. now asks U.S. for running reports on its constructive designs and other manufacturing experience, in order that U.K. after the war is ended and its present strain of other construction is over, may be in a position to prepare itself to promptly produce against the danger of a new threat or a new war.
5. Should the U.S. grant this request unequivocally? Should it seek safeguards against any use of product except under political restrictions? Should it refuse the request as entirely uncalled for, under the original agreement between the President and Prime Minister?

The Prime Minister remarked that this was a trenchant analysis of the situation. The Prime Minister then suggested that he would be in favor of an agreement between himself and the President of the United States having the following points:

1. A free interchange to the end that the matter be a completely joint enterprise.
2. That each Government should agree not to use this invention against the other.
3. That each Government should agree not to give information to any other parties without the consent of both.
4. That they should agree not to use it against any other parties without the consent of both.
5. That the commercial or industrial uses of Great Britain should be limited in such manner as the President might consider fair and equitable in view of the large additional expense incurred by the U.S.

[4]Based on the policy of restricting information to those able to use it in furthering the war effort.
[5]Note by General Groves: It was clear to me that Mr. Akers was thinking primarily of commercial advantages of Britain after the war during his conferences in the fall of 1942. [Footnote in the source text.]

The Secretary stated that he was not in a position to express any U.S. Government views on these suggestions but would be glad to present these to the President of the United States for his consideration.

After the adjournment to the meeting, Dr. Bush and I waited with Lord Cherwell while the Secretary was talking with the Prime Minister on other matters, and I pointed out to Lord Cherwell the great difficulty of the President making any promises which were not strictly within the war powers and the political danger of such promises in the President's relation with Congress which might later seriously prejudice any attempt to reach a fair agreement between the United States and Great Britain.

H[ARVEY] H. B[UNDY]

ROOSEVELT PAPERS: TELEGRAM

President Roosevelt to Prime Minister Churchill[1]

SECRET   [WASHINGTON,] July 26, 1943.

326. Personal and secret to the Former Naval Person[2] from the President.

   In reply to your 354, I have arranged satisfactorily for the TUBE ALLOYS. Unless you have the proper person in this country now, it might be well if your top man in this enterprise comes over to get full understanding from our people.

ROOSEVELT

---

[1]Channel of transmission not indicated.
[2]Roosevelt's nickname for Winston Churchill, who had served as First Lord of the Admiralty earlier in his career.

Articles of Agreement Governing Collaboration between the Authorities of the U.S.A. and the U.K. in the matter of Tube Alloys

Whereas it is vital to our common safety in the present War to bring the Tube Alloys project to fruition at the earliest moment; and whereas this may be more speedily achieved if all available British and American brains and resources are pooled; and whereas owing to war conditions it would be an improvident use of war resources to duplicate plants on a large scale on both sides of the Atlantic and therefore a far greater expense has fallen upon the United States;

It is agreed between us

First, that we will never use this agency against each other.

Secondly, that we will not use it against third parties without each other's consent.

Thirdly, that we will not either of us communicate any information about Tube Alloys to third parties except by mutual consent.

Fourthly, that in view of the heavy burden of production falling upon the United States as the result of a wise division of war effort, the British Government recognise that any post-war advantages of an industrial or commercial character shall be dealt with as between the United States and Great Britain on terms to be specified by the President of the United States to the Prime Minister of Great Britain. The Prime Minister expressly disclaims any interest in these industrial and commercial aspects beyond what may be considered by the President of the United States to be fair and just and in harmony with the economic welfare of the world.

And Fifthly, that the following arrangements shall be made to ensure full and effective collaboration between the two countries in bringing the project to fruition:

(a) There shall be set up in Washington a Combined Policy Committee composed of:

The Secretary of War	(United States)
Dr Vannevar Bush	(United States)
Dr James B. Conant	(United States)
Field-Marshal Sir John Dill, G.C.B., C.M.G., D.S.O.	(United Kingdom)
Colonel the Right Hon. J. J. Llewellin, C.B.E., M.C., M.P.	(United Kingdom)
The Honourable C. D. Howe	(Canada)

The functions of this Committee, subject to the control of the respective Governments, will be:

(1) To agree from time to time upon the programme of work to be carried out in the two countries.

(2) To keep all sections of the project under constant review.

(3) To allocate materials, apparatus and plant, in limited supply, in accordance with the requirements of the programme agreed by the Committee.

(4) To settle any questions which may arise on the interpretation or application of this Agreement.

(*b*) There shall be complete interchange of information and ideas on all sections of the project between members of the Policy Committee and their immediate technical advisers.

(*c*) In the field of scientific research and development there shall be full and effective interchange of information and ideas between those in the two countries engaged in the same sections of the field.

(*d*) In the field of design, construction and operation of large-scale plants, interchange of information and ideas shall be regulated by such *ad hoc* arrangements as may, in each section of the field, appear to be necessary or desirable if the project is brought to fruition at the earliest moment. Such *ad hoc* arrangements shall be subject to the approval of the Policy Committee.

<u>Thursday, September 9, 1943</u>
<u>Page 2</u>

●　●　●

　　　　We had a scare about S-1. CIO[1] is trying to unionize the workers
in the laboratory at the University of California at Berkeley and they are
already getting information about vital secrets and sending them to Russia.
So I called up the President and told him that this was a vital danger and
asked him if he would not get hold of Phil Murray[2] and tell him that this group
simply cannot be unionized. He was much impressed and promised to do so at
once.

●　●　●

[1]Congress of Industrial Organization, a union of industrial workers.
[2]President of the C.I.O.

THE WHITE HOUSE
WASHINGTON

October 26, 1943.

MEMORANDUM FOR

THE SECRETARY OF WAR

When you spoke to me about

the Union activities at the

Laboratory at the University of

California, I took it up at once

and was assured by Phil Murray

that this would end at once.

I will check again.

F. D. R.

Mr Bundy.   10/28/43
The Sec. has not read
this as yet
Sec noted 10/28/43. MoB

Friday, February 18, 1944.

After a preliminary conference with General Clay, Dr. Bush, Bundy,
and Marshall, in order to polish up on the subject, Bush, Marshall and I went
up to Speaker Rayburn's office in the Capitol where we met John McCormack,
Democratic leader in the House, and Joe Martin, the Republican leader. Then
for the first time we disclosed to them in outline what we were doing in S-1.
I acted as the introductory spokesman, telling them the history of the situation.
Bush followed with the scientific details and Marshall gave the military importance
of the situation. The whole meeting went off satisfactorily and the three
gentlemen whom we had met professed to be completely satisfied that we were
right and should have the money which we asked. We discussed with them the
best ways of doing it and they agreed to take the matter of breaking the way
for us with the members of the Appropriations Committee into their own hands.
Marshall is to get a draft of the itemized program of these appropriations
as we shall present it to the Appropriations Committee and Rayburn, Martin,
and McCormack are to see that the Committee does not discuss them in public.

```
C
 O
  P
   Y.
```

UNITED STATES SENATE

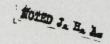

Special Committee Investigating
the National Defense Program

March 10, 1944.

Dear Mr. Stimson:

About June 15, 1943 the Committee requested of the
War Department information with respect to the project in
the neighborhood of Pasco, Washington, and you will recall
that you made a specific request upon me that the Committee
not make any investigation whatever as to that project
because of your fear that important secrets might become
known to the enemy.

Since that time, the Committee has received, both
directly and from five members of the Senate, not members
of the Committee, suggestions that the undertaking at Pasco
is being carried out in a wasteful manner.

Bearing in mind your desire for secrecy, the Committee
several weeks ago suggested that Brigadier General Frank
Lowe and Lieutenant Colonel Harry Vaughan be sent by the
Committee to the Pasco project solely for the purpose of
investigating questions of waste with respect to the construction of housing roads and other matters not relating to the
processes of manufacture or other secrets connected with the
project.

This suggestion was made because General Lowe had
been assigned by the Chief of Staff of the Army as Executive
Officer to the Committee for the purpose of carrying out
assignments made by the Committee in which it was expected
that his personal experience and qualifications and his
duties in the War Department especially would qualify him.
The detail was not sought by General Lowe nor by the Committee
but was welcomed by the Committee because the Committee
believed that General Lowe could serve a valuable function.

In this instance, I thought that General Lowe would be
especially valuable because he is an officer of the Army and

his obligations as such certainly preclude any assumption that he could not be safely permitted to examine into the non-secret portions of the Pasco project, especially as those portions are being constructed by thousands of civilians who have access thereto.

I understand that Mr. Julius Amberg on your behalf has notified the Committee that you personally oppose any examination into this project, and that you have decided that General Lowe, if sent to the project, would be barred from entering it. I understand further that you suggest that any investigation desired by the Committee be conducted by personnel of the War Department to be chosen by it. If such personnel is limited to those in charge of the construction of the project, it is my opinion that no useful purpose would be served by asking them to investigate themselves. If such investigation is to be conducted by any other personnel, I do not understand why it would be expected that the secrets would be any safer with such other personnel than with General Lowe, in whom the Committee has the utmost confidence.

If General Lowe is not to be permitted to serve the functions for which he was detailed, a serious question arises as to whether his detail should not be reviewed by the War Department insofar as his duties with this Committee affect the War Department.

The decision which has been made by the War Department with respect to the Pasco project, if it has been made as indicated above, is a serious one. It may be necessary for the Committee to consider the appointment of a subcommittee to investigate the project. On your urgent request, that usual procedure will not be adopted at this time. The responsibility therefor and for any waste or improper action which might otherwise be avoided rests squarely upon the War Department.

Very truly yours,

/sgd/ HARRY S. TRUMAN
U.S.S.

Honorable Henry L. Stimson
The Secretary of War

Washington, D.C.

SECRET

March 13, 1944.

Honorable Harry S. Truman,
The United States Senate,
Washington, D. C.

Dear Senator Truman:

I have your letter of March 10th. I remember
very well my pleasant talk with you on June 15, 1943, and your
ready acquiescence in my request that you trust my assurance as
to the character and importance of the Pasco project, and to
not make any investigation into it until the purpose of the
project be accomplished.

I am sorry that your committee is being pressed by
members of the Congress with suggestions that the project is
being carried out in a wasteful manner. I assure you that this
question as to such waste cannot be justly or properly ascertained
until the project has been carried out and its necessity and
purpose understood.

In declining to take into my confidence any further
persons, whether Army officers or civilians, I am merely carrying out the express directions of the President of the United
States.

With much regret that I cannot properly accede to
your request in respect to General Lowe and Colonel Vaughn, I
shall have to accept the responsibility suggested in your letter.

Very sincerely yours,

HENRY L. STIMSON

Secretary of War.

<u>Monday, March 13, 1944.</u>
<u>Page 2.</u>

● ● ●

Today I also sent off my letter to Senator Truman politely telling him that I could not consent to telling the story of S-1 to one of his aides, General Lowe, whom he wished me to take into my confidence. He had threatened me with dire consequences. I told him I had to accept the responsibility for those consequences because I had been directed by the President to do just what I did do. Truman is a nuisance and a pretty untrustworthy man. He talks smoothly but he acts meanly.

● ● ●

Mr. Bundy's file copy

May 12, 1944.

TOP SECRET

Dear Mr. President:

When the question of the suit brought by the
United States against Dupont and the Imperial Chemical Company
came before the Cabinet last Thursday, I regret that I did not
recall that this Company was connected with S-1 project,
sometimes referred to as Tube Alloys. As a matter of fact
the Dupont Company has entire charge of the construction and
operation of the two main installations, and the top executives
are the key to the successful operation of this project.
In my opinion any diversion of their time would be disastrous.
We have been urging upon them that there must be no delay even
for a day in the progress of this project.

By imposing upon them at the present time the
time-consuming burden which would inevitably be involved in preparing for this litigation¹, we would be taking a position so at
variance to that which we have been heretofore strenuously taking
with them in regard to the necessity of haste that I think it
would inevitably cause a slackening up in promptitude in the
completion of the work. I therefore strongly urge that the
litigation be stayed entirely for the present.

I do not think the Attorney General is familiar with
the implications of this S-1 situation and I have not undertaken
to advise him because of its peculiar nature. I enclose herewith a memorandum received from Judge Patterson which goes into
somewhat more detail on this litigation.

Faithfully yours,

HENRY L. STIMSON

Secretary of War.

Encl: Memo. from
  Judge Patterson 5/22/44.

*Mr. Bundy handled sending above
to White House thru Col. McCarthy*

The President,
The White House

copies to Miss Neary, C. + R. Bur., + Judge Patterson

¹A possible anti-trust suit.

• • •

Jimmy Byrnes called me up to tell me that the President had laid
before him the matter which I had protested against, namely the prosecution of
the Duponts for violation of the anti-trust law. The Duponts are very busy with
very important work for us and the Attorney General refused to recognize this and
has been making good headway with the President apparently to go on with his case.
But I wrote a letter and I got Vannevar Bush to join in a letter too to the
President pointing out that these men were doing such important work for us in
S-1 that it would be the height of folly to have them harassed by a suit just at
present when the thing ought to be postponed. Justice Byrnes told me now that he
had agreed with me and had told the President so and the President evidently has
been given pause on his headlong career by this action. He is very obstinate and
when he once starts with a prejudice it is awfully hard to make him stop and he
hasn't yet given his final decision here but I think that we have got him.

Saturday, June 10, 1944.

After sitting with the Staff meeting until they had given me the
news on the beachhead in France and the situation in Italy, I went in and prepared myself for a few minutes with the aid of Bundy and then went up to the
Hill to Senator Barkley's room, where I had asked him to call a meeting of
himself, Senator White (the leader of the Minority on the floor), and Senator
Thomas of Oklahoma (the chairman of the sub-committee on Appropriations relating

to military matters), and Senator Bridges of New Hampshire, being the senior
Minority member of that sub-committee. I took with me General Richards, the
Budget Officer for the War Department, and Dr. Bush met me up there. Our purpose
was to do in respect to the Senators what we had successfully accomplished with
the aid of the Speaker of the House and the two leaders of the floor in the House,
namely to keep from there being any public discussion of the item in regard to
S-1 which was in the budget. Fortunately we have saved out of our appropriations
for past years a surplus unused of an amount more than necessary to cover the
amount we are asking to finish the S-1 project, but we felt that we ought not to
go any further now without at least taking into our confidence the leaders of both
Houses of Congress so that they would know what it was all about. That was the
purpose of this meeting. The meeting was very successful. I outlined to them
the problem as it had come since I was first asked by the President when I came
four years ago to become one of the group that handled it. I then told them a
sketchy history of the project and of what we were driving at; how the Germans
knew it before the war and got started on it about six months ahead of us; how
by bombing successfully their installation we have probably put them back, so that
they were not ahead of us; but it was a race as to which one would finish first;
and how in the successful completion of the research and construction of the
instruments themselves lay the possible ultimate success of the war in case of a
deadlock. The four gentlemen who met us were very much impressed. They none
of them knew anything about it and they promised that they would help and keep
absolute silence about it and prevent discussion in public as to what it was
about. Dr. Bush followed what I said and gave more definitely and accurately
the scientific nature of the element in question.

Declaration of Trust

THIS AGREEMENT AND DECLARATION OF TRUST is made the thirteenth day of June One thousand nine hundred and forty four by FRANKLIN DELANO ROOSEVELT on behalf of the Government of the United States of America, and by WINSTON LEONARD SPENCER CHURCHILL on behalf of the Government of the United Kingdom of Great Britain and Northern Ireland. The said Governments are hereinafter referred to as 'the Two Governments';

WHEREAS an agreement (hereinafter called the Quebec Agreement) was entered into on the Nineteenth day of August One thousand nine hundred and forty three by and between the President of the United States and the Prime Minister of the United Kingdom; and

WHEREAS it is an object vital to the common interests of those concerned in the successful prosecution of the present war to insure the acquisition at the earliest practicable moment of an adequate supply of uranium and thorium ores; and

WHEREAS it is the intention of the Two Governments to control to the fullest extent practicable the supplies of uranium and thorium ores within the boundaries of such areas as come under their respective jurisdictions; and

WHEREAS the Government of the United Kingdom of Great Britain and Northern Ireland intends to approach the Governments of the Dominions and the Governments of India and of Burma for the purpose of securing that such Governments shall bring under control deposits of the uranium and thorium ores within their respective territories; and

WHEREAS it has been decided to establish a joint organisation for the purpose of gaining control of the uranium and thorium supplies in certain areas outside the control of the Two Governments and of the Governments of the Dominions and of India and of Burma;

Now IT IS HEREBY AGREED AND DECLARED AS FOLLOWS:

1. (1)There shall be established in the City of Washington, District of Columbia, a Trust to be known as 'The Combined Development Trust'.
   (2)The Trust shall be composed of and administered by six persons who shall be appointed, and be subject to removal, by the Combined Policy Committee established by the Quebec Agreement.
2. The Trust shall use its best endeavours to gain control of and develop the production of the uranium and thorium supplies situate in certains areas other than the areas under the jurisdiction of the Two Governments and of the Governments of the Dominions and of India and of Burma and for that purpose shall take such steps as it may in the common interest think fit to:
   a. Explore and survey sources of uranium and thorium supplies.
   b. Develop the production of uranium and thorium by the acquisition of mines and ore deposits, mining concessions or otherwise.
   c. Provide with equipment any mines or mining works for the production of uranium and thorium.
   d. Survey and improve the methods of production of uranium and thorium.
   e. Acquire and undertake the treatment and disposal of uranium and thorium and uranium and thorium materials.
   f. Provide storage and other facilities.
   g. Undertake any functions or operations which conduce to the effective carrying out of the purpose of the Trust in the common interest.

3. (1)The Trust shall carry out its functions under the direction and guidance of the Combined Policy Committee, and as its agent, and all uranium and thorium and all uranium and thorium ores and supplies and other property acquired by the Trust shall be held by it in trust for the Two Governments jointly, and disposed of or otherwise dealt with in accordance with the direction of the Combined Policy Committee.
(2)The Trust shall submit such reports of its activities as may be required from time to time by the Combined Policy Committee.

4. For the purpose of carrying out its functions, the Trust shall utilize whenever and wherever practicable the established agencies of any of the Two Governments, and may employ and pay such other agents and employees as it considers expedient, and may delegate to any agents or employees all or any of its functions.

5. The Trust may acquire and hold any property in the name of nominees.

6. All funds properly required by the Trust for the performance of its functions shall be provided as to one-half by the Government of the United States of America and the other half by the Government of the United Kingdom of Great Britain and Northern Ireland.

7. In the event of the Combined Policy Committee ceasing to exist, the functions of the Committee under the Trust shall be performed by such other body or person as may be designated by the President for the time being of the United States of America and the Prime Minister for the time being of the United Kingdom of Great Britain and Northern Ireland.

8. The signatories of this Agreement and Declaration of Trust will, as soon as practicable after the conclusion of hostilities, recommend to their respective Governments the extension and revision of this war-time emergency agreement to cover post war conditions and its formalization by treaty or other proper method. This Agreement and Declaration of Trust shall continue in full force and effect until such extension or revision.

[Signed] FRANKLIN D. ROOSEVELT
ON BEHALF OF THE GOVERNMENT OF THE UNITED STATES OF AMERICA

[Signed] WINSTON S. CHURCHILL
ON BEHALF OF THE GOVERNMENT OF THE UNITED KINGDOM OF
GREAT BRITAIN AND NORTHERN IRELAND

PART 2

Frankfurter's account of Bohr
and his meeting with Roosevelt.
Roosevelt-Churchill Hyde Park
aide-mémoire. Bush-Conant interest
in postwar control. Question of
Russia. Continuing concern with
Congress. Stimson's last advice to
Roosevelt. Churchill insists on
secrecy.

Quest for Postwar Planning

Niels Bohr

**Yalta Conference - Winston Churchill,
Franklin D. Roosevelt, and Joseph Stalin**

Long before the Manhattan Project reached its conclusion, soldiers, civilians, and scientists began to think about the postwar world. Their quest for an atomic energy policy turned out to be more haphazard than calculated—the product of circumstance, bargaining, and anxiety. Worry about the industrial world after the war led to an early decision to exclude Great Britain from the Manhattan Project entirely. Americans feared that British industry might use atomic secrets for commercial advantage after the war. The British, angry and indignant, demanded full partnership as recognition of their critical contributions at the start (see Document 12). In the summer of 1943, through the Quebec Agreement, they became junior partners, but only after promising not to use technical information for postwar profit (see Document 14). This agreement and the subsequent Declaration of Trust (see Document 23) laid the foundation for an atomic alliance between Great Britain and the United States. Here, as elsewhere, wartime accords helped to shape the postwar world.

The fate of the atomic bomb—as opposed to the fate of atomic energy—received simultaneous attention. Apprehensiveness again prompted early action. As early as 1943, some of the most distinguished scientists associated with the project began to see a fatal potential in their effort. If the British and Americans secretly developed atomic weapons during the war, an arms race with the Soviet Union might follow willy-nilly. Danish physicist Niels Bohr became the busiest prophet of gloom. Shuttling between Washington and London in 1943 and 1944, Bohr warned both Franklin Roosevelt and Winston Churchill of the need to inform Russian Premier Joseph Stalin of the Manhattan Project. According to Bohr, keeping its existence hidden from Stalin would lead to corrosive wartime mistrust and deadly postwar competition (see Document 25). Bohr's junkets succeeded in raising the question of arms control but failed to produce anything other than suspicion of his intentions (see Documents 26 and 27). In time, influential scientist-administrators such as Vannevar Bush and James B. Conant endorsed Bohr's suggestions, but to no avail (see Documents 30 and 31). By the end of the war, the Russians had still received no official word of the Manhattan Project.

Early efforts to fashion postwar atomic policy came incrementally, step by small step. Without an overall plan, the momentum of past decisions became the principal guide to the future. Incrementalism was not simply a function of the special circumstances of war; it also derived from the personality of the President. Whenever possible, Franklin Roosevelt wanted to be "on a 24-hour basis." He made no decisions that could be deferred; he kept his own counsel; and, as with the Quebec Agreement, he barely informed his staff of understandings he had already reached. Roosevelt always gave himself room to maneuver so that he could stay firmly in command, especially at the critical last moments.

The technique carried a hidden liability. It left his successor with a sorry road map for what was to become a dangerous journey. In the case of the atomic bomb, Roosevelt set the governing terms of the Manhattan Project—secrecy and military control of the project—but he came to no conclusions about some of the most important questions: Should military men or civilians control the weapon? Should the secret be shared before it was used? Should the bomb be used at all? No one knows what Roosevelt would have done if he had lived to see the Trinity test. We do know that he was aware of subtle domestic pressures (as well as obvious military ones) to use the weapon. High officials fretted over the political fallout from an atomic dud. James F. Byrnes, in particular, worried that the enormous cost of the Manhattan Project—hidden from most of Congress—might lead to angry investigations after the war (see Document 33). Such evidence has led some historians to the extreme conclusion that a latent motive for dropping the bomb was to legitimize wartime expenditures.

Because Roosevelt never addressed this issue of domestic politics directly, its effect on him remains uncertain. And the record indicates that whichever way he may have been leaning, he had not decided what to do with the weapon by the time of his death. In private conversation, he mused about simply threatening the Japanese with it (see Document 28). (The timetable for completion of the bomb made its use against Germany unlikely.) The single commitment he put in writing—the Hyde Park aide-mémoire of September 18, 1944—obligated him only to consider the possibility of employing the weapon against Japan (see Document 26). After Roosevelt's death, his scanty and ambiguous legacy left the momentum of the Manhattan Project as a compelling pressure for dropping the bomb.

One aspect of Roosevelt's legacy was crystal clear, however. Though he had told Felix Frankfurter that the arms race Bohr feared "worried him to death" (see Document 25), Roosevelt agreed with Churchill on a critical point. "The suggestion," the two leaders wrote from Hyde Park on September 18, 1944, "that the world should be informed regarding Tube Alloys [the British code name for the atomic bomb], with a view to an international agreement regarding its control and use, is not accepted" (see Document 26). They also stressed that "steps [be] taken to ensure that he [Bohr] is responsible for no leakage of information, particularly to the Russians." Roosevelt, who has been charged by some historians with being naive over the intentions of the Russians, felt distrustful enough to exclude them from the Manhattan Project. Amid those suspicions lay at least some seeds of the cold war.

Such distrust also introduced a new age of science. Despite Bohr's lobbying, the prewar convention of freely flowing information in the world of science ceased to operate automatically. A closed system, imposed by nations that sought military superiority through scientific advances, supplanted the previously open network. As the cold war deepened, more and more researchers found themselves funded, directed, and restricted by their respective governments. Competition replaced cooperation in the realm of international science.

The newest interpretive wrinkle in the issues raised in this section of documents is the notion of a "lost chance" for an international agreement on atomic weaponry. This line of reasoning has been developed most cogently by Martin V. Sherwin in *A World Destroyed: The Atomic Bomb and the Grand Alliance* (1977).Sherwin argues, as Bohr did before him, that by keeping the atomic bomb a secret, the United States squandered an opportunity to avoid the atomic-arms race that developed after the war. The principal weakness of the argument lies in the dubious assumption that any single act, even one as important as sharing knowledge of the atomic bomb, would have reduced the distrust that prevailed between Russia and the west enough to have mattered. The more general subject of Roosevelt's wartime diplomacy is well covered in Robert Dallek's *Franklin D. Roosevelt and American Foreign Policy, 1932–1945* (1979).

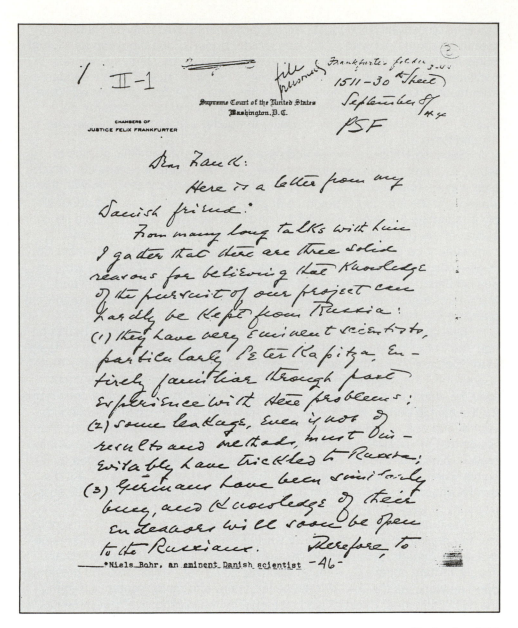

September 8/44

Dear Frank:

Here is a letter from my Danish friend.[1]

From many long talks with him I gather that there are three solid reasons for believing that knowledge of the pursuit of our project can hardly be kept from Russia: (1) they have very eminent scientists, particularly Peter Kapitza, entirely familiar through past experience with these problems; (2) some leakage, even if not of results and methods, must inevitably have trickled to Russia; (3) Germans have been similarly busy, and knowledge of their endeavors will soon be open to the Russians. Therefore, to open the subject with Russia, without of course mak-

[1]Niels Bohr, eminent Danish physicist. The letter from Bohr has not been included.

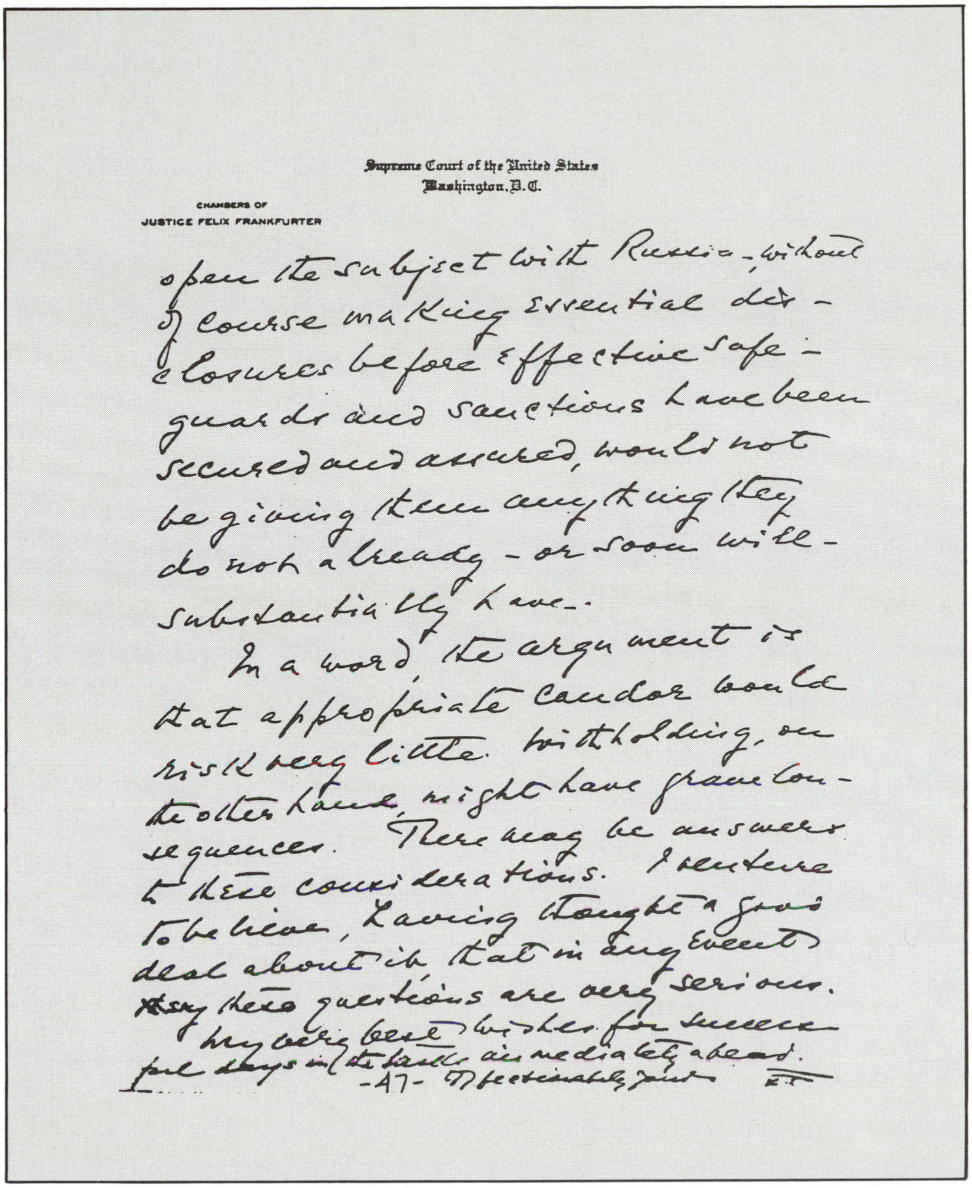

Supreme Court of the United States
Washington, D.C.

CHAMBERS OF
JUSTICE FELIX FRANKFURTER

open the subject with Russia—without
of course making essential disclosures before effective safeguards and sanctions have been
secured and assured, would not
be giving them anything they
do not already—or soon will—
substantially have.

In a word, the argument is
that appropriate candor would
risk very little. Withholding, on
the other hand, might have grave consequences. There may be answers
to these considerations. I venture
to believe, having thought a good
deal about it, that in any event
these questions are very serious.

My very best wishes for successful days in the tasks immediately ahead.

-A7- Affectionately yours F.F.

ing essential disclosures before effective safeguards and sanctions have been secured and arranged, would not be giving them anything they do not already—or soon will—substantially have.

In a word, the argument is that appropriate candor would risk very little. Withholding, on the other hand, might have grave consequences. There may be answers to these considerations. I venture to believe, having thought a good deal about it, that in any event these questions are very serious.

My very best wishes for successful days in the tasks immediately ahead.

Affectionately yours,

<u>Strictly</u> <u>Private</u>

During my year at Oxford (1933-34), as the George Eastman Visiting Professor, I made the acquaintance of Professor Niels Bohr, the renowned Danish physicist and Nobel prize winner. We met again when Professor Bohr visited Washington in the spring of 1939. Professor Bohr, who has lived most of his life in the laboratory and in the fellowship of other men of scientific distinction, is a shy man, but we happened to hit it off at this second meeting, largely, I suspect, because he found in me a sympathetic response to his anxieties about the gathering clouds of the European War and Hitler's brutal purposes. As a result, our acquaintance developed into a warm friendly relation. But we had no communication after he left this country, and I knew nothing of his fate after the war broke out until I learned from the press of his successful escape to Sweden when the Nazis began their deportations and massacres in Denmark.

Some time thereafter, the Danish minister, Mr. de Kauffmann, asked my wife and me to a small tea to meet Professor Bohr. (The exact date is easily ascertainable but at the moment I have not time for running it down.) A handful of people was present, including the Crown Princess Martha. I had no chance of any private word with Professor Bohr, but on leaving I expressed the hope that I would have an opportunity to talk with him and invited him to lunch at my Chambers. A time was fixed and he duly turned up. We talked about the recent events in Denmark, the probable course of the war, the state of England (for I knew of his affectionate devotion to England--one of the things that brought us together was his deep regard for Lord Rutherford whom I had the good fortune to know), our certainty of German defeat and what lay ahead. Professor Bohr never remotely hinted the purpose of his visit to this country.

Some time before Professor Bohr's arrival in this country I had been approached by some distinguished American scientists, because of past academic

TOP SECRET

TOP SECRET

- 2 -

associations, to advise them on a matter that seemed to them of the greatest importance to our national interest and presented to them difficulties with which they, as scientists, were unable to cope since they were problems not within their technical competence. I had thus become aware of X--aware, that is, that there was such a thing as X and of its significance, but I have never been told and do not at this moment know anything that could convey to anyone any valuable information about it. Knowing, however, the general range of Professor Bohr's work in the field of physics, I had reason for assuming that his gifts were being availed of for the common cause.

And so, in the course of the lunch to which I have just referred, I made a very oblique reference to X so that if I was right in my assumption that Professor Bohr was sharing in it, he would know that I knew something about it, and, if not, I could easily turn my question into other channels. He likewise replied in an innocent remote way, but it soon became clear to both of us that two such persons, who had been so long and so deeply preoccupied with the menace of Hitlerism and who were so deeply engaged in the common cause, could talk about the implications of X without either making any disclosure to the other. The conversation proceeded on this basis and Professor Bohr then expressed to me his conviction that X might be one of the greatest boons to mankind or might become the greatest disaster. This has been the core of his talk with me in the many conversations that I have since had with him. These conversations have all been variations of the same theme. He never disclosed anything that anybody could even remotely call a secret. He never told me anything that might be deemed a piece of information regarding X nor ever discussed any technical matter with me. Throughout, he has been concerned entirely with the political problem of so controlling X as to make it a beneficial instead of a disastrous contribution by science. He was a man weighed down with a conscience and with an almost over-whelming solicitude for the dangers of our people.

He infected me with his solicitude, and finally I deemed it my duty to

TOP SECRET

TOP SECRET

-3-

communicate to President Roosevelt what had come to me through the American
scientists and Professor Bohr. Accordingly, I saw the President and told him in
full detail what I have just summarized and put to him the central worry of Professor Bohr, that it might be disastrous to the whole endeavor of achieving
sound international relations with Russia, if Russia should learn on her own about
X rather than that the existence of X should be utilized by this country and
Great Britain as a means of exploring the possibility of effective international
arrangements with Russia. Professor Bohr made me feel that it would not be too
difficult, on the basis of the scientific situation antedating the war, for
Russia to gain the necessary information, to say nothing of other factors that
militate against assuring non-disclosure.

The President was plainly impressed by my account of the matter. I was
with the President for about an hour and a half, (having made two or three efforts
to terminate the visit), and practically all of it was consumed by this subject.
He told me that the whole thing "worried him to death" (I remember the phrase
vividly), and said he was most eager for help in dealing with the problem. He
said he would like to see Professor Bohr and asked me whether I would arrange it.
When I suggested to him that the solution of this problem might be more important
than all the schemes for a world organization, he agreed and authorized me to tell
Professor Bohr that he, Bohr, might tell our friends in London that the President
was anxious to explore ways for achieving proper safeguards in relation to X.

It is unnecessary to go into details by which the desire of the President
to see Professor Bohr was carried out. Suffice it to say that the President did
see Bohr for about an hour and a quarter shortly before the Quebec Conference.
Bohr gave me a full account of his conference with the President, who, plainly,
could not have been more friendly or more open in his discussion of the political
problems raised by X. The President asked Professor Bohr to feel entirely free
to communicate with him at any time on the subject and to do so either through
"Mr. Justice Frankfurter, or, if the latter was away from Washington during the

TOP SECRET

-4-   **TOP SECRET**

summer, through the Danish Minister." After Professor Bohr's interview with the President, General Watson[1] told me of it and said that if I had any communication from Professor Bohr to the President, I was to give it to him, the General, who would see to it that it got directly into the President's hands. Professor Bohr did, as a matter of fact, write a letter to the President which he asked me to get into the latter's hands. I saw General Watson in his apartment the day before he left for the Quebec Conference and gave him Bohr's letter. General Watson said, "I will carry that letter on my person and will personally give it to the President."

Then followed Quebec. About happenings there regarding this matter I have no first-hand information.

Felix Frankfurter

April 18, 1945

TOP SECRET

---

[1] A Roosevelt aide.

10 Downing Street,
Whitehall.

<u>TOP SECRET</u>

<u>TUBE ALLOYS</u> [1]

Aide-memoire of conversation between the President and the

Prime Minister at Hyde Park, September 18, 1944.

1.   The suggestion that the world should be informed

regarding Tube Alloys, with a view to an international

agreement regarding its control and use, is not accepted.

The matter should continue to be regarded as of the utmost

secrecy; but when a "bomb" is finally available, it might

perhaps, after mature consideration, be used against the

Japanese, who should be warned that this bombardment will be

repeated until they surrender.

2.   Full collaboration between the United States and the

British Government in developing Tube Alloys for military

and commercial purposes should continue after the defeat of

Japan unless and until terminated by joint agreement.

3.   Enquiries should be made regarding the activities of

Professor Bohr and steps taken to ensure that he is responsible

for no leakage of information, particularly to the Russians.

[1]British code name for the atomic bomb.

September 22, 1944

MEMORANDUM OF CONFERENCE:

I was called to the White House but not given a subject. Present at the conference were the President, Admiral Leahy, Lord Cherwell, and myself. The President stated that the Admiral had recently been given full information on the special project. The purpose of the conference became apparent after some preliminary general discussion which does not need to be noted.

The President stated that Mr. Justice Frankfurter had visited him a few weeks ago and expressed himself as very much worried about the future handling in the post-war period of matters pertaining to the secret project. The President apparently professed ignorance of what Frankfurter was talking about, although I do not know how far this went, and I certainly gained the impression that the President did not tell Frankfurter any more than he knew when he came. Frankfurter insisted that Bohr should see the President, as he and Bohr had discussed the future state of the world from this standpoint and Bohr had some very striking ideas. This was apparently arranged and the President had seen Bohr for a short time and listened to him. The President, however, was very much disturbed in regard to security and wished to know how far Bohr had been taken into the matter, whether he was trusted, and also how Mr. Frankfurter happened to know anything about the subject whatever. Lord Cherwell traced the history of Bohr's escape from Denmark, his introduction to this country, and so on. He stated that Bohr had similarly seen the Prime Minister after having insisted on doing so in Britain and had told him his ideas about future handling of this subject. These ideas, I believe, revolve about immediate disclosure of the subject, its use as a threat against Germany, and similar matters, and also a control by the British and Americans of the subject after the war, and I judge the maintenance of a peace by the Anglo-Americans on this basis. I then traced the way Bohr had been introduced into this country and in particular the care that had been taken to be sure that he was handled in such a manner that we became sure of his discretion before introducing him to parts of the project. Both Cherwell and I brought out the fact that he was a very important physicist who had been able to contribute and also that he had given us some ideas as to what was going on in Germany that were quite valuable. It also appeared in this discussion that Bohr had been invited by the Russians to visit Russia but had declined.

I then told the President that I thought I could recite how Mr. Frankfurter knew about the project. I reminded him of the individual whose name I could not remember who had insisted on seeing the President, and the President interrupted and said, "Yes, he saw my wife". I reminded him that at the same time this particular individual was in touch with Mr. Frankfurter and that Frankfurter undoubtedly received his knowledge of the subject in that way if not in others. I told the President that we had had a group of physicists who were somewhat disgruntled but that I believed the matter had been handled properly and adequately and that we had not recently had any evidence of further inclinations on the part of this group to talk to people outside of the project in order to attempt to enforce their own ideas. I told him that I did not know how Bohr and Frankfurter had gotten together, but I could probably find out if it was a matter of interest. Both Cherwell and I emphasized that a great deal was known about this subject all over the world from the standpoint of the general physics involved, and I

Memorandum of Conference   page 2.

also brought out that it was quite generally known in this country that the
government had a good deal of activity going on since it was impossible not to
have this occur with the many commercial people involved, but that the military
aspects of the matter were very securely guarded and I felt sure that neither
the general public, Mr. Frankfurter, nor similar people knew about this.

    The President then started discussing the subject quite generally. I was
very much embarrassed, for he discussed international relations on this matter
after the war, and introduced parts of this that we had not discussed at any
time. I was hence much embarrassed to find myself discussing this subject in
the presence of a British representative before having had an opportunity to advise
the President on it privately. The President was very much in favor of complete
interchange with the British on this subject after the war in all phases, and in
fact apparently on a basis where it would be used jointly or not at all. He told
of some of his discussions with Mr. Churchill at Quebec along these lines. On
this I was of course in no position whatever to state what was actually in my
mind, namely that too close collaboration with the British, without considering
simultaneously the entire world situation, might lead to a very undesirable
relationship indeed on the subject with Russia. I did, however, get the opportunity to say that after the war I knew there would be free and open publication
of the scientific aspects of this entire subject, that there would be great
progress all over the world, that the art would change rapidly, and that I hoped
that this scientific discussion would be participated in also by the Russians.
The President mentioned also commercial use, and both Cherwell and I pointed out
the great dangers of commercial use from a safety standpoint and stated that
we did not feel there would be important industrial use for perhaps ten years.
The President then talked of the necessity for control in this country because
of the dangers involved. I told him that Conant and I had given a considerable
amount of thought to this subject, and that we had in fact only a few days
before given to the Secretary of War a memorandum summarizing our thoughts on the
matter and I believed that the Secretary planned to see the President on the
subject shortly. I stated, and the President agreed, that it was not too early
to start on this matter. The President, in fact, felt that legislation should
be obtained while the war was on, and we had some discussion of the possibilities
of this. I said that I felt that when the end of the war came, or when this
became used, there should be a full disclosure of almost all aspects of it, and
that we were doing some preliminary work so that the President would have available
a basis for such a statement as would then become necessary, and the President
said he was glad this was being done. I said I did not know what the Secretary's
opinion was in regard to the memorandum which Conant and I had given him since
we had had no opportunity to discuss the matter with him since he had had time
to read it. I offered, however, to see the Secretary, tell him that the subject
is very much on the President's mind, and urge him to discuss it with the
President shortly. The President replied that he thought this was very desirable
and that he would like to discuss it with us. I did not tell the President
that, in this document to the Secretary, Conant and I had also discussed the
need for a treaty with Britain, for Lord Cherwell was present and I feared that
the extent and nature of the matter might become discussed in a way that would
be very embarrassing. The President's own statements in regard to post-war
collaboration with Britain on the subject were very general indeed, but went very
far. He pointed out his belief of the necessity for maintaining the British
Empire strong, and went into some of the methods by which this could be brought
about, which are not pertinent to this subject. As usual there were a number of
other non-pertinent matters such as statements in regard to the discussions at
Quebec.

page 3.

At the end of the conference I discussed what had occurred with Dr. Conant. Both he and I was much disturbed that the President has apparently been talking post-war relations with Britain at Quebec quite at length with the Prime Minister and with Lord Cherwell, without having obtained the opinions of the Secretary of War and others concerned with this matter in private consultation beforehand. It is hence very necessary that discussions occur, and I plan to speak to the Secretary of War soon. Both Conant and I feel that the very broad world-wide implications of this subject need careful evaluation, and that while good relations with Britain are certainly important in this it is certainly far from being the entire story.

Vannevar Bush

September 23, 1944

MEMORANDUM TO DR. CONANT:

There are some points on which I should post you further, concerning the subject of my memorandum yesterday, for of course you may be brought into the present discussions and I would like to keep you fully posted.

This morning I visited General Groves. I acquainted him with the part of the conversation which occurred yesterday, and which is recited in yesterday's memorandum, concerning the contacts of Dr. Bohr and of Justice Frankfurter. The General had no further information to give me concerning the way in which Bohr had gotten in contact with Frankfurter and similar matters. We discussed security somewhat at length. We both felt that there was little danger that Bohr would be indiscreet in regard to the more secret parts of the project, and felt that he had probably based his discussions with Frankfurter only on the physics, which is well known. General Groves also told me about another leak which has occurred, but this he will probably advise you of separately.

I then visited Mr. Bundy. I told him of the general nature and scope of the conference, but we had a brief talk and I did not go into many of the points that are in the memorandum of yesterday. I did tell him that I had told the President that you and I had recently given a memorandum to the Secretary on the subject of post-war control[1], and that the President had indicated that he would like to discuss this with us. I understand that he meant that he would like to talk it with the Secretary and that he assumed you or I would also be present, although he was not explicit. I told Mr. Bundy that the President talked international matters concerning the relations of Britain and the United States on this subject in the post-war period, and that he did so in the presence of Lord Cherwell without giving me any prior information that this was to occur and that he told of some of his conversations with Mr. Churchill at Quebec, and that Lord Cherwell had made remarks which showed that he had been present at at least some of these conversations. I told Mr. Bundy that I felt this was a highly dangerous situation and that the Secretary should be apprised at once, and Mr. Bundy stated that he would get me in touch with the Secretary, probably on Monday. Mr. Bundy agreed with me that it was an extraordinary thing to discuss these British relations without having previously sought the careful advice of those closely associated with the project who have given it close thought and those who are his normal advisers on such matters, and that it was particularly extraordinary to open this subject and make broad statements to me in the presence of Lord Cherwell, when I was in no position to make statements on points on which I might be in disagreement as to the appropriate American point of view. We referred back to the previous instance at the time when the previous Quebec conference was held at which time the President did an almost parallel thing. You will remember that I worked with Sir John Anderson on a war-time agreement for interchange, and that we did so on the basis of a memorandum prepared by the Prime Minister in which he included also some points having political aspects and points having post-war aspects, and that in my letter in which I placed this matter before the President I recommended that we make the arrangements as indicated for war-time interchange, but expressly stated that I was not advising in regard to the points in the Prime Minister's memorandum which went beyond this aspect, and in fact stated, I believe, that I assumed that the President would call for such advice on these aspects as might be desired. It is my memory that the Secretary saw the President before the Quebec conference and advised rather strongly on certain aspects of this matter, and Mr. Bundy this morning agreed that such a conference did occur, and agreed that he would look up to see whether the Secretary had an appropriate memorandum of that conversation. The result was, as we know, the so-called Quebec

agreement. Beyond this information that I here recite I have no knowledge as to
what advice the President secured before entering into that agreement. I have
the feeling, however, that he did so, having been advised quite completely in
regard to the war-time aspects of it, but without full advice in regard to some
of the political clauses or post-war clauses. This, taken together with the
incident of yesterday, renders me very much disturbed. The working out of post-
war relationships on this matter in order to secure as far as possible good international understanding and to provide for the peace of the world with this element
present warrants the attention of some of the best possible minds that the President can bring to bear upon it, and I greatly fear that he is proceeding without
such advice. I hence intend to tell the Secretary that that is my feeling when
I see him on Monday. As I analyze this matter, you and I are called upon to advise
in regard to the technical aspects and in regard to various phases of the war-time
handling of this subject, but we are not the normal advisers of the President in
regard to international relations on the subject generally or on post-war matters,
and he has not indicated that we have any duty thus to advise. Nevertheless, I
think, if you agree with me, that the time has come when we should say quite
definitely to those who are his normal advisers on such matters that we feel that
they should insist upon giving their advice even if it is not called for.

There was one other matter which came up in the conversation yesterday which
I neglected to put in the memorandum. The conference lasted for about an hour and
a half and it was of course difficult to record it in full, although I believe
I recorded the essential points accurately. At one time in the conversation the
President raised the question of whether this means should actually be used against
the Japanese or whether it should be used only as a threat with full-scale
experimentation in this country. He did so, I believe, in connection with Bohr's
apparent urging that a threat be employed against Germany, which would of course,
I think, be futile. I stated that there were many sides to this question, that
fortunately we did not need to approach it for some time, for certainly it would
be inadviasble to make a threat unless we were distinctly in a position to follow
it up if necessary, since a threat which had no effect and was not followed up
would have the contrary effect to that intended, and that it seemed to me that the
matter warranted very careful discussion, but this could be postponed for quite
a time, and the President agreed that the matter did not now need to be discussed.

                    V. Bush

September 25, 1944

MEMORANDUM FOR DR. CONANT:

This afternoon I conferred with Secretary Stimson. I told him the essential points of the interview at the White House which I recited to you in my memorandum. In **particular**, I said that I was much disturbed because it appeared that the President had negotiated with Mr. Churchill at Quebec very definitely in regard to post-war US-UK relations on the secret project, with no technical representatives present except Lord Cherwell, and without having the advice of the American group that have studied deeply into this matter. I said that I was also appalled because it seemed to me that the President had thought the matter only part way through, and that I had been much embarrassed when he called me in and presented some of his conclusions as to the post-war relationships with Lord Cherwell present, so that I did not have an opportunity to state what seemed to me to be appropriate U.S. policy. I told him that the matter of internal controls had also been introduced, that I had told the President that you and I had given him a memorandum on this subject, but did not know his views, and that the President had said he would like to discuss this matter with us. Mr. Stimson was equally disturbed, I believe, and feels that the appropriate post-war relationship is going to be very difficult to work out, and that it should be done with the best possible advice and consultation. He felt, however, that it would be very difficult indeed to get the President to really consult or to get his attention for a sufficient length of time to give him the reasoned thinking of people who have been studying the subject. He recited to me several instances where the President has recently gone ahead in negotiation and where it has been very difficult indeed to see that he gave attention to the opinion of American advisers. The Secretary is very much harrassed at the present time with a number of exceedingly difficult problems, and he is particularly worried because on some of these where a frank discussion with the President is indicated, he has been unable to get his serious attention. He asked me why I was disturbed at the President's point of view. I told him primarily because it seemed to me it was being arrived at without adequate review of the various possibilities in a situation of great difficulty and complexity, and also because it seemed to me that it was an extreme point of view which might lead to trouble. In fact, I stated that it seemed to me that the President had evidently thought he could join with Churchill in bringing about a US-UK post-war agreement on this subject by which it would be held closely and presumably to control the peace of the world, and I felt that this extreme attitude might well lead to extraordinary efforts on the part of Russia to establish its own position in the field secretly, and might lead to a clash, say 20 years from now. On the other hand, I felt that if there were complete scientific interchange on this subject among all countries that there would be much less danger of a secret race on military applications as the art changes. I also felt that there might be a possibility that an international agreement involving all countries for the control of this affair might have some hope of success, and that it most certainly ought to be explored and carefully analyzed. The Secretary agreed with this last statement completely and was apparently in agreement with a large part of my statement in regard to a reasonable approach, although of course I would not wish to record here any considered opinion on his part, for I have not any direct statement from him on which to base it completely, and he should state his own opinion in any case. We discussed somewhat at length what might be done. He was very pessimistic indeed in regard to the possibility of getting the President's serious consideration for a sufficient interval to get to the bottom of the subject. On the other hand, he felt that we ought to make some attempt even if it did no more than to make the record complete. He certainly has not the strength nor the time with the many

pressing matters now before him to get this subject formulated. I therefore
suggested, if he wished us to do so, that you and I might draft a brief statement
of what we consider would be a reasonable approach to the international problem
on this subject for his review, and he grasped at this and said that he would
be much indebted to us if we would do so and that he felt that some such brief
statement after he had had a chance to discuss it ought to get into the President's
hands and that it might cause at least a pause for further study. I judge that
such a document would not need to recommend an explicit plan, but would rather
analyze alternatives, point out dangers, and also point out possibilities. It
seems to me that you and I ought to make the attempt to get something of the sort
together. I doubt, however, if the Secretary can get his mind on the matter
immediately.

There were incidental matters touched on. I told him very briefly of the
matter concerning Justice Frankfurter. I did not discuss the security violation
which General Groves brought up as I thought he ought to report that himself. I
told him that Admiral Leahy had now been brought into the matter.

V. Bush

                                        September 30, 1944.
                                        Top Secret

                    M E M O R A N D U M

To: The Secretary of War
From: V. Bush and J. B. Conant
Subject: Salient Points Concerning Future International
           Handling of Subject of Atomic Bombs.

    1. Present Military Potentialities. There is every reason
to believe that before August 1, 1945, atomic bombs will have
been demonstrated and that the type then in production would
be the equivalent of 1,000 to 10,000 tons of high explosive
in so far as general blast damage is concerned. This means
that one B-29 bomber could accomplish with such a bomb the
same damage against weak industrial and certain civilian
targets as 100 to 1,000 B-29 bombers.
    2. Future Military Potentialities. We are dealing with an
expanding art and it is difficult to predict the future. At
present we are planning atomic bombs utilizing the energy
involved in the fission of the uranium atom. It is believed
that such energy can be used as a detonator for setting off
the energy which would be involved in the transformation of
heavy hydrogen atoms into helium. If this can be done a
factor of a thousand or more would be introduced into the
amount of energy released. This means that one such super-
super bomb would be equivalent in blast damage to 1,000 raids
of 1,000 B-29 Fortresses delivering their load of high
explosive on one target. One must consider the possibility
of delivering either the bombs at present contemplated or the
super-super bomb on an enemy target by means of a robot plane
or guided missile. When one considers these possibilities we
see that very great devastation could be caused immediately
after the outbreak of hostilities to civilian and industrial
centers by an enemy prepared with a relatively few such bombs.
That such a situation presents a new challenge to the world is
evident.
    3. Present Advantage of United States and Great Britain
Temporary. Unless it develops that Germany is much further
along than is now believed it is probable that the present
developments in the United States undertaken in cooperation
with Great Britain put us in a temporary position of great
ascendancy. It would be possible, however, for any nation
with good technical and scientific resources to reach our
present position in three or four years. Therefore it would
be the height of folly for the United States and Great Britain
to assume that they will always continue to be superior in
this new weapon. Once the distance between ourselves and those

who have not yet developed this art is eliminated the accidents of research could give another country a temporary advantage as great as the one we now enjoy.

4. Impossibility of maintaining complete secrecy after the war is over. In order to accomplish our present gigantic technical and scientific task it has been necessary to bring a vast number of technical men into the project. Information in regard to various aspects of it is therefore widespread. Furthermore, all the basic facts were known to physicists before the development began. Some outside the project have undoubtedly guessed a great deal of what is going on. Considerable information is already in the hands of various newspaper men who are refraining from writing our stories only because of voluntary censorship. In view of this situation it is our strong recommendation that plans be laid for complete disclosure of the history of the development and all but the manufacturing and military details on the bombs as soon as the first bomb has been demonstrated. This demonstration might be over enemy territory, or in our own country, with subsequent notice to Japan that the materials would be used against the Japanese mainland unless surrender was forthcoming.

5. Dangers of partial secrecy and international armament race. It is our contention that it would be extremely dangerous for the United States and Great Britain to attempt to carry on in complete secrecy further developments of the military applications of this art. If this were done Russia would undoubtedly proceed in secret along the same lines and so too might certain other countries, including our defeated enemies. We do not believe that over a period of a decade the control of the supply could be counted on to prevent such secret developments in other countries. This is particularly true if the super-super bomb were developed for the supply of heavy hydrogen is essentially unlimited and the rarer materials such as uranium and thorium would be used only as detonators. If a country other than Great Britain and the United States developed the super-super bomb first we should be in a terrifying situation if hostilities should occur. The effect on public reaction of the uncertainties in regard to an unknown threat of this new nature would be very great.

6. Proposed international exchange of information. In order to meet the unique situation created by the development of this new art we would propose that free interchange of all scientific information on this subject be established under the auspices of an international office deriving its power from whatever association of nations is developed at the close of the present war. We would propose further that as soon as practical the technical staff of this office be given free access in all countries not only to the scientific

laboratories where such work is contained, but to the military
establishments as well. We recognize that there will be
great resistance to this measure, but believe the hazards
to the future of the world are sufficiently great to warrant
this attempt. If accurate information were available as to
the development of these atomic bombs in each country,
public opinion would have true information about the status
of the armament situation. Under these conditions there is
reason to hope that the weapons would never be employed
and indeed that the existence of these weapons might decrease
the chance of another major war.

                        [sgd] J. B. CONANT
                        [sgd] V. BUSH

<u>Sunday, December 31, 1944</u>
<u>Page 5</u>

• • •

     While we were on the question of troubles with Russia, I took
occasion to tell him[1] of Deane's[2] warning to us in the Department that we
would not gain anything at the present time by further easy concessions to
Russia and recommending that we should be more vigorous on insisting upon
a quid pro quo.[3] And in this connection I told him of my thoughts as to the
future of S-1 in connection with Russia; that I knew they were spying on our
work but that they had not yet gotten any real knowledge of it and that,
while I was troubled about the possible effect of keeping from them even now
that work, I believed that it was essential not to take them into our confidence until we were sure to get a real quid pro quo[2] from our frankness.
I said I had no illusions as to the possibility of keeping permanently such
a secret but that I did not think it was yet time to share it with Russia.
He said he thought he agreed with me.

• • •

[1]Roosevelt.
[2]General John R. Deane, stationed at the time in Moscow.
[3]Literally "this for that"; in diplomatic terminology, an exchange or trade-off.

• • •

Then a little later in the morning Patterson brought me a new
trouble in Congress. This time it is Congressman Engel who is insisting
on going to see our installations of S-1. Patterson had had an interview
with him on Saturday and had held him off till I got back. Engel is a sincere
man but a rather self-seeking man and he wants to break through and see the
installations which everybody else has been kept away from. So I called in
Patterson this morning with General Styer and Madigan, who is Patterson's
expert, and Bundy, and they told me about their interview on Saturday and I
got ready to handle Engel. He had written a letter to me which was a very
improper one in some ways because in it he gave away some of the secrets of S-1
which he had heard rumors of. But they say he is honest so I decided to see
him. He is on the Committee on Appropriations and he is threatening to oppose
the passage of the deficiency bill which has in it some of the money which we
need, and it also has in it authority to transfer funds from one operation to
another which we also need for this operation. I tried to get Speaker Rayburn
on the telephone to get his advice, with whom I had my conference a year or so
ago when this thing was first coming up and who promised us to hold on to his
bad actors in the House; but he is away in Texas and won't be back here till
some time in March. So then I talked with Congressman John Taber who is a
fellow Republican with Engel and also on the same Appropriations Committee, and
Taber is a fine conservative loyal fellow and took the right attitude. I asked
him if he would bring Engel down to see me and I would talk with them together.

So they came at three o'clock in the afternoon and in the meanwhile I had
gotten hold of General Groves and had gotten preparations made which gave
me the things that I could tell them in the shape of the way in which
we had used the money in housing and roads and which gave the items of expenditures which would not convey any knowledge to an outsider or a spy as to
what the real secret was; and then when they came at three o'clock I had a
long talk for an hour and a half with them in which I appealed to Engel's
decency and loyalty and told him the history of S-1 so far as I could tell
it without giving the secret away, and got him into a more amenable frame of
mind. Finally he agreed not to make his objection to the House appropriations tomorrow and I told him that I would take under consideration giving him
a visit just to the outside installations so that he could see that those
were all right. He promised by all that was holy that he wouldn't talk anything about it; that his only remark would be that he would go along with
the appropriation in case anybody asked him what he had seen. I have got to
see Rayburn about it on account of my talk with him last year, and therefore
today we agreed to let the thing ride for some few days in regard to his visit
to the installations. I told him I would consider the visit and let him know.

OFFICE OF WAR MOBILIZATION
Washington D.C.

March 3, 1945   TOP SECRET

James F. Byrnes
Director

MEMORANDUM FOR THE PRESIDENT

FROM: JAMES F. BYRNES

    I understand that the expenditures for the Manhattan project
are approaching 2 billion dollars with no definite assurance yet of
production.

    We have succeeded to date in obtaining the cooperation of
Congressional Committees in secret hearings. Perhaps we can continue
to do so while the war lasts.

    However, if the project proves a failure, it will then be sub-
jected to relentless investigation and criticism.

    I know little of the project except that it is supported by
eminent scientists. Even eminent scientists may continue a project
rather than concede its failure. Also, it may be feasible to continue the experiment on a reduced scale.

    In any event, no harm could come from an impartial investiga-
tion and review by a small group of scientists not already identified
with the project.

    Such a review might hurt the feelings of those now engaged in the
project. Still 2 billion dollars is enough money to risk such hurt.
I think Dr. Bush would be glad to have two or three scientists whose
pride was in no way involved in the project, check it and report that
results justify continuance of the project.

    A favorable finding would justify continuance, regardless of
future success or failure. An unfavorable finding would at least indicate the need for further justification by those who are responsible for
the project.

    In any event, it would be clear that we were mindful of the tre-
mendous expenditure of men and materials.

TOP SECRET

Thursday, March 15, 1945.

• • •

Then afterwards I had a talk with George Harrison and Harvey Bundy.
Harrison had just come back from his long illness and thinks that he will be
able to go on with the work in regard to S-1, particularly in laying out a
plan of operations there, and we discussed that.

I spent part of the morning in getting ready for an interview with
the President on this subject of S-1. I had asked Miss Tully to get the
date fixed for my talk with him this week which the President had suggested
last Saturday that he would have with me. She proposed tomorrow, Friday, or
Saturday and I said either one would do. But then at the last minute after
half past twelve I got a telephone message from the White House and she told
me that the President had suggested that I come over to lunch today. That
upset my schedule a little and made me hustle like fury to get ready on the
S-1 matter before I went over; but I finally did so and got the papers all
ready. When I got there I had to wait half an hour for him because he is
lunching nowadays in the main building of the White House and he often gets
detained in the Executive Office with tardy appointments. But we sat down at
about ten minutes of two.

First I took up with him a memorandum which he sent to me from
Jimmy Dunn[1] who had been alarmed at the rumors of extravagance in the Manhattan
project. Jimmy suggested that it might become disastrous and he suggested
that we get a body of "outside" scientists to pass upon the project because

[1]Stimson is actually referring to James Byrnes. See Document 33.

rumors are going around that Vannevar Bush and Jim Conant have sold the
President a lemon on the subject and ought to be checked up on. It was
rather a jittery and nervous memorandum and rather silly, and I was prepared
for it and I gave the President a list of the scientists who were actually
engaged on it to show the very high standing of them and it comprised four
Nobel Prize men, and also how practically every physicist of standing was
engaged with us in the project. Then I outlined to him the future of it and
when it was likely to come off and told him how important it was to get
ready. I went over with him the two schools of thought that exist in respect
to the future control after the war of this project in case it is successful,
one of them being the secret close-in attempted control of the project by
those who control it now, and the other being the international control based
upon freedom both of science and of access. I told him that those things
must be settled before the first projectile is used and that he must be ready
with a statement to come out to the people on it just as soon as that is done.
He agreed to that. I told him how I had settled Engel's rebellion a few
weeks ago when he was threatening to make a speech on the subject in the
House and I had invited him down to the office and showed him some of the
cost figures and tamed him down. Then I told him that I was proposing to lay
the project for the same method of treatment before Sam Rayburn, the Speaker
of the House, when it comes time for the next big appropriation which will be
probably in April. I told him that I thought we would probably propose to
send four men of the House through the establishment, namely outside of the
buildings, and let them see the construction and generally let them be able
to say that they have been through it. On the whole the talk I had with the
President was successful.

10 Downing Street,
WHITEHALL.
March 25, 1945

FOREIGN SECRETARY

1. I certainly do not agree that this secret should be imparted to the French. My agreement with President Roosevelt in writing forbids either party to reveal to anyone else the secret. I believe you underrate the lead which has been obtained by the United States, in which we participate, through their vast expenditure of money—I believe above four hundred million pounds.

2. *I was shocked at Yalta too when the President in a casual manner spoke of revealing the secret to Stalin on the grounds that de Gaulle, if he heard of it, would certainly double-cross us with Russia.*[1]

3. In all the circumstances our policy should be to keep the matter so far as we can control it in American and British hands and leave the French and Russians to do what they can. The Chancellor said that the Frenchmen whom he had interviewed would never betray the secret to de Gaulle, and he vouched for their good behaviour. Now we are threatened that the Russians will be told. But anyhow there is all the difference between having certain paper formulae and having a mightly [sic] plant in existence, and perhaps soon in working order. Once you tell them they will ask for the very latest news, and to see the plants. This will speed them up by two years at least. You may be quite sure that any power that gets hold of the secret will try to make the article and that this touches the existence of human society.

4. I am getting rather tired of all the different kinds of things that we must do or not do lest Anglo-French relations suffer. *One thing I am sure that there is nothing that de Gaulle would like better than to have plenty of T.A. to punish Britain, and nothing he would like less than to arm Communist Russia with the secret.* This matter is out of all relation to anything else that exists in the whole world, and I could not think of participating in any disclosure to third or fourth parties at the present time. I do not believe there is anyone in the world who can possibly have reached the position now occupied by us and the United States.

5. As to questions of honour as between us and France. At that time France was represented by Vichy and de Gaulle had no status to speak for her. I have never made the slightest agreement with France or with any Frenchman. I shall certainly continue to urge the President not to make or permit the slightest disclosure to France or Russia. *Even six months will make a difference should it come to a show-down with Russia, or indeed with de Gaulle.*

[Signed] W.C.C.

---

[1]Churchill's draft reply to Foreign Secretary Anthony Eden's Minute of March 20. Paragraph 2 and sections of paragraphs 4 and 5 (identified here by italics) were edited out of the final draft.

PART 3

Stimson's conference with President
Truman. Target considerations.
The "Committee of Three" projects
effect of bomb on Russia. Creation
and early sessions of the Interim
Committee. Compton's account of
the Interim Committee meeting and
the report of the Scientific Advisory
Panel. The Interim Committee
decides on terms for using bomb.
Stimson and Truman discuss
upcoming summit (Potsdam) and
effect of bomb on Russians. Question
of "unconditional surrender."

Planning
the Drop

J. Robert Oppenheimer

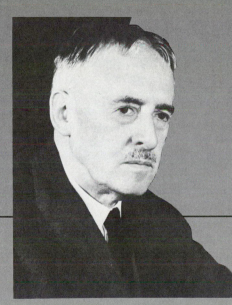

Henry Stimson

Los Alamos National Laboratory

Policy-makers never systematically addressed the question of whether to drop the atomic bombs on Japan. No one expected Germany to survive long enough to become a target, so little attention was paid to German sites. Historian Gregg Herken, in *The Winning Weapon: The Atomic Bomb in the Cold War, 1945–1950*, cites other factors militating against a drop on Germany: (1) German scientists, more sophisticated than their Japanese counterparts, would be able to analyze a "dud" with greater accuracy; (2) there were no B-29 bombers in Europe at the time to carry the weapon; and (3) the Japanese fleet was a more attractive target than German cities. Racism against Asians did not, as some historians have charged, doom the Japanese and save the Germans. According to Leslie Groves, "President Roosevelt asked if we were prepared to drop bombs on Germany if it was necessary to do so and we replied that we would be prepared to do so if necessary." As it turned out, the Nazis surrendered on May 7, 1945, more than two months before the test of the bomb.

Despite Roosevelt's pledge in 1944 to give the issue "mature consideration" (see Document 26), using the weapon was a foregone conclusion by the time of his death. Two weeks after Harry Truman became President, he was informed of the details of the Manhattan Project in a brief, secret meeting with Stimson and Groves. Truman listened quietly and then appointed an ad hoc advisory group called the Interim Committee. Its original charge was to counsel the President on temporary wartime controls and publicity for the bomb as well as on postwar legislation and organization regarding atomic energy. Eventually, the Interim Committee broadened its own mandate by recommending that the bomb be dropped on Japan as soon as possible and without any warning or prior demonstration (see Document 41). The committee made no careful examination of options. Aside from a handful of scientists and Navy under secretary Ralph A. Bard, no one challenged the prevailing assumption that the bomb would be used (see Documents 43, 61, and 76). In this respect, one of the most important acts of the war resulted from a "nondecision."

Events and attitudes made dropping the bomb almost an automatic consequence of the decision to develop it. In the midst of a bloody struggle, it seemed unreasonable, even unpatriotic, to think about withholding a weapon that might win the war. President Truman, who took ultimate responsibility, never expressed a doubt. As he saw it, American ends required atomic means. The matter boiled down to simple arithmetic. "We have used [the bomb]," Truman said after Hiroshima, "in order to shorten the agony of war, in order to save the lives of thousands and thousands of young Americans." In his memoirs—a section of which is reproduced in Part 6 (see Document 76)—Truman maintained that thousands of Japanese lives were spared, as well, because the atomic victory made a suicidal defense of the home islands unnecessary.

Secretary of War Henry Stimson, writing for *Harper's* in February 1947, seconded Truman's explanation, and, together, the two highest-ranking officials associated with the Manhattan Project provided the basis for orthodox historical accounts, such as Herbert Feis's *The Atomic Bomb and the End of World War II* (1966). Accepting the inevitability of use, Feis and others of this school focused their attention on the beneficial results—a quick end to the war; a minimal loss of American lives; and a reduction of the diplomatic risks of a prolonged struggle. In their accounts, doubts about the drop are duly recorded, but none is seriously explored.

In the following three sections, skepticism among some scientists begins to emerge and soon ripens into dissent. These second thoughts—from questions of morality to diplomatic strategy—never penetrated the inner circle of political power, but they did have an impact. An offhand remark at lunch by science adviser Arthur Holly Compton led Henry Stimson, chairman of the Interim Committee, to open a discussion of whether it might be possible to arrange a nonmilitary demonstration of the bomb (see Document 43). A scientific panel was asked whether they could devise an atomic alternative that would still cow Japan. They could devise no substitute for the drop.

The selection of targets received much more attention. Among the principal considerations were size (a smaller city would yield more precise results), location (a flat plane would afford fewer natural obstructions), weather (clear skies would permit the bombing to be carried out visually), industry and population (an industrial base would allow workers to report the demoralizing effects of the first atomic blast), and history (a city free of past bombing would promote maximum devastation). A small, strictly military target was ruled out, said one report, to avoid "undue risks of the weapon being lost due to bad placing of the bomb" (see Document 39).

By May 1945, five cities had emerged as leading candidates. Nigata received a "B" ranking. Yokohama, a seaport and industrial center, and the Kokura Arsenal received "A" rankings. The top "AA" rankings went to Hiroshima, with its army depot and port, and to the ancient religious capital of Kyoto. So far, none of these cities had been touched, not because of any strategic decision but because either the Army Air Corps simply had not gotten around to them yet or, as in the case of Yokohama, they were situated in areas protected by heavy antiaircraft fire (see Document 39).[1]

One issue surfaces again in this section of documents—the question of Russia. As the war drew to a close, Soviet-American relations assumed greater importance and became more entwined with the bomb. In the previous section, Henry Stimson first made the connection between diplomacy and the bomb in a conversation with President Roosevelt in December 1944. The bomb, Stimson suggested, could be used to horse-trade with the Russians. He left the terms of such a bargain vague (see Document 31). In this section, Stimson begins to elaborate this line of thinking. Citing difficulties in dealing with the Soviet Union over the fate of the far east, Stimson now refers to the bomb as the "master card" (see Document 40). He is unwilling, he says, "to gamble with such big stakes in diplomacy" without it and so presses President Truman to postpone the upcoming Allied summit meeting at Potsdam until after the weapon has been tested.

Historian Gar Alperovitz in *Atomic Diplomacy: Hiroshima and Potsdam* (1965) calls postponement the "strategy of a delayed showdown." It was the first stab at an "atomic diplomacy" designed to "make Russia more manageable." At the time, this was a startling revision of the orthodox interpretation, raising as it did questions about American motives. To the conventional notion that the United States dropped the bomb to win the war was now added the revisionist charge that the bomb was also used to manipulate the peace.

---

[1]Nagasaki was a late addition to the target list, probably doomed because of the requirement for visual bombing. Less than four hundred fifty miles southwest of Nigata and two hundred twenty miles southwest of Hiroshima, Nagasaki was close enough to be within striking distance and far enough to be clear if clouds covered either of those two target cities. Nagasaki had the further misfortune of having been untouched by conventional bombs as of late July 1945, when the final list was compiled.

The New York Times.

LATE CITY EDITION
Clearing and warm today. Fair, continued warm tomorrow.
Temperature Yesterday—Max. 74; Min. 54
Sunrise today, 6:11 A. M.; Sunset, 7:12 P. M.

Copyright, 1945, by The New York Times Company.

VOL. XCIV...No. 31,856.   Entered as Second-Class Matter, Postoffice, New York, N. Y.   NEW YORK, FRIDAY, APRIL 13, 1945.   THREE CENTS IN NEW YORK CITY

PRESIDENT ROOSEVELT IS DEAD;
TRUMAN TO CONTINUE POLICIES;
9TH CROSSES ELBE, NEARS BERLIN

U. S. AND RED ARMIES DRIVE TO MEET

Americans Across the Elbe in Strength Race Toward Russians Who Have Opened Offensive From Oder

WEIMAR TAKEN, RUHR POCKET SLASHED

Third Army Reported 19 Miles From Czechoslovak Border—British Drive Deeper in the North, Seizing Celle—Canadians Freeing Holland

By DREW MIDDLETON
By Wireless to The New York Times.

PARIS, April 12—Thousands of tanks and a half million doughboys of the United States First, Third and Ninth Armies are racing through the heart of the Reich on a front of 150 miles, threatening Berlin, Leipsig and the last citadels of the Nazi power.

The Second Armored Division of the Ninth Army has crossed the Elbe River in force and is striking eastward toward Berlin, whose outskirts lie less than sixty miles to the east, according to reports from the front. [A report quoted by The United Press placed the Americans less than fifty miles from the capital.]

Beyond Berlin the First White Russian Army has crossed the Oder on a wide front and a junction between the western and eastern Allies is not far off.

[The Moscow radio reported that heavy battles were raging west of the Oder before Berlin, indicating that Marshal Gregory K. Zhukoff had launched his drive toward the Reich's capital. The Soviet communiqué announced further progress by the Red Army forces in and around Vienna.]

Paris is wild with excitement tonight. A special edition of the newspaper France-Soir carries a report by the radio station "Voice of America" that places American forces fifteen and five-eighths miles from Berlin after an airborne landing that had linked up with Lieut. Gen. William H. Simpson's forces advancing eastward from the Elbe. This would put American forces only seventy-five miles from the Red Army vanguard.

No Confirmation at Headquarters

There was no confirmation of this report at Allied Supreme Headquarters, which by its own admission was thirty-six hours behind developments on some sectors of the front.

Resistance was continuing only on the northern and southern flanks. The center had burst wide open. Weimar fell to Lieut. Gen. George S. Patton's infantry, and reports from the front said Erfurt also had been cleared. Schweinfurt and Heilbronn, two German bastions on the south, had fallen to United States Seventh Army forces, who were driving on Bamberg, while farther north Third Army forces were about thirty-five miles from the Czechoslovak frontier in the area east of Coburg.

[The German radio reported American Third Army forces at Lichtenberg, nineteen miles from the Czechoslovak border, The United Press said.]

The offensives to liberate the Netherlands and reduce the Ruhr was imminent.

Continued on Page 15, Column 3

OUR OKINAWA GUNS DOWN 118 PLANES

Japanese Fliers Start 'Suicide' Attacks on Fleet, Sink a Destroyer, Hit Other Ships

By W. H. LAWRENCE
By Wireless to The New York Times.

GUAM, Friday, April 13—Japanese attempting to halt the American march to Tokyo, have started "desperate, suicidal" aerial attacks upon our ships and men in the Okinawa area, losing 118 planes on Thursday alone, Fleet Admiral Chester W. Nimitz announced today.

The Japanese succeeded in sinking a destroyer and damaging several other surface units, the communiqué said. All of the damaged vessels remained in action.

It was the first time that the Navy had revealed the suicidal nature of the Japanese air missions against our ships and men. The Japanese radio has been saying that this type of assault was being carried on by a "special attack corps" known in Japanese as "kamakasi," which, translated literally, means "divine wind."

Attack at Low Levels

The Japanese fliers launched their attacks upon our ships and men at a high speed and from low levels, diving directly into a ship before their bombs as they crashed.

There was no official estimate of the total number of enemy aircraft engaged in the Okinawa area attack other than the report of the 118 enemy planes destroyed.

Admiral Nimitz reported that the attacks began early on April 12 (Eastern Longitude time) with seven enemy planes shot down during the morning in the vicinity of the Hagushi beaches.

The tempo of the attacks stepped up in the afternoon as the Japanese bore in on our ships in wave after wave. Admiral Nimitz said that ships' guns, carrier aircraft and shore-based anti-aircraft shot down 111 of the attackers.

The revelation of the suicidal Japanese air attacks was the highlight of Admiral Nimitz' regular morning communiqué, which also disclosed the identity of two Marine and two Army divisions that have gone into action on Okinawa. These included the Twenty-seventh Army Division, formed from New York National Guard units, which are seeing action for the first time since the Saipan campaign and previously had engaged in the Gilbert Islands assault. It is composed...

Continued on Page 13, Column 2

Army Leaders See Reich End at Hand

By The Associated Press.
WASHINGTON, April 12—High Army officials told Senators today that the end of organized fighting in Germany probably would come within a few days.

Describing the pell-mell dash of American Armies across Germany, General Staff officers expressed the opinion to members of the Senate Military Committee that a collapse of German arms was imminent.

Those who attended said the army chiefs declared that they were so sure of the results that orders had been drawn for a drastic reduction in shipments of durable equipment to Europe.

Continued on Page 13, Column 3

Franklin Delano Roosevelt
1882-1945

© Perable

SECURITY PARLEY WON'T BE DELAYED

State Department Urges That World Be Shown We Plan No Changes in Policy

By JAMES B. RESTON
Special to The New York Times.

WASHINGTON, April 12—The United Nations Security Conference will open in San Francisco on April 25, despite the death of President Roosevelt, Secretary of State Edward R. Stettinius Jr. announced tonight.

Mr. Stettinius said that he had been authorized by President Harry Truman to make this announcement after a meeting of the Cabinet at the White House.

Most of the overseas delegations to the San Francisco conference have either arrived in this country or are now on their way, but while this was said to have been a factor in the decision to proceed with the conference, State Department officials urged that every attempt be made to give immediate evidence to the world that President Roosevelt's foreign policy would be sustained by the new Administration.

President Roosevelt immediately called a meeting at the White House at which the new Cabinet members pledged their support. Mr. Roosevelt's policies would be continued, that the war down.

The revelation of President Roosevelt's policy would be...

Continued on Page 2, Column 1

War News Summarized

FRIDAY, APRIL 13, 1945

President Roosevelt died yesterday afternoon, suddenly and unexpectedly. He was stricken with a massive cerebral hemorrhage at Warm Springs, Ga., on the eve of his greatest military and diplomatic successes—the impending fall of Berlin and the opening of the San Francisco Conference to set up a World Security Organization that would make the world free from martial and economic strife [1:7-8.]

Mr. Roosevelt had been sitting in front of the fireplace of his Little White House, having gone to Warm Springs on March 30 for a three-week rest. About 2:15 Eastern war time he said, "I have a terrific headache," lost consciousness in a few moments and died at 4:35. He was 63 years old. [1:6.]

The tragic word spread quickly around the world. Expressions of sorrow poured in from all sections. [4:5.] American soldiers and sailors refused to believe the reports until there was no longer doubt that their Commander-in-Chief had gone. [4:2-3.]

Harry S. Truman was sworn in as President at 7:09 o'clock last night, and a few minutes later Mrs. Roosevelt left for Warm Springs. [1:7.] The new President immediately called a Cabinet meeting and declared that Mr. Roosevelt's policies would be continued, that the war would be carried on until Germany and Japan surrendered unconditionally and that the San Francisco Conference would open April 25 as scheduled. [1:3.]

Some 500,000 American soldiers of the Third and Ninth Armies, and thousands of tanks, sped along a 150-mile front toward Berlin and Leipsig. The Ninth, surging across the Elbe, according to delayed reports was less than fifty miles from the...

German capital and 115 from the Russians along the Oder. The Third Army captured Weimar, home of the late German Republic, and was twenty-three miles below Leipsig, with the First closing a pincers from the north. [1:1-2; map P. 2.]

The Moscow radio reported that the Red Army was waging fierce battles east of Berlin, indicating resumption of the drive on that city. Elsewhere Russian troops scored wide gains and cut the last escape railroad from Vienna. [13:1.]

Open cities were ruled out and every German was ordered by Himmler to fight to the death, although Goebbels said "the war cannot last much longer." [12:6-7.]

The Ninth Air Force destroyed at least 117 more German planes yesterday. [11:5.]

In Italy the Eighth Army advanced along a thirty-mile front toward Bologna and the Po Valley; the Fifth Army also made good gains and was eleven miles from La Spezia. [13:8, with map.]

Japanese planes resumed their suicide attacks on American ships off Okinawa, sinking a destroyer and damaging several other vessels. One hundred and eighteen enemy planes were shot down. [1:2.] The American Division invaded Bohol, last of the enemy-held central Philippines. [18:6.] The B-29 attack on Kortyama, 110 miles north of Tokyo, set a new Superfortress distance record. [18:2.]

Clashes between Right and Left wing elements in Iran were reported from Moscow. [13:2.]

LAST WORDS: 'I HAVE TERRIFIC HEADACHE'

Roosevelt Was Posing for Artist When Hemorrhage Struck—He Died in Bedroom

WARM SPRINGS, Ga., April 12 —President Franklin D. Roosevelt's last words were:

"I have a terrific headache."

He spoke them to Comdr. Howard G. Bruenn, naval physician.

Mr. Roosevelt was sitting in front of a fireplace in the Little White House here atop Pine Mountain when what was described as a massive cerebral hemorrhage struck him.

The President's Negro valet, Arthur Prettyman, and a Filipino messboy carried him to his bedroom. He was unconscious at the end. It came without pain.

Dr. Bruenn said that he saw the President this morning and he was in excellent spirits at 9:30 A. M.

"At 1 o'clock," Dr. Bruenn added, "he was sitting in a chair while sketches were being made of him by an artist. He suddenly complained of a very severe occipital headache (back of the head).

"Within a very few minutes he lost consciousness. He was seen by me at 1:30 P. M., fifteen minutes after the episode had started.

"He did not regain consciousness, and he died at 3:35 P. M. (Georgia time)."

The artist sketching Mr. Roosevelt was N. Robbie of 530 West 139th Street, New York.

Only others present in the cottage were Comdr. George Fox, White House pharmacist and long an attendant on the President; William D. Hassett, Presidential secretary; Miss Grace Tully, con-

Continued on Page 4, Column 3

END COMES SUDDENLY AT WARM SPRINGS

Even His Family Unaware of Condition as Cerebral Stroke Brings Death to Nation's Leader at 63

ALL CABINET MEMBERS TO KEEP POSTS

Funeral to Be at White House Tomorrow, With Burial at Hyde Park Home—Impact of News Tremendous

By ARTHUR KROCK
Special to The New York Times.

WASHINGTON, April 12—Franklin Delano Roosevelt, War President of the United States and the only Chief Executive in history who was chosen for more than two terms, died suddenly and unexpectedly at 4:35 P. M. today at Warm Springs, Ga., and the White House announced his death at 5:48 o'clock. He was 63.

The President, stricken by a cerebral hemorrhage, passed from unconsciousness to death on the eighty-third day of his fourth term and in an hour of high triumph. The armies and fleets under his direction as Commander in Chief were at the gates of Berlin and the shores of Japan's home islands as Mr. Roosevelt died, and the cause he represented and led was nearing the conclusive stage of success.

Less than two hours after the official announcement, Harry S. Truman of Missouri, the Vice President, took the oath as the thirty-second President. The oath was administered by the Chief Justice of the United States, Harlan F. Stone, in a one-minute ceremony at the White House. Mr. Truman immediately let it be known that Mr. Roosevelt's Cabinet is remaining in office at his request, and that he had authorized Secretary of State Edward R. Stettinius Jr. to proceed with plans for the United Nations Conference on international organization at San Francisco, scheduled to begin April 25. A report was circulated that he leans somewhat to the idea of a coalition Cabinet, but this is unsubstantiated.

Funeral Tomorrow Afternoon

It was disclosed by the White House that funeral services for Mr. Roosevelt would take place at 4 P. M. (E. W. T.) Saturday in the East Room of the Executive Mansion. The Rev. Angus Dun, Episcopal Bishop of Washington; the Rev. Howard S. Wilkinson of St. Thomas's Church in Washington, and the Rev. John G. McGee of St. John's in Washington will conduct the services.

The body will be interred at Hyde Park, N. Y., Sunday, the Rev. George W. Anthony of St. James Church officiating. The time has not yet been fixed.

Jonathan Daniels, White House secretary, said Mr. Roosevelt's body would not lie in state. He added that, in view of the limited size of the East Room, which holds only about 200 persons, the list of those attending the funeral services would be limited to high Government officials, representatives of the membership of the...

Continued on Page 3, Column 2

TRUMAN IS SWORN IN THE WHITE HOUSE

Members of Cabinet on Hand as Chief Justice Stone Administers the Oath

By C. P. TRUSSELL
Special to The New York Times.

WASHINGTON, April 12—Vice President Harry S. Truman of Missouri, standing erect, with his sharp features taut and looking straight ahead through his large, round glasses, became the thirty-second President of the United States in a ceremony lasting not more than a minute in the Cabinet Room of the White House at 7:09 o'clock tonight.

The oath was administered by Chief Justice Harlan F. Stone two hours and thirty-four minutes after the sudden death of President Roosevelt. Mr. Truman had picked up a Bible from the end of the big Cabinet conference table, held it with his left hand and placed his right hand upon the upper cover. After repeating the oath, he bowed his head, lifted the Bible to his lips and kissed it.

Even before he had taken the oath Mr. Truman had asked President Roosevelt's Cabinet to continue in service. He also authorized Edward R. Stettinius Jr., Secretary of State, to announce that the United Nations Conference for International Organization would go on as scheduled.

To the newsmen at the White House he sent this word, through Stephen Early, press secretary:

"For the time being I prefer not to hold a press conference. It will be my effort to carry on as I believe the President would have done, and to that end I have asked the Cabinet to stay on with me."

Soon after he became President, Mr. Truman left the White House for the five-room Connecticut Avenue apartment where he has resided with Mrs. Truman and their 20-year-old daughter, Mary Margaret, for four years. He said he was "going home, to bed."

It was shortly after he had finished presiding over the Senate debate on the United States-Mexican Water Treaty late this afternoon that Mr. Truman received word from the White House of President Roosevelt's death. This was at about 5:15 P. M., a half hour before the news was made public. Reaching for his hat, he dashed out of the office, calling back to his staff that he was going to the White House.

Arriving at the White House, the...

Continued on Page 5, Column 2

Byrnes May Take Post With Truman

Special to The New York Times.
WASHINGTON, April 12—James F. Byrnes, recently resigned as Director of War Mobilization and Reconversion, known to be one of President Truman's warmest friends in official Washington, is expected to be called to the White House for consultation, and, possibly to take an important post in the Cabinet, in the immediate future.

President Truman's administration of former Justice Byrnes is well known here. He is said to take a successor to Cordell Hull as Secretary of State.

<u>Wednesday, April 25, 1945.</u>

I spent the first part of the morning going over with Harrison and Bundy the brief memorandum on S-1 which I had drafted with Bundy yesterday.[1] I also showed it to Marshall and to Groves who came in. Finally when we got it approved by all, I set it aside and called it a job. A copy of this memorandum will be annexed to this day's diary when the security control is taken off the subject.

● ● ●

At twelve o'clock noon I went over for my conference with the President[2] at the White House over S-1. General Groves was to meet me there, but he had to take a secret road around because if the newspaper men, who are now gathered in great numbers every morning in the President's anteroom, should see us both together there they would be sure to guess what I was going to see the President about. So Colonel McCarthy, the Secretary of the General Staff, arranged to have General Groves conducted around through underground passages to a room near the President and there wait till I had got far on in my talk with the President. The talk worked very well indeed. First of all I showed the President the paper that I had drawn yesterday and this morning. It is on the political aspects of the S-1 performance and the problems which are involved with the public.

[1]See Document 38.
[2]Harry S Truman, who succeeded Roosevelt upon his death on April 12, 1945.

<u>Wednesday, April 25, 1945.</u>
<u>Page 2</u>

He read it carefully and was very much interested in it. I then produced

General Groves and his account of the manufacturing operation, and Groves and

I and this report explained the matter to the President. The President took

one copy and we took the other and we went over it and answered his questions

and told him all about the process and about the problems that are coming up

and in fact I think very much interested him. He was very nice about it.

He remembered the time that I refused to let him go into this project when

he was chairman of the Truman Committee and was investigating it, and he said

that he understood now perfectly why it was inadvisable for me to have taken

any other course than I had taken.

        After three-quarters of an hour with the President, I left the

White House and drove up to Woodley for lunch alone, hoping to get a restful

nap afterwards. But is was barely two o'clock when I was called out of my nap

by Colonel Kyle to say that this active President of ours had come to the

Pentagon Building and was wandering at large in the building. It turned out

that he was there on a telephone call to London. Nevertheless I got up and

hurried down to the Pentagon in case that he might want me, and I did see him

for a minute and chatted with him as he was going.

● ● ●

<u>Memorandum discussed with the President</u>
<u>April 25, 1945</u>

1. Within four months we shall in all probability have completed the most terrible weapon ever known in human history, one bomb of which could destroy a whole city.

2. Although we have shared its development with the UK, physically the US is at present in the position of controlling the resources with which to construct and use it and no other nation could reach this position for some years.

3. Nevertheless it is practically certain that we could not remain in this position indefinitely.

   a. Various segments of its discovery and production are widely known among many scientists in many countries, although few scientists are now acquainted with the whole process which we have developed.

   b. Although its construction under present methods requires great scientific and industrial effort and raw materials, which are temporarily mainly within the possession and knowledge of US and UK, it is extremely probable that much easier and cheaper methods of production will be discovered by scientists in the future, together with the use of materials of much wider distribution. As a result, it is extremely probable that the future will make it possible to be constructed by smaller nations or even groups, or at least by a large nation in a much shorter time.

4. As a result, it is indicated that the future may see a time when such a weapon may be constructed in secret and used suddenly and effectively with devastating power by a wilful nation or group against an unsuspecting nation or group of much greater size and material power. With its aid even a very powerful unsuspecting nation might be conquered within a very

few days by a very much smaller one, although probably the only nation
which could enter into production within the next few years is Russia.

5. The world in its present state of moral advancement compared
with its technical development would be eventually at the mercy of such a
weapon. In other words, modern civilization might be completely destroyed.

6. To approach any world peace organization of any pattern now
likely to be considered, without an appreciation by the leaders of our
country of the power of this new weapon, would seem to be unrealistic. No
system of control heretofore considered would be adequate to control this
menace. Both inside any particular country and between the nations of the
world, the control of this weapon will undoubtedly be a matter of the greatest
difficulty and would involve such thorough-going rights of inspection and
internal controls as we have never heretofore contemplated.

7. Furthermore, in the light of our present position with reference
to this weapon, the question of sharing it with other nations and, if so shared,
upon what terms, becomes a primary question of our foreign relations. Also
our leadership in the war and in the development of this weapon has placed a
certain moral responsibility upon us which we cannot shirk without very serious
responsibility for any disaster to civilization which it would further.

8. On the other hand, if the problem of the proper use of this weapon
can be solved, we would have the opportunity to bring the world into a pattern
in which the peace of the world and our civilization can be saved.

9. As stated in General Groves' report, steps are under way looking
towards the establishment of a select committee of particular qualifications
for recommending action to the Executive and legislative branches of our
government when secrecy is no longer in full effect. The committee
would also recommend the actions to be taken by the War Department prior
to that time in anticipation of the postwar problems. All recommendations
would of course be first submitted to the President.

TOP SECRET   TOP SECRET

12 May 1945

Memorandum For: Major General L. R. Groves

Subject: Summary of Target Committee Meetings on 10 and 11 May 1945

1. The second meeting of the Target Committee convened at 9:00 AM
10 May in Dr. Oppenheimer's office at Site Y with the following present:

General Farrell   Dr. C. Lauritsen
Colonel Seeman   Dr. Ramsey
Captain Parsons   Dr. Dennison
Major Derry   Dr. Von Neumann
Dr. Stearns   Dr. Wilson
Dr. Tolman   Dr. Penney
Dr. Oppenheimer

Dr. Bethe and Dr. Brode were brought into the meeting for discussion of Item A
of the agenda. During the course of the meeting panels were formed from the
committee members and others to meet in the afternoon and develop conclusions
to items discussed in the agenda. The concluding meeting was held at 10:00 AM
11 May in Dr. Oppenheimer's office with the following present:

Colonel Seeman   Dr. Stearns
Captain Parsons   Dr. Von Neumann
Major Derry   Dr. Dennison
Dr. Tolman   Dr. Penney
Dr. Oppenheimer   Dr. Ramsey
                Dr. Wilson
2. The agenda for the meetings presented by Dr. Oppenheimer consisted of
the following:

A. Height of Detonation

B. Report on Weather and Operations

C. Gadget Jettisoning and Landing

D. Status of Targets

E. Psychological Factors in Target Selection

F. Use Against Military Objectives

G. Radiological Effects

H. Coordinated Air Operations

- continued on next page -

TOP SECRET

TOP SECRET   - 2 -

2. The agenda for the meetings --- continued

        I.   Rehearsals

        J.   Operating Requirements for Safety of Airplanes

        K.   Coordination with 21st Program

3. Height of Detonation

    A. The criteria for determining height selection were discussed. It
was agreed that conservative figures should be used in determining the height
since it is not possible to predict accurately the magnitude of the explosion
and since the bomb can be detonated as much as 40% below the optimum with a
reduction of 25% in area of damage whereas a detonation 14% above the optimum
will cause the same loss in area. It was agreed that fuses should be prepared
to meet the following possibilities:

        (1) For the Little Boy the detonation height should correspond
             to a pressure of 5 psi, a height of the Mach-stem of 100 feet
             and a magnitude of detonation of either 5,000 or 15,000 tons
             of H.E. equivalent. With present knowledge the fuse setting
             corresponding to 5,000 tons equivalent would be used but
             fusing for the other should be available in case more is
             known at the time of delivery. The heights of detonation
             corresponding to 5,000 and 15,000 tons are 1550 feet and
             2400 feet, respectively.

        (2) For the Fat Man the detonation heights should correspond
             to a pressure of 5 psi, a height of the Mach-stem of
             100 feet, and a magnitude of explosion of 700, 2,000, or
             5,000 tons of H.E. equivalent. With the present information
             the fuse would be set at 2,000 tons equivalent but fusing
             for the other values should be available at the time of
             final delivery. The heights of detonation corresponding to
             700, 2,000, and 5,000 tons are 580 feet, 1,000 feet and
             1,550 feet, respectively. Trinity data will be used for this gadget.

    B. In the case of the Fat Man delay circuits are introduced into the
unit for other purposes which make the detonation of the bomb 400 feet below the height
at which the fuse is set. For this reason as far as the Fat Man is concerned
the fuse settings should be 980 feet, 1,400 feet, or 1,950 feet.

    C. In view of the above it was agreed by all present that fuses should be
available at four (4) different height settings. These heights are 1,000 feet,
1,400 feet, 2,000 feet and 2,400 feet. With present information the 1,400 feet
fuse would be most likely to be used for both the Fat Man and the Little Boy.
(Later data presented by Dr. Brode modify the above conclusions on fusing and
detonating heights; the differential height for the Little Boy is 210 feet and
for the Fat Man 500 feet. For this reason some of the above figures must be
revised).

TOP SECRET

- 3 -

TOP SECRET

4. Report on Weather and Operations

     A. Dr. Dennison reported on the above subject. His report essentially
covered the materials in his Top Secret memo of 9 May - Subject: "Preliminary
Report on Operational Procedures". For this reason his report will not be
repeated here but is attached as an appendix. It was agreed by those present
that the mission if at all possible should be a visual bombing mission. For
this we should be prepared to wait until there is a good weather forecase in
one or more of three alternative targets. There is only a 2% chance in this
case that we will have to wait over two weeks. When the mission does take
place there should be spotter aircraft over each of three alternative targets
in order that an alternative target may be selected in the last hour of
flight if the weather is unpromising over the highest priority target.

     B. In case the aircraft reaches the target and finds, despite these
precautions that visual bombing is impossible, it should return to its base
provided it is in good operating condition. Only if the aircraft is in
sufficiently bad shape that it is unlikely that it can return to base and
make a safe landing or if it is essential that the drop be made that day
should the drop be made with radar equipment. For this purpose it may be
desirable to have an Eagle radar equipped airplane accompany the mission in
order that formation bombing with the Eagle plane in the lead can be made to
obtain the increased accuracy from Eagle. A final decision as to the
desirability of this emergency procedure can only be made after further combat
experience is obtained with Eagle aircraft. In any case every effort should
be made to have the mission such that blind bombing will be unnecessary.

     C. It was agreed that Dr. Stearns and Dr. Dennison should keep themselves
continuously informed as to radar developments. If at any time new developments
are available which show in combat a marked improvement of accuracy the basic
plan may be altered.

     D. It was agreed that Shoran was a very promising development for the
21st Bomber Command but that we should make no plans to use Shoran until its
success is fully confirmed in normal bombing missions in that area.

     E. The plan to use the gadget with visual bombing even though this may
require a one day to three weeks delay requires that the gadget be such that
for a period of at least three weeks it can be held in readiness in such a state
that on twelve hours notice it can be prepared for a combat mission. No
difficulty in this regard was foreseen by those present.

5. Gadget Jettisoning and Landing

     A. It was agreed that if the aircraft has to return to its base with the
gadget and if it is in good condition when it has reached there, it should make
a normal landing with the greatest possible care and with such precautions as
stand-by fire equipment being held in readiness on the ground. This operation
will inevitably involve some risks to the base and to the other aircraft parked
on the field. However, the chance of a crash when the aircraft is in good
condition and the chances of the crash initiating a high order explosion are both
sufficiently small that it was the view of those present that the landing operation
with the unit under these circumstances was a justifiable risk. Frequent landings
with inert and H.E. filled units have been made in the past. Training in landing
with the unit should be given to all crews who carry an active unit.

TOP SECRET

- 4 -

TOP SECRET

5. <u>Gadget Jettisoning and Landing</u>   continued

B. In case the aircraft returns to its base and then finds that it cannot make a normal landing it may be necessary to jettison the bomb. In the case of the Fat Man this can probably best be accomplished by dropping the bomb into shallow water from a low altitude. Tests on this will be carried out with both inert and live units. In the case of the Little Boy the situation is considerably more complicated since water leaking into the Little Boy will set off a nuclear reaction, and since the American held territory in the vicinity of the base is so densely filled that no suitable jettisoning ground for the Little Boy has been found which is sufficiently devoid of mositure, which is sufficiently soft that the projectile is sure not to seat from the impact, and which is sufficiently remote from extremely important American installations whose damage by a nuclear explosion would seriously affect the American war effort. The best emergency procedure that has so far been proposed is considered to be the removal of the gun powder from the gun and the execution of a crash landing. In this case there is no danger of fire setting off the gun and the accelerations should be sufficiently small to prevent seating of the projectile by the impact. Tests on the feasibility of unloading the gun powder in flight will be conducted.

C. It was agreed that prior to actual delivery some form of instructions should be prepared as a guide to the senior man on the aircraft as to procedures to be followed in cases of different types of disasters.

6. <u>Status of Targets</u>

A. Dr. Stearns described the work he had done on target selection. He has surveyed possible targets possessing the following qualifications: (1) they be important targets in a large urban area of more then three miles diameter, (2) they be capable of being damaged effectively by a blast, and (3) they are likely to be unattacked by next August. Dr. Stearns had a list of five targets which the Air Forces would be willing to reserve for our use unless unforeseen circumstances arise. These targets are:

   (1) <u>Kyoto</u> - This target is.an urban industrial area with a population of 1,000,000. It is the former capital of Japan and many people and industries are now being moved there as other areas are being destroyed. From the psychological point of view there is the advantage that Kyoto is an intellectual center for Japan and the people there are more apt to appreciate the significance of such a weapon as the gadget. (Classified as an AA target)

   (2) <u>Hiroshima</u> - This is an important army depot and port of embarkation in the middle of an urban industrial area. It is a good radar target and it is such a size that a large part of the city could be extensively damaged. There are adjacent hills which are likely to produce a focusing effect which would considerably increase the blast damage. Due to rivers it is not a good incendiary target. (Classified as an AA target)

TOP SECRET

- 5 -

TOP SECRET

6.   Status of Targets - continued

(3)   Yokohama - This target is an important urban industrial area
which has so far been untouched. Industrial activities include
aircraft manufacture, machine tools, docks, electrical equipment
and oil refineries. As the damage to Tokyo has increased
additional industries have moved to Yokohama. It has the disadvantage of the most important target areas being separated by
a large body of water and of being in the heaviest anti-aircraft
concentration in Japan. For us it has the advantage as an
alternative target for use in case of bad weather of being rather
far removed from the other targets considered. (Classified as
an A Target)

(4)   Kokura Aresenal - This is one of the largest arsenals in Japan
and is surrounded by urban industrial structures. The arsenal
is important for light ordnance, anti-aircraft and beach head
defense materials. The dimensions of the arsenal are
4100' x 2000'. The dimensions are such that if the bomb were
properly placed full advantage could be taken of the higher
pressures immediately underneath the bomb for destroying the
more solid structures and at the same time considerable blast
damage could be done to more feeble structures further away.
(Classified as an A Target)

(5)   Nigata - This is a port of embarkation on the N.W. coast of
Honshu. Its importance is increasing as other ports are damaged.
Machine tool industries are located there and it is a potential
center for industrial despersion. It has oil refineries and
storage. (Classified as a B Target)

(6)   The possibility of bombing the Emperor's palace was discussed.
It was agreed that we should not recommend it but that any
action for this bombing should come from authorities on military
policy. It was agreed that we should obtain information from
which we could determine the effectiveness of our weapon against
this target.

   B. It was the recommendation of those present at the meeting that the first
four choices of targets for our weapon should be the following:

                    a. Kyoto
                    b. Hiroshima
                    c. Yokohama
                    d. Kokura Arsenal

   C. Dr. Stearns agreed to do the following: (1) brief Colonel Fisher
thoroughly on these matters, (2) request reservations for these targets, (3) find
out more about the target area including exact locations of the strategic
industries there, (4) obtain further photo information on the targets, and (5)
to determine the nature of the construction, the area, heights, contents and roof
coverage of the buildings. He also agreed to keep in touch with the target data as
it develops and to keep the committee advised of other possible target areas.
He will also check on locations of small military targets and obtain further
details on the Emperor's palace.

TOP SECRET

- 6 -

TOP SECRET

7. <u>Psychological Factors in Target Selection</u>

A. It was agreed that psychological factors in the target selection were of great importance. Two aspects of this are (1) obtaining the greatest psychological effect against Japan and (2) making the initial use sufficiently spectacular for the importance of the weapon to be internationally recognized when publicity on it is released.

B. In this respect Kyoto has the advantage of the people being more highly intelligent and hence better able to appreciate the significance of the weapon. Hiroshima has the advantage of being such a size and with possible focusing from nearby mountains that a large fraction of the city may be destroyed. The Emperor's palace in Tokyo has a greater fame than any other target but is of least strategic value.

8. <u>Use Against "Military" Objectives</u>

A. It was agreed that for the initial use of the weapon any small and strictly military objective should be located in a much larger area subject to blast damage in order to avoid undue risks of the weapon being lost due to bad placing of the bomb.

9. <u>Radiological Effect</u>

A. Dr. Oppenheimer presented a memo he had prepared on the radiological effects of the gadget. This memo will not be repeated in this summary but is being sent to General Groves as a separate exhibit. The basic recommendations of this memo are (1) for radiological reasons no aircraft should be closer than 2-1/2 miles to the point of detonation (for blast reasons the distance should be greater) and (2) aircraft must avoid the cloud of radio-active materials. If other aircraft are to conduct missions shortly after the detonation a monitoring plane should determine the areas to be avoided.

10. <u>Coordinated Air Operations</u>

A. The feasibility of following the raid by an incendiary mission was discussed. This has the great advantage that the enemies' fire fighting ability will probably be paralyzed by the gadget so that a very serious conflagration should be capable of being started. However, until more is learned about the phenomena associated with a detonation of the gadget, such as the extent to which there will be radio-active clouds, an incediary mission immediately after the delivery of the gadget should be avoided. A coordinated incendiary raid should be feasible on the following day at which time the fire raid should still be quite effective. By delaying the coordinated raid to the following day, the scheduling of our already contemplated operations will not be made even more difficult, photo reconnaissance of the actual damage directly caused by our device can be obtained without confusion from the subsequent fire raid, and dangers from the radio-active clouds can be avoided.

B. Fighter cover should be used for the operation as directed by the 21st Bomber Command.

TOP SECRET

- 7 -

TOP SECRET

11.   Rehearsals

A.   It was agreed by all that very complete rehearsals of the entire
operation are essential to its success. It is possible for thirty (30)
pumpkin units for this purpose to be shipped from this country in June with
perhaps sixty (60) being shipped in July. These rehearsals overseas should
take place beginning in July. At least some of the rehearsals should be
very complete including the placing of spotter aircraft over the alternative
targets, use of fighter cover, etc. Even though it is hoped that radar
will not be used some rehearsals of radar operations are required in
order that the operations may be carried out successfully if emergency
arises for which they are required.

12.   Operating Requirements for Safety of Aircraft

A.   Dr. Penney reported some very encouraging information he had just
received from England in this respect. His previous information was that
no one could guarantee the safety of a large aircraft at blast pressures
greater than 1/2 lb. per square inch. However, in some recent experiments
in England large aircraft have been flown over detonations of 2,000 lbs.
of TNT and pilots have not objected to going as low as 900 feet. On this
basis with a 100,000 ton total equivalent energy release or a 64,000 ton
equivalent blast energy 23,000 feet would be a safe altitude on the basis
of these experiments if allowance is made for the rarefaction of the
atmosphere at high altitudes. However, due to the greater duration of the
blast in our case, the safe height will probably be somewhat greater.

13.   Coordination with 21st Program

A.   This matter was included as part of the other discussion and is
included in previous paragraphs of this summary.

14.   It was agreed that the next meeting of the Target Committee should
take place at 9:00 AM EST on 28 May in Room 4E200 of the Pentagon Building
in Washington. Dr. Oppenheimer recommended and others agreed that either
Captain Parsons and/or Dr. Ramsey should attend this meeting.

15.   In view of the high classification of the minutes of this meeting
it was agreed that copies should not be sent to those present but that instead
one copy should be kept on file in General Groves' office, one copy in
Dr. Oppenheimer's office, and one copy in Captain Parsons' office.

J. A. Derry, Maj. C.E.
N. F. Ramsey

Major J. A. Derry
Dr. N. F. Ramsey

dc

Distribution:
 Copy 1: Maj Gen L. R. Groves
 Copy 2: Capt. Parsons
 Copies 3 & 4: J. R. Oppenheimer

TOP SECRET

<u>Tuesday, May 15, 1945</u>

At 9:30 we went into our meeting of the Committee of Three,-
Grew, Forrestal and myself being present with McCloy as recorder. Averill
Harriman, the Ambassador to Russia, came with Grew; also William Phillips,
formerly Under Secretary of State years ago. Forrestal brought Major Correa.
We had a pretty red hot session first over the questions which Grew had pro-
pounded to us in relation to the Yalta Conference and our relations with Russia.
They have been entered in the diary here so I will not repeat them. I tried
to point out the difficulties which existed and I thought it was premature to
ask those questions; at least we were not yet in a position to answer them.
The trouble is that the President has now promised apparently to meet Stalin
and Churchill on the first of July[1] and at that time these questions will become
burning and it may be necessary to have it out with Russia on her relations to
Manchuria and Port Arthur and various other parts of North China and also the
relations of China to us. Over any such tangled wave of problems the S-1 secret
would be dominant and yet we will not know until after that time probably,
until after that meeting, whether this is a weapon in our hands or not. We
think it will be shortly afterwards, but it seems a terrible thing to gamble
with such big stakes in diplomacy without having your master card in your hand.
The best we could do today was to persuade Harriman not to go back until we had
had time to think over these things a little bit harder.

[1]The upcoming Allied summit meeting in Potsdam, Germany.

TOP SECRET

NOTES OF THE INTERIM COMMITTEE MEETING
THURSDAY, 31 MAY 1945
10:00 A.M. to 1:15 P.M. - 2:15 P.M. to 4:15 P.M.

PRESENT:

Members of the Committee

Secretary Henry L. Stimson, Chairman
Hon. Ralph A. Bard
Dr. Vannevar Bush
Hon. James F. Byrnes
Hon. William L. Clayton
Dr. Karl T. Compton
Dr. James B. Conant
Mr. George L. Harrison

Invited Scientists

Dr. J. Robert Oppenheimer
Dr. Enrico Fermi
Dr. Arthur H. Compton
Dr. E. O. Lawrence

By Invitation

General George C. Marshall
Major Gen. Leslie R. Groves
Mr. Harvey H. Bundy
Mr. Arthur Page

I. OPENING STATEMENT OF THE CHAIRMAN:

Secretary Stimson explained that the Interim Committee

had been appointed by him, with the approval of the President to

make recommendations on temporary war-time controls, public announce-

ment, legislation and post-war organization. The Secretary gave

high praise to the brilliant and effective assistance rendered to

the project by the scientists of the country and expressed great

TOP SECRET

TOP SECRET

- 2 -

appreciation to the four scientists present for their great contributions to the work and their willingness to advise on the many complex problems that the Interim Committee had to face. He expressed the hope that the scientists would feel completely free to express their views on any phase of the subject.

The Committee had been termed an "Interim Committee" because it was expected that when the project became more widely known a permanent organization established by Congressional action or by treaty arrangements would be necessary.

The Secretary explained that General Marshall shared responsibility with him for making recommendations to the President on this project with particular reference to its military aspects; therefore, it was considered highly desirable that General Marshall be present at this meeting to secure at first hand the views of the scientists.

The Secretary expressed the view, a view shared by General Marshall, that this project should not be considered simply in terms of military weapons, but as a new relationship of man to the universe. This discovery might be compared to the discoveries of the Copernican theory and of the laws of gravity, but far more important than these in its effect on the lives of men. While the advances in the field to date had been fostered by the needs of war, it was important to realize that the implications of the project went far beyond the needs of the present war. It must be controlled if possible to make it an assurance of future peace rather than a menace to civilization.

TOP SECRET

TOP SECRET

- 3 -

The Secretary suggested that he hoped to have the
following questions discussed during the course of the meeting:

1. Future military weapons.

2. Future international competition.

3. Future research.

4. Future controls.

5. Future developments, particularly non-military.

II. STAGES OF DEVELOPMENT:

As a technical background for the discussions, Dr. A. H.
Compton explained the various stages of development. The first
stage involved the separation of uranium 235. The second stage
involved the use of "breeder" piles to produce enriched materials
from which plutonium or new types of uranium could be obtained.
The first stage was being used to produce material for the present
bomb while the second stage would produce atomic bombs with a
tremendous increase in explosive power over those now in production.
Production of enriched materials was now on the order of pounds or
hundreds of pounds and it was contemplated that the scale of operations
could be expanded sufficiently to produce many tons. While bombs
produced from the products of the second stage had not yet been
proven in actual operation, such bombs were considered a scientific
certainty. It was estimated that from January 1946 it would take
one and one-half years to prove this second stage in view of certain
technical and metallurgical difficulties, that it would take three

TOP SECRET

TOP SECRET

- 4 -

years to get plutonium in volume, and that it would take perhaps

six years for any competitor to catch up with us.

Dr. Fermi estimated that approximately twenty pounds of

enriched material would be needed to carry on research in current

engineering problems and that a supply of one-half to one ton would

be needed for research on the second stage.

In response to the Secretary's question, Dr. A. H. Compton

stated that the second stage was dependent upon vigorous exploitation

of the first stage and would in no way vitiate the expenditure

already made on the present plant.

Dr. Conant mentioned a so-called "third stage" of develop-

ment in which the products of the "second stage" would be used simply

as a detonator for heavy water. He asked Dr. Oppenheimer for an

estimate of the time factor involved in developing this phase.

Dr. Oppenheimer stated that this was a far more difficult development

than the previous stages and estimated that a minimum of three years

would be required to reach production. He pointed out that heavy

water (hydrogen)was much cheaper to produce than the other materials

and could eventually be obtained in far greater quantity.

Dr. Oppenheimer reviewed the scale of explosive force

involved in these several stages. One bomb produced in the first

stage was estimated to have the explosive force of 2,000 - 20,000

tons of TNT. The actual blast effect would be accurately measured

when the test was made. In the second stage the explosive force

TOP SECRET

TOP SECRET

- 5 -

was estimated to be equal to 50,000 - 100,000 tons of TNT. It was considered possible that a bomb developed from the third stage might produce an explosive force equal to 10,000,000 - 100,000,000 tons of TNT.

III. DOMESTIC PROGRAM:

  Dr. Lawrence expressed his great appreciation for the fact that the leaders of the Government had been willing to take the chances inherent in the development of this program. He expressed a view that if the United States were to stay ahead in this field it was imperative that we knew more and did more than any other country. He felt that research had to go on unceasingly. There were many unexplored possibilities in terms of new methods and new materials beyond thorium and uranium. In fact, all heavy elements held potentialities for exploitation in this field. He thought it might be possible one day to secure our energy from terrestrial sources rather than from the sun. Dr. Lawrence pointed out that there was no real doubt about the soundness of the program. Any failures that had occurred or would occur in the future were nothing more than temporary setbacks and there was every reason to believe that such setbacks would be quickly overcome.

  Dr. Lawrence recommended that a program of plant expansion be vigorously pursued and at the same time a sizable
       and material
stock pile of bombs/should be built up. For security reasons

TOP SECRET

TOP SECRET

- 6 -

plants that were built should be widely scattered throughout the country. Every effort should be made to encourage industrial application and development. Only by vigorously pursuing the necessary plant expansion and fundamental research, and by securing adequate government support could this nation stay out in front. With this view Dr. A. H. Compton expressed complete agreement.

Dr. Karl T. Compton, summarizing the views expressed above, suggested the following program:

1. Expand production under the first stage to produce bombs for stock pile and to furnish material for research.

2. Intensify "second stage" research.

3. Build necessary "second stage" pilot plants.

4. Produce the new product.

Dr. Oppenheimer pointed out that one of the difficult problems involved in guiding a future domestic program would be the allocation of materials as between different uses. Dr. Karl T. Compton added further that every effort should be made to encourage industrial progress in order that our fundamental research program would be strengthened.

The Secretary summarized the views of the group concerning our domestic program as follows:

1. Keep our industrial plant intact.

2. Build up sizable stock piles of material for military use and for industrial and technical use.

3. Open the door to industrial development.

TOP SECRET

TOP SECRET

- 7 -

IV.   FUNDAMENTAL RESEARCH:

Dr. Oppenheimer felt that the work now being done under
war pressure was simply a process of plucking the fruits of earlier
research. In order to exploit more fully the potentialities of this
field, it was felt that a more leisurely and a more normal research
situation should be established. Dr. Oppenheimer strongly urged
that numbers of the present staff should be released to go back to
their universities and research laboratories in order to explore
the many ramifications of this field, to avoid the sterility of
the present orientation to specific problems only, and to develop
cheaper and simpler methods of production. Dr. Bush expressed the
view that while it is imperative in war time to concentrate on
specific problems such a narrowing of the field in peace time was
completely wrong. He agreed with Dr. Oppenheimer that only a nucleus
of the present staff should be retained and that as many as possible
should be released for broader and freer inquiry. Drs. A. H. Compton
and Fermi reenforced this view by emphasizing that we could never
be sure of the tremendous possibilities in this field until thorough
fundamental research could be brought to bear.

V.   PROBLEMS OF CONTROL AND INSPECTION:

The Secretary inquired what other potentialities beyond
purely military uses might be exploited. In reply Dr. Oppenheimer
pointed out that the immediate concern had been to shorten the war.
The research that had lead to this development had only opened the
door to future discoveries. Fundamental knowledge of this subject
was so wide spread throughout the world that early steps should

TOP SECRET

TOP SECRET

- 8 -

be taken to make our developments known to the world. He thought
it might be wise for the United States to offer to the world free
interchange of information with particular emphasis on the development of peace-time uses. The basic goal of all endeavors in the
field should be the enlargement of human welfare. If we were to
offer to exchange information before the bomb was actually used,
our moral position would be greatly strengthened.

The Secretary stated that an understanding of the nonmilitary potentialities was a necessary background to the consideration
of the question of interchange of information and international cooperation. He referred to the Bush-Conant memorandum which had
stressed the role of science in securing a policy of self-restraint.
This memorandum had recommended that in any international organization
which might be established complete scientific freedom should be
provided for and the right of inspection should be given to an
international control body. The Secretary asked what kind of
inspection might be effective and what would be the position of
democratic governments as against totalitarian regimes under such
a program of international control coupled with scientific freedom.
The Secretary said that it was his own feeling that the democratic
countries had fared pretty well in this war. Dr. Bush indorsed
this view vigorously, pointing out that our advantage over totalitarian states had been tremendous. Evidence just in from Germany
revealed that she was far behind us in the technology of this
field and in other scientific fields. He said that our tremendous
advantage stemmed in large measure from our system of team work

TOP SECRET

TOP SECRET

- 9 -

and free interchange of information by which we had won out and
would continue to win out in any competitive scientific and
technological race. He expressed some doubt, however, of our
ability to remain ahead permanently if we were to turn over completely to the Russians the results of our research under free
competition with no reciprocal exchange. Dr. Karl T. Compton
felt that we would hold our advantage at least to the extent of
the construction lag, but, in any event, he felt that secrets of
this nature could not be successfully kept for any period of time
and that we could safely share our knowledge and still remain ahead.

Dr. A. H. Compton stated that the destructive applications
of these discoveries were perhaps easier to control than the constructive ones. He referred to the nuclonics prospectus prepared
some time ago in which were indicated certain other potential uses
in such fields as naval propulsion, health, chemistry, and industrial
development. He pointed out/Faraday's hopes and predictions in the
field of electro-dynamics were realized by Edison only after the
lapse of several decades. Such a lag in this field with as yet
uncharted possibilities seemed likely. He stressed the impossibility
of keeping technological advances secret, as witness the experience
of industry. The fundamental knowledge in the field was known
in many countries and a policy of restraint, of the nationalization
of scientific ideas could not work. Unless scientists were able
to keep abreast of advances in the field throughout the world they
would probably lose out on many developments.

Dr. Conant felt that international control in this field

TOP SECRET

TOP SECRET

- 10 -

would require the power of inspection and that international arrangements among scientists would be by a means of strengthening this power. Dr. Oppenheimer expressed doubts concerning the possibility of knowing what was going on in this field in Russia, but expressed the hope that the fraternity of interest among scientists would aid in the solution.

General Marshall cautioned against putting too much faith in the effectiveness of the inspection proposal. Mr. Clayton also expressed considerable doubt on this point.

VI. RUSSIA:

In considering the problem of controls and international collaboration the question of paramount concern was the attitude of Russia. Dr. Oppenheimer pointed out that Russia had always been very friendly to science and suggested that we might open up this subject with them in a tentative fashion and in the most general terms without giving them any details of our productive effort. He thought that we might say that a great national effort had been put into this project and express a hope for cooperation with them in this field. He felt strongly that we should not prejudge the Russian attitude in this matter.

At this point General Marshall discussed at some length the story of charges and counter-charges that have been typical of our relations with the Russians, pointing out that most of these allegations have proven unfounded. The seemingly uncooperative attitude of Russia in military matters stemmed from the necessity

TOP SECRET

TOP SECRET

- 11 -

of maintaining security. He said that he had accepted this reason
for their attitude in his dealings with the Russians and had acted
accordingly. As to the post-war situation and in matters other
than purely military, he felt that he was in no position to express
a view. With regard to this field he was inclined to favor the
building up of a combination among like-minded powers, thereby
forcing Russia to fall in line by the very force of this coalition.
General Marshall was certain that we need have no fear that the
Russians, if they had knowledge of our project, would disclose
this information to the Japanese. He raised the question whether
it might be desirable to invite two prominent Russian scientists
to witness the test.

Mr. Byrnes expressed a f ear that if information ~~was~~ WERE
given to the Russians, even in general terms, Stalin would ask
to be brought into the partnership. He felt this to be particularly
likely in view of our commitments and pledges of cooperation with
the British. In this connection Dr. Bush pointed out that even
the British do not have any of our blue prints on plants. Mr. Byrnes
expressed the view, which was generally agreed to by all present,
that the most desirable program would be to push ahead as fast as
possible in production and research to make certain that we stay
ahead and at the same time make every effort to better our political
relations with Russia.

VII. INTERNATIONAL PROGRAM:

Dr. A. H. Compton stressed very strongly the need for

TOP SECRET

- 12 -

maintaining ourselves in a position of superiority while at the same time working toward adequate political agreements. He favored freedom of competition and freedom of research activity to as great an extent as possible consistent with security and/the international situation. To maintain rigid security over this project would result in a certain sterility of research and a very real competitive disadvantage to the nation. He felt that within the larger field of freedom for research it would still be possible to maintain close security of the military aspects of the field. We could maintain our technical advantage over other nations only by drawing on the free interchange of scientific investigation and curiosity. He urged the view, expressed earlier by General Marshall, that we should secure agreements for cooperation with other like-minded nations and at the same time work toward solidifying our relations with the Russians.

Dr. A. H. Compton recommended that roughly the following program should be adopted for at least a decade:

1. Freedom of research be developed to the utmost consistent with national security and military necessity.

2. A combination of democratic powers be established for cooperation in this field.

3. A cooperative understanding be reached with Russia.

The meeting adjourned for luncheon at 1:15 P.M. and resumed at 2:15 P.M. All who attended the

TOP SECRET

TOP SECRET

- 13 -

morning session were present with the exception
of General Marshall.

VIII. <u>EFFECT OF THE BOMBING ON THE JAPANESE AND THEIR WILL TO FIGHT</u>:

It was pointed out that one atomic bomb on an arsenal
would not be much different from the effect caused by any Air Corps
strike of present dimensions. However, <u>Dr. Oppenheimer</u> stated
that the visual effect of an atomic bombing would be tremendous.
It would be accompanied by a brilliant luminescence which would
rise to a height of 10,000 to 20,000 feet. The neutron effect of
the explosion would be dangerous to life for a radius of at least
two-thirds of a mile.

After much discussion concerning various types of
targets and the effects to be produced, <u>the Secretary expressed</u>
<u>the conclusion, on which there was general agreement, that we could</u>
<u>not give the Japanese any warning; that we could not concentrate</u>
<u>on a civilian area; but that we should seek to make a profound</u>
<u>psychological impression on as many of the inhabitants as possible.</u>
<u>At the suggestion of Dr. Conant the Secretary agreed that the most</u>
<u>desirable target would be a vital war plant employing a large number</u>
<u>of workers and closely surrounded by workers' houses.</u>

There was some discussion of the desirability of attempting
several strikes at the same time. <u>Dr. Oppenheimer's</u> judgment was
that several strikes would be feasible. <u>General Groves</u>, however,
expressed doubt about this proposal and pointed out the following
objections: (1) We would lose the advantage of gaining additional

TOP SECRET

TOP SECRET

- 14 -

knowledge concerning the weapon at each successive bombing; (2) such a program would require a rush job on the part of those assembling the bombs and might, therefore, be ineffective; (3) the effect would not be sufficiently distinct from our regular Air Force bombing program.

IX. <u>HANDLING OF UNDESIRABLE SCIENTISTS</u>:

General Groves stated that the program has been plagued since its inception by the presence of certain scientists of doubtful discretion and uncertain loyalty. It was <u>agreed</u> that nothing could be done about dismissing these men until after the bomb has actually been used or, at best, until after the test has been made. After some publicity concerning the weapon was out, steps should be taken to sever these scientists from the program and to proceed with a general weeding out of personnel no longer needed.

X. <u>CHICAGO GROUP</u>:

Dr. A. H. Compton outlined briefly the nature and size of the Chicago program. In line with directives from General Groves it was intended to limit the operations at Chicago to those useful in the prosecution of this war. Its activities fell into the following categories:

1. Aid to the Hanford project on plutonium development.

2. Aid to the Santa Fe group.

3. Research on a thorium using pile.

4. Preliminary investigations of the extension of uranium piles.

TOP SECRET

TOP SECRET

- 15 -

5. Studies of the health of personnel
working with these materials.

It was pointed out that programs 3 and 4 above did not
bear directly on current war use, but that they comprised only
about 20 per cent of the work being carried on in Chicago and that
it was considered desirable in terms of future development to continue this work.

It was the consensus of the meeting that the Committee
should lean on the recommendations of Drs. Conant and Bush as to
what should be done with the Chicago group. Dr. Bush, as seconded
by Dr. Conant, recommended that the present programs, including
Chicago, should be continued at their present levels until the
end of the war. It was agreed that this recommendation should
be transmitted to the Secretary of War.

XI. POSITION OF THE SCIENTIFIC PANEL:

Mr. Harrison stated that the Scientific Panel had been
called in at the suggestion of Drs. Bush and Conant and with the
heartiest approval of all members of the Committee. It was considered a continuing Panel which was free to present its views
to the Committee at any time. The Committee was particularly
anxious to secure from the scientists their ideas of just what
sort of organization should be established to direct and control
this field. The Committee requested the Panel to prepare as speedily
as possible a draft of their views on this subject. In this connection
Dr. Bush pointed out that there would be no need at this time in
drawing up a draft of an organization in this field to consider

TOP SECRET

TOP SECRET

- 16 -

relationships with the Research Board for National Security.
Dr. Karl T. Compton suggested that the organization could be
tied in later to the Research Board for National Security through
its section on nuclear physics.

The question was raised as to what the scientists might
tell their people about the Interim Committee and their having been
called before it. It was agreed that the four scientists should
feel free to tell their people that an Interim Committee appointed
by the Secretary of War and with the Secretary of War as Chairman
had been established to deal specifically with the problems of
control, organization, legislation, and publicity. The identity
of the members of the Committee should not be divulged. The
scientists should be permitted to explain that they had met with
this Committee and had been given complete freedom to present
their views on any phase of the subject. The impression should
definitely be left with their people that the Government was taking
a most active interest in this project.

XII. NEXT MEETING:

The next meeting of the Committee was scheduled for
Friday, 1 June 1945, at 11:00 A.M. in the office of the Secretary
of War. The purpose of this meeting was to secure the views of
four representatives from industry.

The meeting adjourned at 4:15 P.M.

R. Gordon Arneson

R. GORDON ARNESON
2nd Lieutenant, A.U.S.
Secretary

TOP SECRET

<u>Thursday, May 31, 1945.</u>

Another nice clear day. I got down to the Department quite
early at eight-forty and had a talk with George Harrison and General Marshall
before the meeting called for the Interim Committee of S-1, and I prepared
for the meeting as carefully as I could because on me fell the job of opening it and telling them what it was and telling what we expected of these
scientists in getting them started and talking. . . .

•   •   •

I told the invited scientists who the Committee was, the Interim
Committee, what it was established for, and then I switched over and told them
what we wanted of them, the invited scientists; first, to congratulate and
thank them for what they have done and then to get them started in talking and
questioning. It was a little slow sledding at first but I think I got some
wrinkles out of their heads in regard to my own attitude and that of the
Army towards this new project. I told them that we did not regard it as a new
weapon merely but as a revolutionary change in the relations of man to the
universe and that we wanted to take advantage of this; that the project might
even mean the doom of civilization or it might mean the perfection of civilization;
that it might be a Frankenstein which would eat us up or it might be a project
"by which the peace of the world would be helped in becoming secure".
Well after a while the talk went pretty well. I had Marshall in and during
a time when I had to be absent to go over to the White House he took a
vigorous hand in the discussion and I think impressed himself very much upon
them. I think we made an impression upon the scientists that we were
looking at this like statesmen and not like merely soldiers anxious to win
the war at any cost. On the other hand, they were a fine lot of men as
can be seen from their records. Dr. Fermi, Dr. Lawrence, and Dr. Compton
were all Nobel prize winners; and Dr. Oppenheimer, though not a Nobel
prize winner, was really one of the best of the lot.

•   •   •

'Gentlemen, it is our responsibility to recommend action that may turn the course of civilization. In our hands we expect soon to have a weapon of wholly unprecedented destructive power. Today's prime fact is war. Our great task is to bring this war to a prompt and successful conclusion. We may assume that our new weapon puts in our hands overwhelming power. It is our obligation to use this power with the best wisdom we can command. To us now the matter of first importance is how our use of this new weapon will appear in the long view of history.'

This, as accurately as I can recall it, was the statement made by Secretary of War Henry L. Stimson as he presented to the 'Interim Committee' the question of what should be done with the atomic bomb. The place was the Secretary's office in Washington. The date was 31 May 1945.

● ● ●

THE INTERIM COMMITTEE CONSIDERS. After Secretary Stimson's opening statement at the meeting of 31 May 1945, he turned the committee's attention immediately to what the atomic bomb could do and how it might be used. Oppenheimer explained that the simplest kind of bomb was necessarily the objective of this first development. Such a bomb could be exploded above the ground with the help of the newly developed proximity fuse. Its greatest military effect would be in destroying structures by the blast of the explosion. The kind of target on which such a weapon would have the greatest military effect seemed to be either a concentration of troops or war plants whose buildings could be put out of commission by the explosion. Oppenheimer noted that if the bomb were exploded over a city their estimates indicated that some 20,000 people would probably be killed.[1] He was giving a technical reply to a technical question. Stimson's response was that of a man of wide culture and broad sympathy, to whom Japan was a living reality. To him Japan was not just a place on the map, not only a nation that must be defeated. The objective was military damage, he pointed out, not civilian lives. To illustrate his point he noted that Kyoto was a city that must not be bombed. It lies in the form of a cup and thus would be exceptionally vulnerable. But this city, he said, is no military target. It is exclusively a place of homes and art and shrines.

General Marshall stated that from the point of view of the postwar safety of the nation he would have to argue against the use of the bomb in World War II, at least if its existence could be kept secret. Such use, he said, would show our hand. We would be in a stronger position with regard to future military action if we did not show the power we held.

This led to a discussion about the possibility of maintaining secrecy about our development of atomic weapons. The members of the Scientific Panel were unanimous in the opinion that so many persons already knew of the wartime atomic studies that soon after the war it would be common knowledge that nuclear energy could be released and that it could not be long before an atomic explosion would somewhere be tried.

This reply did not, however, answer fully General Marshall's objection to the use of the bomb. Even though the knowledge of the availability of atomic energy might become widespread, perhaps the details of the bomb itself would not be known outside of the United States and Britain. In any case, if the bomb were not

[1]It was not anticipated that when the attack was made practically no one would have sought shelter. This was the major reason for the considerable error in this estimate when compared with the roughly 100,000 killed at Hiroshima and 40,000 at Nagasaki. The estimates were based on experience with previous bomb attacks. The deadly fire raids that caused such complete destruction in densely populated Tokyo took just as many lives. But, because the area of destruction in Tokyo was four times as great, the number of lives lost per square mile at Tokyo was only one-fourth as great as at Hiroshima and Nagasaki.

used in the present war the compelling incentive for its development by other nations would be lacking.

Though General Marshall was thus noting a real military objection to any demonstration of the bomb, he seemed to accept the view that its use was nevertheless important. This I verified in subsequent discussions. He was fully convinced at this time that the bomb should be used. This was primarily to bring the war quickly to a close and thereby to save lives. He never believed that the Japanese would surrender solely as a result of further naval operations and conventional air attacks. At this meeting, however, Marshall was careful to avoid any statement that might prejudice the thinking of the civilian committee. It was their verdict that was being sought as to whether the lives that the bomb might save were more or less important than the possible advantage of holding a powerful secret weapon.

Throughout the morning's discussions it seemed to be a foregone conclusion that the bomb would be used. It was regarding only the details of strategy and tactics that differing views were expressed. At the luncheon following the morning meeting, I was seated at Mr. Stimson's left. In the course of the conversation I asked the Secretary whether it might not be possible to arrange a nonmilitary demonstration of the bomb in such a manner that the Japanese would be so impressed that they would see the uselessness of continuing the war. The Secretary opened this question for general discussion by those at the table. Various possibilities were brought forward. One after the other it seemed necessary that they should be discarded.

It was evident that everyone would suspect trickery. If a bomb were exploded in Japan with previous notice, the Japanese air power was still adequate to give serious interference. An atomic bomb was an intricate device, still in the developmental stage. Its operation would be far from routine. If during the final adjustments of the bomb the Japanese defenders should attack, a faulty move might easily result in some kind of failure. Such an end to an advertised demonstration of power would be much worse than if the attempt had not been made. It was now evident that when the time came for the bombs to be used we should have only one of them available, followed afterwards by others at all-too-long intervals. We could not afford the chance that one of them might be a dud. If the test were made on some neutral territory, it was hard to believe that Japan's determined and fanatical military men would be impressed. If such an open test were made first and failed to bring surrender, the chance would be gone to give the shock of surprise that proved so effective. On the contrary, it would make the Japanese ready to interfere with an atomic attack if they could. Though the possibility of a demonstration that would not destroy human lives was attractive, no one could suggest a way in which it could be made so convincing that it would be likely to stop the war.

After luncheon the Interim Committee went into executive session. Our Scientific Panel was then again invited in. We were asked to prepare a report as to whether we could devise any kind of demonstration that would seem likely to bring the war to an end without using the bomb against a live target.

Ten days later, at Oppenheimer's invitation, Lawrence, Fermi, and I spent a long week end at Los Alamos. We were keenly aware of our responsibility as the scientific advisers to the Interim Committee. Among our colleagues were the scientists who supported Franck in suggesting a nonmilitary demonstration only. We thought of the fighting men who were set for an invasion which would be so very costly in both American and Japanese lives. We were determined to find, if we could, some effective way of demonstrating the power of an atomic bomb without loss of life that would impress Japan's warlords. If only this could be done!

Ernest Lawrence was the last one of our group to give up hope for finding such a solution. The difficulties of making a purely technical demonstration that would carry its impact effectively into Japan's controlling councils were indeed great. We had to count on every possible effort to distort even obvious facts. Experience with the determination of Japan's fighting men made it evident that the war would not be stopped unless these men themselves were convinced of its futility.

Our hearts were heavy as on 16 June we turned in this report to the Interim Committee. We were glad and proud to have had a part in making the power of the atom available for the use of man. What a tragedy it was that this power should become available first in time of war and that it must first be used for human destruction. If, however, it would result in the shortening of the war and the saving of lives—if it would mean bringing us closer to the time when war would be abandoned as a means of settling international disputes—here must be our hope and our basis for courage.

One of the young men who had been with us at Chicago and had transferred to Los Alamos came into my Chicago office in a state of emotional stress. He said he had heard of an effort to prevent the use of the bomb. Two years earlier I had persuaded this young man, as he was graduating with a major in physics, to cast his lot with our project. The chances are, I had told him, that you will be able to contribute more toward winning the war in this position than if you should accept the call to the Navy that you are considering. He had heeded my advice. Now he was sorely troubled: 'I have buddies who have fought through the battle of Iwo Jima. Some of them have been killed, others wounded. We've got to give these men the best weapons we can produce.' Tears came to his eyes. 'If one of these men should be killed because we didn't let them use the bombs, I would have failed them. I just could not make myself feel that I had done my part.' Others, though less emotional, felt just as deeply.

TOP SECRET

NOTES OF THE INTERIM COMMITTEE MEETING
FRIDAY, 1 JUNE 1945
11:00 A.M. - 12:30 P.M., 1:45 P.M. - 3:30 P.M.

PRESENT:

Members of the Committee

Secretary Henry L. Stimson, Chairman
Hon. Ralph A. Bard
Dr. Vannevar Bush
Hon. James F. Byrnes
Hon. William L. Clayton
Dr. Karl T. Compton
Dr. James B. Conant
Mr. George L. Harrison

Invited Industrialists

Mr. George H. Bucher, President
of Westinghouse - manufacture
of equipment for the electromagnetic process.

Mr. Walter S. Carpenter, President
of Du Pont Company - construction
of the Hanford Project.

Mr. James Rafferty, Vice President
of Union Carbide - construction
and operation of gas diffusion
plant in Clinton.

Mr. James White, President of Tennessee
Eastman - production of basic chemicals
and construction of the RDX plant at
Holston, Tennessee.

By Invitation

General George C. Marshall
Major Gen. Leslie H. Groves
Mr. Harvey H. Bundy
Mr. Arthur Page

CONFIDENTIAL

TOP SECRET

TOP SECRET

- 8 -

The Committee reassembled at 2:15 P.M. in
Mr. Harrison's office.[1]

IV. <u>POST-WAR ORGANIZATION - COMMITTEE DISCUSSION</u>:

<u>Dr. Conant</u> reported that the four scientists had com-
pleted their memorandum on post-war organization and were submitting it to the Secretary of War through Mr. Harrison. Dr.
Conant stressed the great complexity of this problem and the
need for securing as members of the board of directors men of the
highest competence and wisdom.

<u>Dr. Bush</u> stated that the organization proposed by the
four scientists need not be concerned at this time with the problem
of an over-all post-war research organization for national security.
He said that one of the problems with which the board of directors
would have to concern itself was the question of the allocation
of material, such as loans to universities and other research groups.
He pointed out that the universities not only would want access to
certain quantities of material for research purposes, but also access
to pilot plants.

<u>Dr. Compton</u> expressed the conviction, which was agreed
to by <u>Dr. Conant</u>, that the Interim Committee was not competent to
decide upon these detailed questions, but rather that it was responsible
for recommendations leading to the establishment of a permanent organi-

CONFIDENTIAL

TOP SECRET

TOP SECRET

- 9 -

zation which would be competent to deal with these questions.
It was <u>agreed</u> that the organization paper from the scientists,
when received, should be considered a basis for the drafting of the
necessary legislation.

V. <u>CURRENT APPROPRIATIONS</u>:

      <u>General Groves</u> reported that current appropriations for
the project would run through June of 1946. Mr. Byrnes pointed
out, however, that in the event that the war ended before the end
of June 1946 Congress would be disposed to cancel all outstanding
authorizations. In this event the Committee would be faced with
the immediate problem of taking up with Congress the question of
continuing appropriations and in so doing it would be necessary to
furnish an estimate of the costs involved.

      <u>General Groves</u> reported that the five Congressmen whom
he recently took on a visit to the project in Tennessee were very
much impressed with the plant and appeared to be most appreciative
of the magnitude and national importance of the program.

VI. <u>USE OF THE BOMB</u>:

      <u>Mr. Byrnes</u> <u>recommended</u>, and the Committee <u>agreed</u>, that
the Secretary of War should be advised that, while recognizing that
the final selection of the target was essentially a military decision,
the present view of the Committee was that the bomb should be used
against Japan as soon as possible; that it be used on a war plant

CONFIDENTIAL
TOP SECRET

TOP SECRET

- 10 -

surrounded by workers' homes; and that it be used without prior
warning. It was the understanding of the Committee that the
small bomb would be used in the test and that the large bomb (gun
mechanism) would be used in the first strike over Japan.

VII. PUBLICITY:

Mr. Harrison pointed out that the discussions and
tentative conclusions of yesterday's meeting had already rendered
obsolete the draft Presidential statement prepared by Arthur Page.
In the past few days the Secretary had held discussions with
Generals Marshall and Arnold concerning targets and would probably
discuss this question further with Admiral King and General Marshall.
This Committee was not considered competent to make a final decision
on the matter of targets, this being a military decision. Accordingly,
Mr. Harrison suggested that he be empowered by the Committee to confer
with those members of the Committee who would be available as the
situation with regard to targets developed and to have prepared
new draft statements for the consideration of the full Committee
at its next meeting.

VIII. LEGISLATION:

Mr. Harrison urged that prompt consideration be given to
the problem of drafting the necessary legislation. It was suggested
that the memorandum of the four scientists could be used as a basis
for the draft. The Committee agreed that Mr. Harrison should proceed,

CONFIDENTIAL

TOP SECRET

TOP SECRET

- 11 -

with the assistance of those members of the Committee who were
available, with the preparation of an outline of major points
to be included in a bill for study by the Committee at its next
meeting.

IX.   NEXT MEETING:

It was <u>agreed</u> that the next meeting should be held at
9:30 A.M. Thursday, 21 June 1945, the place of the meeting depending
upon the schedule of the Secretary of War.

It was <u>agreed</u> that the Committee should consider
organization proposals and the requirements of legislation.
The Committee would also consider at that time the situation
with regard to publicity.

The meeting was adjourned at 3:30 P.M.

R. Gordon Arneson

R. GORDON ARNESON
1st Lieutenant, A.U.S.
Secretary

CONFIDENTIAL

TOP SECRET

Memorandum of talk with the President,
June 6, 1945

     2. I then took up the matters on my agenda, telling him
first of the work of the Interim Committee meetings last week. He said
that Byrnes had reported to him already about it and that Byrnes seemed
to be highly pleased with what had been done. I then said that the
points of agreement and views arrived at were substantially as follows:

     a. That there should be no revelation to Russia or
anyone else of our work in S-1 until the first bomb had been
successfully laid on Japan.

     b. That the greatest complication was what might
happen at the meeting of the Big Three. He told me he had
postponed that until the 15th of July on purpose to give us more
time. I pointed out that there might still be delay and if there
was and the Russians should bring up the subject and ask us to
take them in as partners, I thought that our attitude was to do
just what the Russians had done to us, namely to make the simple
statement that as yet we were not quite ready to do it.

     c. I told him that the only suggestion which our Com-
mittee had been able to give as to future control of the situation
was that each country should promise to make public all work that
was being done on this subject and that an international committee
of control should be constituted with full power of inspection of
all countries to see whether this promise was being carried out.
I said I recognized that this was imperfect and might not be assented
to by Russia, but that in that case we were far enough ahead of
the game to be able to accumulate enough material to serve as
insurance against being caught helpless.

     d. I said that of course no disclosure of the work should
be made to anyone until all such promises of control were made and
established. We then also discussed further quid pro quos which
should be established in consideration for our taking them into
partnership. He said he had been thinking of that and mentioned
the same things that I was thinking of, namely the settlement of
the Polish, Rumanian, Yugoslavian, and Manchurian problems.

     3. He then asked me if I had heard of the accomplishment
which Harry Hopkins had made in Moscow and when I said I had not
he told me there was a promise in writing by Stalin that Manchuria
should remain fully Chinese except for a 99 year lease of
Port Arthur and the settlement of Dairea which we had hold of. I
warned him that with the 50-50 control of the railways running
across Manchuria, Russia would still be likely to outweight the
Chinese in actual power in that country. He said he would ok that
but the promise was perfectly clear and distinct.

     4. I told him that I was busy considering our conduct
of the war against Japan and I told him how I was trying to hold
the Air Force down to precision bombing but that with the Japanese

method of scattering its manufacture it was rather difficult to prevent area bombing. I told him I was anxious about this feature of
the war for two reasons: first, because I did not want to have the
United States get the reputation of outdoing Hitler in atrocities;
and second, I was a little fearful that before we could get ready
the Air Force might have Japan so thoroughly bombed out that the new
weapon would not have a fair background to show its strength. He
laughed and said he understood.

TOP SECRET

From "Interim Committee: Log"
    compiled by Lieut. R. Gordon Arneson

7 June 1945.

Harrison discussed with S/W[1] the recommendations of the
Committee agreed at the 31 May and 1 June meetings: (1) the
present program, including Chicago, be continued at present levels
for the duration of the war; (2) the bomb be used without prior
warning against Japan at earliest opportunity, the targets to
be a military target surrounded by workers houses; (3) a Military
Panel be established, and (4) work be started promptly on legislation. The S/W was in agreement on (1) and (2). He did not
favor establishing a Military Panel. With regard to (4) the
S/W wanted first priority given to legislation for <u>domestic</u>
control, with the problems of international relations and controls
to be dealt with by the Permanent Post-War Commission that would
be established by law.

[1]Secretary of War Henry Stimson.

```
                      MINUTES OF MEETING
                           OF THE
                      COMMITTEE OF THREE

                        June 12, 1945
```

The Secretary of War spoke of the letter which Herbert Hoover sent to the President regarding the treatment of Japan. Mr. Forrestal said he thought the note we should take was one of avoiding a frozen position which might result in our not being able to take advantage of developments in Japan: that the question of issuing warnings to Japan of what the continuation of the war would mean was a matter of coordination and timing. He felt that real thought should be given to this matter so that we did not find ourselves in the position where we might be encouraging the militant group in Japan to build strength for themselves amongst the populace. He had in mind the somewhat mystical relationship of the people to the Emperor and the general religious background of some of the Japanese nationalism.

The Secretary of War said this matter was occupying his mind; that he had talked with General Marshall about the subject. Thereupon some discussion ensued as to the wisdom of the continuation of the phrase "unconditional surrender". He said he felt that if we could accomplish all of our strategic objectives without the use of this phrase, we should have no hesitation in abandoning it, although the feeling was that occupation of the main Japanese islands was a necessity if there was to be a real attempt to demilitarize Japan. Mr. Grew likewise felt that occupation was necessary, but stressed again the possibility of enlisting the better elements in Japan toward the adoption of more peaceful and democratic policies.

P A R T 4

Dissent at Metlab. The Franck
Report. Recommendations of the
Scientific Advisory Panel. Military
projections of invasion of Kyushu.
Informing the Russians.
Under-Secretary of the Navy Bard's
dissent. Stimson's ideas on how to
induce the Japanese to surrender.
The Szilard dissent and petition. A
poll of scientific opinion on use of
weapon. Intelligence estimate of
enemy situation.

The
Scientists'
Debate

Einstein and Oppenheimer

Ernest O. Lawrence
and J. Robert Oppenheimer

Enrico Fermi,
Ernest O. Lawrence,
and Isidor L. Rabi

The scientists of the Manhattan Project formed a "scientific community" only in the loosest sense of that term. They were actually a cadre of theorists and technicians drawn together by the war and moved by the call to duty. Some had no idea what they were working on. Those who did found what Oppenheimer called the "technically sweet problem" of turning an idea into a weapon captivating and sought the solution with obsessive single-mindedness, giving little thought to the consequences of their pursuit.

Shared fervor gave the scientists a collective identity that obscured their considerable differences. In fact, they came from vastly different backgrounds, even from different countries. Several, such as Niels Bohr and Leo Szilard, were Europeans who had already established eminent reputations. Others were promising young Americans, like twenty-five-year-old Richard P. Feynman, a flamboyant thinker who would win a Nobel Prize in physics in 1965 for his research in quantum electrodynamics. Some were self-effacing and retiring, others self-promoting prima donnas. Their expertise varied as much as did their personal profiles. Among them were physicists, mathematicians, metallurgists, chemists, engineers, and draft-deferred graduate students. They held to no single philosophy of politics and had no one view of foreign affairs. What drove them most of all was fear—the fear of an atomic bomb in the hands of Adolf Hitler.

By the spring of 1945, both the fear and the fervor had diminished. The defeat of Germany brought a collective sigh of relief from scientists with nightmares of a Nazi bomb. No longer were they in a race to the death. They had, moreover, just about licked the technical problem of building an atomic bomb. Some sections were nearly done with their work. Such was the case with the Metallurgical Laboratory at the University of Chicago, called Metlab. Metlab had been responsible for developmental work on chain reactions and on plutonium. With their mission largely completed, Metlab scientists had had time to think, and Leo Szilard, for one, had developed fears of an atomic-arms race. Unaware of Niels Bohr's efforts to forestall that possibility, the General (as his staff called him) had begun to stir the consciences of his colleagues with second thoughts about using the bomb. One result was their appointment of James Franck, associate director of the chemistry division of Metlab, as chairman of a committee to explore the political and social implications of the yet-untested bomb.

The committee report, submitted to the secretary of war in June of 1945, proceeded from a simple yet terrifying premise: that the atom bomb opened the way to "total mutual destruction" of all nations (see Document 49). As the seven scientists on the committee saw it, the military conventions of the past were irrelevant. Even "a quantitative advantage in reserves of bottled destructive power will not make us safe from sudden attack." Their reasoning was clear: "In no other type of warfare does the advantage lie so heavily with the aggressor." They advocated an "international agreement on total prevention of nuclear warfare." The alternative was so frightening that "only lack of mutual trust, and not lack of desire" could stand in the way.

The Franck Report also urged policymakers to refrain from using the bomb against Japan without a demonstration before "the eyes of representatives of all the United Nations." "It may be very difficult," the report read, "to persuade the world that a nation which was capable of secretly preparing and suddenly releasing a weapon as indiscriminate as the rocket bomb and a million times more destructive, is to be trusted in its proclaimed desire of having such weapons abolished by international agreement."

Not all scientists working on the bomb shared this conclusion of the Franck committee. In mid-June, a scientific panel appointed by the Interim Committee recommended "direct military use" of the weapon and denied that as scientists, its members had any "claim to special competence in solving the political, social, and military problems which are presented by the advent of atomic power" (see Document 51). On the Interim Committee itself, only Under Secretary of the Navy Ralph A. Bard voted against unannounced use of the weapon (see Document 56); then he resigned.

A month later, an opinion poll of one hundred fifty scientists working on the project revealed that 46 percent believed a "military demonstration" should be given in Japan "to be followed by a renewed opportunity for surrender before full use of the weapons is employed" (see Document 61). Another 15 percent thought the weapons should be used "in the manner that is from the military point of view most effective in bringing about prompt Japanese surrender." And so it went in a scientist's game of point and counterpoint.

The logic or merits of the cases made by dissenters changed nothing. Not one of their briefs, including a series of petitions circulated by Szilard against using the bomb, ever reached President Truman because by the summer of 1945, a more powerful logic had taken hold. Casualty reports from the April invasion of Okinawa had given policymakers a sense of things to come. The banana-shaped island of Okinawa lay just three hundred fifty miles southwest of Japan. It was sixty miles long, mountainous, and honeycombed with hideouts. Endless mazes of mutually supporting strong points, thousands of caves and tunnels piled high with arms and filled with men, and seven hundred assault planes (half of them suicidal kamikazes) had made the American attack a nightmare. Fanatical Japanese resistance had resulted in terrible losses on both sides. Seven thousand American soldiers and marines (including the commanding general of the invading force) and five thousand sailors were killed in the two-month battle. Seventy thousand Japanese died, along with eighty thousand Okinawans, most of them civilians.

It was assumed that an assault on the Japanese home islands, some of whose terrain was similar to Okinawa's, would exact an even higher price. The dimensions of the bloodbath to come could be deduced from the forces being mustered to resist an American landing: 2,350,000 soldiers of the regular Japanese army, backed by 250,000 garrison troops, the entire remnants of the navy, and the 7000 airplanes that were left; 4 million civilian employees of the two services; and the whole civilian militia of 28 million men, women, and boys. Estimates of American casualties ran between 500,000 and 1 million. In the face of such estimates, concern over the long-term dangers of dropping the atomic bomb, even pressure to warn the Japanese of its impending use, seemed a deadly indulgence.

The work of the scientists is best treated in Alice Kimball Smith's *A Peril and a Hope: The Scientists' Movement in America, 1945–1947* (1971). The details of their debate are recorded in Peter Wyden's *Day One: Before Hiroshima and After* (1984) and Richard Rhodes's *The Making of the Atomic Bomb* (1987). Leo Szilard offers his side of the story in *Leo Szilard: His Version of the Facts* (1978), edited by Spencer R. Weart and Gertrude Weiss Szilard. For a clear and coherent account of the war in the Pacific, see Ronald H. Spector's *Eagle Against the Sun: The American War with Japan* (1985).

Metallurgical Laboratory
P.O. BOX 5207
CHICAGO 80, ILLINOIS

June 12, 1945

BUTTERFIELD 4300

To: Secretary of War – Attention: Mr. George Harrison

From: Arthur H. Compton

In re: Memorandum on "Political and Social Problems" from Members of the
     "Metallurgical Laboratory" of the University of Chicago. [1]

Dear Mr. Secretary:

I have submitted to you a memorandum which has been prepared on short
notice by certain key members of the scientific staff of the Metallurgical
Laboratory of the University of Chicago. It deals with the long-term
consequences of use of the new weapons with which we are concerned. I am
submitting this at the request of the Laboratory, for the attention of
your Interim Advisory Committee. The memorandum has not yet been considered by other members of the "Scientific Panel." This will be done
within a few days, and a report by the panel dealing with the matter in
question will be submitted. In the meantime, however, because time is
short for making the necessary decisions, I have personally taken the
liberty of transmitting this memorandum to you for the consideration
of your committee.

The main point of this memorandum is the predominating importance of
considering the use of nuclear bombs as a problem of long-range policy
rather than for its military advantage in this war. Their use should
thus be directed primarily toward bringing about some international control
of the means of nuclear warfare.

The proposal is to make a technical but not military demonstration,
preparing the way for a recommendation by the United States that the military use of atomic explosives be outlawed by firm international agreement.
It is contended that its military use by us now will prejudice the world
against accepting any future recommendation by us that its use be not
permitted.

I note that two important considerations have not been mentioned:

(1)   that failure to make a military demonstration of the
      new bombs may make the war longer and more expensive
      of human lives, and

(2)   that without a military demonstration it may be impossible
      to impress the world with the need for national sacrifices
      in order to gain lasting security.

[1] See Document 49.

Metallurgical Laboratory

P.O. BOX 5207
CHICAGO 80, ILLINOIS

BUTTERFIELD 4300

To: Secretary of War – Page 2

Nevertheless, the importance of the problem considered, and the weight of the arguments presented for never permitting the bombs to be used in war, are such that I have considered it wise to bring the memorandum immediately to your attention.

Yours very truly,

Arthur H. Compton

KT   Arthur H. Compton

I. PREAMBLE

The only reason to treat nuclear power differently from all the other developments in the field of physics is the possibility of its use as a means of political pressure in peace and sudden destruction in war. All present plans for the organization of research, scientific and industrial development, and publication in the field of nucleonics are conditioned by the political and military climate in which one expects those plans to be carried out. Therefore, in making suggestions for the postwar organization of nucleonics, a discussion of political problems cannot be avoided. The scientists on this Project do not presume to speak authoritatively on problems of national and international policy. However, we found ourselves, by the force of events during the last five years, in the position of a small group of citizens cognizant of a grave danger for the safety of this county as well as for the future of all the other nations, of which the rest of mankind is unaware. We therefore feel it our duty to urge that the political problems, arising from the mastering of nuclear power, be recognized in all their gravity, and that appropriate steps be taken for their study and the preparation of necessary decisions. We hope that the creation of the Committee[1] by the Secretary of War to deal with all aspects of nucleonics, indicates that these implications have been recognized by the government. We believe that our acquaintance with the scientific elements of the situation and prolonged preoccupation with its world-wide political implications, imposes on us the obligation to offer to the Committee some suggestions as to the possible solution of these grave problems.

Scientists have often before been accused of providing new weapons for the mutual destruction of nations, instead of improving their well-being. It is undoubtedly true that the discovery of flying, for example, has so far brought much more misery than enjoyment and profit to humanity. However, in the past, scientists could disclaim direct responsibility for the use to which mankind had put their disinterested discoveries. We feel compelled to take a more active stand now because the success which we have achieved in the development of nuclear power is fraught with infinitely greater dangers than were all the inventions of the past. All of us, familiar with the present state of nucleonics, live with the vision before our eyes of sudden destruction visited on our own country, of a Pearl Harbor disaster repeated in thousand-fold magnification in every one of our major cities.

In the past, science has often been able to provide also new methods of protection against new weapons of aggresson it made possible, but it cannot promise such efficient protection against the destructive use of nuclear power. This protection can come only from the political organization of the world. Among all the arguments calling for an efficient international organization for peace, the existence of nuclear weapons is the most compelling one. *In the absence of an international authority which would make all resort to force in international conflicts impossible, nations could still be diverted from a path which must lead to total mutual destruction, by a specific international agreement barring a nuclear armaments race.*

II. PROSPECTS OF ARMAMENTS RACE

It could be suggested that the danger of destruction by nuclear weapons can be avoided—at least as far as this country is concerned—either by keeping our discoveries secret for an indefinite time, or else by developing our nucleonic ar-

---

[1]The Interim Committee.

maments at such a pace that no other nations would think of attacking us from fear of overwhelming retaliation.

The answer to the first suggestion is that although we undoubtedly are at present ahead of the rest of the world in this field, the fundamental facts of nuclear power are a subject of common knowledge. British scientists know as much as we do about the basic wartime progress of nucleonics—if not of the specific processes used in our engineering developments—and the role which French nuclear physicists have played in the pre-war development of this field, plus their occasional contact with our Projects, will enable them to catch up rapidly, at least as far as basic scientific discoveries are concerned. German scientists, in whose discoveries the whole development of this field originated, apparently did not develop it during the war to the same extent to which this has been done in America; but to the last day of the European war, we were living in constant apprehension as to their possible achievements. The certainty that German scientists are working on this weapon and that their government would certainly have no scruples against using it when available, was the main motivation of the initiative which American scientists took in urging the development of nuclear power for military purposes on a large scale in this country. In Russia, too, the basic facts and implications of nuclear power were well understood in 1940, and the experience of Russian scientists in nuclear research is entirely sufficient to enable them to retrace our steps within a few years, even if we should make every attempt to conceal them. Furthermore, we should not expect too much success from attempts to keep basic information secret in peacetime, when scientists acquainted with the work on this and associated Projects will be scattered to many colleges and research institutions and many of them will continue to work on problems closely related to those on which our developments are based. In other words, even if we can retain our leadership in basic knowledge of nucleonics for a certain time by maintaining secrecy as to all results achieved on this and associated Projects, it would be foolish to hope that this can protect us for more than a few years.

It may be asked whether we cannot prevent the development of military nucleonics in other countries by a monopoly on the raw materials of nuclear power. The answer is that even though the largest now known deposits of uranium ores are under the control of powers which belong to the "western" group (Canada, Belgium, and British India), the old deposits in Czechoslovakia are outside this sphere. Russia is known to be mining radium on its own territory; and even if we do not know the size of the deposits discovered so far in the USSR, the probability that no large reserves of uranium will be found in a country which covers $\frac{1}{5}$ of the land area of the earth (and whose sphere of influence takes in additional territory), is too small to serve as a basis for security. *Thus, we cannot hope to avoid a nuclear armament race either by keeping secret from the competing nations the basic scientific facts of nuclear power or by cornering the raw materials required for such a race.*

We now consider the second of the two suggestions made at the beginning of this section, and ask whether we could not feel ourselves safe in a race of nuclear armaments by virtue of our greater industrial potential, including greater diffusion of scientific and technical knowledge, greater volume and efficiency of our skilled labor corps, and greater experience of our management—all the factors whose importance has been so strikingly demonstrated in the conversion of this country into an arsenal of the Allied Nations in the present war. The answer is that all that these advantages can give us is the accumulation of a large number of bigger and better atomic bombs—and this only if we produce these bombs at the maximum of our capacity in peace time, and do not rely on conversion of a peace-time nucleonics industry to military production after the beginning of hostilities.

However, such a quantitative advantage in reserves of bottled destructive power will not make us safe from sudden attack. Just because a potential enemy will be afraid of being "outnumbered and outgunned," the temptation for him may be overwhelming to attempt a sudden unprovoked blow—particularly if he should suspect us of harboring aggressive intentions against his security or his sphere of influence. In no other type of warfare does the advantage lie so heavily with the aggressor. He can place his "infernal machines" in advance in all our major cities and explode them simultaneously, thus destroying a major part of our industry and a large part of our population, aggregated in densely populated metropolitan districts. Our possibilities of retaliation—even if retailiation should be considered adequate compensation for the loss of millions of lives and destruction of our largest cities—will be greatly handicapped because we must rely on aerial transportation of the bombs, and also because we may have to deal with an enemy whose industry and population are dispersed over a large territory.

In fact, if the race for nuclear armaments is allowed to develop, the only apparent way in which our country can be protected from the paralyzing effects of a sudden attack is by dispersal of those industries which are essential for our war effort and dispersal of the populations of our major metropolitan cities. As long as nuclear bombs remain scarce (i.e., as long as uranium and thorium remain the only basic materials for their fabrication), efficient dispersal of our industry and the scattering of our metropolitan population will considerably decrease the temptation to attack us by nuclear weapons.

Ten years hence, it may be that atomic bombs containing perhaps 20 kg of active material can be detonated at 6% efficiency, and thus each have an effect equal to that of 20,000 tons of TNT. One of these bombs could then destroy something like 3 square miles of an urban area. Atomic bombs containing a larger quantity of active material but still weighing less than one ton may be expected to be available within ten years which could destroy over ten square miles of a city. A nation able to assign 10 tons of atomic explosives for the preparation of a sneak attack on this country, can then hope to achieve the destruction of all industry and most of the population in an area from 500 square miles upwards. If no choice of targets, with a total area of five hundred square miles of American territory, contains a large enough fraction of the nation's industry and population to make their destruction a crippling blow to the nation's war potential and its ability to defend itself, then the attack will not pay, and may not be undertaken. At present, one could easily select in this country a hundred areas of five square miles each whose simultaneous destruction would be a staggering blow to the nation. Since the area of the United States is about three million square miles, it should be possible to scatter its industrial and human resources in such a way as to leave no 500 square miles important enough to serve as a target for nuclear attack.

We are fully aware of the staggering difficulties involved in such a radical change in the social and economic structure of our nation. We felt, however, that the dilemma had to be stated, to show what kind of alternative methods of protection will have to be considered if no successful international agreement is reached. It must be pointed out that in this field we are in a less favorable position than nations which are either now more diffusely populated and whose industries are more scattered, or whose governments have unlimited power over the movement of population and the location of industrial plants.

If no efficient international agreement is achieved, the race for nuclear armaments will be on in earnest not later than the morning after our first demonstration of the existence of nuclear weapons. After this, it might take other nations three or four years to overcome our present head start, and eight or ten years to draw even with us if we continue to do intensive work in this field. This might be all the time we would have to bring about the regroupment of our population and industry. Obviously, no time should be lost in inaugurating a study of this problem by experts.

III. PROSPECTS OF AGREEMENT

The consequences of nuclear warfare, and the type of measures which would have to be taken to protect a country from total destruction by nuclear bombing, must be as abhorrent to other nations as to the United States. England, France, and the smaller nations of the European continent, with their congeries of people and industries, would be in a particularly desperate situation in the face of such a threat. Russia and China are the only great nations at present which could survive a nuclear attack. However, even though these countries may value human life less than the peoples of Western Europe and America, and even though Russia, in particular, has an immense space over which its vital industries could be dispersed and a government which can order this dispersion the day it is convinced that such a measure is necessary—there is no doubt that Russia will shudder at the possibility of a sudden disintegration of Moscow and Leningrad and of its new industrial cities in the Urals and Siberia. Therefore, only lack of mutual *trust*, and not lack of *desire* for agreement, can stand in the path of an efficient agreement for the prevention of nuclear warfare. The achievement of such an agreement will thus essentially depend on the integrity of intentions and readiness to sacrifice the necessary fraction of one's own sovereignty, by all the parties to the agreement.

From this point of view, the way in which the nuclear weapons now being secretly developed in this country are first revealed to the world appears to be of great, perhaps fateful importance.

One possible way—which may particularly appeal to those who consider nuclear bombs primarily as a secret weapon developed to help win the present war—is to use them without warning on an appropriately selected object in Japan. It is doubtful whether the first available bombs, of comparatively low efficiency and small size, will be sufficient to break the will or ability of Japan to resist, especially given the fact that the major cities like Tokyo, Nagoya, Osaka and Kobe already will largely have been reduced to ashes by the slower process of ordinary aerial bombing. Although important tactical results undoubtedly can be achieved by a sudden introduction of nuclear weapons, we nevertheless think that the question of the use of the very first available atomic bombs in the Japanese war should be weighed very carefully, not only by military authorities, but by the highest political leadership of this country. If we consider international agreement on total prevention of nuclear warfare as the paramount objective, and believe that it can be achieved, this kind of introduction of atomic weapons to the world may easily destroy all our chances of success. Russia, and even allied countries which bear less mistrust of our ways and intentions, as well as neutral countries may be deeply shocked. It may be very difficult to persuade the world that a nation which was capable of secretly preparing and suddenly releasing a weapon as indiscriminate as the rocket bomb and a million times more destructive, is to be trusted in its proclaimed desire of having such weapons abolished by international agreement. We have large accumulations of poison gas, but do not use them, and recent polls have shown that public opinion in this country would disapprove of such a use even if it would accelerate the winning of the Far Eastern war. It is true that some irrational element in mass psychology makes gas poisoning more revolting than blasting by explosives, even though gas warfare is in no way more "inhuman" than the war of bombs and bullets. Nevertheless, it is not at all certain that American public opinion, if it could be enlightened as to the effect of atomic explosives, would approve of our own country being the first to introduce such an indiscriminate method of wholesale destruction of civilian life.

Thus, from the "optimistic" point of view—looking forward to an international agreement on the prevention of nuclear warfare—the military advantages and the saving of American lives achieved by the sudden use of atomic bombs against Japan may be outweighed by the ensuing loss of confidence and by a wave of horror and repulsion sweeping over the rest of the world and perhaps even dividing public opinion at home.

From this point of view, a demonstration of the new weapon might best be made, before the eyes of representatives of all the United Nations, on the desert or a barren island. The best possible atmosphere for the achievement of an international agreement could be achieved if America could say to the world, "You see what sort of a weapon we had but did not use. We are ready to renounce its use in the future if other nations join us in this renunciation and agree to the establishment of an efficient international control."

After such a demonstration the weapon might perhaps be used against Japan if the sanction of the United Nations (and of public opinion at home) were obtained, perhaps after a preliminary ultimatum to Japan to surrender or at least to evacuate certain regions as an alternative to their total destruction. This may sound fantastic, but in nuclear weapons we have something entirely new in order of magnitude of destructive power, and if we want to capitalize fully on the advantage their possession gives us, we must use new and imaginative methods.

It must be stressed that if one takes the pessimistic point of view and discounts the possibility of an effective international control over nuclear weapons at the present time, then the advisability of an early use of nuclear bombs against Japan becomes even more doubtful—quite independently of any humanitarian considerations. If an international agreement is not concluded immediately after the first demonstration, this will mean a flying start toward an unlimited armaments race. If this race is inevitable, we have every reason to delay its beginning as long as possible in order to increase our head start still further. It took us three years, roughly, under forced draft of wartime urgency, to complete the first stage of production of nuclear explosives—that based on the separation of the rare fissionable isotope U^{235}, or its utilization for the production of an equivalent quantity of another fissionable element. This stage required large-scale, expensive constructions and laborious procedures. We are now on the threshold of the second stage—that of converting into fissionable material the comparatively abundant common isotopes of thorium and uranium. This stage probably requires no elaborate plans and may provide us in about five or six years with a really substantial stockpile of atomic bombs. Thus it is to our interest to delay the beginning of the armaments race at least until the successful termination of this second stage. The benefit to the nation, and the saving of American lives in the future, achieved by renouncing an early demonstration of nuclear bombs and letting the other nations come into the race only reluctantly, on the basis of guesswork and without definite knowledge that the "thing does work," may far outweigh the advantages to be gained by the immediate use of the first and comparatively inefficient bombs in the war against Japan. On the other hand, it may be argued that without an early demonstration it may prove difficult to obtain adequate support for further intensive development of nucleonics in this country and that thus the time gained by the postponement of an open armaments race will not be properly used. Furthermore one may suggest that other nations are now, or will soon be, not entirely unaware of our present achievements, and that consequently the postponement of a demonstration may serve no useful purpose as far as the avoidance of an armaments race is concerned, and may only create additional mistrust, thus worsening rather than improving the chances of an ultimate accord on the international control of nuclear explosives.

Thus, if the prospects of an agreement will be considered poor in the immediate future, the pros and cons of an early revelation of our possession of nuclear weapons to the world—not only by their actual use against Japan, but also by a prearranged demonstration—must be carefully weighed by the supreme political and military leadership of the country, and the decision should not be left to military tacticians alone.

One may point out that scientists themselves have initiated the development of this "secret weapon" and it is therefore strange that they should be reluctant to try it out on the enemy as soon as it is available. The answer to this question was given above—the compelling reason for creating this weapon with such speed was our fear that Germany had the technical skill necessary to develop such a weapon, and that the German government had no moral restraints regarding its use.

Another argument which could be quoted in favor of using atomic bombs as soon as they are available is that so much taxpayers' money has been invested in these Projects that the Congress and the American public will demand a return for their money. The attitude of American public opinion, mentioned earlier, in the matter of the use of poison gas against Japan, shows that one can expect the American public to understand that it is sometimes desirable to keep a weapon in readiness for use only in extreme emergency; and as soon as the potentialities of nuclear weapons are revealed to the American people, one can be sure that they will support all attempts to make the use of such weapons impossible.

Once this is achieved, the large installations and the accumulation of explosive material at present earmarked for potential military use will become available for important peace time developments, including power production, large engineering undertakings, and mass production of radioactive materials. In this way, the money spent on wartime development of nucleonics may become a boon for the peacetime development of national economy.

IV. METHODS OF INTERNATIONAL CONTROL

We now consider the question of how an effective international control of nuclear armaments can be achieved. This is a difficult problem, but we think it soluble. It requires study by statesmen and international lawyers, and we can offer only some preliminary suggestions for such a study.

Given mutual trust and willingness on all sides to give up a certain part of their sovereign rights, by admitting international control of certain phases of national economy, the control could be exercised (alternatively or simultaneously) on two different levels.

The first and perhaps simplest way is to ration the raw materials—primarily, the uranium ores. Production of nuclear explosives begins with the processing of large quantities of uranium in large isotope separation plants or huge production piles. The amounts of ore taken out of the ground at different locations could be controlled by resident agents of the international Control Board, and each nation could be allotted only an amount which would make large scale separation of fissionable isotopes impossible.

Such a limitation would have the drawback of making impossible also the development of nuclear power for peace-time purposes. However, it need not prevent the production of radioactive elements on a scale sufficient to revolution-ize the industrial, scientific and technical use of these materials, and would thus not eliminate the main benefits which nucleonics promises to bring to mankind.

An agreement on a higher level, involving more mutual trust and under-standing, would be to allow unlimited production, but keep exact bookkeeping on the fate of each pound of uranium mined. Some difficulty with this method of control will arise in the second stage of production, when one pound of pure fissionable isotope will be used again and again to produce additional fissionable material from thorium. These could be overcome by extending control to the min-ing and use of thorium, even though the commercial use of this metal may cause complications.

If check is kept on the conversion of uranium and thorium ore into pure fissionable materials, the question arises as to how to prevent accumulation of large quantities of such materials in the hands of one or several nations. Accu-mulations of this kind could be rapidly converted into atomic bombs if a nation should break away from international control. It has been suggested that a com-pulsory denaturation of pure fissionable isotopes may be agreed upon by diluting them, after production, with suitable isotopes to make them useless for military purposes, while retaining their usefulness for power engines.

One thing is clear: any international agreement on prevention of nuclear armaments must be backed by actual and efficient controls. No paper agreement can be sufficient since neither this or any other nation can stake its whole exis-tence on trust in other nations' signatures. Every attempt to impede the interna-tional control agencies would have to be considered equivalent to denunciation of the agreement.

It hardly needs stressing that we as scientists believe that any systems of control envisaged should leave as much freedom for the peacetime development of nucleonics as is consistent with the safety of the world.

SUMMARY

The development of nuclear power not only constitutes an important addition to the technological and military power of the United States, but also creates grave political and economic problems for the future of this country.

Nuclear bombs cannot possibly remain a "secret weapon" at the exclusive disposal of this country for more than a few years. The scientific facts on which their construction is based are well known to scientists of other countries. Unless an effective international control of nuclear explosives is instituted, a race for nuclear armaments is certain to ensue following the first revelation of our posses-sion of nuclear weapons to the world. Within ten years other countries may have nuclear bombs, each of which, weighing less than a ton, could destroy an urban area of more than ten square miles. In the war to which such an armaments race is likely to lead, the United States, with its agglomeration of population and indus-try in comparatively few metropolitan districts, will be at a disadvantage com-pared to nations whose population and industry are scattered over large areas.

We believe that these considerations make the use of nuclear bombs for an early unannounced attack against Japan inadvisable. If the United States were to be the first to release this new means of indiscriminate destruction upon mankind, she would sacrifice public support throughout the world, precipitate the race for armaments, and prejudice the possibility of reaching an international agreement on the future control of such weapons.

Much more favorable conditions for the eventual achievement of such an agreement could be created if nuclear bombs were first revealed to the world by a demonstration in an appropriately selected uninhabited area.

In case chances for the establishment of an effective international control of nuclear weapons should have to be considered slight at the present time, then not only the use of these weapons against Japan, but even their early demonstration, may be contrary to the interests of this country. A postponement of such a demonstration will have in this case the advantage of delaying the beginning of the nuclear armaments race as long as possible. If, during the time gained, ample support can be made available for further development of the field in this country, the postponement will substantially increase the lead which we have established during the present war, and our position in an armament race or in any later attempt at international agreement would thus be strengthened.

On the other hand, if no adequate public support for the development of nucleonics will be available without a demonstration, the postponement of the latter may be deemed inadvisable, because enough information might leak out to cause other nations to start the armament race, in which we would then be at a disadvantage. There is also the possibility that the distrust of other nations may be aroused if they know that we are conducting a development under cover of secrecy, and that this will make it more difficult eventually to reach an agreement with them.

If the government should decide in favor of an early demonstration of nuclear weapons, it will then have the possibility of taking into account the public opinion of this country and of the other nations before deciding whether these weapons should be used in the war against Japan. In this way, other nations may assume a share of responsibility for such a fateful decision.

To sum up, we urge that the use of nuclear bombs in this war be considered as a problem of long-range national policy rather than of military expediency, and that this policy be directed primarily to the achievement of an agreement permitting an effective international control of the means of nuclear warfare.

The vital importance of such a control for our country is obvious from the fact that the only effective alternative method of protecting this country appears to be a dispersal of our major cities and essential industries.

J. FRANCK, CHAIRMAN
D. J. HUGHES
J. J. NICKSON
E. RABINOWITCH
G. T. SEABORG
J. C. STEARNS
L. SZILARD

From "Interim Committee: Log":

                                        12 June 1945.

        Arneson met with A. H. Compton concerning a memorandum
prepared by certain of the Chicago scientists on "Social and
Political Problems."

                                        15 June 1945.

        Arneson reported to Harrison on his discussions with
Compton and Byrnes. Harrison decided that the Scientific Panel
and not the Committee should consider the memorandum from the
Chicago scientists.

        Arneson turned over to Harrison the first draft of
the proposed public statement of the S/W.

                                        15 June 1945.

        Harrison talked with A. H. Compton by telephone concerning
the Chicago memorandum, stating that he thought the Committee
should consider it only after the Scientific Panel had made its
comments. Compton agreed and promised to have available for
Committee consideration at the next meeting the views of the
Panel on the subject memorandum. He also agreed to submit the
Panel's recommendation as to the disposition of the Chicago group
after the war.

TOP SECRET

RECOMMENDATIONS ON THE IMMEDIATE USE OF NUCLEAR WEAPONS

A. H. Compton
E. O. Lawrence
J. R. Oppenheimer
E. Fermi

J R Oppenheimer

J. R. Oppenheimer
For the Panel

June 16, 1945

TOP SECRET

TOP SECRET

You have asked us to comment on the initial use of the new weapon. This use, in our opinion, should be such as to promote a satisfactory adjustment of our international relations. At the same time, we recognize our obligation to our nation to use the weapons to help save American lives in the Japanese war.

(1) To accomplish these ends we recommend that before the weapons are used not only Britain, but also Russia, France, and China be advised that we have made considerable progress in our work on atomic weapons, that these may be ready to use during the present war, and that we would welcome suggestions as to how we can cooperate in making this development contribute to improved international relations.

(2) The opinions of our scientific colleagues on the initial use of these weapons are not unanimous: they range from the proposal of a purely technical demonstration to that of the military application best designed to induce surrender. Those who advocate a purely technical demonstration would wish to outlaw the use of atomic weapons, and have feared that if we use the weapons now our position in future negotiations will be prejudiced. Others emphasize the opportunity of saving American lives by immediate military use, and believe that such use will improve the international prospects, in that they are more concerned with the prevention of war than with the elimination of this specific weapon. We find ourselves closer to these latter views; we can propose no technical demonstration likely to bring an end to the war; we see no acceptable alternative to direct military use.

(3) With regard to these general aspects of the use of atomic energy, it is clear that we, as scientific men, have no proprietary rights. It is true that we are among the few citizens who have had occasion to give thoughtful consideration to these problems during the past few years. We have, however, no claim to special competence in solving the political, social, and military problems which are presented by the advent of atomic power.

TOP SECRET

Meeting of the President, Secretary of War Stimson, Secretary
of the Navy Forrestal, John J. McCloy, and the Joint Chiefs of
Staff; June 18, 1945

THE PRESIDENT stated that he had called a meeting for the purpose of
informing himself with respect to the details of the campaign against Japan
set out in Admiral Leahy's memorandum to the Joint Chiefs of Staff of June
14. He asked General Marshall if he would express his opinion.
GENERAL MARSHALL pointed out that the present situation with respect
to operations against Japan was practically identical with the situation which
had existed in connection with the operations proposed after Normandy. He
then read, as an expression of his views, the following digest of a memorandum prepared by the Joint Chiefs of Staff for presentation to the President:

. . . .

General MacArthur and Admiral Nimitz are in agreement with the Chiefs
of Staff in selecting 1 November as the target date to go into Kyushu because
by that time:
  a. If we press preparations we can be ready.
  b. Our estimates are that our air action will have smashed practically every industrial target worth hitting in Japan as well as destroying
huge areas in the Jap cities.
  c. The Japanese Navy, if any still exists, will be completely powerless.
  d. Our rear action and air power will have cut the Jap reinforcement
capability from the mainland to negligible proportions.

Important considerations bearing on the 1 November date rather than a
later date are the weather and cutting to a minimum Jap time for preparation
for defense. If we delay much after the beginning of November, the weather
situation in the succeeding months may be such that the invasion of Japan,
and hence the end of the war, will be delayed up to 6 months.
An outstanding military point about attacking Korea is the difficult
terrain and beach conditions which appear to make the only acceptable assault
area Fusan in the southeast corner and Keijo, well up the western side. To
get to Fusan, which is a strongly fortified area, we must move large and vulnerable assault forces past heavily fortified Japanese areas. The operation
appears more difficult and costly than the assault on Kyushu. Keijo appears
an equally difficult and costly operation. After we have undertaken either
one of them we will will not be as far forward as going into Kyushu.
The Kyushu operation is essential to a strategy of strangulation and
appears to be the least costly worthwhile operation following Okinawa. The
basic point is that a lodgement in Kyushu is essential, both to tightening
our stranglehold of blockade and bombardment of Japan and to forcing capitulation by invasion of the Tokyo Plain.
We are bringing to bear against the Japanese every weapon and all
the force we can employ and there is no reduction in our maximum possible application of bombardment and blockade, while at the same time we are pressing
invasion preparations. It seems that if the Japanese are ever willing to
capitulate short of complete military defeat in the field they will do it
when faced with the completely hopeless prospect occasioned by (1) destruction

2.

already wrought by air bombardment and sea blockade, coupled with (2) a landing on Japan indicating the firmness of our resolution, and also perhaps
coupled with (3) the entry or threat of entry of Russia into the war.

  With reference to clean-up of the Asiatic mainland, our objectives
should be to get the Russians to deal with the Japs in the interior (and Korea
if necessary) and to vitalize the Chinese to a point where, with assistance of
American air power and some supplies, they can mop out their own country.

  CASUALTIES. Our experience in the Pacific War is so diverse as to
casualties that it is considered wrong to give any estimate in numbers.
Using various combinations of Pacific experience the War Department staff
reaches the conclusion that the cost of securing a worthwhile position in
Korea would almost certainly be greater than the cost of the Kyushu operation.
Points on the optimistic side of the Kyushu operation are that: General Mac-
Arthur has not yet accepted responsibility for going ashore where there would
be disproportionate casualties. The nature of the objective area gives room
for maneuver, both on land and by sea. As to any discussion of specific operations, the following data are pertinent.

Campaign	U.S. Casualties Killed, wounded, missing	Jap Casualties Killed and Prisoners (NOT including wounded)	Ratio U.S. to Japan
Leyte	17,000	78,000	1:4.6
Luson	31,000	156,000	1:5.0
Iwo Jima	20,000	25,000	1:1.25
Okinawa	34,000 (Ground)	81,000	
	7,700 (Navy)	(not a complete count)	1:2
Normandy (first 30 days)	42,000	----	----

  The record of General MacArthur's operation from 1 March 1944 through
1 May 1945 shows 13,742 US killed compared to 320,165 Japanese killed, or a
ratio of 22:1.

  There is reason to believe that the first 30 days in Kyushu should not
exceed the price we have paid for Luson. It is a grim fact that there is not
an easy, bloodless way to victory in war and it is the thankless task of the
leaders to maintain their firm outward front which holds the resolution of
their subordinates. Any irresolution in the leaders may result in costly
weakening and indecision in the subordinates.

  An important point about Russian participation in the war is that the
impact of Russian entry on the already hopeless Japanese may well be the decisive action levering them into capitulation at that time or shortly thereafter
if we land in Japan.

  GENERAL MARSHALL said that it was his personal view that the operation
against Kyushu was the only course to pursue. He felt that air power alone
was not sufficient to put the Japanese out of the war. It was unable alone to
put the Germans out. General Eaker and General Eisenhower both agreed to this.
Against the Japanese, scattered through mountainous country, the problem would
be much more difficult than it had been in Germany. He felt that this plan

3.

offered the only way the Japanese could be forced into a feeling of utter helplessness. The operation would be difficult but not more so than the assault in Normandy. He was convinced that every individual moving to the Pacific should be indoctrinated with a firm determination to see it through.

....

ADMIRAL KING called attention to what he considered an important difference between Okinawa and Kyushu. There had been only one way to go on Okinawa. This meant that straight frontal attack against a highly fortified position. On Kyushu, however, landings would be made on three fronts simultaneously and there would be much more room for maneuver. It was his opinion that a realistic casualty figure for Kyushu would lie somewhere between the number experienced by General MacArthur in the operation on Luson and the Okinawa casualties.

GENERAL MARSHALL pointed out that the total assault groups for the Kyushu campaign were shown in the memorandum prepared for the President at 766,700. He said, in answer to the President's question as to what opposition could be expected on Kyushu, that it was estimated at 8 Jap divisions or about 350,000 troops. He said that divisions were still being raised in Japan and that reinforcements from other areas were possible but it was becoming increasingly difficult and painful.

THE PRESIDENT then asked the Secretary of War for his opinion.

MR. STIMSON agreed with the Chiefs of Staff that there was no other choice. He felt that he was personally responsible to the President more for political than for military considerations. It was his opinion that there was a large submerged class in Japan who do not favor the present war and whose full opinion and influence have never yet been felt. He felt sure that this submerged class would fight and fight tenaciously if attacked on their own ground. He was concerned that something should be done to arouse them and to develop any possible influence they might have before it became necessary to come to grips with them.

THE PRESIDENT stated that this possibility was being worked on all the time. He asked if the invasion of Japan by white men would not have the effect of more closely uniting the Japanese.

MR. STIMSON thought there was every prospect of this. He agreed with the plan proposed by the Joint Chiefs of Staff as being the best thing to do but he still hoped for some fruitful accomplishment through other means.

....

THE PRESIDENT said that he considered the Kyushu plan all right from a military standpoint, and, so far as he was concerned, the Joint Chiefs of Staff could go ahead with it; but we can do this operation and then decide as to the final action later.

<u>Monday, June 18, 1945.</u>

• • •

I also had a short conference with General Groves and Harvey Bundy
as to the progress of matters in S-1 and at three-thirty in the afternoon I
went to the White House and attended a most important meeting of the President
with the Chiefs of Staff, only Forrestal, McCloy, and I being present besides
the Chiefs of Staff. The Chiefs of Staff presented their views of the plans
for the campaign against Japan and on the President's request I gave my views
on the big political question lying apart from the military plans, namely
as to whether we had grounds for thinking that there was a liberal-minded section
of the Japanese people with whom we can make proper terms for the future life
of Japan. I spoke very briefly of my relations with some of the Japanese
leaders and told the President that I should like to give him more fully my
views at some other time.

• • •

<u>Tuesday, June 19, 1945</u>

We had a good meeting of the Committee of Three although unfortunately Forrestal was absent at a meeting on the Hill, but Grew, Cates, and myself were there together with McCloy and Correa in attendance. I took up the question as to what position the three Departments should take on what you might call the civil military questions of the war against Japan. The Chiefs of Staff had taken their position at the meeting on Monday, and Forrestal and I have agreed to it as far as the purely military side of it goes. But there was a pretty strong feeling that it would be deplorable if we have to go through the military program with all its stubborn fighting to a finish. We agreed that it is necessary now to plan and prepare to go through, but it became very evident today in the discussion that we all feel that some way should be found of inducing Japan to yield without a fight to the finish and that was the subject of the discussion today. Grew read us a recent report he had made to the President on the subject in which he strongly advocated a new warning to Japan as soon as Okinawa has fallen, but apparently that does not meet with the President's plans in respect to the coming meeting with Churchill and Stalin. My only fixed date is the last chance warning which must be given before an actual landing of the ground forces on Japan, and fortunately the plans provide for enough time to bring in the sanctions to our warning in the shape of heavy ordinary bombing attack and an attack of S-1.

I had a talk with Marshall after the meeting of the Committee of Three this morning and went over it with him. He is suggesting an additional sanction to our warning in the shape of an entry by the Russians into the war. That would certainly coordinate all the threats possible to Japan. In the afternoon I did a little reading on the subject and started the dictation of a memorandum to the President.

CONFIDENTIAL

TOP SECRET

WAR DEPARTMENT
WASHINGTON

25 June 1945

MEMORANDUM FOR MR. HARRISON:

The notes of the June 21 meeting of the Interim Committee indicate the following action to be taken:

1. Inform the Secretary of War

    (a) That, at the discretion of the Secretary of

         War, he should inform the President that the

         Interim Committee had agreed that, in the

         coming Conference[1] and if suitable opportunity

         arose, the President might mention, subject

         to the agreement of the Prime Minister, that

         this country is working in this field, that

         if results are satisfactory we might use the

         weapon against Japan, that no further infor-

         mation can be given at this time but that it

         is the President's hope that the weapon might

         become an aid to peace and that this aspect of

         the subject might be discussed further at a

         later date.

CONFIDENTIAL
TOP SECRET

[1]The Allied summit meeting at Potsdam, Germany, to be held in mid-July 1945.

TOP SECRET

- 2 - CONFIDENTIAL

(b) That the Committee voted unanimously that
the Secretary of War be advised that the
Interim Committee favored revocation of Clause
Two of the Quebec Agreement   (secondly, that
we will not use it against third parties without each other's consent) by appropriate action.

(c) That the Committee reaffirmed the position taken
at the May 31 and June 1 meetings that the
weapon should be used against Japan at the
earliest opportunity, that it be used without
warning, <u>and that it be used on a dual target,
namely, a military installation or war plant
surrounded by or adjacent to homes or other
buildings most susceptible to damage.</u>

(d) That the Committee approved the recommendation
of the Scientific Panel that the directive to
the Manhattan District be extended to include
work of post-war importance, such work not to
exceed an annual budget of $20,000,000.

2. Appoint a sub-committee to rework the publicity statements, the members of the sub-committee to be Mr. Page
and a representative from General Groves' office.
This sub-committee is to be responsible for future
releases in line with general policies laid down by
the Committee. General Groves is to prepare a list

CONFIDENTIAL
TOP SECRET

TOP SECRET

- 3 -

CONFIDENTIAL

of rules to be followed which will be submitted to
the Committee for approval.

3. Write Dr. A. H. Compton rejecting the petition that
Dr. Urey be added to the Scientific Panel but pointing out that the Panel will consult Dr. Urey
concerning his special field of competence.

4. Appoint Mr. Marbury, General Royall, and a representative from General Groves' office as a sub-
committee to study the problem of post-war control
and to draft the legislation necessary to establish
a Post-War Control Commission.

>   R. Gordon Arneson
>   1st Lieut., A.U.S.
>   Interim Committee Secretary

CONFIDENTIAL

TOP SECRET

WAR DEPARTMENT
WASHINGTON

26 June 1945

MEMORANDUM FOR THE SECRETARY OF WAR:

Many of the scientists who have been working on S-1 have expressed considerable concern about the future dangers of the development of atomic power. Some are fearful that no safe system of international control can be established. They, therefore, envisage the possibility of an armament race that may threaten civilization.

One group of scientists, working in the Chicago Laboratories, urges that we should not make use of the bomb, so nearly completed, against any enemy country at this time. They feel that to do so might sacrifice our whole moral position and thus make it more difficult for us to be the leaders in proposing or enforcing any system of international control designed to make this tremendous force an influence towards the maintenance of world peace rather than an uncontrollable weapon of war.

This anonymous statement of the Chicago scientists was submitted for comment to the Panel of Scientists appointed by the Interim Committee. Their answer was that they saw no acceptable alternative to direct military use since they believe that such

- 2 -   TOP SECRET

use would be an obvious means of saving American lives and
shortening the war.

It is interesting that practically all of the scientists,
including those on the panel, feel great concern for the future
if atomic power is not controlled through some effective international mechanism. Accordingly, most of then believe that one
of the effective steps in establishing such a control is the
assurance that, after this war is over, there shall be a free
interchange of scientific opinion throughout the world supplemented,
if possible, by some system of inspection. This they admit is a
problem of the future. In the meantime, however, they feel that
we must, even before actual use, briefly advise the Russians of
our progress.

This matter of notice to the Russians was made a subject
of thorough discussion at the last meeting of the Interim Committee
on June 21. It was unanimously agreed that in view of the importance of securing an effective future control, and in view of
the fact that most of the story, other than production secrets,
will become known in _____ in any event, there would be considerable advantage, if a suitable opportunity arises at the "Big
Three" meeting, in having the President advise the Russians simply
that we are working intensely on this weapon and that, if we succeed
as we think we will, we plan to use it against the enemy. Such a
statement might will be supplemented by the statement that in the
future, after this war, we would expect to discuss the matter further
with a view to insuring that this means of warfare will become a
substantial aid in preserving the peace of the world rather than a

TOP SECRET

- 3 -   TOP SECRET

weapon of terror and destruction.

It was felt by the Committee that if the Russians should ask for more details now rather than later or if they should raise questions as to timetables, methods of production, etc., they should be told that we are not yet ready to discuss the subject beyond the simple statement suggested above. Our purpose is merely to let them know that we did not wish to proceed with actual use without giving them prior information that we intend to do so. Not to give them this prior information at the time of the "Big Three" Conference and within a few weeks thereafter to use the weapon and to make fairly complete statements to the world about its history and development, might well make it impossible ever to enlist Russian cooperation in the set-up of future international controls over this new power.

It was agreed by the Committee that in view of the provisions of the Quebec Agreement it would be desirable to discuss this whole aspect of the question with the Prime Minister in advance of the "Big Three" Conference.

GEORGE L. HARRISON

SECRET   TOP SECRET   SECRET

<u>MEMORANDUM ON THE USE OF S-1 BOMB</u>:

Ever since I have been in touch with this program I have
had a feeling that before the bomb is actually used against
Japan that Japan should have some preliminary warning for **say**
two or three days in advance of use. The position of the
United States as a great humanitarian nation and the fair play
attitude of our people generally is responsible in the main for
this feeling.

During recent weeks I have also had the feeling very definitely
that the Japanese government may be searching for some opportunity which they could use as a medium of surrender. Following the
three-power conference emissaries from this country could contact
representatives from Japan somewhere on the China Coast and make
representations with regard to Russia's position and at the same
time give them some information regarding the proposed use of atomic
power, together with whatever assurances the President might care
to make with regard to the Emperor of Japan and the treatment of
the Japanese nation following unconditional surrender. It seems
quite possible to me that this presents the opportunity which the
Japanese are looking for.

I don't see that we have anything in particular to lose in following such a program. The stakes are so tremendous that it is my
opinion very real consideration should be given to some plan of
this kind. I do not believe under present circumstances existing
that there is anyone in this country whose evaluation of the chances
of the success of such a program is worth a great deal. The only
way to find out is to try it out.

RALPH A. BARD[1]

27 June 1945

TOP SECRET

---

[1]Ralph A. Bard, undersecretary of the Navy.

<u>Tuesday, June 26th to</u>
<u>Saturday, June 30, 1945</u>

At the meeting this morning of the Committee of Three, Forrestal,
Grew and I were present with McCloy as recorder and Correa as legal adviser
for the Navy. I took up at once the subject of trying to get Japan to
surrender by giving her a warning after she had been sufficiently pounded
possibly with S-1. This is a matter about which I feel very strongly and
feel that the country will not be satisfied unless every effort is made to
shorten the war. I had made a draft of a letter to the President on the
subject and I read this to the Committee and a long thorough discussion
followed. When we got through, both Forrestal and Grew said that they
approved of the propsed step and the general substance of the letter. We
then appointed a sub-committee consisting of McCloy for the War Department,
Dooman and Ballantine for the State Department, and Correa for the Navy, to
draft an actual warning to be sent when the time came.

●   ●   ●

<u>Monday, July 2, 1945.</u>

●   ●   ●

At eleven o'clock I went to the White House, telling the President
I had two important subjects I wanted to talk with him about; one, our plans
in regard to Japan, and the other our treatment of Germany. He was very
agreeable to both and said that he was troubled over both of them and wanted
my views. I then took out this bunch of papers which I had been preparing
during the past week and started on the problem of, first, whether it was
worthwhile to try to warn Japan into surrender. The President read my memorandum
to him which we had discussed last Tuesday at the Committee of Three and evidently
was impressed with it. A copy is attached hereto. He also examined the
draft warning which, as I pointed out, was merely a tentative draft and
necessarily could not be completed until we knew what was going to be done

with S-1. I also showed him the draft which had been prepared by the
Interim Committee for a Presidential statement after the first bomb is
dropped on Japan. This he read carefully. I then went into the subject
of the attitude of the members of the Interim Committee on our attitude
towards Russia in respect to S-1. By this time my allotted time was approaching its end and people were fretting at the door. The President told me
that these matters were so important that he wanted me to come again tomorrow
when we would have plenty of time to finish them. I told him in a word
of the importance of time in respect to both of these matters in their relation to his coming trip abroad and his conference with Stalin and Churchill.
I pointed out that practically every subject on the "Germany agenda" was a
matter handled by the War Department and I asked him to tell me frankly whether
he was afraid to ask me to come to those meetings on account of the fear that
I could not take the trip. He laughed and said "Yes", that was just it;
that he wanted to save me from over-exertion at this time and I told him of
my relations with the Surgeon General and of his endorsement of my condition
and said that I did not wish to push into his, the President's, party at all
but I thought that he ought to be able to get advice from people on the
Secretarial level from the War Department who were not purely military but
were civilian. On this subject he seemed to agree with me and said that we
would discuss the matter at our next meeting which he fixed for the following
day at 2:45.

His attitude throughout was apparently very well satisfied with the way in which the subjects were presented and he was apparently acquiescent with my attitude towards the treatment of Japan and pronounced the paper which I had written as a very powerful paper.

I regard these two subjects, viz: the effort to shorten the Japanese war by a surrender and the proper handling of Germany so as not to create such harshness in seeking vengeance as to make it impossible to lay the foundations of a new Germany which will be a proper member of the family of nations, as two of the largest and most important problems that I have had since I have been here. In the first one I have to meet and overcome the zeal of the soldier, and in the second the zeal of the Jewish American statesman seeking for vengeance. And in both cases I have to meet the feeling of war passion and hysteria which seizes hold of a nation like ours in the prosecution of such a bitter war. The President so far has struck me as a man who is trying hard to keep his balance. He certainly has been very receptive to all my efforts in these directions. On the other hand, I have been recently much troubled by the attitude which Barney Baruch has taken in regard to Germany. I have hitherto regarded him as an able economist and statesman who could rise above the impulses of racial seeking for vengeance. But he has just lately made some statements before the Kilgore Committee which have disappointed me sadly and his influence is so great in all our Cabinet circle that I fear for the consequences of this lapse.

●   ●   ●

TOP SECRET

(WASHINGTON,) July 2, 1945.

Dear Mr. President: I am enclosing herewith a memorandum to
you on the matter of the proposed warning to Japan, a subject which
I have heretofore discussed with you. I have tried to state as suc-
cinctly as possible how the matter lies in my mind, and in the course
of preparing the memorandum, I have consulted with the Secretary
of the Navy and the Acting Secretary of State, each of whom has approved the tenor of the memorandum and has subscribed to the recommendations contained in it.

I have also had prepared a proposed form of proclamation which
has been discussed with representatives of the State Department and
the Navy Department, as well as with officers of the General Staff but
which has not been placed in final form or in any sense approved as a
final document by the Secretary of State or the Secretary of Navy
or the Joint Chiefs of Staff. It has been drafted merely to put on
paper something which would give us some idea of how a warning of
the character we have in mind might appear. You will note that it
is written without specific relation to the employment of any new
weapon. Of course it would have to be revamped to conform to
the efficacy of such a weapon if the warning were to be delivered, as
would almost certainly be the case, in conjunction with its use.

As these papers were primarily prepared as a possible background
for some of your discussions at the forthcoming conference, this added
element was not included, but a suitable provision could be readily
added at the appropriate time.

I shall continue to discuss this matter with the Secretary of State,
and the Secretary of Navy, as well as with the representatives of the
Joint Chiefs of Staff, and will of course keep you currently informed
of any further suggestions we may have.

Faithfully yours,

Henry L. Stimson

TOP SECRET

(WASHINGTON,) July 2, 1945

MEMORANDUM FOR THE PRESIDENT

PROPOSED PROGRAM FOR JAPAN

1. The plans of operation up to and including the first landing have been authorized and the preparations for the operation are now actually going on. This situation was accepted by all members of your conference on Monday, June 18th.

2. There is reason to believe that the operation for the occupation of Japan following the landing may be a very long, costly and arduous struggle on our part. The terrain, much of which I have visited several times, has left the impression on my memory of being one which would be susceptible to a last ditch defense such as has been made on Iwo Jima and Okinawa and which of course is very much larger than either of those two areas. According to my recollection it will be much more unfavorable with regard to tank maneuvering than either the Philippines or Germany.

3. If we once land on one of the main islands and begin a forceful occupation of Japan, we shall probably have cast the die of last ditch resistance. The Japanese are highly patriotic and certainly susceptible to calls for fanatical resistance to repel an invasion. Once started in actual invasion, we shall in my opinion have to go through with an even more bitter finish fight than in Germany. We shall incur the losses incident to such a war and we shall have to leave the Japanese islands even more thoroughly destroyed than was the case with Germany. This would be due both to the difference in the Japanese and German personal character and the differences in the size and character of the terrain through which the operations will take place.

4. A question then comes: Is there any alternative to such a forceful occupation of Japan which will secure for us the equivalent of an unconditional surrender of her forces and a permanent destruction of her power again to strike an agressive blow at the "peace of the Pacific"? I am inclined to think that there is enough such chance to make it well worthwhile our giving them a warning of what is to come and a definite opportunity to capitulate. As above suggested, it should be tried before the actual forceful occupation of the homeland islands is begun and furthermore the warning should be given in ample time to permit a national reaction to set in.

We have the following enormously favorable factors on our side—factors much weightier than those we had against Germany:

Japan has no allies.

Her navy is nearly destroyed and she is vulnerable to a surface and underwater blockade which can deprive her of sufficient food and supplies for her population.

She is terribly vulnerable to our concentrated air attack upon her crowded cities, industrial and food resources.

She has against her not only the Anglo-American forces but the rising forces of China and the ominous threat of Russia.

We have inexhaustible and untouched industrial resources to bring to bear against her diminishing potential.

We have great moral superiority through being the victim of her first sneak attack.

The problem is to translate these advantages into prompt and economical achievement of our objectives. I believe Japan _is_ susceptible to reason in such a crisis to a much greater extent than is indicated by our current press and other current comment. Japan is not a nation composed wholly of mad fanatics of an entirely different mentality from ours. On the contrary, she has within the past century shown herself to possess extremely intelligent people, capable in an unprecedentedly short time of adopting not only the complicated technique of Occidental civilization but to a substantial extent their culture and their political and social ideas. Her advance in all these respects during the short period of sixty or seventy years has been one of the most astounding feats of national progress in history—a leap from the isolated feudalism of centuries into the position of one of the six or seven great powers of the world. She has not only built up powerful armies and navies. She has maintained an honest and effective national finance and respected position in many of the sciences in which we pride ourselves. Prior to the forcible seizure of power over her government by the fanatical military group in 1931, she had for ten years lived a reasonably responsible and respectable international life.

My own opinion is in her favor on the two points involved in this question.

a. I think the Japanese nation has the mental intelligence and versatile capacity in such a crisis to recognize the folly of a fight to the finish and to accept the proffer of what will amount to an unconditional surrender; and

b. I think she has within her population enough liberal leaders (although now submerged by the terrorists) to be depended upon for her reconstruction as a responsible member of the family of nations. I think she is better in this last respect than Germany was. Her liberals yielded only at the point of the pistol and, so far as I am aware, their liberal attitude has not been personally subverted in the way which was so general in Germany.

On the other hand, I think that the attempt to exterminate her armies and her population by gunfire or other means will tend to produce a fusion of race solidity and antipathy which had no analogy in the case of Germany. We have a national interest in creating, if possible, a condition wherein the Japanese nation may live as a peaceful and useful member of the future Pacific community.

5. It is therefore my conclusion that a carefully timed warning be given to Japan by the chief representatives of the United States, Great Britain, China and, if then a belligerent, Russia, calling upon Japan to surrender and permit the occupation of her country in order to insure its complete demilitarization for the sake of the future peace.

This warning should contain the following elements:

The varied and overwhelming character of the force we are about to bring to bear on the islands.

The inevitability and completeness of the destruction which the full application of this force will entail.

The determination of the allies to destroy permanently all authority and influence of those who have deceived and misled the country into embarking on world conquest.

The determination of the allies to limit Japanese sovereignty to her main islands and to render them powerless to mount and support another war.

The disavowal of any attempt to extirpate the Japanese as a race or to destroy them as a nation.

A statement of our readiness, once her economy is purged of its militaristic influences, to permit the Japanese to maintain such industries, particularly of a light consumer character, as offer no threat of aggression against their neighbors, but which can produce a sustaining economy, and provide a reasonable standard of living. The statement should indicate our willingness, for this purpose, to give Japan trade access to external raw materials, but no longer any control over, the sources of supply outside her main islands. It should also indicate our willingness, in accordance with our now established foreign trade policy, in due course to enter into mutually advantageous trade relations with her.

The withdrawal from their country as soon as the above objectives of the allies are accomplished, and as soon as there has been established a peacefully inclined government, of a character representative of the masses of the Japanese people. I personally think that if in saying this we should add that we do not exclude a constitutional monarchy under her present dynasty, it would substantially add to the chances of acceptance.

6. Success of course will depend on the potency of the warning which we give her. She has an extremely sensitive national pride and, as we are now seeing every day, when actually locked with the enemy will fight to the very death. For that reason the warning must be tendered before the actual invasion has occurred and while the impending destruction, though clear beyond peradventure, has not yet reduced her to fanatical despair. If Russia is a part of the threat, the Russian attack, if actual, must not have progressed too far. Our own bombing should be confined to military objectives as far as possible.

•   •   •

I then finished up what was left unfinished the day before in respect to

S-1. That was the question of what the President should do to Stalin at

this coming conference, and I finally summed it up informally that he should

look sharp and, if he found that he thought that Stalin was on good enough

terms with him, he should shoot off at him what we had arranged, George Harrison

and I, in the aide memoire. In other words, simply telling him that we were

busy with this thing working like the dickens and we knew he was busy with

this thing and working like the dickens, and that we were pretty nearly ready

and we intended to use it against the enemy, Japan; that if it was satis-

factory we proposed to then talk it over with Stalin afterwards, with the

purpose of having it make the world peaceful and safe rather than to destroy

civilization. If he pressed for details and facts, Truman was simply to

tell him that we were not yet prepared to give them. The President listened

attentively and he understood and he thought that was the best way to do it.

•   •   •

July 4, 1945

Dear

     Inclosed is the text of a petition which will be submitted to the President of the United States. As you will see, this petition is based on purely moral considerations.

     It may very well be that the decision of the President whether or not to use atomic bombs in the war against Japan will largely be based on considerations of expediency. On the basis of expediency, many arguments could be put forward both for and against our use of atomic bombs against Japan. Such arguments could be considered only within the framework of a thorough analysis of the situation which will face the United States after this war and it was felt that no useful purpose would be served by considering arguments of expediency in a short petition.

     However small the chance might be that our petition may influence the course of events, I personally feel that it would be a matter of importance if a large number of scientists who have worked in this field want clearly and unmistakably on record as to their opposition on moral grounds to the use of these bombs in the present phase of the war.

     Many of us are inclined to say that individual Germans share the guilt for the acts which Germany committed during this war because they did not raise their voices in protest against those acts. Their defense that their protest would have been of no avail hardly seems acceptable even though these Germans could not have protests without running risks to life and liberty. We are in a position to raise our voices without incurring any such risks even though we might incur the displeasure of some of those who are at present in charge on controlling the work on "atomic power".

     The fact that the people of the United States are unaware of the choice which faces us increases our responsibility in this matter since those who have worked on "atomic power" represent a sample of the population and they alone are in a position to form an opinion and declare their stand.

     Anyone who might wish to go on record by signing the petition ought to have an opportunity to do so and, therefore, it would be appreciated if you could give every member of your group an opportunity for signing.

Leo Szilard

P.S.--Anyone who wants to sign the petition ought to sign both attached copies and ought to read not only the petition but also this covering letter letter.

SECRET

July 13, 1945

To: A. H. Compton

From: Farrington Daniels

Re: Poll on the use of weapon

Following the suggestions of your letter, AC-2757, I took copies of excerpts of your letter individually to the eight different section chiefs and asked them to show the questions individually to some of the members of their group. These extracts which went to the section chiefs were marked "Secret", delivered in person, and all copies returned and destroyed.

Each person polled read the questions and placed in an envelope the number which most closely represented his choice. All the balloting was done on Thursday afternoon, July 18. The ballots were returned to me, and the counts are as follows:

Suggestion No.:	No. of Votes:	% of Total Vote:
(1)	23	15
(2)	69	46
(3)	39	26
(4)	16	11
(5)	3	2
	150	100

The Argonne Laboratory and the Patent Division were not polled. Approximately 2/3 of the remaining academic personnel voted.

The suggested procedures were as follows:

(1) Use the weapons in the manner that is from the military point of view most effective in bringing about prompt Japanese surrender at minimum human cost to our armed froces.

(2) Give a military demonstration in Japan, to be followed by a renewed opportunity for surrender before full use of the weapons is employed.

(3) Given an experimental demonstration in this country, with representatives of Japan present; followed by a new opportunity for surrender before full use of the weapons is employed.

(4) Withhold military use of the weapons, but make public experimental demonstration of their effectiveness.

(5) Maintain as secret as possible all developments of our new weapons, and refrain from using them in this war.

SECRET

Farrington Daniels

SECRET

Metallurgical Laboratory

P.O. BOX 5207
CHICAGO 80, ILLINOIS

July 24, 1945

BUTTERFIELD 4300

To: Colonel K. D. Nichols

From: Arthur H. Compton

In re: Transmittal of Petitions addressed to the President

I have been requested to transmit the enclosed petition to the President of the United States. At the suggestion of General Groves, I am herewith handing it to you for disposition. Since the matter presented in the petition is of immediate concern, the petitioners desire the transmittal to occur as promptly as possible. It will be appreciated if you will inform me with regard to its disposition.

You will note that the signed draft of the petition is enclosed within a sealed envelope. I have personally verified that this envelope contains only signed copies of a petition, identical in text with the carbon copy attached, together with receipt forms for classified material. Mr. Szilard, in his covering letter, has requested that this envelope be opened only by those authorized to read the President's mail.

You have requested me to evaluate this petition and likewise those submitted to you by Mr. Whitaker on behalf of certain members of Clinton Laboratories.

The question of use of atomic weapons has been considered by the Scientific Panel of the Secretary of War's Interim Advisory Committee. The opinion which they expressed was that military use of such weapons should be made in the Japanese War. There was not sufficient agreement among the members of the panel to unite upon a statement as to how or under what conditions such use was to be made.

A small group of petitioners initially canvassed certain groups of scientists within the project seeking signatures requesting no use of the new weapons in this war. The response was such as to call forth several counter petitions, of which those submitted through Mr. Whitaker are typical, and to cause the formulator of the original petition to rephrase it so as to approve use of the weapons after giving suitable warning and opportunity for surrender under known conditions.

In order to obtain a fair expression of the opinion of a typical group of scientists, an opinion poll was conducted on a group of 150. The results are described in the enclosed memo to me from Dr. Daniels. You will note that the strongly favored procedure is to "give a military demonstration in Japan, to be followed by a renewed opportunity for surrender before full use of the weapons is employed." This coincides with my own preference, and is, as nearly as I can judge, the procedure that has found most favor in all informed groups where the subject has been discussed.

KT

Arthur H. Compton

SECRET

SECRET   July 17, 1945

A PETITION TO THE PRESIDENT OF THE UNITED STATES[1]

Discoveries of which the people of the United States are not aware may affect the welfare of this nation in the near future. The liberation of atomic power which has been achieved places atomic bombs in the hands of the Army. It places in your hands, as Commander-in-Chief, the fateful decision whether or not to sanction the use of such bombs in the present phase of the war against Japan.

We, the undersigned scientists, have been working in the field of atomic power. Until recently we have had to fear that the United States might be attacked by atomic bombs during this war and that her only defense might lie in a counterattack by the same means. Today, with the defeat of Germany, this danger is averted and we feel impelled to say what follows:

The war has to be brought speedily to a successful conclusion and attacks by atomic bombs may very well be an effective method of warfare. We feel, however, that such attacks on Japan could not be justified, at least not unless the terms which will be imposed after the war on Japan were made public in detail and Japan were given an opportunity to surrender.

If such public announcement gave assurance to the Japanese that they could look forward to a life devoted to peaceful pursuits in their homeland and if Japan still refused to surrender our nation might then, in certain circumstances, find itself forced to resort to the use of atomic bombs. Such a step, however, ought not to be made at any time without seriously considering the moral responsibilities which are involved.

The development of atomic power will provide the nations with new means of destruction. The atomic bombs at our disposal represent only the first step in this direction, and there is almost no limit to the destructive power which will become available in the course of their future development. Thus a nation which sets the precedent of using these newly liberated forces of nature for purposes of destruction may have to bear the responsibility of opening the door to an era of devastation on an unimaginable scale.

If after this war a situation is allowed to develop in the world which permits rival powers to be in uncontrolled possession of these new means of destruction, the cities of the United States as well as the cities of other nations will be in continuous danger of sudden annihilation. All the resources of the United States, moral and material, may have to be mobilized to prevent the advent of such a world situation. Its prevention is at present the solemn responsibility of the United States--singled out by virtue of her lead in the field of atomic power.

The added material strength which this lead gives to the United States brings with it the obligation of restraint and if we were to violate this obligation our moral position would be weakened in the eyes of the world and in our own eyes. It would then be more difficult for us to live up to our responsibility of bringing the unloosened forces of destruction under control.

In view of the foregoing, we, the undersigned, respectfully petition: first, that you exercise your power as Commander-in-Chief, to rule that the United States shall not resort to the use of atomic bombs in this war unless the terms which will be imposed upon Japan have been made public in detail and Japan knowing these terms has refused to surrender; second, that in such an event the question whether or not to use atomic bombs be decided by you in the light of the considerations presented in this petition as well as all the other moral responsibilities which are involved.

---

[1]Neither this form nor any of the petitions signed by scientists ever reached the President.

Combined Intelligence Committee, "Estimate of the Enemy Situation,"
July 8, 1945

11. <u>Probable Military Strategy</u>. The primary preoccupation of the
Japanese High Command at present is the defense of the home islands, especially
Kyushu and Honshu. For this defense they may dispose by the end of 1945 more
than 35 active divisions plus 14 depot divisions, which, with army troops,
will total over 2,000,000 men. Except possibly in case of Hokkaido, all available aircraft will be employed in the defense of the home islands, mainly in
suicide operations. Their air effort might amount initially to 400-500 sorties
of combat-type aircraft and 200-300 sorties of trainer-type aircraft during
any 24 hour period: this effort will, however, decline rapidly. Similarly
all remaining naval units will be employed in suicide operations in defense of
the homeland.

. . . .

All other areas will be regarded as of minor importance only. They
will not be reinforced from the Inner Zone, but their garrisons will be ordered
to resist to the last in order to contain allied forces which might otherwise
be used against Japan, and in order to deny to the allies strategic materials
and bases in their areas. Strategy in these outlying areas will, therefore, be
designed to keep Japanese forces in being rather than to defend particular objectives to the last or to undertake more than, at the most, local counteroffen-
sives.

12. <u>Probable Political Strategy</u>. In general, Japan will use all political means for avoiding complete defeat or unconditional surrender. During
the next few months the political strategy of the Government will exhibit the
following aims to,
   a. Continue and even increase its attempts to secure complete political
      unity within the empire, possibly through personal rule, real or ap-
      parent, of the Emperor.
   b. Attempt to foster a belief among Japan's enemies that the war will
      prove costly and long drawn out if the United Nations insist on
      fighting until the complete conquest of Japan.
   c. Make desperate efforts to persuade the USSR to continue her neutra-
      lity, if necessary by offering important territorial or other
      concessions, while at the same time making every effort to sow dis-
      cord between the American and British on one side and the Russians
      in the other. As the situation deteriorates still further, Japan
      may even make a serious attempt to use the USSR as a mediator in
      ending the war.
   d. Put out intermittent peace feelers, in an effort to bring the war to
      an acceptable end, to weaken the determination of the United Nations
      to fight to the bitter end, or to create inter-allied dissension.
   e. Take all possible advantages of estranged relations between Communists
      and Kuomintang factions in China.

13. <u>Possibility of Surrender</u>. The Japanese ruling group are aware of the
desperate military situation and are increasingly desirous of a compromise peace,
but still find unconditional surrender unacceptable. The basic policy of the

2.

present government is to fight as long and as desperately as possible in the hope of avoiding complete defeat and of acquiring a better bargaining position in a negotiated peace. Japanese leaders are now playing for time in the hope that Allied war weariness, Allied disunity, or some "miracle" will present an opportunity to arrange a compromise peace.

We believe that a considerable portion of the Japanese population now consider absolute military defeat to be probable. The increasing effects of sea blockade and the cumulative devastation wrought by strategic bombing, which has already rendered millions homeless, and has destroyed from 25 to 50% of the built up areas of Japan's most important cities, should make this realization increasingly general. An entry of the Soviet Union into the war would finally convince the Japanese of the inevitability of complete defeat. Although individual Japanese willingly sacrifice themselves in the service of the nation we doubt that the nation as a whole is predisposed toward national suicide. Rather, the Japanese as a nation have a strong concept of national survival, regardless of the fate of individuals. They would probably prefer national survival, even through surrender, to virtual extinction.

The Japanese believe, however, that unconditional surrender would be the equivalent of national extinction. There are as yet no indications that the Japanese are willing to accept such terms. The idea of foreign occupation of the Japanese homeland, foreign custody of the person of the Emperor, and the loss of prestige entailed by the acceptance of the terms of unconditional surrender are most revolting to the Japanese. To avoid these conditions, if possible, and, in any event, to insure survival of the institution of the Emperor, the Japanese might well be willing to withdraw from all territory they have seized on the Asiatic continent and in the southern Pacific, and even to agree to the independence of Korea and to the practical disarmament of their military forces.

PART

Truman and Stimson learn of
successful test. Stimson's
recommendations for policy toward
the Japanese and Russians. Grove's
report of test. The Interim
Committee considers postwar control
of atomic energy. Stimson observes
Truman's new confidence and
discusses relations with Russia,
Russian entry into the war against
Japan, terms for a Japanese
surrender, and hopes for postwar
cooperation from Japan. The
Potsdam Declaration. Byrnes's
opposition to Russian entry.

The first atomic bomb

Successful Test, the Potsdam Summit, and Preparations for Use

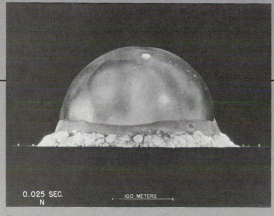

Bomb test, Alamagordo, New Mexico

Potsdam Conference –
Churchill, Truman, and Stalin

Coming in the wake of Germany's surrender and straddling the successful test of the atomic bomb, the Potsdam summit conference has received much scholarly but little popular attention. The following section of documents picks up the story of the atomic bomb as it became more and more entwined with diplomacy. Nowhere during the war was the connection closer than at Potsdam, Germany, in the summer of 1945. Harry Truman and his advisers learned of the successful test of the atomic bomb in the midst of the conference, and, at its close, the Allies, with the weapon in their hands, issued their final demand for surrender to Japan.

From Herbert Feis's *Between War and Peace: The Potsdam Conference* (1960) to Gar Alperovitz's *Atomic Diplomacy: Hiroshima and Potsdam* (1965) and Charles L. Mee's *Meeting at Potsdam* (1975), historians have paid considerable attention to this final summit of the Allies, and properly so. Though little of substance was decided (which probably accounts for its relative popular anonymity), the Potsdam conference was a dress rehearsal for the future. Potsdam, more than any other wartime diplomatic encounter, foreshadowed postwar relations between the United States and the Soviet Union. Soviet Premier Joseph Stalin relentlessly pressed for advantage—maximum influence in Austria and eastern Europe, bases in Turkey, and heavy reparations from Germany. Harry Truman blocked each thrust, condemning Soviet control of Poland and the Balkans, refusing Soviet Mediterranean claims, and rejecting the call for punitive payments from Germany. The Second World War was not yet over, but at Potsdam the opening rounds of the cold war were already being fought.

The Potsdam conference also marked the coming out of Harry Truman. British Prime Minister Winston Churchill and other observers commented on Truman's new-found confidence during the meeting. Ever since, historians have argued over how to account for it. One point to keep in mind is that Potsdam was really Truman's second coming out. Less than two weeks after his swearing in, he unceremoniously dressed down Soviet Foreign Minister Vyacheslav Molotov at the White House. "I've never been talked to that way in my life," Molotov protested. "Carry out your agreements and you won't get talked to like that," Truman snorted. More suspicious and less deft than Roosevelt, Harry Truman was prepared to be firm with the Russians from the beginning.

If anything, firmness hardened into resolve at Potsdam. Churchill noticed the change the moment Truman learned of the successful atomic test at Alamogordo. The President, observed the prime minister, suddenly took control of the meeting. Had the bomb become Truman's "big stick," a secret whose mere possession transformed an unseasoned President into a hard-nosed diplomat? This seems unlikely. It was not simply—or even mainly—the power of the weapon as a tool of diplomacy that produced a "new" Truman. Rather the potential of the bomb for inducing quick victory probably toughened the already blunt bargainer. Before the test, American policy had been predicated on the need to bring the Soviet Union into the Pacific war as soon as possible. Since 1941, when the Russians signed a neutrality pact with Japan, they had stayed out of the Asian theater. As the European war wound down, Allied hopes grew that Soviet entry alone might force the Japanese to capitulate.

At the Yalta conference in February 1945, Roosevelt and Churchill had secured Stalin's pledge to begin a far eastern campaign three months after the cessation of hostilities in Europe. Until late spring, American policymakers had

180

looked on Potsdam as an opportunity to ensure that the Russians kept their promise. By June 1945, when a test of the new weapon appeared imminent, American thinking had changed. The probability of having an atomic bomb made Russian intervention less appealing. Some American policymakers now saw Russian entry as downright dangerous. James Byrnes, who was fast becoming Truman's most trusted adviser, feared that a Soviet declaration of war against Japan might promote an undesired and troublesome Russian presence in Asia. "Once in there," he told Secretary of the Navy James Forrestal after the Potsdam conference, "it would not be easy to get them out." It would be better, he felt, "to get the Japanese affair over with before the Russians got in" (see Document 75).

Potsdam also gave the western Allies their last chance to tell Stalin about the bomb. For reasons that still remain obscure, Truman avoided full disclosure and relied, instead, on a veiled reference to a new weapon of "unusual destructive force" (see Document 76). This sly admission followed the precedent of past decisions. The secret of the bomb was kept to the end, not only from Stalin but from the Japanese as well. When the United States, Great Britain, and China issued an ultimatum to Japan at the close of the conference, they made no mention of the atomic bomb, noting simply that if the Japanese refused to surrender, "prompt and utter destruction" would follow (see Document 74).

"Utter destruction" was no longer to be the fate of one proposed target, however. Almost from the start, Henry Stimson had opposed the atomic bombing of Kyoto, one of the original "AA" targets. During the 1920s, Stimson had been so taken with Kyoto that he visited it on three separate occasions. Its 3000 shrines symbolized the sacred esteem in which the Japanese held the city. Stimson knew that bombing Kyoto would be regarded as an act of blasphemy, not simply of war. The consequent bitterness, he argued to Truman at Potsdam, "might make it impossible during the long post war period to reconcile the Japanese to us in that area rather than to the Russians" (see Document 75). Truman agreed, and Kyoto was spared, another indication of how the atomic bomb and postwar diplomacy were entwined.

All the while, Japan had been seeking a negotiated settlement. The principal aim was to guarantee the retention of the Emperor, who was considered a deity in Japanese culture. As early as February 1945, the Japanese approached the Russians about acting as go-betweens in arranging a peace with the western powers. In April 1945, a new Japanese government came to power under Kantaro Suzuki, a seventy-seven-year-old retired admiral. His expressed purpose was to make peace. Though the Japanese cabinet still remained divided, Prime Minister Suzuki asked the Russians again in late spring to serve as intermediaries. A week before the Potsdam conference, the Emperor himself, impatient with Russian inaction, decided to send an envoy to Moscow.

At Potsdam, Stalin told Truman and Churchill about the Japanese peace feelers. The western leaders, holding to their demand for unconditional surrender, replied with the Potsdam Declaration (see Document 74). While debate within its cabinet continued, Japan answered the Declaration with the time-honored and confusing policy of *mokusatsu*. There is no exact equivalent in English for this word, which can mean anything from "withhold comment" to "unworthy of public notice." Japanese opponents of peace pushed the harsher meaning in the press, and the Allies interpreted it as an outright rejection. As historians James Crowley and Akira Iriye have demonstrated, cultural ignorance and misperception helped to bring on the Japanese-American conflict. Ignorance and misperception also contributed, perhaps tragically, at its end.

TOP SECRET

16 July 1945.

At 8:00 A.M. E.W.T. Groves called Harrison[1] reporting success of the test. At 9:00 A.M. Groves called in further details. Results even better than expected. Harrison prepared a cable to s end to the S/W which he turned over to Pasco to prepare for transmittal. At 9:30 A.M. Harrison showed a copy of the cable to Lovett[2] and then to Patterson.[3] After Patterson's approval, Harrison authorized dispatch of cable at 11:15 A.M.

At 1:00 P.M. Consodine[4] came over to show Harrison a copy of the statement that had been released to the local press in New Mexico at 11:00 A.M. M.W.T.

Harrison had tried to get in touch with Makins during the morning. At 3:00 P.M. Makins came over and was shown the telegram. Harrison told him about the press release that had been issued in New Mexico to cover the curiosity that had been aroused locally. It was agreed that Makins should inform Halifax[5] immediately but only in very general terms to the effect that the test had been successful and that results had exceeded expectations. It was understood further that Chadwicks[6] report would be transmitted to Makins through Groves.

TOP SECRET

[1]George Harrison, special assistant to the Secretary of War.
[2]Robert Lovett, Assistant Secretary of War (for air).
[3]Robert Patterson, Under Secretary of War.
[4]William Consodine, major in the U.S. Army attached to the Manhattan Project.
[5]Lord Halifax, British ambassador to the United States.
[6]James Chadwick, head of the British mission to Los Alamos.

WAR DEPARTMENT

CLASSIFIED MESSAGE CENTER

OUTGOING MESSAGE

Secretary, General Staff
Col. Pasco 3542

16 July 1945

TERMINAL

Number WAR 32887

To Humelsine for Colonel Kyle's EYES ONLY from Harrison for Stimson.

Operated on this morning. Diagnosis not yet complete but results seem satisfactory and already exceed expectations. Local press release necessary as interest extends great distance. Dr. Groves pleased. He returns tomorrow. I will keep you posted.

End.

Stimson's notes for his diary,
July 16, 1945:

    Also received important paper in re Japanese
maneuverings for peace.

    At 7:30 p.m. Mr. Harrison's first message
arrived. Took it to the White House[1] to President and
Byrnes, and delivered it to the President who kept it.
Both he and Byrnes were delighted with it.

[1]Stimson refers here not to the White House in Washington, D.C., but to President Truman's quarters for the Potsdam Conference, nicknamed the "Little White House."

<u>Memorandum for the President</u>

<u>The Conduct of the War with Japan</u>

With the great needs of rehabilitation both domestically and abroad facing us, we still find ourselves engaged in war with a major Pacific power. The length and limitation upon our lines of communications to the Pacific combat areas aggravate the strains upon our resources which the wastes of war always impose. The Japanese soldier has proved himself capable of a suicidal, last ditch defense, and will no doubt continue to display such a defense on his homeland. Yet we have enormous factors in our favor and any step which can be taken to translate those advantages into a prompt and successful conclusion of the war should be taken. I have already indicated in my memorandum to you of 2 July 1945,[1] the reasons which impel me to urge that warnings be delivered to Japan, designed to bring about her capitulation as quickly as possible. While that war is going on, it will be most difficult politically and econom- ically to make substantial contributions to the reestablishment of stable conditions abroad. The longer that war progresses, the smaller will our surpluses become, and the more our over-all resources will be strained.

<u>Warning to Japan</u>

It seems to me that we are at the psychological moment to commence our warnings to Japan. The great marshalling of our new air and land forces in the combat area in the midst of the ever greater blows she is receiving from the naval and already established Army forces, is bound to provoke thought even among their military leaders. Added to this is the effect induced by this Conference and the impending threat of Russia's participation, which it accentuates.

[1]See Document 58.

Moreover, the recent news of attempted approaches on the
part of Japan to Russia, impels me to urge prompt delivery of our
warning. I would therefore urge that we formulate a warning to
Japan to be delivered during the course of this Conference, and
rather earlier than later, along the lines of the draft prepared
by the War Department and now approved, I understand, by both the
State and Navy Departments. In the meantime our tactical plans
should continue to operate without let up, and if the Japanese per-
sist, the full force of our newer weapons should be brought to bear
in the course of which a renewed and even heavier warning, backed
by the power of the new forces and possibly the actual entrance of
the Russians in the war, should be delivered.

Whether the Russians are to be notified of our intentions
in advance in this regard, would depend upon whether an agreement
satisfactory to us had been reached with the Russians on the terms
of their entry into the Japanese war.

The Yalta Agreements

As for the Russian participation and the so-called Yalta
Agreements, I believe that these agreements, so long as they are
interpreted consistently with our traditional policy toward China,
should not cause us any concern from a security point of view, assuming always we keep clear our control over the Pacific Islands. By
our traditional policy toward China I refer, or course, to the Open
Door and the recognition of Chinese sovereignty over Manchuria.

. . .

<u>Allied ^Occupation of the ^Main _Japanse Islands</u>

I would hope that our occupation of the Japanese islands
would not involve the government of the country as a whole in any
such manner as we are committed in Germany. I am afraid we would
make a hash of it if we tried. The Japanese are an oriental people
with an oriental mind and religion. Our occupation should be limited
to that necessary to (a) impress the Japanese, and the orient as a
whole, with the fact of Japanse defeat, (b) demilitarize the country,
and (c) punish war criminals, including those responsible for the
perfidy of Pearl Harbor.

If the Russians seek joint occupation after a creditable
participation in the conquest of Japan, I do no see how we could
refuse at least a token occupation. I feel, however, that no prolonged occupation by the Soviet should be approved and, indeed, any
occupation by any major ally which exceeds our own, either in the
strength of forces employed or in duration. I would approve their
occupation of the Kuriles or indeed their cession to Russia, but I
do not relish Russian occupation further south. If there is to be
occupation of the main islands, the conditions and terms must certainly be determined by us. If the Kuriles are to be ceded to
Russia, we should retain permanent landing rights therein, as the
islands are located in a great circle route to Japan from the United
States, and would substantially shorten our mileage on air voyages
following this route.

                              /s/ Henry L. Stimson
                              The Secretary of War

The Commanding General, MANHATTAN DISTRICT Project (Groves) to the Secretary of War (Stimson)

TOP SECRET   WASHINGTON, 18 July 1945.

MEMORANDUM FOR THE SECRETARY OF WAR

Subject: The Test.

1. This is not a concise, formal military report but an attempt to recite what I would have told you if you had been here on my return from New Mexico.

2. At 0530, 16 July 1945, in a remote section of the Alamogordo Air Base, New Mexico, the first full scale test was made of the implosion type atomic fission bomb. For the first time in history there was a nuclear explosion. And what an explosion! . . . The bomb was not dropped from an airplane but was exploded on a platform on top of a 100-foot high steel tower.

3. The test was successful beyond the most optimistic expectations of anyone. Based on the data which it has been possible to work up to date, I estimate the energy generated to be in excess of the equivalent of 15,000 to 20,000 tons of TNT; and this is a conservative estimate. Data based on measurements which we have not yet been able to reconcile would make the energy release several times the conservative figure. There were tremendous blast effects. For a brief period there was a lighting effect within a radius of 20 miles equal to several suns in midday; a huge ball of fire was formed which lasted for several seconds. This ball mushroomed and rose to a height of over ten thousand feet before it dimmed. The light from the explosion was seen clearly at Albuquerque, Santa Fe, Silver City, El Paso and other points generally to about 180 miles away. The sound was heard to the same distance in a few instances but generally to about 100 miles. Only a few windows were broken although one was some 125 miles away. A massive cloud was formed which surged and billowed upward with tremendous power, reaching the substratosphere at an elevation of 41,000 feet, 36,000 feet above the ground, in about five minutes, breaking without interruption through a temperature inversion at 17,000 feet which most of the scientists thought would stop it. Two supplementary explosions occurred in the cloud shortly after the main explosion. The cloud contained several thousand tons of dust picked up from the ground and a considerable amount of iron in the gaseous form. Our present thought is that this iron ignited when it mixed with the oxygen in the air to cause these supplementary explosions. Huge concentrations of highly radioactive materials resulted from the fission and were contained in this cloud.

4. A crater from which all vegetation had vanished, with a diameter of 1200 feet and a slight slope toward the center, was formed. In the center was a shallow bowl 130 feet in diameter and 6 feet in depth. The material within the crater was deeply pulverized dirt. The material within the outer circle is greenish and can be distinctly seen from as much as 5 miles away. The steel from the tower was evaporated. 1500 feet away there was a four-inch iron pipe 16 feet high set in concrete and strongly guyed. It disappeared completely.

5. One-half mile from the explosion there was a massive steel test cylinder weighing 220 tons. The base of the cylinder was solidly encased in concrete. Surrounding the cylinder was a strong steel tower 70 feet high, firmly anchored to concrete foundations. This tower is comparable to a steel building bay that would be found in typical 15 or 20 story skyscraper or in warehouse construction. Forty tons of steel were used to fabricate the tower which was 70 feet high, the height of a six story building. The cross bracing was much stronger than that normally used in ordinary steel construction. The absence of the solid walls of a building gave the blast a much less effective surface to push against. The blast tore the tower from its foundations, twisted it, ripped it apart and left it flat on the ground. The effects on the tower indicate that, at that distance, unshielded permanent steel and masonry buildings would have been destroyed. I no longer consider the Pentagon a safe shelter from such a bomb. Enclosed are a sketch showing the tower before the explosion and a telephotograph showing what it looked like afterwards. None of us had expected it to be damaged.

6. The cloud traveled to a great height first in the form of a ball, then mush-roomed, then changed into a long trailing chimney-shaped column and finally was sent in several directions by the variable winds at the different elevations. It deposited its dust and radioactive materials over a wide area. It was followed and monitored by medical doctors and scientists with instruments to check its radio-active effects. While here and there the activity on the ground was fairly high, at no place did it reach a concentration which required evacuation of the population. Radioactive material in small quantities was located as much as 120 miles away. The measurements are being continued in order to have adequate data with which to protect the Government's interests in case of future claims. For a few hours I was none too comfortable about the situation.

7. For distances as much as 200 miles away, observers were stationed to check on blast effects, property damage, radioactivity and reactions of the popu-lation. While complete reports have not yet been received, I now know that no persons were injured nor was there any real property damage outside our Gov-ernment area. As soon as all the voluminous data can be checked and corre-lated, full technical studies will be possible.

8. Our long range weather predictions had indicated that we could expect weather favorable for our tests beginning on the morning of the 17th and continu-ing for four days. This was almost a certainty if we were to believe our long range forecasters. The prediction for the morning of the 16th was not so certain but there was about an 80% chance of the conditions being suitable. During the night there were thunder storms with lightning flashes all over the area. The test had been originally set for 0400 hours and all the night through, because of the bad weather, there were urgings from many of the scientists to postpone the test. Such a delay might well have had crippling results due to mechanical difficulties in our complicated test set-up. Fortunately, we disregarded the urgings. We held firm and waited the night through hoping for suitable weather. We had to delay an hour and a half, to 0530, before we could fire. This was 30 minutes before sun-rise.

9. Because of bad weather, our two B-20 observation airplanes were unable to take off as scheduled from Kirtland Field at Albuquerque and when they finally did get off, they found it impossible to get over the target because of the heavy clouds and the thunder storms. Certain desired observations could not be made and while the people in the airplanes saw the explosion from a distance, they were not as close as they will be in action. We still have no reason to anticipate the loss of our plane in an actual operation although we cannot guarantee safety.

10. Just before 1100 the news stories from all over the state started to flow into the Albuquerque Associated Press. I then directed the issuance by the Commanding Officer, Alamogordo Air Base of a news release as shown on the inclosure. With the assistance of the Office of Censorship we were able to limit the news stories to the approved release supplemented in the local papers by brief stories from the many eyewitnesses not connected with our project. One of these was a blind woman who saw the light.

11. Brigadier General Thomas F. Farrell was at the control shelter located 10,000 yards south of the point of explosion. His impressions are given below:

> "The scene inside the shelter was dramatic beyond words. In and around the shelter were some twenty-odd people concerned with last minute arrangements prior to firing the shot. Included were: Dr. Oppenheimer, the Director who had borne the great scientific burden of developing the weapon from the raw materials made in Tennessee and Washington and a dozen of his key assistants—Dr. Kistiakowsky, who developed the highly special explosives; Dr. Bainbridge, who supervised all the detailed arrangements for the test; Dr. Hubbard, the weather expert, and several others. Besides these, there were a handful of soldiers, two or three Army officers and one Naval officer. The shelter was cluttered with a great variety of instruments and radios.

> "For some hectic two hours preceding the blast, General Groves stayed with the Director, walking with him and steadying his tense excitement. Every time the Director would be about to explode because of some untoward happening, General Groves would take him off and walk with him in the rain, counselling with him and reassuring him that everything would be all right. At twenty minutes before zero hour, General Groves left for his station at the base camp, first because it provided a better observation point and second, because of our rule that he and I must not be together in situations where there is an element of danger, which existed at both points.

> "Just after General Groves left, announcements began to be broadcast of the interval remaining before the blast. They were sent by radio to the other groups participating in and observing the test. As the time interval grew smaller and changed from minutes to seconds, the tension increased by leaps and bounds. Everyone in that room knew the awful potentialities of the thing that they thought was about to happen. The scientists felt that their figuring must be right and that the bomb had to go off but there was in everyone's mind a strong measure of doubt. The feeling of many could be expressed by 'Lord, I believe; help Thou mine unbelief.' We were reaching into the unknown and we did not know what might come of it. It can be safely said that most of those present—Christian, Jew and Atheist—were praying and praying harder than they had ever prayed before. If the shot were successful, it was a justification of the several years of intensive effort of tens of thousands of people—statesmen, scientists, engineers, manufacturers, soldiers, and many others in every walk of life.

"In that brief instant in the remote New Mexico desert the tremendous effort of the brains and brawn of all these people came suddenly and startlingly to the fullest fruition. Dr. Oppenheimer, on whom had rested a very heavy burden, grew tenser as the last seconds ticked off. He scarcely breathed. He held on to a post to steady himself. For the last few seconds, he stared directly ahead and then when the announcer shouted 'Now!' and there came this tremendous burst of light followed shortly thereafter by the deep growling roar of the explosion, his face relaxed into an expression of tremendous relief. Several of the observers standing back of the shelter to watch the lighting effects were knocked flat by the blast.

"The tension in the room let up and all started congratulating each other. Everyone sensed 'This is it!' No matter what might happen now all knew that the impossible scientific job had been done. Atomic fission would no longer be hidden in the cloisters of the theoretical physicists' dreams. It was almost full grown at birth. It was a great new force to be used for good or for evil. There was a feeling in that shelter that those concerned with its nativity should dedicate their lives to the mission that it would always be used for good and never for evil.

"Dr. Kistiakowsky, the impulsive Russian,[1] threw his arms around Dr. Oppenheimer and embraced him with shouts of glee. Others were equally enthusiastic. All the pent-up emotions were released in those few minutes and all seemed to sense immediately that the explosion had far exceeded the most optimistic expectations and wildest hopes of the scientists. All seemed to feel that they had been present at the birth of a new age—The Age of Atomic Energy—and felt their profound responsibility to help in guiding into right channels the tremendous forces which had been unlocked for the first time in history.

"As to the present war, there was a feeling that no matter what else might happen, we now had the means to insure its speedy conclusion and save thousands of American lives. As to the future, there had been brought into being something big and something new that would prove to be immeasurably more important than the discovery of electricity or any of the other great discoveries which have so affected our existence.

"The effects could well be called unprecedented, magnificent, beautiful, stupendous and terrifying. No man-made phenomenon of such tremendous power had ever occurred before. The lighting effects beggared description. The whole country was lighted by a searing light with the intensity many times that of the midday sun. It was golden, purple, violet, gray and blue. It lighted every peak, crevasse and ridge of the nearby mountain range with a clarity and beauty that cannot be described but must be seen to be imagined. It was that beauty the great poets dream about but describe most poorly and inadequately. Thirty seconds after the explosion came first, the air blast pressing hard against the people and things, to be followed almost immediately by the strong, sustained, awesome roar which warned of doomsday and made us feel that we puny things were blasphemous to dare tamper with the forces heretofore reserved to The Almighty. Words are inadequate tools for the job of acquainting those not present with the physical, mental and psychological effects. It had to be witnessed to be realized."

---

[1]At this point is the following manuscript interpolation by Groves: "an American and Harvard professor for many years".

12. My impressions of the night's high points follow:

After about an hour's sleep I got up at 0100 and from that time on until about five I was with Dr. Oppenheimer constantly. Naturally he was nervous, although his mind was working at its usual extraordinary efficiency. I devoted my entire attention to shielding him from the excited and generally faulty advice of his assistants who were more than disturbed by their excitement and the uncertain weather conditions. By 0330 we decided that we could probably fire at 0530. By 0400 the rain had stopped but the sky was heavily overcast. Our decision became firmer as time went on. During most of these hours the two of us journeyed from the control house out into the darkness to look at the stars and to assure each other that the one or two visible stars were becoming brighter. At 0510 I left Dr. Oppenheimer and returned to the main observation point which was 17,000 yards from the point of explosion. In accordance with our orders I found all personnel not otherwise occupied massed on a bit of high ground.

At about two minutes of the scheduled firing time all persons lay face down with their feet pointing towards the explosion. As the remaining time was called from the loud speaker from the 10,000 yard control station there was complete silence. Dr. Conant said he had never imagined seconds could be so long. Most of the individuals in accordance with orders shielded their eyes in one way or another. There was then this burst of light of a brilliance beyond any comparison. We all rolled over and looked through dark glasses at the ball of fire. About forty seconds later came the shock wave followed by the sound, neither of which seemed startling after our complete astonishment at the extraordinary lighting intensity. Dr. Conant reached over and we shook hands in mutual congratulations. Dr. Bush, who was on the other side of me, did likewise. The feeling of the entire assembly was similar to that described by General Farrell, with even the uninitiated feeling profound awe. Drs. Conant and Bush and myself were struck by an even stronger feeling that the faith of those who had been responsible for the initiation and the carrying on of this Herculean project had been justified. I personally thought of Blondin crossing Niagara Falls on his tight rope, only to me this tight rope had lasted for almost three years and of my repeated confident-appearing assurances that such a thing was possible and that we would do it.

13. A large group of observers were stationed at a point about 27 miles north of the point of explosion. Attached is a memorandum written shortly after the explosion by Dr. E. O. Lawrence which may be of interest.[2]

14. While General Farrell was waiting about midnight for a commercial airplane to Washington at Albuquerque—120 miles away from the site—he overheard several airport employees discussing their reaction to the blast. One said that he was out on the parking apron; it was quite dark; then the whole southern sky was lighted as though by a bright sun; the light lasted several seconds. Another remarked that if a few exploding bombs could have such an effect, it must be terrible to have them drop on a city.

[2]Not printed.

15. My liaison officer at the Alamogordo Air Base, 60 miles away, made the following report:

"There was a blinding flash of light that lighted the entire northwestern sky. In the center of the flash, there appeared to be a huge billow of smoke. The original flash lasted approximately 10 to 15 seconds. As the first flash died down, there arose in the approximate center of where the original flash had occurred an enormous ball of what appeared to be fire and closely resembled a rising sun that was three-fourths above a mountain. The ball of fire lasted approximately 15 seconds, then died down and the sky resumed an almost normal appearance.

"Almost immediately, a third, but much smaller, flash and billow of smoke of a whitish-orange color appeared in the sky, again lighting the sky for approximately 4 seconds. At the time of the original flash, the field was lighted well enough so that a newspaper could easily have been read. The second and third flashes were of much lesser intensity.

"We were in a glass-enclosed control tower some 70 feet above the ground and felt no concussion or air compression. There was no noticeable earth tremor although reports overheard at the Field during the following 24 hours indicated that some believed that they had both heard the explosion and felt some earth tremor."

16. I have not written a separate report for General Marshall as I feel you will want to show this to him. I have informed the necessary people here of our results. Lord Halifax after discussion with Mr. Harrison and myself stated that he was not sending a full report to his government at this time. I informed him that I was sending this to you and that you might wish to show it to the proper British representatives.

17. We are all fully conscious that our real goal is still before us. The battle test is what counts in the war with Japan.

18. May I express my deep personal appreciation for your congratulatory cable to us[3] and for the support and confidence which I have received from you ever since I have had this work under my charge.

19. I know that Colonel Kyle will guard these papers with his customary extraordinary care.

L R GROVES

[Enclosure 3]

BULLETIN[4]

Alamogordo, N. M., July 16—William O. Eareckson, commanding officer of the Alamogordo Army Air Base, made the following statement today:

"Several inquiries have been received concerning a heavy explosion which occurred on the Alamogordo Air Base reservation this morning.

"A remotely located ammunition magazine containing a considerable amount of high explosive and pyrotechnics exploded.

"There was no loss of life or injury to anyone, and the property damage outside of the explosives magazine itself was negligible.

"Weather conditions affecting the content of gas shells exploded by the blast may make it desirable for the Army to evacuate temporarily a few civilians from their homes."

[3]Not printed.
[4]Identified in the source copy as a clipping from *The Albuquerque Tribune* for July 16, 1945.

Thursday, July 19, 1945.

• • •

At twelve o'clock Lord Cherwell[1] called, and he and Bundy and I
sat out under the trees and talked over S-1. He was very reasonable on the
subject of notification to the Russians, feeling about as doubtful as we.
He reported Churchill as being much pleased with our luncheon together last
Monday and much cheered by the talk.

• • •

Later in the afternoon at a quarter to five McCloy, Bundy, and
I had a long and interesting discussion on our relations with Russia; what
the cause of the constant differences between the countries are, and how to
avoid them. As a result, I dictated a memorandum on the subject to serve
as a sort of analysis and possible basis for action. It boiled down to the
possibility of getting the Russians to see that the real basis of the evil
was the absence of freedom of speech in their regime, and the **iron-bound rule**
of the OGPU.[2] I have been very much impressed on this visit with the atmosphere of repression that exists everywhere, and which is felt by all who come
in contact with the Russian rule in Germany. While the Russian soldiers and
American soldiers seem to like each other individually when they meet, the
people who have to deal with the Russian officials feel very differently, and
it greatly impairs the cooperation between our two countries. Churchill is
very rampant about it, and most of our people who have seen the Russians most
intimately think we have been too easy and that they have taken advantage of it.

[1] Science adviser to British Prime Minister Winston Churchill.
[2] Russian secret police.

It is a very difficult problem because they are crusaders for their own system and suspicious of everybody outside trying to interfere with it. At the same time it is becoming more and more evident to me that a nation whose system rests upon free speech and all the elements of freedom, as does ours, cannot be sure of getting on permanently with a nation where speech is strictly controlled and where the government uses the iron hand of the secret police. The question is very important just now, and the development of S-1 is bringing it to a focus. I am beginning to feel that our committee which met in Washington on this subject and was so set upon opening communications with the Russians on the subject may have been thinking in a vacuum. Today's talk with McCloy and Bundy was a good one and opened up the situation.

TOP SECRET

NOTES OF THE INTERIM COMMITTEE MEETING
Thursday, 19 July 1945
10:00 A.M. - 1:15 P.M.

PRESENT:

Members of Committee

Dr. Vannevar Bush
Dr. Karl T. Compton
Dr. James B. Conant
Mr. George L. Harrison, Acting Chairman

By Invitation

Maj. Gen. Leslie R. Groves
Brig. Gen Kenneth C. Royall)
Mr. William L. Marbury   ) Consideration
Lt. George S. Allan   )   of IV.
Lt. George M. Duff, Jr.   )

I. RECOMMENDATIONS FROM SCIENTIFIC PANEL:

The Committee considered a memorandum prepared by

Dr. Bush in consultation with Dr. Conant which they proposed

should be sent by the Committee to the Scientific Panel. The

memorandum requested the Panel to study in some detail the

future program of research and development in this field with

particular reference to the scale of effort that should be planned

for in terms of scientific and technical personnel and financial

outlay. Dr. Bush explained that it was thought desirable to secure

at this time the recommendations of the Panel in detail so that the

Committee might gain a more specific understanding of the dimensions

of this subject and its implications to the scientific resources

of the nation and thus be in a position to consider the balance

that must be struck between this program and other fields of

scientific research in the post-war period. The Committee

agreed that, subject to minor verbal changes, the memorandum

should go forward from Mr. Harrison to the Scientific Panel.

TOP SECRET

TOP SECRET

- 2 -

II. <u>BUSH-CONANT MEMORANDUM CONCERNING INTERNATIONAL RELATIONS</u>:

<u>Drs. Bush and Conant</u> placed before the Committee a memorandum dealing with the question of establishing in the United Nations organization some mechanism for international control in this field. They pointed out in the discussion which followed that the memorandum constituted only a tentative proposal designed simply to raise the issue. In receiving the memorandum the Committee felt, as did Drs. Bush and Conant, that consideration of this question should be deferred until after the Potsdam Conference when the full Committee membership would be available.

III. <u>EXCHANGE OF CABLES WITH THE SECRETARY OF WAR</u>:

As a matter of information, Mr. Harrison read to the Committee his exchanges of cables with the Secretary of War regarding the outcome of the test. In this connection Mr. Harrison raised the question whether a letter of congratulations should be sent on behalf of the Secretary of War to Dr. Oppenheimer. The Committee unanimously <u>agreed</u> this should be done.

IV. <u>LEGISLATION</u>:

<u>Dr. Bush</u> reported that Senator Magnuson of Washington was that day introducing a bill which followed closely the recommendations made to the President in Dr. Bush's report "Science - The Endless Frontier." Senator Kilgore probably would also introduce a bill which would not follow the report so closely.

At this point General Royall and Mr. Marbury, and two lawyers from the Manhattan District, Lt. Allan and Lt. Duff, joined

TOP SECRET

TOP SECRET

- 3 -

the meeting to go over the draft bill which had been drawn up by
General Royall and Mr. Marbury. It was learned that Lts. Allan
and Duff had been working for some time in New York gathering
together materials pertaining to such legislation and had compiled
a most comprehensive document. It was felt that they would be
aided in their work by having the benefit of the Committee's
discussion of the Royall/Marbury draft.

   Mr. Harrison suggested that the Committee should not
concern itself at this time with a line by line consideration of
the bill but should confine its discussion to general principles.

   a. Name of Organization. It was agreed that the
organization established by legislation should be known
as the "Commission on Atomic Energy."

   b. Compensation. With regard to members of
the Commission it was felt that they should not receive
a salary but rather a per diem so as to avoid making the
positions susceptible to political pressure. With
regard to the administrator and deputy administrator
it was agreed that salaries should be on the order of
$15,000 and $12,000 respectively.

   c. Composition. While it was agreed that no
member should be named as a representative of any
particular agency or interest, some divergence of
view developed concerning the provision in the draft
for two Army and two Navy officers out of a total of
nine members. Dr. Bush favored a commission composed
only of civilians, as did Dr. Conant; while General

TOP SECRET

TOP SECRET

- 4 -

Royall pointed out that in view of the preponderance
of the military aspect of this field and the greater
likelihood of prompt Congressional action if this fact
were reflected in the composition of the Commission,
he felt that strong military representation was desirable.
Mr. Harrison suggested that the military interest would
probably be adequately protected by the existing provision
for a Military Board plus a new proviso to the effect that
the President should be empowered to turn this field over
to the military in time of war or threatened emergency.
General Groves expressed the view that it would be desirable
to provide that some members should have military experience
but not that such members necessarily serve as representatives
of the Services.

d.   Control Over Research in the Universities.
Dr. Conant expressed concern about the sweeping powers
given to the Commission over research. While he recognized
the need for control of the material, he felt that it should
be possible to devise some quantitative measure whereby
university laboratories could use material and conduct
experiments in this field without endangering national
security while at the same time preserving considerable
freedom to pursue basic research. Dr. Compton suggested
that such a measure might be devised in terms of energy
release. The Committee agreed that the bill should make
some positive statement requiring the Commission to define
some quantitative borderline. All agreed that the emphasis

TOP SECRET

TOP SECRET

- 5 -

should be in the direction of freedom of research in universities to an extent not incompatible with national security

    e. <u>Basic Research.</u> <u>Dr. Bush</u> strongly urged that the
bill should contain a positive statement of intent to the
effect that the Commission should normally depend on the
universities to carry forward the basic research program
in this field. He pointed out that unless this were done
the bill would be in direct conflict with his Foundation
bill, and would be a serious deterrent to the healthy advance
of fundamental knowledge in this field. The Committee was
in <u>general agreement</u> with this view.

    f. <u>Censorship</u>. <u>Dr. Bush</u> felt that the censorship
and security provisions of the bill were too broad. He
suggested that the law should permit any publication of
information in this field which did not endanger national
security and should require the Commission to draw up rules
which would implement this principle. It was <u>generally
agreed</u> that the advantage which the United States has in
this field might be lost if publication were too narrowly
restricted.

    g. <u>Patents</u>. It was <u>generally agreed</u> that the section
on patents should empower the Commission to impose secrecy
orders on patents and prevent issue if and when the Commission
determined such action was necessary in the national interest.

    h. <u>Assets of the Combined Development Trust</u>. It was
<u>agreed</u> that provision should be made in the law to empower
the Commission to take over American interests in any exist-

TOP SECRET

TOP SECRET

- 6 -

ing international agreements.

i. International Relations. Mr. Marbury pointed out that it was not necessary to spell out in the bill any powers with regard to entering into international agreements, for the power to enter into any treaties in this field would automatically stem from the law.

j. General Accounting Office. It was agreed that the bill should provide that the Commission would have relationships to the General Accounting Office similar to those of the TVA, namely, that while the Commission would be accountable to the GAO it should be empowered to certify that certain expenditures were necessary in the national interest and not subject to detailed accounting.

k. Miscellaneous. Other suggestions made by the Committee members were as follows:

(1) General Groves. -- In addition to the four Boards named in the bill the Commission should be empowered to name "such other boards" as in its discretion appear necessary.

(2) General Groves. -- The Administrator should operate under general rules laid down by the Commission; he should not be required to secure specific approval from the Commission for individual decisions.

(3) General Groves. -- It would not be possible to render a "complete" inventory of the holdings of the Manhattan District in three months as provided in the subject draft. The reporting period should also

TOP SECRET

TOP SECRET

- 7 -

be put on a fiscal rather than a calendar year basis.

(4) <u>Dr. Bush</u>. -- Clerical and administrative personnel should b e under Civil Service, but scientific, technical, and legal personnel should be exempt.

<u>General Royall</u> pointed out that the bill did not give the Commission any quasi-judicial power. The Committee <u>agreed</u> that it should not have such powers. The Committee also <u>agreed</u> with General Royall's view that no power need be given the Commission in the bill over exports and imports. It was <u>agreed</u> that the language of the law should permit the Commission to make payments for local taxes when circumstances so warranted.

It was <u>agreed</u> that Lts. Allan and Duff should redraft the bill so as to reflect the suggestions brought out at the meeting as well as the more extended comments which Dr. Bush and General Groves w ould prepare in writing.

V. <u>NEXT MEETING</u>:

No definite time was set for the next meeting. <u>Dr. Conant</u> suggested that 2 August would be desirable from his point of view.

R. Gordon Arneson

R. GORDON ARNESON
1st Lieutenant, AUS
Secretary to the Committee.

TOP SECRET

July 21, 1945

At eleven thirty-five General Groves special report was
received by special courier. It was an immensely powerful document, clearly and well written and with supporting documents of
the highest importance. It revealed far greater destructive
power than we expected in S1. While I was reading it with Bundy,
Joseph E. Davies came in by appointment, and I had to break off
and discuss with him matters purely related to a call of courtesy.
I talked with him of the character of the Russians as he had
observed it in his Ambassadorship in Russia, and he was a little
bit more encouraging than Harriman. But I had to break away as
quickly as I could in order to get back to the reading of the
report. I made an appointment with the President for as soon as
he could see me, which was at three thirty

• • •

At three o'clock I found that Marshall had returned from
the Joint Chiefs of Staff, and to save time I hurried to his house
and had him read Groves' report and conferred with him about it.

I then went to the 'Little White House' and saw President
Truman. I asked him to call in Secretary Byrnes and then I read
the report in its entirety and we then discussed it. They were

TOP SECRET

TOP SECRET

immensely pleased. Truman said it gave him an entirely new
feeling of confidence, and he thanked me for having come to
the Conference and being present to help him in this way.

I then left the 'Little White House', picked up Bundy, and
went to the Prime Minister's house where we conferred with him and
Lord Cherwell. I turned over the paper to Churchill and he began
reading it, but was interrupted a few minutes before five in order
to hurry to the Big Three Conference at five o'clock. He asked
me to return on the following morning to finish up the report.

Massage and dinner, and then in the evening about ten thirty,
two short cables came in from Harrison indicating that operations
would be ready **earlier** than expected, and also asking me to reverse
my decision as to one of the proposed topics. I cabled, saying I
saw no new factors for reversing myself, but, on the contrary, the
new factors seemed to confirm it.

<u>Sunday, 22 July 1945.</u>

Called on President Truman at nine twenty. The foregoing day
I had left with him my paper on reflections as to our relations
with Russia, copy of which is hereto attached. I had told him that
this paper was in no sense an official paper: that it did not
even contain my matured opinions, but that it represented an
analysis which I thought was correct and a program of what I
hoped might **s**ometime be done. With that understanding he asked
me to see it and I left it with him, and this morning picked it
up. He gave it to me, stating he had read it and agreed with it.

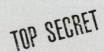

TOP SECRET

I also discussed with him Harrison's two messages. He was
intensely pleased by the accelerated timetable. As to the
matter of the special target which I had refused to permit,
he strongly confirmed my view, and said he felt the same way.

At ten forty Bundy and I again went to the British
headquarters and talked to the Prime Minister and Lord Cherwell
for over an hour. Churchill read Groves' report in full. He
told me that he had noticed at the meeting of the three yesterday,
Truman was evidently much fortified by something that had happened,
and that he stood up to the Russians in a most emphatic and
decisive manner, telling them as to certain demands that they
absolutely could not have, and that the United States was entirely
against them. Churchill said he now understood how this pepping
up had taken place and that he felt the same way. His own attitude
confirmed this admission. He now not only was not worried about
giving the Russians information of the matter, but was rather
inclined to use it as an argument in our favor in the negotiations.
The sentiment of the four of us was unanimous in thinking that it
was advisable to tell the Russians at least that we were working
                         if and when it was successfully
on that subject, and intended to use it ~~until~~ finished.

At twelve fifteen I called General Arnold over, showed him
Harrison's two cables, showed him my answer to them and showed
him Groves' report, which he read in its entirety. He told me
that he agreed with me about the target which I had struck off
the program. He said that it would take considerable hard work
to organize the operations now that it was to move forward.

TOP SECRET

Reflections on the Basic Problems which Confront us

1. With each International Conference that passes and, in fact, with each month that passes between conferences, it becomes clearer that the great basic problem of the future is the stability of the relations of the Western democracies with Russia.

2. With each such time that passes it also becomes clear that that problem arises out of the fundamental differences between a nation of free thought, free speech, free elections, in fact, a really free people with a nation which is not basically free but which is systematically controlled from above by Secret Police and in which free speech is not permitted.

3. It also becomes clear that no permanently safe international relations can be established between two such fundamentally different national systems. With the best of efforts we cannot understand each other. Furthermore, in an autocratically controlled system, policy cannot be permanent. It is tied up with the life of one man. Even if a measure of mental accord is established with one head the resulting agreement is liable to be succeeded by an entirely different policy coming from a different successor.

4. Daily we find our best efforts for coordination and sympathetic understanding with Russia thwarted by the suspicion which basically and necessarily must exist in any controlled organization of man.

5. Thus every effort we make at permanent organization of such a world composed of two such radically different systems is subject to frustration by misunderstandings arising out of mutual suspicion.

6. The great problem ahead is how to deal with this basic difference which exists as a flaw in our desired accord. I believe we must not accept

the present situation as permanent for the result will then almost
inevitably be a new war and the destruction of our civilization.

I believe we should direct our thoughts constantly to the
time and method of attacking the basic difficulty and the means we may
have in hand to produce results. That something can be accomplished is
not an idle dream. STALIN has shown an indication of his appreciation
of our system of freedom by his proposal of a free constitution to be
established among the Soviets. To read this Constitution would lead one
to believe that Russia had in mind the establishing of free speech, free
assembly, free press and the other essential elements of our Bill of Rights
and would not have forever resting upon every citizen the stifling hand of
autocracy. He has thus given us an opening.

The questions are:

a. When can we take any steps without doing more harm
than good?

b. By what means can we proceed?

1. By private diplomatic discussion of the reasons for
our distrust.

2. By encouraging open public discussions.

3. By setting conditions for any concessions which
Russia may ask in respect to –

(a) Territorial concessions

(b) Loans

(c) Bases

(d) Any other concessions.

How far these conditions can extend is a serious problem. At the start it may be possible to effect only some amelioration of the local results of ^{R}ussia's Secret Police State.

_7._ The foregoing has a vital bearing upon the control of the vast and revolutionary discovery of ___X_____ which is now confronting us. Upon the successful control of that energy depends the future successful development or destruction of the modern civilized world. The Committee appointed by the War Department which has been considering that control has pointed this out in no uncertain terms and has called for an international organization for that purpose. After careful reflection I am of the belief that _no_ world organization containing as one of its dominant members a nation whose people are not possessed of free speech but whose governmental action is controlled by the autocratic machinery of a secret political police, cannot give effective control of this new agency with its devastating possibilities.

I therefore believe that before we share our new discovery with Russia we should consider carefully whether we can do so safely under any system of control until Russia puts into effective action the proposed constitution which I have mentioned. If this is a necessary condition, we must go slowly in any disclosures or agreeing to any Russian participation whatsoever and constantly explore the question how our head-start in ___X___ and the Russian desire to participate can be used to bring us nearer to the removal of the basic difficulties which I have emphasized.

TOP SECRET

Monday, 23 July 1945.

At ten o'clock Secretary Byrnes called me up, asking me
as to the timing of the S1 program. I told him the effect of
the two cables, and that I would try to get further definite
news. I dictated a cable to Harrison asking him to let us know
immediately when the time was fixed.

At ten fifteen Ambassador Harriman arrived, and he and
McCloy, Bundy, and I had a talk over the situation, Harriman
giving us the information of yesterday afternoon's meetings.
He commented on the increasing cheerfulness evidently caused
by the news from us, and confirmed the expanding demands being
made by the Russians. They are throwing aside all their previous
restraint as to being only a Continental power and not interested
in any further acquisitions, and are now apparently seeking to
branch in all directions. Thus they have not only been vigorously
seeking to extend their influence in Poland, Austria, Rumania,
and Bulgaria, but they are seeking bases in Turkey and now are
putting in demands for the Italian colonies in the Mediterranean
and elsewhere. He told us that Stalin had brought up yesterday
the question of Korea again and was urging an immediate trusteeship. The British and the French are refusing to consider a
trusteeship on Hong Kong and Indo-China, and I foresee that if
that is continued, the Russians will probably drop their proposal
for trusteeship of Korea and ask for solitary control of it.

- 14 -

TOP SECRET

TOP SECRET

At eleven o'clock I went down to the 'Little White House' to try to see the President or Byrnes. I am finding myself crippled by not knowing what happens in the meetings in the late afternoon and evening. This is particularly so now that the program for S1 is tying in what we are doing in all fields. When I got there I found Byrnes out, and I asked for the President who saw me at once. I told him that it would be much more conven- ient for me to form my program on the military side if I could drop in early every morning and talk with him or Byrnes of the events of the preceding day. He told me at once to come; that he would be glad to see me every morning and talk over these matters with me. I then told him of matters that came up in the conference with Mr. Harriman this morning which I just referred to, and told him that I had sent for further, more definite, information as to the time of operation from Harrison. He told me that he had the warning message which we prepared on his desk, and had accepted our most recent change in it, and that he proposed to shoot it out as soon as he heard the definite day of the operation. We had a brief discussion about Stalin's recent expansions and he confirmed what I have heard. But he told me that the United States was standing firm and he was apparently relying greatly upon the information as to S1. He evidently thinks a good deal of the new claims of the Russians are bluff, and told me what he thought the real claims were confined to.

After lunch and a short rest I received Generals Marshall and Arnold, and had in McCloy and Bundy at the conference. The Presi-

TOP SECRET

TOP SECRET

dent had told me at a meeting in the morning that he was very
anxious to know whether Marshall felt that we needed the Russians
in the war or whether we could get along without them, and that
was one of the subjects we talked over. Of course Marshall could
not answer directly or explicitly. We had desired the Russians to
come into the war originally for the sake of holding up in Manchuria
the Japanese Manchurian Army. That was now being accomplished as
the Russians have amassed their forces on that border, Marshall said,
and were poised, and the Japanese were moving up positions in their
Army. But he pointed out that even if we went ahead in the war
without the Russians, and compelled the Japanese to surrender to
our terms, that would not prevent the Russians from marching into
Manchuria anyhow and striking, thus permitting them to get virtually
what they wanted in the surrender terms. Marshall told us during
our conference that he thought thus far in the military conference
they had handled only the British problems and that these are
practically all settled now and probably would be tied up and
finished tomorrow. He suggested that it might be a good thing,
something which would call the Russians to a decision one way
or the other, if the President would say to Stalin tomorrow
that "inasmuch as the British have finished and are going home,
I suppose I might as well let the American Chiefs of Staff go
away also" that might bring the Russians to make known what
their position wasand what they were going to do, and of course,
that indicated that Marshall felt as I felt sure he would, that

- 16 -

TOP SECRET

TOP SECRET

now with our new weapon we would not need the assistance of the
Russians to conquer Japan.

There was further talk about the war in the Pacific in the
conference. Apparently they have been finding it very hard to
get along with MacArthur, and Marshall has been spending most of
his time in conferences in smoothing down the Navy.

I talked to Marshall about the preparation of S1 and he gave
us a bad picture of the rainy season weather in Japan at this time,
and said that one thing that might militate against our attack was
the low ceiling and heavy clouds, although there were breaks and
good days in between.

After the conference I took a short drive with Col. Kyle
accompanied by Captain Cabilia, Russian interpreter, past the
Potsdam marshalling yards to the Schloss Cecilienhof. This
Schloss was where the meetings of the present Conference were
held. The drive was a refreshing one.

In the evening I received a telegram from Harrison giving
me the exact dates as far as possible when they expected to have
S1 ready, and I answered it with a further question as to further
future dates of the possibility of accumulation of supplies.

<u>Tuesday, 24 July 1944.</u>

At nine twenty I went to the Little White House and was at
once shown into the President's room where he was alone with his
work, and he told me about the events of yesterday's meeting

- 17 -

TOP SECRET

with which he seemed to be very well satisfied. I then told him
of my conference with Marshall and the implication that could be
inferred as to his feeling that the Russians were not needed.
I also told the President of the question which Marshal had
suggested might be put to Stalin as to the Americans going home,
and he said that he would do that this afternoon at the end of
the hearing, but he told me that there had been a meeting called
by Leahy of the Military Staffs to meet either this afternoon,
and, I think, tomorrow morning.

The President was frank about his desire to close the
Conference and get away. He told me Churchill was going away
Wednesday and was coming back Friday, and that he hoped to get
the whole thing closed up and get away either Sunday or Monday.
I told him that I thought I had done all that I could see in
sight, and that as Churchill was going away, I was thinking of
going down to see Patton's troops in Bavaria for a day or so,
and then if he did not telegraph me that he would like me to
come back, I thought I would go on home. He said that arrangement
was perfectly agreeable to him, and if he wanted to have me come
back, he would let me know at Patton's.

I then showed him the telegram which had come last evening
from Harrison giving the dates of the operations. He said that
was just what he wanted, that he was highly delighted and that
it gave him his cue for his warning. He said he had just sent
his warning to Chiang Kai Shek[1] to see if he would join in it,
and as soon as that was cleared by Chiang, he, Truman, would

- 18 -

TOP SECRET

[1]President of the Republic of China.

TOP SECRET

release the warning and that would fit right in time with the program we had received from Harrison.

I then spoke of the importance which I attributed to the reassurance of the Japanese on the continuance of their dynasty, and I had felt that the insertion of that in the formal warning was important and might be just the thing that would make or mar their acceptance, but that I had heard from Byrnes that they preferred not to put it in, and that now such a change was made impossible by the sending of the message to Chiang. I hoped that the President would watch carefully so that the Japanese might be reassured verbally through diplomatic channels if it was found that they were hanging fire on that one point. He said that he had that in mind, and that he would take care of it.

We had a few words more about the S1 program, and I again gave him my reasons for eliminating one of the proposed targets.[1] He again reiterated with the utmost emphasis his own concurring belief on that subject, and he was particularly emphatic in agreeing with my suggestion that if elimination was not done, the bitterness which would be caused by such a wanton act might make it impossible during the long post war period to reconcile the Japanese to us in that area rather than to the Russians. It might thus, I pointed out, be the means of preventing what our policy demanded, namely, a sympathetic Japan to the United States in case there should be any aggression by Russia in Manchuria.

TOP SECRET

[2]Kyoto, a Japanese cultural center.

Proclamation Defining Terms for the Japanese Surrender, Signed at Potsdam and Issued by the President of the United States (Truman) and the Prime Minister of the United Kingdom (Attlee) and Concurred in by the President of the National Government of China (Chiang), July 26, 1945.

(1) We—the President of the United States, the President of the National Government of the Republic of China, and the Prime Minister of Great Britain, representing the hundreds of millions of our countrymen, have conferred and agree that Japan shall be given an opportunity to end this war.

(2) The prodigious land, sea and air forces of the United States, the British Empire and of China, many times reinforced by their armies and air fleets from the west, are poised to strike the final blows upon Japan. This military power is sustained and inspired by the determination of all the Allied Nations to prosecute the war against Japan until she ceases to resist.

(3) The result of the futile and senseless German resistance to the might of the aroused free peoples of the world stands forth in awful clarity as an example to the people of Japan. The might that now converges on Japan is immeasurably greater than that which, when applied to the resisting. Nazis, necessarily laid waste to the lands, the industry and the method of life of the whole German people. The full application of our military power, backed by our resolve, *will* mean the inevitable and complete destruction of the Japanese armed forces and just as inevitably the utter devastation of the Japanese homeland.

(4) The time has come for Japan to decide whether she will continue to be controlled by those self-willed militaristic advisers whose unintelligent calculations have brought the Empire of Japan to the threshold of annihilation, or whether she will follow the path of reason.

(5) Following are our terms. We will not deviate from them. There are no alternatives. We shall brook no delay.

(6) There must be eliminated for all time the authority and influence of those who have deceived and misled the people of Japan into embarking on world conquest, for we insist that a new order of peace, security and justice will be impossible until irresponsible militarism is driven from the world.

(7) Until such a new order is established *and* until there is convincing proof that Japan's war-making power is destroyed, points in Japanese territory to be designated by the Allies shall be occupied to secure the achievement of the basic objectives we are here setting forth.

(8) The terms of the Cairo Declaration[1] shall be carried out and Japanese sovereignty shall be limited to the islands of Honshu, Hokkaido, Kyushu, Shikoku and such minor islands as we determine.

(9) The Japanese military forces, after being completely disarmed, shall be permitted to return to their homes with the opportunity to lead peaceful and productive lives.

(10) We do not intend that the Japanese shall be enslaved as a race or destroyed as a nation, but stern justice shall be meted out to all war criminals, including those who have visited cruelties upon our prisoners. The Japanese Government shall remove all obstacles to the revival and strengthening of democratic tendencies among the Japanese people. Freedom of speech, of religion, and of thought, as well as respect for the fundamental human rights shall be established.

TOP SECRET

[1] The allied policy of unconditional surrender established at the Cairo summit (1943).

(11) Japan shall be permitted to maintain such industries as will sustain her economy and permit the exaction of just reparations in kind, but not those which would enable her to re-arm for war. To this end, access to, as distinguished from control of, raw materials shall be permitted. Eventual Japanese participation in world trade relations shall be permitted.

(12) The occupying forces of the Allies shall be withdrawn from Japan as soon as these objectives have been accomplished and there has been established in accordance with the freely expressed will of the Japanese people a peacefully inclined and responsible government.

(13) We call upon the government of Japan to proclaim now that unconditional surrender of all Japanese armed forces, and to provide proper and adequate assurances of their good faith in such action. The alternative for Japan is prompt and utter destruction.

```
28 July 1945                                European Trip
   ...He (Mr. Truman) said he was being very realistic with
the Russians and found Stalin not difficult to do business with.
I asked who he thought would be Stalin's successor, but he
said that he doubted if anyone knew.  He felt that when that
time came there would be revolution in Russia and a struggle
for power.  Stalin regards all dictatorships except his own as
dangerous, particularly Franco's.¹ He referred to an effort on
Russia's part to draw the distinction between good and bad
dictators.  "This, however, is a distinction without a difference."

                        . . . .


   Talked with Byrnes (now at Potsdam as American Secretary
of State, having succeeded Mr. Stettinius on the conclusion of
the San Francisco Conference)....Byrnes said he was most
anxious to get the Japanese affair over with before the Rus-
sians got in, with particular reference to Dairen and Port Ar-
thur.  Once in there, he felt, it would not be easy to get them
out

                        . . . .
```

¹The fascist regime of Francisco Franco in Spain.

PART 6

Truman's memoir account of events leading to the drop on Hiroshima. A victim describes the atomic bombing of Hiroshima. Russian declaration of war against Japan. Bombing of Nagasaki. U.S. Strategic Bombing Survey reports on effects of the atomic bombs. Japan's surrender.

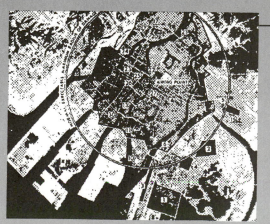
Diagram of damaged area of Hiroshima

The Drops and the Surrender of Japan

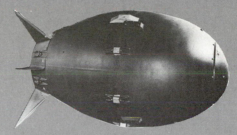

"Little Boy"

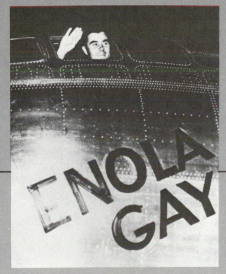

"Fat Man"

The Enola Gay

Truman announcing Japanese surrender
and end of World War 2

Ο

ne of the most vexing and persistent historical problems of the Second World War is Japan's decision to surrender. The complex and mannered nature of Japanese politics, the suicidal quality of Japanese warfare, the unprecedented intervention of the Emperor, and Russia's last-minute declaration of war make the defeat of Japan an irresistible subject for speculation.

The atomic bomb must enter into any discussion of Japan's final days. The devastation it wrought naturally has enhanced the allure of other options. A uranium bomb (nicknamed Little Boy) destroyed Hiroshima with a force equal to 13,500 tons of TNT. The city was not the exclusively military target President Truman had hoped to attack. Most of its 350,000 residents were civilians. It was a center of communications, a storage area, and an assembly point for troops. It was also headquarters of the Second Army, responsible for the defense of southern Japan. By August 1945, approximately 43,000 soldiers were stationed there. The atomic blast, coupled with the ensuing fires and radiation, killed about 140,000 by the end of 1945.[1]

Nagasaki was the target of the second atomic bomb (a plutonium weapon nicknamed Fat Man). In fact, the city was doomed by cloud cover over the primary objective, the Kokura Arsenal on the coast of Kyushu. Unlike Hiroshima, there was no question of Nagasaki's military value. It was a vital port, the "San Francisco of Japan," and a shipbuilding center, where the Mitsubishi torpedoes that had sunk the American fleet at Pearl Harbor were manufactured. Its hilly terrain and many concrete structures reduced the impact of the blast. With a force roughly equivalent to Little Boy's, Fat Man killed fewer people—between 60,000 and 70,000 of the nearly 240,000 residents.[2]

Such terrible effects have compelled analysts to make a microscopic examination of the use of the weapon. Among the questions they have asked: What role did the two atomic bombs play in the fall of Japan? Might dropping them have been avoided? Were two bombs required? Did President Truman and his advisers, well aware of Japanese exhaustion, order the atomic attacks simply to impress the Russians with a massive display of new American power?

There are no conclusive answers. Japan had been maneuvering for peace since early 1945. The primary stumbling blocks were the Allied insistence on unconditional surrender and the Japanese demand for retention of their Emperor. As it turned out, a diplomatic bargain was struck, albeit implicitly. While severely restricting the Emperor's status, the Allies accepted his continued existence (see Document 87). Perhaps a negotiated settlement could have been reached earlier if the demand for unconditional surrender had been abandoned.

Here the strength of the peace faction within the Japanese government must be measured. Even historians critical of Allied atomic policy, such as Barton Bernstein and Martin J. Sherwin, have conceded that the bombing of Hiroshima provided a needed catalyst for the advocates of peace and for the

[1]Among the casualties were twenty American airmen held as prisoners of war.
[2]Richard Rhodes reports a last-minute effort to warn Japanese citizens of impending atomic destruction in the wake of the bombing of Hiroshima. On August 8, 1945, Allied radio stations at Saipan began braodcasting a message at fifteen-minute intervals describing the atomic bomb and threatening its continued use. In addition, 6 million leaflets were ordered to be dropped on forty-seven cities with populations over 100,000. Printing the leaflets took so much time that Nagasaki did not receive its full share until August 10, 1945, the day after the second bomb was dropped.

unprecedented intervention of Emperor Hirohito. The Emperor himself had to break the cabinet deadlock. Even then, fanatical army officers attempted a last-minute coup at the imperial palace in Tokyo to avoid the shameful surrender.

Between the bombings of Hiroshima and Nagasaki, another element became part of the far eastern equation—Russia. Japanese leaders had been counting on Soviet neutrality while they bargained with the other Allies, but on August 8, 1945, two days after Hiroshima was bombed, Russia declared war on Japan. Perhaps the Russian declaration itself could have tipped the final balance in favor of peace. The emerging historical consensus is that two bombs—in addition to Russian participation—were probably unnecessary.

Some critics have even suggested that the second atomic attack was launched to minimize the impact of Russian entry. Yet as historian Mark H. Lytle has argued, the atomic bombing of Nagasaki was actually the result of standard military operating procedure. In the closing phases of the operation, control over precise targets automatically shifted from Washington to the staging island of Tinian in the Marianas, where meteorological and other conditions could be assessed quickly and accurately. The only instructions received from the Pentagon were to deliver the "first special bomb as soon as weather will permit visual bombing after about 3 August 1945 on one of the targets: Hiroshima, Kokura, Niigata and Nagasaki. . . . Additional bombs will be delivered on the above targets as soon as made ready by the project staff" (see Document 76). "It was weather," Lytle concludes, "and not diplomatic or military strategy, that sealed Nagasaki's fate."

Maybe Japan could have been beaten by conventional air and sea power—without Russia, the atomic bombs, or an invasion of the home islands. If so, it is hard to imagine how continued aerial bombardment and a naval blockade would have cost fewer lives than the two atomic bombs. A single incendiary air strike on Tokyo in March 1945 killed 84,000 Japanese, injured another 41,000, and burned out nearly sixteen square miles of the city. It is also helpful to remember that strategic bombing by itself failed to defeat Germany, which was subjected to a more intensive aerial campaign than Japan. German production actually increased until the last few weeks of fighting. The infantry, along with air and sea assaults, was needed to end the war in Europe. Whether Japan would have surrendered without the atomic attacks or an invasion remains uncertain.

We do know, as Peter Wyden reveals in *Day One: Before Hiroshima and After* (1984), that American authorities thought it might require as many as fifty nuclear bombs to force Japan out of the war. Two bombs were available by mid-August 1945, with a third on the verge of shipment to the South Pacific staging island. According to Wyden, the United States was prepared to manufacture more of the plutonium weapons in assembly-line fashion at the rate of at least seven per month. They were scheduled to be used as soon as possible.

Whether such plans ever would have been put into effect is also a matter of conjecture, which hinges partly on an assessment of Harry Truman. Truman had no doubts and showed no remorse about dropping the weapon on Hiroshima and Nagasaki. "When you have to deal with a beast," he later wrote the Federal Council of Churches in defense of his decision, "you have to treat him as a beast. . . ." Yet it is also clear from the record that after Nagasaki, Truman also had no stomach for more carnage. According to Secretary of Commerce Henry A. Wallace, Truman ordered a halt to the atomic bombing because "the thought of wiping out another 100,000 people was too horrible. He didn't like the idea of killing, as he said, 'all those kids' " (see Document 86).

Chapter 26

The historic message of the first explosion of an atomic bomb was flashed to me in a message from Secretary of War Stimson on the morning of July 16. The most secret and the most daring enterprise of the war had succeeded. We were now in possession of a weapon that would not only revolutionize war but could alter the course of history and civilization. This news reached me at Potsdam the day after I had arrived for the conference of the Big Three.

Preparations were being rushed for the test atomic explosion at Alamogordo, New Mexico, at the time I had to leave for Europe, and on the voyage over I had been anxiously awaiting word on the results. I had been told of many predictions by the scientists, but no one was certain of the outcome of this full-scale atomic explosion. As I read the message from Stimson, I realized that the test not only met the most optimistic expectation of the scientists but that the United States had in its possession an explosive force of unparalleled power.

Stimson flew to Potsdam the next day to see me and brought with him the full details of the test. I received him at once and called in Secretary of State Byrnes, Admiral Leahy, General Marshall, General Arnold, and Admiral King to join us at my office at the Little White House. We reviewed our military strategy in the light of this revolutionary development. We were not ready to make use of this weapon against the Japanese, although we did not know as yet what effect the new weapon might have, physically or psychologically, when used against the enemy. For that reason the military advised that we go ahead with the existing military plans for the invasion of the Japanese home islands.

At Potsdam, as elsewhere, the secret of the atomic bomb was kept closely guarded. We did not extend the very small circle of Americans who knew about it. Churchill naturally knew about the atomic bomb project from its very beginning, because it had involved the pooling of British and American technical skill.

On July 24 I casually mentioned to Stalin that we had a new weapon of unusual destructive force. The Russian Premier showed no special interest. All he said was that he was glad to hear it and hoped we would make "good use of it against the Japanese."

A month before the test explosion of the atomic bomb the service Secretaries and the Joint Chiefs of Staff had laid their detailed plans for the defeat of Japan before me for approval. There had apparently been some differences of opinion as to the best route to be followed, but these had evidently been reconciled, for when General Marshall had presented his plan for a two-phase invasion of Japan, Admiral King and General Arnold had supported the proposal heartily.

The Army plan envisaged an amphibious landing in the fall of 1945 on the island of Kyushu, the southernmost of the Japanese home islands. This would be accomplished by our Sixth Army, under the command of General Walter Krueger. The first landing would then be followed approximately four months later by a second great invasion, which would be carried out by our Eighth and Tenth Armies, followed by the First Army transferred from Europe, all of which would go ashore in the Kanto plains area near Tokyo. In all, it had been estimated that it would require until the late fall of 1946 to bring Japan to her knees.

This was a formidable conception, and all of us realized fully that the fighting would be fierce and the losses heavy. But it was hoped that some of Japan's forces would continue to be preoccupied in China and others would be prevented from reinforcing the home islands if Russia were to enter the war.

There was, of course, always the possibility that the Japanese might choose to surrender sooner. Our air and fleet units had begun to inflict heavy damage on industrial and urban sites in Japan proper. Except in China, the armies of the

Mikado had been pushed back everywhere in relentless successions of defeats.

Acting Secretary of State Grew had spoken to me in late May about issuing a proclamation that would urge the Japanese to surrender but would assure them that we would permit the Emperor to remain as head of the state. Grew backed this with arguments taken from his ten years' experience as our Ambassador in Japan, and I told him that I had already given thought to this matter myself and that it seemed to me a sound idea. Grew had a draft of a proclamation with him, and I instructed him to send it by the customary channels to the Joint Chiefs and the State-War-Navy Co-ordinating Committee in order that we might get the opinions of all concerned before I made my decision.

On June 18 Grew reported that the proposal had met with the approval of his Cabinet colleagues and of the Joint Chiefs. The military leaders also discussed the subject with me when they reported the same day. Grew, however, favored issuing the proclamation at once, to coincide with the closing of the campaign on Okinawa, while the service chiefs were of the opinion that we should wait until we were ready to follow a Japanese refusal with the actual assault of our invasion forces.

It was my decision then that the proclamation to Japan should be issued from the forthcoming conference at Potsdam. This, I believed, would clearly demonstrate to Japan and to the world that the Allies were united in their purpose. By that time, also, we might know more about two matters of significance for our future effort: the participation of the Soviet Union and the atomic bomb. We knew that the bomb would receive its first test in mid-July. If the test of the bomb was successful, I wanted to afford Japan a clear chance to end the fighting before we made use of this newly gained power. If the test should fail, then it would be even more important to us to bring about a surrender before we had to make a physical conquest of Japan. General Marshall told me that it might cost half a million American lives to force the enemy's surrender on his home grounds.

My own knowledge of these developments had come about only after I became President, when Secretary Stimson had given me the full story. He had told me at that time that the project was nearing completion and that a bomb could be expected within another four months. It was at his suggestion, too, that I had then set up a committee of top men and had asked them to study with great care the implications the new weapon might have for us.

Secretary Stimson headed this group as chairman, and the other members were George L. Harrison, president of the New York Life Insurance Company, who was then serving as a special assistant to the Secretary of War; James F. Byrnes, as my personal representative; Ralph A. Bard, Under Secretary of the Navy; Assistant Secretary William L. Clayton for the State Department; and three of our most renowned scientists—Dr. Vannevar Bush, president of the Carnegie Institution of Washington and Director of the Office of Scientific Research and Development; Dr. Karl T. Compton, president of the Massachusetts Institute of Technology and Chief of Field Service in the Office of Scientific Research and Development; and Dr. James B. Conant, president of Harvard University and chairman of the National Defense Research Committee.

This committee was assisted by a group of scientists, of whom those most prominently connected with the development of the atomic bomb were Dr. Oppenheimer, Dr. Arthur H. Compton, Dr. E. O. Lawrence, and the Italian-born Dr. Enrico Fermi. The conclusions reached by these men, both in the advisory committee of scientists and in the larger committee, were brought to me by Secretary Stimson on June 1.

It was their recommendation that the bomb be used against the enemy as soon as it could be done. They recommended further that it should be used without specific warning and against a target that would clearly show its devastating strength. I had realized, of course, that an atomic bomb explosion would inflict damage and casualties beyond imagination. On the other hand, the scientific advisers of the committee reported, "We can propose no technical demonstration likely to bring an end to the war; we see no acceptable alternative to direct military use." It was their conclusion that no technical demonstration they might propose, such as over a deserted island, would be likely to bring the war to an end. It had to be used against an enemy target.

The final decision of where and when to use the atomic bomb was up to me. Let there be no mistake about it. I regarded the bomb as a military weapon and never had any doubt that it should be used. The top military advisers to the President recommended its use, and when I talked to Churchill he unhesitatingly told me that he favored the use of the atomic bomb if it might aid to end the war.

In deciding to use this bomb I wanted to make sure that it would be used as a weapon of war in the manner prescribed by the laws of war. That meant that I wanted it dropped on a military target. I had told Stimson that the bomb should be dropped as nearly as possibly upon a war production center of prime military importance.

Stimson's staff had prepared a list of cities in Japan that might serve as targets. Kyoto, though favored by General Arnold as a center of military activity, was eliminated when Secretary Stimson pointed out that it was a cultural and religious shrine of the Japanese.

Four cities were finally recommended as targets: Hiroshima, Kokura, Niigata, and Nagasaki. They were listed in that order as targets for the first attack. The order of selection was in accordance with the military importance of these cities, but allowance would be given for weather conditions at the time of the bombing. Before the selected targets were approved as proper for military purposes, I personally went over them in detail with Stimson, Marshall, and Arnold, and we discussed the matter of timing and the final choice of the first target.

General Spaatz, who commanded the Strategic Air Forces, which would deliver the bomb on the target, was given some latitude as to when and on which of the four targets the bomb would be dropped. That was necessary because of weather and other operational considerations. In order to get preparations under way, the War Department was given orders to instruct General Spaatz that the first bomb would be dropped as soon after August 3 as weather would permit. The order to General Spaatz read as follows:

24 July 1945

To: General Carl Spaatz
Commanding General
United States Army Strategic Air Forces

1. The 509 Composite Group, 20th Air Force will deliver its first special bomb as soon as weather will permit visual bombing after about 3 August 1945 on one of the targets: Hiroshima, Kokura, Niigata and Nagasaki. To carry military and civilian scientific personnel from the War Department to observe and record the effects of the explosion of the bomb, additional aircraft will accompany the airplane carrying the bomb. The observing planes will stay several miles distant from the point of impact of the bomb.

2. Additional bombs will be delivered on the above targets as soon as made ready by the project staff. Further instructions will be issued concerning targets other than those listed above.

3. Dissemination of any and all information concerning the use of the weapon against Japan is reserved to the Secretary of War and the President of the United States. No communique on the subject or release of information will be issued by Commanders in the field without specific prior authority. Any news stories will be sent to the War Department for special clearance.

4. The foregoing directive is issued to you by direction and with the approval of the Secretary of War and the Chief of Staff, U.S.A. It is desired that you personally deliver one copy of this directive to General MacArthur and one copy to Admiral Nimitz for their information.

/s/ THOS. T. HANDY
General, GSC
Acting Chief of Staff

With this order the wheels were set in motion for the first use of an atomic weapon against a military target. I had made the decision. I also instructed Stimson that the order would stand unless I notified him that the Japanese reply to our ultimatum was acceptable.

A specialized B-29 unit, known as the 509th Composite Group, had been selected for the task, and seven of the modified B-29's, with pilots and crews, were ready and waiting for orders. Meanwhile ships and planes were rushing the materials for the bomb and specialists to assemble them to the Pacific island of Tinian in the Marianas.

On July 28 Radio Tokyo announced that the Japanese government would continue to fight. There was no formal reply to the joint ultimatum of the United States, the United Kingdom, and China. There was no alternative now. The bomb was scheduled to be dropped after August 3 unless Japan surrendered before that day.

On August 6, the fourth day of the journey home from Potsdam, came the historic news that shook the world. I was eating lunch with members of the *Augusta's* crew when Captain Frank Graham, White House Map Room watch officer, handed me the following message:

TO THE PRESIDENT
FROM THE SECRETARY OF WAR

Big bomb dropped on Hiroshima August 5 at 7:15 P.M. Washington time. First reports indicate complete success which was even more conspicuous than earlier test.

I was greatly moved. I telephoned Byrnes aboard ship to give him the news and then said to the group of sailors around me, "This is the greatest thing in history. It's time for us to get home."

"All the News That's Fit to Print"

The New York Times.

LATE CITY EDITION
Partly cloudy, less humid today. Cloudy and warm tomorrow.
Temperatures Yesterday—Max., 72; Min., 66
Sunrise today, 5:17 A. M.; Sunset, 8:06 P. M.

VOL. XCIV..No. 31,972. Entered as Second-Class Matter, Postoffice, New York, N. Y. NEW YORK, TUESDAY, AUGUST 7, 1945. THREE CENTS IN NEW YORK CITY

FIRST ATOMIC BOMB DROPPED ON JAPAN; MISSILE IS EQUAL TO 20,000 TONS OF TNT; TRUMAN WARNS FOE OF A 'RAIN OF RUIN'

HIRAM W. JOHNSON, REPUBLICAN DEAN IN THE SENATE, DIES

Isolationist Helped Prevent U. S. Entry Into League—Opposed World Charter

CALIFORNIA EX-GOVERNOR

Ran for Vice President With Theodore Roosevelt in '12—In Washington Since '17

Special to The New York Times.

WASHINGTON, Aug. 6—Senator Hiram Warren Johnson of California lifelong isolationist who helped prevent this country's entry into the League of Nations and fought all "foreign entanglements" through a second World War, died in his sleep this morning at Bethesda Naval Hospital, nine days after, ill but consistent, he had paired his vote against ratification of the United Nations Charter. Death was caused by a thrombosis of a cerebral artery. Mrs. Johnson was with him when the end came.

When word reached the Capitol of the passing of the oldest member of the Senate in point of service, save Senator Kenneth McKellar, the President pro tempore, the mourning was deep. With great personal affection colleagues paid humble tribute to his integrity of character, his liberalism and his steadfastness to his ideals and convictions. They joined in declaring that the country had lost a great statesman.

Senator Johnson, who was serving the fourth year of his fifth term in the Senate, would have been 79 years old on Sept. 2. Although his health had been failing during the last two years and though the thundering voice which had conveyed his eloquence through innumerable stirring debates had become little more than a whisper, friends believed he planned to seek a sixth term in 1947.

He went to the hospital July 13. Five days before that he had cast the lone vote in the Foreign Relations Committee, of which he was the ranking minority member, against reporting the new World Charter to the Senate without change. He did not participate in the floor debate on this document, which won Senate approval by a vote of 82—2. However, he clashed spiritedly with colleagues while the hearings were in progress.

Funeral arrangements awaited the arrival of the Senator's son, Lieut. Col. Hiram W. Johnson Jr., who was flying here from California.

Capper Becomes the Dean

The death of Senator Johnson made Senator Arthur Capper of Kansas, who last month marked his eightieth birthday, the Republican dean of the Senate. It also elevated him to the ranking minority membership on the Foreign Relations Committee, with which Senator Johnson had been so conspicuously identified through the many years of his unshaken position on foreign policy. Mr. Capper, too, with Senators McKellar, Carter Glass of Virginia, David I. Walsh of Massachusetts and Peter G. Gerry, was in the League fight of 1919 and 1920. He supported it, with reservations.

The career of Senator Johnson, from his entrance into the Senate from the Governorship of California in March of 1917, was one distinctly lacking in compromise or reservation. In 1912 he had bolted his party with Theodore Roosevelt and had become his running mate on the Bull Moose ticket. In 1932 he again bolted to support Franklin D. Roosevelt for the Presidency but broke bitterly with the President when he ran for his third term.

In 1919 Mr. Johnson joined with Senators Lodge, Borah, Reed,

Continued on Page 23, Column 1

Jet Plane Explosion Kills Major Bong, Top U. S. Ace

Flier Who Downed 40 Japanese Craft, Sent Home to Be 'Safe,' Was Flying New 'Shooting Star' as a Test Pilot

By The United Press.

BURBANK, Calif., Aug. 6—Maj. Richard Bong, America's greatest air ace, died today in the flaming wreckage of a jet propelled fighter plane which crashed while he was testing it.

Only 24 years old, he wore twenty-six decorations including the nation's highest award, the Congressional Medal of Honor. He had survived countless air battles and shot down forty Japanese planes without a scratch.

The knowledge he gained in those battles was too valuable to risk, so he was brought home to "safe" duty. He was on that "safe" duty today when his P-80, the Shooting Star, hurtled over a clump of trees and burst like a bomb in a field.

Witnesses did not agree on the cause of the crash. One Army flier said that Major Bong overshot the Lockheed airport. Another witness, John McKinney of North Hollywood reported that he saw something fall out of the plane's tail.

"The plane started to wobble up and down, then went into a left bank and hit the ground," he stated. "It exploded and burned and scattered wreckage over about a block square."

Major Bong was trying to get out of the ship when it crashed. He had released the escape hatch and was partly clear. He had pulled the ripcord to his parachute, and the silken folds lay about the body as the flames swept over it.

With a roaring sigh, the plane, like a giant blowtorch, shot over the airport just before 3 P. M. and then lurched over the trees and nosed down into the field, a mile away.

Smoke and flame surged up and crowds rushed from the airport. By the time anyone could reach the scene the ship had been almost consumed.

The crash scene was near the intersection of Cahuenga and Oxnard Boulevards and barely out-

Continued on page 15, Column 2

MORRIS IS ACCUSED OF 'TAKING A WALK'

Fusion Official 'Sad to Part Company'—McGoldrick Sees Only Tammany Aided

The No Deal ticket, headed by Council President Newbold Morris, "can only serve the interests of Tammany Hall," Controller Joseph D. McGoldrick, candidate for reelection on the Republican-Liberal-Fusion party slate, declared yesterday in a fresh attack on the third-party ticket injected over the week-end into the city Mayoralty campaign.

A short while later Gabriel A. Wechsler, general secretary of the City Fusion party, which supported Mayor La Guardia and Mr. Morris in previous city campaigns, accused Mr. Morris of "taking a walk away from the good government forces."

To both charges Mr. Morris declared he would stand on his statement of Sunday that he was not interested in "just taking votes" away from Judge Jonah J. Goldstein, Republican-Liberal-Fusion candidate for Mayor, or from William O'Dwyer, his Democratic-American Labor party opponent.

"I have no comment," he said, "since I stand on my statement of Sunday. We are waging an affirmative campaign."

Informed that Hyman Blumberg,

Continued on Page 19, Column 6

CHINESE WIN MORE OF 'INVASION COAST'

Smash Into Port 121 Miles Southwest of Canton—Big Area Open for Landing

By The Associated Press.

CHUNGKING, China, Aug. 6—Chinese troops have broken into the South China port of Yeungkong and cleared a fifty-mile stretch of the Chinese "invasion coast" west of Hong Kong, Generalissimo Chiang Kai-shek's headquarters said today.

Swaying block-by-block street fighting is raging in the strategic coastal highway town, 121 miles southwest of Canton, a communiqué said.

By breaking into Yeungkong Chinese forces won control of a fifty-mile coastal stretch leading west to Tinpak, which lies east of Luichow Peninsula on the South China Sea. The coastal area now is open to a virtually unopposed landing should American forces choose it for a staging point for supplies to the armies of South China.

West of Luichow Peninsula another 145-mile coastal stretch extending to the Indo-China frontier is under Chinese control and observers believe the Chinese soon may launch a concerted drive from the west and east that would seal off the Japanese on the Luichow

Continued on Page 2, Column 7

Turks Talk War if Russia Presses; Prefer Vain Battle to Surrender

By SAM POPE BREWER

By Wireless to The New York Times.

ANKARA, Turkey, Aug. 6—Russo-Turkish relations weigh heavy on Turkish minds these days. All leading editors commented today on various aspects of the Russian claims against Turkey.

The Potsdam conference leaves the situation virtually unchanged so far as the Turks can see, but they seem to agree that they would go to war, however hopeless such a war might be, rather than yield before the threat of force. Suggestions from London and Washington that the Russians have been asked to moderate their demands give little reassurance here.

The Potsdam communiqué created more confusion than confidence and the Turks are still trying to decide whether the fact that the conference did not deal with certain specific questions means that it was a failure.

Many point out that all the really thorny questions still are unsettled. The Turks probably do not see a relative importance among world problems of Russian demands on Turkey, but point out that the important question of principle is involved. The general and apparently official argument is that the status of the Straits cannot be modified by a bilateral agreement but must be discussed at a conference of the signatories of the Montreux Convention, with America replacing Japan. The signatories were Great Britain, France, Russia, Japan, Turkey, Greece, Rumania, Yugoslavia and Bulgaria.

The grounds for the Russian claims to Kars and Ardahan are not clear, but throughout the Near and Mideast in recent months

Continued on Page 13, Column 1

KYUSHU CITY RAZED

Kenney's Planes Blast Tarumizu in Record Blow From Okinawa

ROCKET SITE IS SEEN

125 B-29's Hit Japan's Toyokawa Naval Arsenal in Demolition Strike

By FRANK L. KLUCKHOHN

By Wireless to The New York Times.

MANILA, Tuesday, Aug. 7—More than 400 fighters and bombers, speeding at chimney-top level for two hours Sunday over Tarumizu in southern Kyushu in the largest single attack launched by Gen. George C. Kenney's Far East Air Forces to date, leveled that city's munitions factories and aircraft and munitions storage depots and waterfront installations.

Rockets and demolition bombs were poured by waves of B-26 Invaders, B-25 Mitchells and Mustangs and Thunderbolts of the Fifth and Seventh Air Forces from Okinawa, supported by a few B-24 Liberators carrying big bombs.

[Tarumizu, about 350 miles from Okinawa, appeared to be a site at which the Japanese might be preparing a rocket campaign against the American base, said a United Press dispatch. FEAF pilots reported seeing in the area, which has extensive cave construction, what seemed to be Japanese robot planes and also a huge catapult-like machine, extending over the water, that might be a rocket launcher.

[About 125 B-29's hit the Toyokawa naval arsenal of Japan in a demolition bombing Tuesday noon, Strategic Air Forces headquarters at Guam reported.]

The planes over Tarumizu met scant resistance, as our fliers took their time to assure the highest

Continued on Page 11, Column 2

REPORT BY BRITAIN

'By God's Mercy' We Beat Nazis to Bomb, Churchill Says

ROOSEVELT AID CITED

Raiders Wrecked Norse Laboratory in Race for Key to Victory

The text of Mr. Churchill's statement is on Page 8.

By CLIFTON DANIEL

By Wireless to The New York Times.

LONDON, Aug. 6—The hitherto secret details of the grisly race between Germany and the Allies to find a weapon so destructive that it would insure absolute victory—a race not only between scientists but also between under-cover agents—were recounted in London tonight after it had been disclosed that the first atomic bomb had been dropped on Japan.

"By God's mercy British and American science outpaced all German efforts," said a statement by former Prime Minister Churchill written before he left office and issued from 10 Downing Street by his successor, Clement R. Attlee.

"The possession of these powers by the Germans at any time might have altered the result of the war," Mr. Churchill said, "and profound anxiety was felt by those who were informed."

The British Isles, which endured the terrors of flying bombs and rockets, did hear repeated rumors that Adolf Hitler's V-3 weapon was to be an atomic bomb, but they never knew until tonight how close they came to being the first victims of its destructive power. Much less did they suspect what

Continued on Page 9, Column 1

War News Summarized

TUESDAY, AUGUST 7, 1945

One bomb hit Japan on Sunday night, but it struck with the force of 20,000 tons of TNT. Where it landed had been the city of Hiroshima; what is there now has not yet been learned.

The attack, dramatically announced by President Truman sixteen hours after the missile had struck, was with an atomic bomb, a "harnessing of the basic power of the universe," he said. "The force from which the sun draws its power has been loosed against those who brought war to the Far East. And the end is not yet."

Details of the missile are closely guarded, but the 125,000 workers who saw materials pour into their factories never saw anything go out. The bomb is the result of pooling British-American scientific knowledge begun in 1940. "We have spent two billion dollars on the greatest scientific gamble in history—and won," Mr. Truman said, and warned:

"We are now prepared to obliterate more rapidly and completely every productive enterprise the Japanese have above ground in any city. It was to spare the Japanese public from utter destruction that the ultimatum of July 26 was issued at Potsdam. If they do not now accept our terms they may expect a rain of ruin from the air."

Secretary of War Stimson detailed the story of research and production and forecast improvements to increase the effectiveness of the "atomic bomb" several times. Congress will be asked to establish a committee to control peacetime use.

Hiroshima was a major military target, a city of 318,000 persons thickly settled around a quartermaster's depot, an embarkation port, armament and airplane parts plants. [All the foregoing 1:5.]

All production was in the United States at two plants at Oak Ridge, near Knoxville, Tenn., and one at Richland, Wash. A scientific laboratory was maintained in Sante Fe, N. M. [1:6.]

Former Prime Minister Churchill told of Britain's part, including costly attacks on German "heavy water" plants and the race to outstrip the Nazis. He praised American scientific achievement and gave full credit to President Roosevelt and his advisers. [1:5.]

Tokyo made no mention of what had happened to Hiroshima but rail service in that area was canceled. [1:7.]

Okinawa sent out 400 planes that left Tarumizu, on Kyushu's Kagoshima Bay, in flaming wreckage. About 125 "Superforts" bombed Toyokawa naval arsenal by daylight. [1:4; map p. 11.]

Chinese troops have broken into the port of Yeungkong and have cleared a large stretch of the south China coast west of Hong Kong and east of the Luichow Peninsula. [1:3; map P. 2.]

Moscow, moving to implement Potsdam decisions, has resumed diplomatic relations with Finland and Rumania. [11:4.]

The Germans received an opportunity to develop democratic talents when the United States and Great Britain authorized local trade unions and political parties in their zones of occupation. [12:2.]

France is expected to ratify the United Nations Charter and then the Bretton Woods monetary plan in the near future. [13:6.] Marshal Pétain was accused of having asked Hitler for help in regaining France's colonies. [13:1.]

Argentina has lifted the state of siege in effect since Pearl Harbor. [11:6.]

Steel Tower 'Vaporized' In Trial of Mighty Bomb

Scientists Awe-Struck as Blinding Flash Lighted New Mexico Desert and Great Cloud Bore 40,000 Feet Into Sky

By LEWIS WOOD

Special to The New York Times.

WASHINGTON, Aug. 6—A blinding flash many times as brilliant as the midday sun and a massive, multi-colored cloud boiling up 40,000 feet into the air accompanied the first test firing of an atomic bomb on July 16, three weeks ago today. Set in the remote desertlands of New Mexico, the experiment was seen against a wild background where rain poured in torrents, and lightning pierced the sky up to the zero hour of the explosion at 5:30 A. M.

A steel tower from which the atomic weapon hung was vaporized. In its place was only a huge, sloping crater. At the moment of the explosion a mountain range three miles distant stood out sharply in brilliant light.

"Then," said the War Department in a description, "came a tremendous, sustained roar and a heavy pressure wave which knocked down two men outside the control tower (10,000 yards, or more than five miles, away.)"

Before the detonation scientists waited in tense expectancy. Minutes lengthened seemingly to hours. Lying face downward, with their feet toward the steel tower, the watchers waited, nearly breathless. They were "reaching into the unknown" and did not know what would happen.

On the instant that all was over these men leaped to their feet. The terrible tension ended, they shook hands, embraced each other and shouted in glee. Behind their triumph was sober consciousness of possessing the means to "insure the speedy conclusion of the war and save thousands of American lives."

The scene of the great drama was the Alamogordo Air Base, 120 miles southeast of Albuquerque. Here the scientists strove to unlock the secret upon which $2,000,000,000 had been spent.

Graphic word pictures of the

Continued on Page 5, Column 1

ATOM BOMBS MADE IN 3 HIDDEN 'CITIES'

Secrecy on Weapon So Great That Not Even Workers Knew of Their Product

By JAY WALZ

Special to The New York Times.

WASHINGTON, Aug. 6—The War Department revealed today how three "hidden cities" with a total population of 100,000 inhabitants sprang into being as a result of the $2,000,000,000 atomic bomb project, how they did their work without knowing what it was all about, and how they kept the biggest secret of the war.

One of these, Oak Ridge, situated where only oak and pine trees had dotted small farms before, is today the fifth largest city in Tennessee. Its population of 75,000 persons has thirteen supermarkets, nine drug stores and seven theatres.

A second town of 7,000 was built for reasons of isolation and security on a New Mexico mesa. The third, named Richland Village, houses 17,000 men, women and children on remote banks of the Columbia River in the State of Washington.

None of the people, who came to these developments from homes all the way from Maine to California, had the slightest idea of what they were making in the gigantic Gov-

Continued on Page 3, Column 2

TRAINS CANCELED IN STRICKEN AREA

Traffic Around Hiroshima Is Disrupted — Japanese Still Sift Havoc by Split Atoms

By The United Press.

WASHINGTON, Aug. 6—The Osaka radio, without referring to the atomic bomb dropped on Hiroshima, hinted tonight at the terrific damage it must have caused by announcing that train service in the Hiroshima and other areas had been canceled.

First mention of the bomb came in a Japanese Domei agency dispatch announcing that President Truman and Prime Minister Attlee had disclosed that the new missile had been dropped on Hiroshima.

The Office of War Information began telling the Japanese today what hit them. OWI branch transmitters in San Francisco, Hawaii and Saipan beamed President Truman's statement on the atomic bomb to Japan.

Edward Barrett, director of the OWI's overseas branch, said that the President's announcement and related information on the atomic bomb will dominate the OWI's normal Japanese transmissions for the next several days.

LONDON, Tuesday, Aug. 7 (U.P.)—The Japanese Domei news agency, in a dispatch recorded by the British radio, said today that

Continued on Page 7, Column 3

Reich Exile Emerges as Heroine In Denial to Nazis of Atom's Secret

Special to The New York Times.

WASHINGTON, Aug. 6—How Germany twice narrowly missed the secret of harnessing atomic energy by splitting uranium atoms and releasing the most powerful destructive force on earth was recalled today in War Department reports on the atomic bomb.

Development of the bomb after more than ten years of experimentation and research marks the first time that Prof. Albert Einstein's theory of relativity has been put to practical use outside the laboratory: the equation by which he showed the existence of a definite relationship of matter, energy and the velocity of light.

That the new bomb may be far from its maximum devastating potential was indicated by the War Department's statement that said:

"The energy we are now able to utilize in the atomic bombs, at 100 per cent efficiency, constitutes only one-tenth of 1 per cent of the total energy present in the material. But even one-hundredth of 1 per cent is still the most destructive force by far on this earth."

The principal character in the dramatic story of the long search for a method of releasing atomic energy is Dr. Lise Meitner, a woman physicist whom the Nazis expelled from Germany as a "non-Aryan." With her associates, Dr. Otto Hahn and Dr. F. Strassmann, both chemists, she had been working in the Kaiser Wilhelm Institute in Berlin, bombarding uranium atoms with neutrons and then submitting the uranium to chemical analysis.

As the War Department tells the story:

To their amazement, they found the element barium in the debris of the smashed uranium atoms

Continued on Page 7, Column 1

NEW AGE USHERED

Day of Atomic Energy Hailed by President, Revealing Weapon

HIROSHIMA IS TARGET

'Impenetrable' Cloud of Dust Hides City After Single Bomb Strikes

Truman, Stimson statements on atomic bomb, Page 4.

By SIDNEY SHALETT

Special to The New York Times.

WASHINGTON, Aug. 6—The White House and War Department announced today that an atomic bomb, possessing more power than 20,000 tons of TNT, a destructive force equal to the load of 2,000 B-29's and more than 2,000 times the blast power of what previously was the world's most devastating bomb, had been dropped on Japan.

The announcement, first given to the world in utmost solemnity by President Truman, made it plain that one of the scientific landmarks of the century had been passed, and that the "age of atomic energy," which can be a tremendous force for the advancement of civilization as well as for destruction, was at hand.

At 10:45 o'clock this morning, a statement by the President was issued at the White House that sixteen hours earlier—about the time that citizens on the Eastern seaboard were sitting down to their Sunday suppers—an American plane had dropped the single atomic bomb on the Japanese city of Hiroshima, an important army center.

Japanese Solemnly Warned

What happened at Hiroshima is not yet known. The War Department said it "as yet was unable to make an accurate report" because "an impenetrable cloud of dust and smoke" masked the target area from reconnaissance planes. The Secretary of War will release the story "as soon as accurate details of the results of the bombing become available."

But in a statement vividly describing the results of the first test of the atomic bomb in New Mexico, the War Department told how an immense steel tower had been "vaporized" by the tremendous explosion, how a 40,000-foot cloud rushed into the sky, and two observers were knocked down at a point 10,000 yards away. And President Truman solemnly warned:

"It was to spare the Japanese people from utter destruction that the ultimatum of July 26 was issued at Postdam. Their leaders promptly rejected that ultimatum. If they do not now accept our terms, they may expect a rain of ruin from the air the like of which has never been seen on this earth."

Most Closely Guarded Secret

The President referred to the joint statement issued by the heads of the American, British and Chinese Governments, in which terms of surrender were outlined to the Japanese and warning given that rejection would mean complete destruction of Japan's power to make war.

[The atomic bomb weighs about 400 pounds and is capable of utterly destroying a town, a representative of the British Ministry of Aircraft Production said in London, the United Press reported.]

What is this terrible new weapon, which the War Department also calls the "Cosmic Bomb"? It is the harnessing of the energy of the atom, which is the basic power of the universe. As President Truman said, "The force from which the sun draws its power has been loosed against those who brought war to the Far East."

"Atomic fission"—in other

Continued on Page 2, Column 2

6 AUGUST

What had happened?

All over the right side of my body I was cut and bleeding. A large splinter was protruding from a mangled wound in my thigh, and something warm trickled into my mouth. My cheek was torn, I discovered as I felt it gingerly, with the lower lip laid wide open. Embedded in my neck was a sizable fragment of glass which I matter-of-factly dislodged, and with the detachment of one stunned and shocked I studied it and my blood-stained hand.

Where was my wife?

Suddenly thoroughly alarmed, I began to yell for her: "Yaeko-san! Yaeko-san! Where are you?"

Blood began to spurt. Had my carotid artery been cut? Would I bleed to death? Frightened and irrational, I called out again: "It's a five-hundred-ton bomb! Yaeko-san, where are you? A five-hundred-ton bomb has fallen!"

Yaeko-san, pale and frightened, her clothes torn and blood-stained, emerged from the ruins of our house holding her elbow. Seeing her, I was reassured. My own panic assuaged, I tried to reassure her.

"We'll be all right," I exclaimed. "Only let's get out of here as fast as we can."

She nodded, and I motioned for her to follow me.

The shortest path to the street lay through the house next door so through the house we went—running, stumbling, falling, and then running again until in headlong flight we tripped over something and fell sprawling into the street. Getting to my feet, I discovered that I had tripped over a man's head.

"Excuse me! Excuse me, please!" I cried hysterically.

There was no answer. The man was dead. The head had belonged to a young officer whose body was crushed beneath a massive gate.

We stood in the street, uncertain and afraid, until a house across from us began to sway and then with a rending motion fell almost at our feet. Our own house began to sway, and in a minute it, too, collapsed in a cloud of dust. Other buildings caved in or toppled. Fires sprang up and whipped by a vicious wind began to spread.

It finally dawned on us that we could not stay there in the street, so we turned our steps towards the hospital.[1] Our home was gone; we were wounded and needed treatment; and after all, it was my duty to be with my staff. This latter was an irrational thought—what good could I be to anyone, hurt as I was.

We started out, but after twenty or thirty steps I had to stop. My breath became short, my heart pounded, and my legs gave way under me. An overpowering thirst seized me and I begged Yaeko-san to find me some water. But there was no water to be found. After a little my strength somewhat returned and we were able to go on.

I was still naked, and although I did not feel the least bit of shame, I was disturbed to realize that modesty had deserted me. On rounding a corner we came upon a soldier standing idly in the street. He had a towel draped across his shoulder, and I asked if he would give it to me to cover my nakedness. The

---

[1]Dr. Hachiya's home was only a few hundred meters from the hospital.

soldier surrendered the towel quite willingly but said not a word. A little later I lost the towel, and Yaeko-san took off her apron and tied it around my loins.

Our progress towards the hospital was interminably slow, until finally, my legs, stiff from drying blood, refused to carry me farther. The strength, even the will, to go on deserted me, so I told my wife, who was almost as badly hurt as I, to go on alone. This she objected to, but there was no choice. She had to go ahead and try to find someone to come back for me.

Yaeko-san looked into my face for a moment, and then, without saying a word, turned away and began running towards the hospital. Once, she looked back and waved and in a moment she was swallowed up in the gloom. It was quite dark now, and with my wife gone, a feeling of dreadful loneliness overcame me.

I must have gone out of my head lying there in the road because the next thing I recall was discovering that the clot on my thigh had been dislodged and blood was again spurting from the wound.

The sky became bright as flames from the hospital mounted. Soon the Bureau was threatened and Mr. Sera gave the order to evacuate. My stretcher was moved into a rear garden and placed beneath an old cherry tree. Other patients limped into the garden or were carried until soon the entire area became so crowded that only the very ill had room to lie down. No one talked, and the ominous silence was relieved only by a subdued rustle among so many people, restless, in pain, anxious, and afraid, waiting for something else to happen.

The sky filled with black smoke and glowing sparks. Flames rose and the heat set currents of air in motion. Updrafts became so violent that sheets of zinc roofing were hurled aloft and released, humming and twirling, in erratic flight. Pieces of flaming wood soared and fell like fiery swallows. While I was trying to beat out the flames, a hot ember seared my ankle. It was all I could do to keep from being burned alive.

The Bureau started to burn, and window after window became a square of flame until the whole structure was converted into a crackling, hissing inferno.

Scorching winds howled around us, whipping dust and ashes into our eyes and up our noses. Our mouths became dry, our throats raw and sore from the biting smoke pulled into our lungs. Coughing was uncontrollable. We would have moved back, but a group of wooden barracks behind us caught fire and began to burn like tinder.

The heat finally became too intense to endure, and we were left no choice but to abandon the garden. Those who could fled; those who could not perished. Had it not been for my devoted friends, I would have died, but again, they came to the rescue and carried my stretcher to the main gate on the other side of the Bureau.

Here, a small group of people were already clustered, and here I found my wife. Dr. Sasada and Miss Kado joined us.

Fires sprang up on every side as violent winds fanned flames from one building to another. Soon, we were surrounded. The ground we held in front of the Communications Bureau became an oasis in a desert of fire. As the flames came closer the heat became more intense, and if someone in our group had not had the presence of mind to drench us with water[2] from a fire hose, I doubt if anyone could have survived.

---

[2]The water mains entered the city from the north and since the Communications Bureau was in the northern edge of the city, its water supply was not destroyed.

Hot as it was, I began to shiver. The drenching was too much. My heart pounded; things began to whirl until all before me blurred.

"*Kurushii*," I murmured weakly. "I am done."

The sound of voices reached my ears as though from a great distance and finally became louder as if close at hand. I opened my eyes; Dr. Sasada was feeling my pulse. What had happened? Miss Kado gave me an injection. My strength gradually returned. I must have fainted.

Huge raindrops began to fall. Some thought a thunderstorm was beginning and would extinguish the fires. But these drops were capricious. A few fell and then a few more and that was all the rain we saw.[3]

The first floor of the Bureau was now ablaze and flames were spreading rapidly towards our little oasis by the gate. Right then, I could hardly understand the situation, much less do anything about it.

An iron window frame, loosened by fire, crashed to the ground behind us. A ball of fire whizzed by me, setting my clothes ablaze. They drenched me with water again. From then on I am confused as to what happened.

I do remember Dr. Hinoi because of the pain, the pain I felt when he jerked me to my feet. I remember being moved or rather dragged, and my whole spirit rebelling against the torment I was made to endure.

My next memory is of an open area. The fires must have receded. I was alive. My friends had somehow managed to rescue me again.

A head popped out of an air-raid dugout, and I heard the unmistakable voice of old Mrs. Saeki: "Cheer up, doctor! Everything will be all right. The north side is burnt out. We have nothing further to fear from the fire."

I might have been her son, the way the old lady calmed and reassured me. And indeed, she was right. The entire northern side of the city was completely burned. The sky was still dark, but whether it was evening or midday I could not tell. It might even have been the next day. Time had no meaning. What I had experienced might have been crowded into a moment or been endured through the monotony of eternity.

Smoke was still rising from the second floor of the hospital, but the fire had stopped. There was nothing left to burn, I thought; but later I learned that the first floor of the hospital had escaped destruction largely through the courageous efforts of Dr. Koyama and Dr. Hinoi.

The streets were deserted except for the dead. Some looked as if they had been frozen by death while in the full action of flight; others lay sprawled as though some giant had flung them to their death from a great height.

Hiroshima was no longer a city, but a burnt-over prairie. To the east and to the west everything was flattened. The distant mountains seemed nearer than I could ever remember. The hills of Ushita and the woods of Nigitsu loomed out of the haze and smoke like the nose and eyes on a face. How small Hiroshima was with its houses gone.

The wind changed and the sky again darkened with smoke.

Suddenly, I heard someone shout: "Planes! Enemy planes!"

Could that be possible after what had already happened? What was there left to bomb? My thoughts were interrupted by the sound of a familiar name.

---

[3]There were many reports of a scanty rainfall over the city after the bombing. The drops were described as large and dirty, and some claimed that they were laden with radioactive dust.

A nurse calling Dr. Katsube.

"It is Dr. Katsube! It's him!" shouted old Mrs. Saeki, a happy ring to her voice. "Dr. Katsube has come!"

It was Dr. Katsube, our head surgeon, but he seemed completely unaware of us as he hurried past, making a straight line for the hospital. Enemy planes were forgotten, so great was our happiness that Dr. Katsube had been spared to return to us.

Before I could protest, my friends were carrying me into the hospital. The distance was only a hundred meters, but it was enough to cause my heart to pound and make me sick and faint.

I recall the hard table and the pain when my face and lip were sutured, but I have no recollection of the forty or more other wounds Dr. Katsube closed before night.

They removed me to an adjoining room, and I remember feeling relaxed and sleepy. The sun had gone down, leaving a dark red sky. The red flames of the burning city had scorched the heavens. I gazed at the sky until sleep overtook me.

7 AUGUST

Dr. Tabuchi, an old friend from Ushita, came in. His face and hands had been burned, though not badly, and after an exchange of greetings, I asked if he knew what had happened.

"I was in the back yard pruning some trees when it exploded," he answered. "The first thing I knew, there was a blinding white flash of light, and a wave of intense heat struck my cheek. This was odd, I thought, when in the next instance there was a tremendous blast.

"The force of it knocked me clean over," he continued, "but fortunately, it didn't hurt me; and my wife wasn't hurt either. But you should have seen our house! It didn't topple over, it just inclined. I have never seen such a mess. Inside and out everything was simply ruined. Even so, we are happy to be alive, and what's more Ryoji, our son, survived. I didn't tell you that he had gone into the city on business that morning. About midnight, after we had given up all hope that he could possibly survive in the dreadful fire that followed the blast, he came home. Listen!" he continued, "why don't you come on home with me? My house is certainly nothing to look at now, but it is better than here."

It was impossible for me to accept his kind offer, and I tried to decline in a way that would not hurt his feelings.

"Dr. Tabuchi," I replied, "we are all grateful for your kind offer, but Dr. Katsube has just warned me that I must lie perfectly still until my wounds are healed."

Dr. Tabuchi accepted my explanation with some reluctance, and after a pause he made ready to go.

"Don't go," I said, "Please tell us more of what occurred yesterday."

"It was a horrible sight," said Dr. Tabuchi. "Hundreds of injured people who were trying to escape to the hills passed our house. The sight of them was almost unbearable. Their faces and hands were burnt and swollen; and great sheets of skin had peeled away from their tissues to hang down like rags on a scarecrow.

They moved like a line of ants. All through the night, they went past our house, but this morning they had stopped. I found them lying on both sides of the road so thick that it was impossible to pass without stepping on them."

I lay with my eyes shut while Dr. Tabuchi was talking, picturing in my mind the horror he was describing. I neither saw nor heard Mr. Katsutani when he came in. It was not until I heard someone sobbing that my attention was attracted, and I recognized my old friend. I had known Mr. Katsutani for many years and knew him to be an emotional person, but even so, to see him break down made tears come to my eyes. He had come all the way from Jigozen[4] to look for me, and now that he had found me, emotion overcame him.

He turned to Dr. Sasada and said brokenly: "Yesterday, it was impossible to enter Hiroshima, else I would have come. Even today fires are still burning in some places. You should see how the city has changed. When I reached the Misasa Bridge[5] this morning, everything before me was gone, even the castle. These buildings here are the only ones left anywhere around. The Communications Bureau seemed to loom right in front of me long before I got anywhere near here."

Mr. Katsutani paused for a moment to catch his breath and went on: "I *really* walked along the railroad tracks to get here, but even they were littered with electric wires and broken railway cars, and the dead and wounded lay everywhere. When I reached the bridge, I saw a dreadful thing. It was unbelievable. There was a man, stone dead, sitting on his bicycle as it leaned against the bridge railing. It is hard to believe that such a thing could happen!"

He repeated himself two or three times as if to convince himself that what he said was true and then continued: "It seems that most of the dead people were either on the bridge or beneath it. You could tell that many had gone down to the river to get a drink of water and had died where they lay. I saw a few live people still in the water, knocking against the dead as they floated down the river. There must have been hundreds and thousands who fled to the river to escape the fire and then drowned.

"The sight of the soldiers, though, was more dreadful than the dead people floating down the river. I came onto I don't know how many, burned from the hips up; and where the skin had peeled, their flesh was wet and mushy. They must have been wearing their military caps because the black hair on top of their heads was not burned. It made them look like they were wearing black lacquer bowls.

"And they had no faces! Their eyes, noses and mouths had been burned away, and it looked like their ears had melted off. It was hard to tell front from back. One soldier, whose features had been destroyed and was left with his white teeth sticking out, asked me for some water, but I didn't have any. I clasped my hands and prayed for him. He didn't say anything more. His plea for water must have been his last words. The way they were burned, I wonder if they didn't have their coats off when the bomb exploded."

It seemed to give Mr. Katsutani some relief to pour out his terrifying experiences on us; and there was no one who would have stopped him, so fascinating

---

[4]A village on the Inland Sea about 10 miles southwest of Hiroshima.
[5]A large bridge which crosses the Ora River not far from the old Hiroshima Castle in the northern part of the city and only a few blocks from the Communications Hospital.

was his tale of horror. While he was talking, several people came in and stayed to listen. Somebody asked him what he was doing when the explosion occurred.

"I had just finished breakfast," he replied, "and was getting ready to light a cigarette, when all of a sudden I saw a white flash. In a moment there was a tremendous blast. Not stopping to think, I let out a yell and jumped into an air-raid dugout. In a moment there was such a blast as I have never heard before. It was terrific! I jumped out of the dugout and pushed my wife into it. Realizing something terrible must have happened in Hiroshima, I climbed up onto the roof of my storehouse to have a look."

Mr. Katsutani became more intense and, gesticulating wildly, went on: "Towards Hiroshima, I saw a big black cloud go billowing up, like a puffy summer cloud. Knowing for sure then that something terrible had happened in the city, I jumped down from my storehouse and ran as fast as I could to the military post at Hatsukaichi.[6] I ran up to the officer in charge and told him what I had seen and begged him to send somebody to help in Hiroshima. But he didn't even take me seriously. He looked at me for a moment with a threatening expression, and then do you know what he said? He said, 'There isn't much to worry about. One or two bombs won't hurt Hiroshima.' There was no use talking to that fool!

"I was the ranking officer in the local branch of the Ex-officer's Association, but even I didn't know what to do because that day the villagers under my command had been sent off to Miyajima[7] for labor service. I looked all around to find someone to help me make a rescue squad, but I couldn't find anybody. While I was still looking for help, wounded people began to stream into the village. I asked them what had happened, but all they could tell me was that Hiroshima had been destroyed and everybody was leaving the city. With that I got on my bicycle and rode as fast as I could towards Itsukaichi. By the time I got there, the road was jammed with people, and so was every path and byway.

"Again I tried to find out what had happened, but nobody could give me a clear answer. When I asked these people where they had come from, they would point towards Hiroshima and say, 'This way.' And when I asked where they were going, they would point toward Miyajima and say, 'That way.' Everybody said the same thing.

"I saw no badly wounded or burned people around Itsukaichi, but when I reached Kusatsu, nearly everybody was badly hurt. The nearer I got to Hiroshima the more I saw until by the time I had reached Koi,[8] they were all so badly injured, I could not bear to look into their faces. They smelled like burning hair."

Mr. Katsutani paused for a moment to take a deep breath and then continued: "The area around Koi station was not burned, but the station and the houses nearby were badly damaged. Every square inch of the station platform was packed with wounded people. Some were standing; others lying down. They were all pleading for water. Now and then you could hear a child calling for its mother. It was a living hell, I tell you. It was a living hell!

---

[6]The next village towards Hiroshima from Jigozen.

[7]Miyajima, or "Sacred Island," one of the seven places of superlative scenic beauty in Japan, where the magnificent camphor-wood *torii* of the Itsukushima Shrine rises majestically from the sea as a gateway to the island, is plainly visible to the south of Jigozen.

[8]A railroad station on the very western limits of the city where the slopes of Chausu-yama merge with the Hiroshima delta.

All day I had listened to visitors telling me about the destruction of Hiroshima and the scenes of horror they had witnessed. I had seen my friends wounded, their families separated, their homes destroyed. I was aware of the problems our staff had to face, and I knew how bravely they struggled against superhuman odds. I knew what the patients had to endure and the trust they put in the doctors and nurses, who, could they know the truth, were as helpless as themselves.

By degrees my capacity to comprehend the magnitude of their sorrow, to share with them the pain, frustration, and horror became so dulled that I found myself accepting whatever was told me with equanimity and a detachment I would have never believed possible.

In two days I had become at home in this environment of chaos and despair.

I felt lonely, but it was an animal loneliness. I became part of the darkness of the night. There were no radios, no electric lights, not even a candle. The only light that came to me was reflected in flickering shadows made by the burning city. The only sounds were the groans and sobs of the patients. Now and then a patient in delirium would call for his mother, or the voice of one in pain would breathe out the word *eraiyo*—"the pain is unbearable; I cannot endure it!"

```
C
O
P   WAR  DEPARTMENT
Y   CLASSIFIED MESSAGE CENTER
    INCOMING CLASSIFIED MESSAGE


            TOP  SECRET

            URGENT


                                    Page - 2-



From:  CG, 313th Bomber Wing, Tinian

Nr  :  APCOM 5479                    9 August 1945

      Pilot Sweeney who took an observing airplane on
Hiroshima mission reported that flash was brighter and
bumps greater than Hiroshima.  He was however, somewhat
closer to burst today.  Weather over target was 7 to 8
tenths cloud.

      Bombadier believes his point of aim at time of strike
was about 500 feet south of south end of Mitsubishi steel
works.  He and others report 3 bumps and compared with 2 at
Hiroshima.  One crew member reported 3 shock waves as visible.
Several reported the cloud as brighter than Hiroshima.  It
was a bright orange color with the top mushroom definitely
luminous of orange and pink colors.  Cloud moved up faster
and went higher than Hiroshima.  Cloud burned away the ex-
isting clouds.  Base cloud of dust and smoke was smaller in
area than Hiroshima.  Fires were seen on both east and west
sides of cloud.
                                    End

      Note:  Received by TELECON as msg nbr FN-09-17



ACTION:  Maj Derry

INFO:  Gen Arnold, Gen Hull, Gen Bissell, CofS



CM-IN-9254         (9Aug 45)        DTG:  091500Z   ngr


            TOP  SECRET
```

"All the News That's Fit to Print"

The New York Times.

LATE CITY EDITION
Sunny with low humidity today. Partly cloudy, warmer tomorrow.
Temperatures Yesterday—Max., 77; Min., 66
Sunrise today, 5:59 A. M.; Sunset, 8:02 P. M.

VOL. XCIV .No. 31,974. Entered as Second-Class Matter, Postoffice, New York, N. Y. NEW YORK, THURSDAY, AUGUST 9, 1945. THREE CENTS IN NEW YORK CITY

SOVIET DECLARES WAR ON JAPAN; ATTACKS MANCHURIA, TOKYO SAYS; ATOM BOMB LOOSED ON NAGASAKI

TRUMAN TO REPORT TO PEOPLE TONIGHT ON BIG 3 AND WAR

Half-Hour Speech by Radio to Cover a Wide Range of Problems Facing the World

HE SIGNS PEACE CHARTER

And Thus Makes This Country the First to Complete All Ratification Requirements

By The Associated Press.

WASHINGTON, Aug. 8—President Truman will report to the country on the Potsdam conference over all radio networks at 10 P. M., Eastern war time, tomorrow in a thirty-minute speech.

The Presidential secretary, Charles G. Ross, said today that the speech, which probably would also be short-waved abroad, would go into greater detail than the communiqué issued by the Big Three at the close of the meeting July 26.

Mr. Truman worked on the speech today as well as on a mass of other paper work which accumulated during his month-long absence, and signed into full ratification the United Nations Charter.

He held his calling list to a minimum, including brief conferences with Senators Hatch of New Mexico and Kilgore of West Virginia, and Henry L. Stimson, Secretary of War.

The Stimson conference was devoted to further discussion of the atomic bomb.

Associates of the President indicated that his report on the Potsdam conference would probably mention the new and revolutionary bomb used for the first time against Japan.

Full Appraisal May Be Given

A full appraisal of revised conditions, including Russia's declaration of war against Japan, may come in Mr. Truman's broadcast.

Originally the speech was expected to be primarily a report on the Soviet-British-American agreements announced at the end of the Potsdam conference. These dealt mainly with Europe, keeping Germany under strict surveillance, and the writing of peace treaties.

It became known today that Mr. Truman had four or five names under consideration for the vacancy on the Supreme Court, and the decision appeared imminent.

One of the names is that of Senator Austin, Republican, of Vermont, who has been endorsed by his Democratic colleague, Senator Hatch. It was to renew his suggestion that Mr. Austin be appointed to succeed Justice Owen Roberts, who retired, that brought Mr. Hatch to the White House today.

"Of course the President made no commitments," Mr. Hatch told reporters later, "but he definitely is considering both the appointment of a Republican and Senator Austin. Of course that is only a possibility."

Justice Roberts, appointed by President Hoover in 1930 was one of two Republicans in the present makeup of the high court. Chief Justice Harlan F. Stone is the remaining member of that party.

Charter Goes to Archives

Special to The New York Times.

WASHINGTON, Aug. 8—When President Truman signed today the document by which he ratified the Charter of the United Nations, the United States thereby became the first country to complete its action for bringing the Charter into force.

Several other countries have ratified or taken action with a view to ratification, but no instrument of ratification has yet been received from any of them by the State Department, which is the

Continued on Page 3, Column 5

Foreigners Asked To Stay at Home

Special to The New York Times.

WASHINGTON, Aug. 8—Discouragement of unessential travel by foreigners to the United States was ordered by the Government today through the State Department.

"The Department of State has always traditionally done everything in its power to promote the travel of citizens of other countries of the Western Hemisphere to the United States," said the announcement. "However, the United States Government is now engaged in a gigantic military operation in deploying forces and supplies from the European theatre to the Pacific area. This tremendous task places an unprecedented burden on the transportation system."

The citizens of other countries should realize the situation, the statement said, and postpone trips to the United States unless they were directly connected with the war.

TAMMANY OUSTS LAST OF REBELS

County Committee Ratifies Executive Group's Action—Meeting Picketed

Without the slightest opposition, the New York County Democratic Committee, popularly known as Tammany, last night ratified the selection of an executive committee on which there remained no opposition to the leadership of Edward V. Loughlin or to the influence in the organization repeatedly exercised by Bert Stand, secretary, and Clarence H. Neal Jr., chairman of its elections committee.

In Brooklyn the Kings County Democratic Committee nominated United States Attorney Miles F. McDonald for District Attorney of Kings County to run for the vacancy caused by the resignation of William O'Dwyer, Democratic and American Labor party candidate for Mayor. Mr. McDonald, a graduate of Holy Cross College and Fordham Law School, in accepting the nomination, told the members of the committee that he would resign as United States Attorney.

Nearly 2,000 members, the largest number in recent years, attended the Tammany meeting in the Central Commercial High School, 214 East Forty-second Street. All resolutions presented were adopted unanimously by voice vote.

The committee ratified action taken by the executive committee in seating Robert B. Blaikie as leader of the Seventh Assembly District in place of Joseph H. Broderick and Assemblyman Patrick H. Sullivan, in spite of the claim of Mr. Broderick that he had elected a majority of county com-

Continued on Page 17, Column 2

2D BIG AERIAL BLOW

Japanese Port Is Target in Devastating New Midday Assault

RESULT CALLED GOOD

Foe Asserts Hiroshima Toll Is 'Uncountable' —Assails 'Atrocity'

By W. H. LAWRENCE

By Wireless to The New York Times.

GUAM, Thursday, Aug. 9—Gen. Carl A. Spaatz announced today that a second atomic bomb had been dropped, this time on the city of Nagasaki, and that crew members reported "good results."

The second use of the new and terrifying secret weapon which wiped out more than 60 per cent of the city of Hiroshima and, according to the Japanese radio, killed nearly every resident of that town, occurred at noon today, Japanese time. The target today was an important industrial and shipping area with a population of about 253,000.

The great bomb, which harnesses the power of the universe to destroy the enemy by concussion, blast and fire, was dropped on the second enemy city about seven hours after the Japanese had received a political "roundhouse punch" in the form of a declaration of war by the Soviet Union.

Vital Transshipment Point

GUAM, Thursday, Aug. 9 (AP)—Nagasaki is vitally important as a port for transshipment of military supplies and the embarkation of troops in support of Japan's operations in China, Formosa, Southeast Asia and the Southwest Pacific. It was highly important as a major shipbuilding and repair center for both naval and merchantmen.

The city also included industrial surburbs of Inase and Akunoura on the western side of the harbor, and Urakami. The combined area is nearly double Hiroshima's.

Nagasaki, although only two-thirds as large as Hiroshima in population, is considered more important industrially. With a population now estimated at 253,000, its twelve square miles are jam-packed with the eave-to-eave buildings that won it the name of "sea of roofs."

General Spaatz' communiqué reporting the bombing did not say whether one or more than one "mighty atom" was dropped.

Hiroshima a 'City of Dead'

The Tokyo radio yesterday described Hiroshima as a city of ruins and dead "too numerous to be counted," and put forth the claim that the use of the atomic

Continued on Page 6, Column 3

RED ARMY STRIKES

Foe Reports First Blow by Soviet Forces on Asian Frontier

KEY POINTS BOMBED

Action Believed Aimed to Free Vladivostok Area of Threat

By The United Press.

SAN FRANCISCO, Aug. 8—Russia's mighty Far Eastern Army began hostilities against Japan at 12:10 A. M. Thursday [Russian time], launching a sudden attack along the eastern Soviet-Manchuria border only nine minutes after Moscow's declaration of war became effective, the enemy reported today.

A Kwantung Army headquarters communiqué issued at Changchun [Hsinking] and recorded here reported the attack and also announced that the Red Air Force already was bombing strategic points in Manchurian territory behind Japanese lines.

No details of the attack were given, but presumably the Russians would drive west from the Vladivostok area into Japanese-held territory north of the tip of Korea. Vladivostok is only about twenty miles east of the border, separated from the Japanese by fortified positions along the rugged, mountainous terrain.

The communiqué made it clear that ground forces had opened the attack—part of the Soviet Union's Far Eastern Army of more than 1,000,000 well-equipped troops, who never were called into action against Germany, but remained along the border, a constant threat to Japan.

Although the communiqué did not locate the fighting, it was believed the Russians would strike out as quickly as possible from the Vladivostok region, which is highly

Continued on Page 4, Column 6

CIRCLE OF SPEARHEADS AROUND JAPAN IS COMPLETED

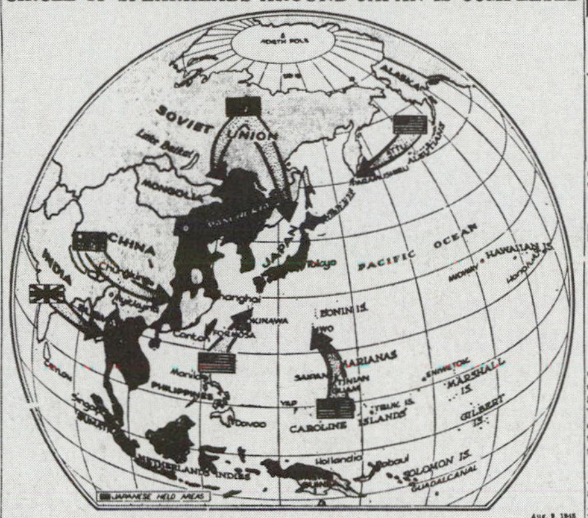

Aug. 9, 1945

With the entry of the Soviet Union into the war against Japan, the enemy is confronted with armed might from new directions—the north and northeast. Japan was already being battered by American power pressing in from the northeast and the south and by Chinese and British power from the west and southwest. The Russians are reported attacking Manchuria.

385 B-29'S SMASH 4 TARGETS IN JAPAN

Tokyo Arsenal and Aircraft Plant Are Seared—Fukuyama and Yawata Cities Ripped

By Wireless to The New York Times.

GUAM, Thursday, Aug. 9—Gen. Carl A. Spaatz, armed with the confirmed knowledge that his Strategic Air Force possesses in the atomic bomb the most powerful destructive agent devised by man since gunpowder was discovered, sent four separate forces

Continued on Page 2, Column 1

U. S. Third Fleet Attacking Targets in Northern Honshu

By ROBERT TRUMBULL

By Wireless to The New York Times.

GUAM, Thursday, Aug. 9—Admiral William F. Halsey's mighty Third Fleet, including British carriers, is now throwing strong air attacks at northern Honshu in the Japanese home islands, where the enemy has twenty to twenty-five airfields, Fleet Admiral Chester W. Nimitz announced this morning.

Although no specific targets were designated, the communiqué said shipping, air installations and "other military targets" were hit by strong air attacks beginning at dawn.

Today's communiqué broke nine days of silence by the Third Fleet after strikes in the Tokyo area July 30. It is possible that persistent fogs, caused by the warm Japanese Current at this time of year, forced Admiral Halsey to desist during that time from the sea-borne attacks carried out in conjunction with land-based air activity over the empire.

Northern Honshu, an area of 30,669 square miles, a little smaller than Maine and populated by 9,500,000 persons, has twenty to twenty-five airfields that are considered operational although some are small, poorly developed bases and probably are used only for the dispersal of the Japanese air force hiding out in that area.

While the northern Honshu district as geographically defined is outside the main military and industrial area of the island there is

Continued on Page 2, Column 8

TRUMAN REVEALS MOVE OF MOSCOW

Announces War Declaration Soon After Russian Action —Capital Is Startled

By FELIX BELAIR JR.

Special to The New York Times.

WASHINGTON, Aug. 8—President Truman announced a few minutes after 3 P. M. today that Russia had just declared war on Japan. The dramatic statement, issued with all the casualness of a routine proclamation, came during the shortest White House press conference on record.

Flanked by Secretary of State James M. Byrnes and Admiral William D. Leahy, his Chief of Staff, the President stood before hastily summoned reporters and in steady, matter-of-fact tones declared: "I have only a simple an-

Continued on Page 3, Column 1

RUSSIA AIDS ALLIES

Joins Pacific Struggle After Spurning Foe's Mediation Plea

SEEKS EARLY PEACE

Molotoff Reveals Move Three Months After Victory in Europe

By BROOKS ATKINSON

By Wireless to The New York Times.

MOSCOW, Aug. 8—Russia declared war on Japan tonight. In a dramatic press conference held at 8:30 P. M., Foreign Commissar Vyacheslaff M. Molotoff read the declaration, which was announced to the public at 10 P. M., Moscow time [3 P. M. New York time].

In view of Japan's refusal of the Allies' demand for unconditional surrender, Mr. Molotoff said, the Allies proposed that the Soviet Union "join the war against Japanese aggression and thus shorten the duration of the war, reduce the number of victims and facilitate the speedy restoration of universal peace.

"Loyal to its Allied duty," the Foreign Commissar continued, "the Soviet Government has accepted the proposal of the Allies and has joined in the declaration of the Allied Powers of July 26. The Soviet Government considers that this policy is the only means able to bring peace nearer, free the people from further sacrifice and suffering and give the Japanese people the possibility of avoiding the dangers and destruction suffered by Germany after her refusal to capitulate unconditionally."

Closing his concise statement, Mr. Molotoff declared:

"In view of the above, the Soviet Government declares that from tomorrow, that is Aug. 9, the Soviet Union will consider itself to be at war with Japan."

The Soviet Government's declaration comes three months after the victory over Germany, supporting rumors that some months ago the Soviet Government intimated it would join in the war against Japan three months after victory was won in Europe.

For the first time Mr. Molotoff revealed that the Japanese Government had asked the Soviet Union to mediate for a cessation of hostilities about the middle of June. Japanese Ambassador Naotaka Sato delivered the message, and also a special message from

Continued on Page 3, Column 2

Tokyo 'Flashes' News 3 Hours After Event

By The Associated Press.

SAN FRANCISCO, Aug. 8—Japan's first recorded wireless reaction to Russia's war declaration was a brief factual announcement of that action by the Domei agency in an English-language transmission to Europe.

The Domei account, broadcast five hours and fifty-five minutes after the Moscow announcement, reported:

"Flash! Flash! Tokyo, Aug. 9—Tass News Agency announced late last night that Foreign Commissar Vyacheslaff M. Molotoff communicated to Naotake Sato, Japanese Ambassador to Russia, that the Soviet Union will consider itself in a state of war with Japan from Thursday, Aug. 9, according to the Moscow radio recorded here this morning."

By the time the "flash" was read, the state of war already had existed for several hours.

Allies Cut Austria Into Four Zones With Vienna Under Joint Control

By LANSING WARREN

Special to The New York Times.

WASHINGTON, Aug. 8—A four-power control machinery, including France with the Big Three, has been established in Austria in accordance with an agreement between the Soviet Union, the United States, the United Kingdom and France, it was announced today.

The system resembles the military control arrangement for Germany. It divides Austria into four zones of occupation and provides that Vienna, the capital city, shall also be occupied by the forces of the four controlling powers. It creates an Allied Council, consisting of the four military commissioners, who will govern Austria as a whole. The commissioners will make the decisions for all Austria and will insure a uniformity of action in the different zones.

[The text of the statement on Austria is on Page 11.]

Under the direction of this combined Allied council each military commander will have full authority in his zone. The council will act through the commanders and through an executive committee, which will advise the council and carry out its decisions.

By this means the agreement seeks to prevent a situation that would separate too rigidly the

Continued on Page 11, Column 5

War News Summarized

THURSDAY, AUGUST 9, 1945

Russia has declared war against Japan because that country is the only great power standing in the way of peace. Foreign Commissar Molotoff so informed Ambassador Sato in Moscow yesterday. He said it was in the interests of shortening the war and bringing peace to the world that Moscow acceded to the Allied request to join the war in the Far East and subscribed to the Potsdam ultimatum of July 26. Mr. Molotoff revealed that Japan had asked the Soviet Union to mediate for peace, but that proposal "lost all foundation" when Tokyo rejected the Potsdam demands. [1:8.]

Hostilities were begun nine minutes after the war declaration went into effect at 12:01 this morning, according to Tokyo, when Soviet troops struck along Manchuria's eastern frontier with Siberia. Air attacks, it was said, quickly followed. [1:4.]

President Truman broke the news when he told a hastily called press conference: "Russia has declared war against Japan—that is all." [1:7.] Secretary of State Byrnes declared there was "still time—but little time—for the Japanese to save themselves from the destruction which threatens them." Mr. Byrnes said the President had convinced Premier Stalin that Russia must enter the war if she was to be responsible for peace. [4:2.]

Congress, jubilant and confident that Russia's aid and the atomic bomb would shorten the war materially, expected to be called back soon. [4:1.]

Japan received another blow when the second atomic bomb to fall struck Nagasaki on Kyushu. Crew members reported good results. "Practically all living things" in Hiroshima were destroyed beyond recognition by heat and pressure from the first atomic bomb, Tokyo reported. [1:3.] Fires leaped seven rivers. [6:3, with map.]

The Third Fleet, after nine days of silence, sent its carrier planes in a strong attack, still continuing at last reports, against northern Honshu and its score of airfields. [1:6-7.] B-29's hit four Japanese cities in twenty-four hours and mined home waters. [1:5; map P. 2.]

Wuhu Island, at the mouth of the Min River east of Foochow, was captured by the Chinese. [8:2, with map.]

Russia, Britain, France and the United States have signed an agreement for the occupation and administration of Austria similar to that in effect in Germany. Complete separation from Germany, restoration of the 1937 frontiers and return of democratic government were set as Allied goals. [1:2-3; maps P. 11.]

A new code of international law was adopted by the Big Four listing wars of aggression as a crime against peace. [1:6-7.]

General de Gaulle and his Cabinet, contrary to the wishes of the Consultative Assembly, will submit the questions of a new constitution and government responsibility to a referendum on Oct. 21. [13:5.]

President Truman signed the United Nations Charter yesterday. He will discuss the Potsdam Conference and the military situation in a broadcast at 10 o'clock tonight. [1:1.]

4 Powers Call Aggression Crime In Accord Covering War Trials

By CHARLES E. EGAN

By Wireless to The New York Times.

LONDON, Aug. 8—A new code of international law, defining aggressive warfare as a crime against the world and providing punishment for those who provoke such wars, was announced here today.

By agreement among representatives of the United States, Great Britain, the Soviet Union and France, the legal framework necessary for the trial of the key German and Italian leaders held by the Allies was promulgated this afternoon. The document sets precedents in international law and, in the words of United States Supreme Court Justice Robert H. Jackson, the American representative, "ought to make clear to the world that those who lead their nations into aggressive war face individual accountability for such acts."

"If we can cultivate in the world the idea that aggressive war making is the way to a prisoners' dock rather than the way to honors," he said "we will have accomplished something toward making peace more secure."

[The texts of the War Crimes Committee report and Mr. Jackson's statement are on Page 10.]

The agreement, upon which the international committee has been laboring since June 26, represents

Continued on Page 11, Column 6

C
O
P
Y

WAR DEPARTMENT
CLASSIFIED MESSAGE CENTER
INCOMING CLASSIFIED MESSAGE

TOP SECRET

URGENT

From: CG, 313th Bomber Wing, Tinian

To: War Department

Nr: APCOM 5479   9 August 1945

To Groves personal from Farrell APCOM 5479 TOPSEC.

Strike and accompanying airplanes have returned to
Tinian. Ashworth's message from Okinawa nr 44 is confirmed
by all observers. Cloud cover was bad at strike and it will
be necessary to await photographs to give exact point of
strike and damage. Strike plane had barely enough fuel to
reach Okinawa.

After listening to the accounts one gets the impression of a supremely tough job carried out with determination,
sound judgement and great skill. It is fortunate for the
success of the mission that its leaders, Ashworth and the
pilot Sweeney were men of stamina and stout heart. Weaker
men could not have done this job. Ashworth's small doubts
reflected in his first strike report were resolved after
checking at Okinawa with crews and observers from all 3
planes. He now feels confident that the bomb was satisfactorily placed and that it did its job well. Some detailed
observations follow:

An observing plane reported that 20 minutes after
explosion the southern edge of cloud was tangent to north
and of Nagasaki harbor with southeastern part of city visible.
There were scattered fires on west side of Nagasaki harbor.
Boats were seen in harbor. Top mushroom of cloud broke off
in a manner similar to cloud at Hiroshima.

CM-IN-9254   (9 Aug 45)

TOP   SECRET

<u>Thursday, August 9, 1945.</u>

When I reached the office this morning I found that the affirmative news for the press conference was so light that Surles thought we had better call the conference off and simply have me make a direct statement on the effect of the success of the atomic bomb on the future size of the Army. It seems as if everybody in the country was getting impatient to get his or her particular soldier out of the Army and to upset the carefully arranged system of points for retirement which we had arranged with the approval of the Army itself. The success of the first atomic bomb and the news of the Russians' entry into the war which came yesterday has rather doubled this crusade. Every industry wishes to get its particular quota of men back and nearly all citizens join in demanding somebody to dig coal for the coming winter. The effect on the morale of the Army is very ticklish. We have instituted a merit system and if, instead of following the fair standards which they proposed in the interest of the men who had served longest and in the most difficult and dangerous circumstances, we now discharge men on the basis of our own needs instead of theirs, there is likely to be trouble. I could see in my recent trip to Europe what a difficult task at best it will be to keep in existence a contented army of occupation and, if mingled with the inevitable difficulties there is a sense of grievance against the unfairness of the government, the situation may become bad. Consequently the paper that we drew last night and continued today was a ticklish one. The bomb and the entrance of the Russians into the war will certainly have an effect on hastening the victory. But just how much that effect is on how long and how many men we will have to keep to accomplish that victory, it is impossible yet to determine. There is a great tendency in the press and among other critics to think that the Army leaders have no feeling for these things and are simply determined to keep a big army in existence because they like it, and therefore it is ticklish to run head on into this feeling with direct counter criticism.

Thursday, August 9, 1945.
Page 4.

    We had news this morning of another successful atomic bomb being dropped on Nagasaki. These two heavy blows have fallen in quick succession upon the Japanese and there will be quite a little space before we intend to drop another. During that time I hope something may be done in negotiating a surrender. I have done the best I could to promote that in my talks with the President and with Byrnes and I think they are both in full sympathy with the aim.

August 9, 1945

MEMORANDUM FOR THE PRESS:

The Secretary of War, the Honorable Henry L. Stimson, today made the following statement:

The press conference this morning was cancelled owing to an engagement which I had at the White House. I had expected to make some general reflections at the conference in reference to the atomic bomb, and certain specific comment in reference to questions which had been asked. My general reflections were as follows:

Great events have happened. The world is changed and it is time for sober thought. It is natural that we should take satisfaction in the achievements of our science, our industry, and our Army in creating the atomic bomb, but any satisfaction we may feel must be overshadowed by deeper emotions.

The result of the bomb is so terrific that the responsibility of its possession and its use must weigh heavily on our minds and on our hearts. We believe that its use will save the lives of American soldiers and bring more quickly to an end the horror of this war which the Japanese leaders deliberately started. Therefore, the bomb is being used.

No American can contemplate what Mr. Churchill has referred to as "this terrible means of maintaining the rule of law in the world" without a determination that after this war is over this great force shall be used for the welfare and not the destruction of mankind.

My specific statement is as follows:

A great many questions have been asked about the effect of the Atomic Bomb and the Declaration of War by Russia on our military strategy and the size of the Army.

The War Department will, of course, appraise the military situation and the size of the Army in the light of the successful use of the bomb and the new Declaration of War. These possibilities have been in our minds for many months. We shall also give heed to any new factors which may develop from day to day. But we shall not do our duty if we plan for the reduction of the Army by even one man below the number which we believe may be needed for the complete defeat of Japan with the least possible loss of American lives.

●   ●   ●

THE EFFECTS OF THE ATOMIC BOMBS

On 6 August and 9 August 1945, the first two atomic bombs to be used for military purposes were dropped on Hiroshima and Nagasaki respectively. One hundred thousand people were killed, 6 square miles or over 50 percent of the built-up areas of the two cities were destroyed. The first and crucial question about the atomic bomb thus was answered practically and conclusively; atomic energy had been mastered for military purposes and the overwhelming scale of its possibilities had been demonstrated. A detailed examination of the physical, economic, and morale effects of the atomic bombs occupied the attention of a major portion of the Survey's staff in Japan in order to arrive at a more precise definition of the present capabilities and limitations of this radically new weapon of destruction.

Eyewitness accounts of the explosion all describe similar pictures. The bombs exploded with a tremendous flash of blue-white light, like a giant magnesium flare. The flash was of short duration and accompanied by intense glare and heat. It was followed by a tremendous pressure wave and the rumbling sound of the explosion. This sound is not clearly recollected by those who survived near the center of the explosion, although it was clearly heard by others as much as fifteen miles away. A huge snow-white cloud shot rapidly into the sky and the scene on the ground was obscured first by a bluish haze and then by a purple-brown cloud of dust and smoke.

Such eyewitness accounts reveal the sequence of events. At the time of the explosion, energy was given off in the forms of light, heat, radiation, and pressure. The complete band of radiations, from X- and gamma-rays, through ultraviolet and light rays to the radiant heat of infra-red rays, travelled with the speed of light. The shock wave created by the enormous pressures built up almost instantaneously at the point of explosion but moved out more slowly, that is at about the speed of sound. The superheated gases constituting the original fire ball expanded outward and upward at a slower rate.

The light and radiant heat rays accompanying the flash travelled in a straight line and any opaque object, even a single leaf of a vine, shielded objects lying behind it. The duration of the flash was only a fraction of a second, but it was sufficiently intense to cause third degree burns to exposed human skin up to a distance of a mile. Clothing ignited, though it could be quickly beaten out, telephone poles charred, thatchroofed houses caught fire. Black or other dark-colored surfaces of combustible material absorbed the heat and immediately charred or burst into flames; white or light-colored surfaces reflected a substantial portion of the rays and were not consumed. The heavy black clay tiles which are an almost universal feature of the roofs of Japanese hourses bubbled at distances up to a mile. Test of samples of this tile by the National Bureau of Standards in Washington indicates that temperatures in excess of 1,800° C. must have been generated in the surface of the tile to produce such an effect. The surfaces of granite blocks exposed to the flash scarred and spalled at distances up to almost a mile. In the immediate area of ground zero (the point on the ground immediately below the explosion), the heat charred corpses beyond recognition.

Penetrating rays such as gamma-rays exposed X-ray films stored in the basement of a concrete hospital almost a mile from ground zero. Symptoms of their effect on human beings close to the center of the explosion, who survived other effects thereof, were generally delayed for two or three days. The bone

---

[1]The Strategic Bombing Survey was a panel of experts commissioned by President Truman to examine the effects of strategic bombing.

marrow and as a result the process of blood formation were affected. The white corpuscle count went down and the human processes of resisting infection were destroyed. Death generally followed shortly thereafter.

The majority of radiation cases who were at greater distances did not show severe symptoms until 1 to 4 weeks after the explosion. The first symptoms were loss of appetite, lassitude and general discomfort. Within 12 to 48 hours, fever became evident in many cases, going as high as 104° to 105° F., which in fatal cases continued until death. If the fever subsided, the patient usually showed a rapid disappearance of other symptoms and soon regained his feeling of good health. Other symptoms were loss of white blood corpuscles, loss of hair, and decrease in sperm count.

Even though rays of this nature have great powers of penetration, intervening substances filter out portions of them. As the weight of the intervening material increases the percentage of the rays penetrating goes down. It appears that a few feet of concrete, or a somewhat greater thickness of earth, furnished sufficient protection to humans, even those close to ground zero, to prevent serious after effects from radiation.

The blast wave which followed the flash was of sufficient force to press in the roofs of reinforced-concrete structures and to flatten completely all less sturdy structures. Due to the height of the explosion, the peak pressure of the wave at ground zero was no higher than that produced by a near-miss of a high-explosive bomb, and decreased at greater distances from ground zero. Reflection and shielding by intervening hills and structures produced some unevenness in the pattern. The blast wave, however, was of far greater extent and duration that that of a high-explosive bomb and most reinforced-concrete structures suffered structural damage or collapse up to 700 feet at Hiroshima and 2,000 feet at Nagasaki. Brick buildings were flattened up to 7,300 feet at Hiroshima and 8,500 feet at Nagasaki. Typical Japanese houses of wood construction suffered total collapse up to approximately 7,300 feet at Hiroshima and 8,200 feet at Nagasaki. Beyond these distances structures received less serious damage to roofs, wall partitions, and the like. Glass windows were blown out at distances up to 5 miles. The blast wave, being of longer duration than that caused by high-explosive detonations, was accompanied by more flying debris. Window frames, doors, and partitions which would have been shaken down by a near-miss of a high-explosive bomb were hurled at high velocity through those buildings which did not collapse. Machine tools and most other production equipment in industrial plants were not directly damaged by the blast wave, but were damaged by collapsing buildings or ensuing general fires.

The above description mentions all the categories of the destructive action by the atomic-bomb explosions at Hiroshima and Nagasaki. There were no other types of action. Nothing was vaporized or disintegrated; vegetation is growing again immediately under the center of the explosions; there are no indications that radio-activity continued after the explosion to a sufficient degree to harm human beings.

Let us consider, however, the effect of these various types of destructive action on the cities of Hiroshima and Nagasaki and their inhabitants.

Hiroshima is built on a broad river delta; it is flat and little above sea level. The total city area is 26 square miles but only 7 square miles at the center were densely built up. The principal industries, which had been greatly expanded during the war, were located on the periphery of the city. The population of the city had been reduced from approximately 340,000 to 245,000 as a result of a civilian defense evacuation program. The explosion caught the city by surprise. An alert had been sounded but in view of the small number of planes the all-clear had been given. Consequently, the population had not taken shelter. The bomb exploded a little northwest of the center of the built-up area. Everyone who was out in the open and was exposed to the initial flash suffered serious burns where not protected by clothing. Over 4 square miles in the center of the city were flattened to the ground with the exception of some 50 reinforced concrete buildings, most of which were internally gutted and many of which suffered structural damage. Most of the people in the flattened area were crushed or pinned down by the collapsing buildings or flying debris. Shortly thereafter, numerous fires started, a few from the direct heat of the flash, but most from overturned charcoal cooking stoves or other secondary causes. These fires grew in size, merging into a general conflagration fanned by a wind sucked into the center of the city by the rising heat. The civilian-defense organization was overwhelmed by the completeness of the destruction, and the spread of fire was halted more by the air rushing toward the center of the conflagration than by efforts of the fire-fighting organization.

Approximately 60,000 to 70,000 people were killed, and 50,000 were injured. Of approximately 90,000 buildings in the city, 65,000 were rendered unusable and almost all the remainder received at least light superficial damage. The underground utilities of the city were undamaged except where they crossed bridges over the rivers cutting through the city. All of the small factories in the center of the city were destroyed. However, the big plants on the periphery of the city were almost completely undamaged and 94 percent of their workers unhurt. These factories accounted for 74 percent of the industrial production of the city. It is estimated that they could have resumed substantially normal production within 30 days of the bombing, had the war continued. The railroads running through the city were repaired for the resumption of through traffic on 8 August, 2 days after the attack.

Nagasaki was a highly congested city built around the harbor and up into the ravines and river valleys of the surrounding hills. Spurs of these hills coming down close to the head of the bay divide the city roughly into two basins. The built-up area was 3.4 square miles of which 0.6 square miles was given over to industry. The peak wartime population of 285,000 had been reduced to around 230,00 [sic] by August 1945, largely by pre-raid evacuations. Nagasaki had been attacked sporadically prior to 9 August by an aggregate of 136 planes which dropped 270 tons of high explosives and 53 tons of incendiary bombs. Some 2 percent of the residential buildings had been destroyed or badly damaged; three of the large industrial plants had received scattered damage. The city was thus comparatively intact at the time of the atomic bombing.

The alarm was improperly given and therefore few persons were in shelters. The bomb exploded over the northwest portion of the city; the intervening hills protected a major portion of the city lying in the adjoining valley. The heat radiation and blast actions of the Nagasaki bomb were more intense than those of the bomb dropped over Hiroshima. Reinforced-concrete structures were structurally damaged at greater distances; the heavy steel-frame industrial buildings of the Mitsubishi steel works and the arms plant were pushed at crazy angles away from the center of the explosion. Contrary to the situation at Hiroshima, the majority of the fires that started immediately after the explosion resulted from direct ignition by the flash.

Approximately 40,000 persons were killed or missing and a like number injured. Of the 52,000 residential buildings in Nagasaki 14,000 were totally destroyed and a further 5,400 badly damaged. Ninety-six percent of the industrial output of Nagasaki was concentrated in the large plants of the Mitsubishi Co. which completely dominated the town. The arms plant and the steel works were located within the area of primary damage. It is estimated that 58 percent of the yen value of the arms plant and 78 percent of the value of the steel works were destroyed. The main plant of the Mitsubishi electric works was on the periphery of the area of greatest destruction. Approximately 25 percent of its value was destroyed. The dockyard, the largest industrial establishment in Nagasaki and one of the three plants previously damaged by high-explosive bombs, was located down the bay from the explosion. The Mitsubishi plants were all operating, prior to the attack, at a fraction of their capacity because of a shortage of raw materials. Had the war continued, and had the raw material situation been such as to warrant their restoration, it is estimated that the dockyard could have been in a position to produce at 80 percent of its full capacity within 3 to 4 months; that the steel works would have required a year to get into substantial production; that the electric works could have resumed some production within 2 months and been back at capacity within 6 months; and that restoration of the arms plant to 60 to 70 percent of former capacity would have required 15 months.

Some 400 persons were in the tunnel shelters in Nagasaki at the time of the explosion. The shelters consisted of rough tunnels dug horizontally into the sides of hills with crude, earth-filled blast walls protecting the entrances. The blast walls were blown in but all the occupants back from the entrances survived, even in those tunnels almost directly under the explosion. Those not in a direct line with the entrance were uninjured. The tunnels had a capacity of roughly 100,000 persons. Had the proper alarm been sounded, and these tunnel shelters been filled to capacity, the loss of life in Nagasaki would have been substantially lower.

The Survey has estimated that the damage and casualties caused at Hiroshima by the one atomic bomb dropped from a single plane would have required 220 B-29s carrying 1,200 tons of incendiary bombs, 400 tons of high-explosive bombs, and 500 tons of anti-personnel fragmentation bombs, if conventional weapons, rather than an atomic bomb, had been used. One hundred and twenty-five B-29s carrying 1,200 tons of bombs would have been required to approximate the damage and casualties at Nagasaki. This estimate presupposed bombing under conditions similar to those existing when the atomic bombs were dropped and bombing accuracy equal to the average attained by the Twentieth Air Force during the last 3 months of the war.

As might be expected, the primary reaction of the populace to the bomb was fear, uncontrolled terror, strengthened by the sheer horror of the destruction and suffering witnessed and experienced by the survivors. Prior to the dropping of the atomic bombs, the people of the two cities had fewer misgivings about the war than people in other cities and their morale held up after it better than might have been expected. Twenty-nine percent of the survivors interrogated indicated that after the atomic bomb was dropped they were convinced that victory for Japan was impossible. Twenty-four percent stated that because of the bomb they felt personally unable to carry on with the war. Some 40 percent testified to various degrees of defeatism. A greater number (24 percent) expressed themselves as being impressed with the power and scientific skill which underlay the discovery and production of the atomic bomb than expressed anger at its use (20 percent). In many instances, the reaction was one of resignation.

The effect of the atomic bomb on the confidence of the Japanese civilian population outside the two cities was more restricted. This was in part due to the effect of distance, lack of understanding of the nature of atomic energy, and the impact of other demoralizing experiences. The role of the atomic bomb in the surrender must be considered along with all the other forces which bore upon that question with Japan.

The Swiss Legation to the Department of State

MEMORANDUM

The Legation of Switzerland in charge of Japanese interests has received an urgent cable from the authorities abroad, requesting that the Department of State be immediately apprised of the following communication from the Japanese Government, reading, in translation, as follows:

"On August 6, 1945, American airplanes released on the residential district of the town of Hiroshima bombs of a new type, killing and injuring in one second a large number of civilians and destroying a great part of the town. Not only is the city of Hiroshima a provincial town without any protection or special military installations of any kind, but also none of the neighboring region of this town constitutes a military objective.

"In a declaration President Truman has asserted that he would use these bombs for the destruction of docks, factories, and installations of transportation. However, this bomb, provided with a parachute, in falling has a destructive force of a great scope as a result of its explosion in the air. It is evident, therefore, that it is technically impossible to limit the effect of its use to special objectives such as designated by President Truman, and the American authorities are perfectly aware of this. In fact, it has been established on the scene that the damage extends over a great area and that combatant and non-combatant men and women, old and young, are massacred without discrimination by the atmospheric pressure of the explosion, as well as by the radiating heat which results therefrom. Consequently there is involved a bomb having the most cruel effects humanity has ever known, not only as far as the extensive and immense damage is concerned, but also for reasons of suffering endured by each victim.

"It is an elementary principle of international public law that in time of war the belligerents do not have unlimited right in the choice of the means of attack and that they cannot resort to projectile arms or any other means capable of causing the enemy needless suffering. These principles are stipulated in the Convention respecting the laws and customs of war on land and in Article 22, as well as under letter (E) of Article 23 of the rules concerning the laws and customs of war on land. Since the beginning of the present war, the American Government has declared on various occasions that the use of gas or other inhuman means of combat were considered illegal in the public opinion of civilized human society and that it would not avail itself of these means before enemy countries resorted to them. The bombs in question, used by the Americans, by their cruelty and by their terrorizing effects, surpass by far gas or any other arm the use of which is prohibited by the treaties for reasons of their characteristics.

"The Americans have effected bombardments of towns in the greatest part of Japanese territory, without discrimination massacring a great number of old people, women, children; destroying and burning down Shinto and Buddhist temples, schools, hospitals, living quarters, etc. This fact alone means that they have shown complete defiance of the essential principles of humanitarian laws, as well as international law. They now use this new bomb, having an uncontrollable and cruel effect much greater than any other arms or projectiles ever used to date. This constitutes a new crime against humanity and civilization. The Government of Japan, in its own name and at the same time in the name of all of humanity and civilization, accuses the American Government with the present note of the use of an inhuman weapon of this nature and demands energetically abstinence from its use."

Reference: I-10
WASHINGTON, August 11, 1945.

From the diary of Henry A. Wallace:

August 10, 1945

...The President, who usually comes to cabinet not later than 2:05, came in about 2:25 saying he was sorry to be late but that he and Jimmie had been busy working on a reply to Japanese proposals. Byrnes then read very slowly the Japanese proposal just as it was printed in the press late in the afternoon.

....

Byrnes stopped while reading the proposal and laid special emphasis on the top dog commander over Hirohito being an American. They were not going to have any chance for misunderstanding as in Europe. They said the proposal had been transmitted to the other Allies and that they had already heard from Bevin[1] and Bevin was in accord. Truman then interjected most fiercely that he didn't think we would hear from the Russians but that we would go ahead without them anyway. Stimson said the Russians were in favor of delay so they could push as far into Manchuria as possible. Truman said it was to our interest that the Russians not push too far into Manchuria. He said there was no agreement with Russia about Manchuria. This surprised me because I remember what Roosevelt used to say in the spring of 1944 about his agreement with Stalin on access to Dairen.

Truman said he had given orders to stop atomic bombing. He said the thought of wiping out another 100,000 people was too horrible. He didn't like the idea of killing, as he said, "all those kids."

Referring to hard and soft terms for Japan, Truman referred to 170 telegrams precipitated by the peace rumor of August 9. 153 of the 170 were for hard terms--unconditional surrender. They were free-will telegrams--not inspired--and were mostly from parents of service-men.

[1]Ernest Bevin, newly elected prime minister of Great Britain.

Exchange of Notes between the Secretary of State (Byrnes) and the
   Swiss Charge d'Affaires ad interim (Grässli) Regarding the Offer
   of Surrender from the Japanese Government.

Note from the Swiss Charge d'Affaires ad interim to the Secretary
   of State, August 10, 1945.

I have the honor to inform you that the Japanese Minister to Switzerland, upon instructions received from his Government, has requested
the Swiss Political Department to advise the Government of the United
States of America of the following:

In obedience to the gracious command of His Majesty the Emperor who, ever
anxious to enhance the cause of world peace, desires earnestly to bring about a
speedy termination of hostilities with a view to saving mankind from the ca-
lamities to be imposed upon them by further continuation of the war, the Japanese
Government several weeks ago asked the Soviet Government, with which neutral
relations then prevailed, to render good offices in restoring peace vis-a-vis the
enemy powers. Unfortunately, these efforts in the interest of peace having failed,
the Japanese Government in conformity with the august wish of His Majesty
to restore the general peace and desiring to put an end to the untold sufferings
entailed by war as quickly as possible, have decided upon the following.
The Japanese Government are ready to accept the terms enumerated in the
joint declaration which was issued at Potsdam on July 26th, 1945, by the heads
of the Governments of the United States, Great Britain, and China, and later
subscribed by the Soviet Government, with the understanding that the said
declaration does not comprise any demand which prejudices the prerogatives of
His Majesty as a Sovereign Ruler.
The Japanese Government sincerely hope that this understanding is warranted
and desire keenly that an explicit indication to that effect will be speedily
forthcoming.

In transmitting the above message the Japanese Minister added that
his Government begs the Government of the United States to forward
its answer through the intermediary of Switzerland. Similar requests
are being transmitted to the Governments of Great Britain and the
Union of Soviet Socialist Republics through the intermediary of Sweden,
as well as to the Government of China through the intermediary of
Switzerland. The Chinese Minister at Berne has already been informed
of the foregoing through the channel of the Swiss Political Department.
Please be assured that I am at your disposal at any time to accept for
and forward to my Government the reply of the Government of the
United States.

Note from the Secretary of State to the Swiss Charge d'Affaires ad
interim, August 11, 1945.

I have the honor to acknowledge receipt of your note of August 10,
and in reply to inform you that the President of the United States has
directed me to send to you for transmission by your Government to the
Japanese Government the following message on behalf of the Governments of the United States, the United Kingdom, the Union of Soviet
Socialist Republics, and China:

With regard to the Japanese Government's message accepting the terms of
the Potsdam proclamation but containing the statement, "with the understanding that the said declaration does not comprise any demand which prejudices
the prerogatives of His Majesty as a soveriegn ruler," our position is as follows:
From the moment of surrender the authority of the Emperor and the Japanese
Government to rule the state shall be subject to the Supreme Commander of
the Allied powers who will take such steps as he deems proper to effectuate the
surrender terms.
The Emperor will be required to authorize and ensure the signature by the
Government of Japan and the Japanese Imperial General Headquarters of the
surrender terms necessary to carry out the provisions of the Potsdam Declaration, and shall issue his commands to all the Japanese military, naval and air
authorities and to all the forces under their control wherever located to cease
active operations and to surrender their arms, and to issue such other orders as
the Supreme Commander may require to give effect to the surrender terms.
Immediately upon the surrender the Japanese Government shall transport
prisoners of war and civilian internees to places of safety, as directed, where
they can quickly be placed aboard Allied transports.
The ultimate form of government of Japan shall, in accordance with the
Potsdam Declaration, be established by the freely expressed will of the Japanese
people.
The armed forces of the Allied Powers will remain in Japan until the purposes
set forth in the Potsdam Declaration are achieved.

The Swiss Charge (Grässli) to the Secretary of State

WASHINGTON, August 14, 1945.

SIR: I have the honor to refer to your note of August 11, in which you requested me to transmit to my Government the reply of the Governments of the United States, the United Kingdom, the Union of Soviet Socialist Republics, and China to the message from the Japanese Government which was communicated in my note of August 10.

At 20.10 today (Swiss Time) the Japanese Minister to Switzerland conveyed the following written statement to the Swiss Government for transmission to the four Allied governments:

"Communication of the Japanese Government of August 14, 1945, addressed to the Governments of the United States, Great Britain, the Soviet Union, and China:

"With reference to the Japanese Government's note of August 10 regarding their acceptance of the provisions of the Potsdam declaration and the reply of the Governments of the United States, Great Britain, the Soviet Union, and China sent by American Secretary of State Byrnes under the date of August 11, the Japanese Government have the honor to communicate to the Governments of the four powers as follows:

"1. His Majesty the Emperor has issued an Imperial rescript regarding Japan's acceptance of the provisions of the Potsdam declaration.

"2. His Majesty the Emperor is prepared to authorize and ensure the signature by his Government and the Imperial General Headquarters of the necessary terms for carrying out the provisions of the Potsdam declaration. His Majesty is also prepared to issue his commands to all the military, naval, and air authorities of Japan and all the forces under their control wherever located to cease active operations, to surrender arms and to issue such other orders as may be required by the Supreme Commander of the Allied Forces for the execution of the above-mentioned terms."

Grässli

The Secretary of State to the Swiss Charge (Grässli)

WASHINGTON, August 14, 1945.

SIR: With reference to your communication of today's date, transmitting the reply of the Japanese Government to the communication
which I sent through you to the Japanese Government on August 11,
on behalf to the Governments of the United States, China, the United
Kingdom, and the Union of Soviet Socialist Republics, which I regard
as full acceptance of the Potsdam Declaration and of my statement
of August 11, 1945, I have the honor to inform you that the President
of the United States has directed that the following message be sent
to you for transmission to the Japanese Government:

"-You are to proceed as follows:
 -(1) Direct prompt cessation of hostilities by Japanese forces,
informing the Supreme Commander for the Allied Powers of the
effective date and hour of such cessation.
 -(2) Send emissaries at once to the Supreme Commander for the
Allied Powers with information of the disposition of the Japanese
forces and commanders, and fully empowered to make any arrangements directed by the Supreme Commander for the Allied Powers
to enable him and his accompanying forces to arrive at the place designated by him to receive the formal surrender.
 -(3) For the purpose of receiving such surrender and carrying
it into effect, General of the Army Douglas MacArthur has been
designated as the Supreme Commander for the Allied Powers, and he
will notify the Japanese Government of the time, place and other
details of the formal surrender."

(JAMES F. BYRNES)

PART 7

Report and recommendations of the Scientific Advisory Panel on future atomic weapons. Byrne rejects international cooporation. Stimson recommends postwar cooporation with the Russians over control of atomic bombs. Public opinion regarding Japan and the postwar world. U.S. Strategic Bombing Survey report on Japan's decision to surrender. An American soldier'7s view of the use of atomic bombs.

Aftermath

Nagasaki

Japanese sign unconditional surrender

Truman with surrender

Nagasaki

Within days of the atomic bombing of Hiroshima and Nagasaki, disturbing reports began to reach Washington from Japan. General Groves, for one, did not know what to make of them. Tokyo Rose, the English-speaking propagandist, had broadcast word of strange injuries and illnesses among the survivors. Soon the reputable Japanese news agency Domei was describing "uncanny effects." "Even those who received minor burns and looked quite healthy at first," one story read, "weakened after a few days for some unknown reason."

The bombs had released an invisible killer—radiation. The results of exposure would take years to understand and assess. Even then, controversy would rage over acceptable limits of tolerance and total number of casualties. At first, the stories from Japan were so unexpected that authorities in the United States doubted what they were hearing. No one thought the atomic bomb would yield more than, in Oppenheimer's words, a "very big bang." Everyone assumed that all casualties would be from a standard explosion. "The region over which there would have been radiation injury was to be a much smaller one than the region of so-called 100% blast kill," recalled Norman Ramsey, former chief of the Delivery Group at Los Alamos. "Any person with radiation damage would have been killed with a brick first."

When news of radiation contamination began to arrive from Tokyo, scientists at Los Alamos were dismayed. The prospect of what they called the "murderous delayed radioactive effects" led them to wire Groves asking for more information. An incredulous Groves suspected a Japanese hoax. After telephoning physicians and other experts, Groves concluded that the reported burns were really the result of heat from the bomb—and a desire for international sympathy. "I think it's good propaganda," one military doctor told him (see Document 92). "The thing is these people got good and burned—good thermal burns." "That's the feeling I have," Groves replied.

Delayed deaths were harder to explain away. Only slowly did Groves, the scientists, and the doctors come to appreciate this unintended consequence of the bomb. Early estimates by the U.S. Strategic Bombing Survey, a panel appointed after the war by President Truman to examine the results of strategic bombing, soon placed the number of deaths from radiation at 15 to 20 percent of the total. Later figures for Hiroshima alone, admittedly conservative, ran as high as 20,000 killed, with another 20,000 sustaining radiation injuries.

Almost immediately, American motives in using the weapon came under attack. One Associated Press article in late August 1945 claimed that the dead were probably "victims of a phenomenon which is well known in the great radiation laboratories of America" (see Document 92). Over the years, as death, cancer, retardation, and abnormalities mounted among the victims, the charge that American policymakers intended to kill and maim through radiation would be repeated. When, in 1955, twenty-five young girls disfigured at Hiroshima were brought for surgery to Mount Sinai Hospital in New York, it was interpreted as an American admission of guilt, not simply a humanitarian gesture. Horrid intent on the part of those who built and dropped the bomb was assumed when, in fact, they had not fully understood the consequences of what they were making.

The American people had less information than did their leaders. Soon after the occupation of Japan began, General Douglas MacArthur temporarily suspended the publication of two leading Japanese dailies, *Asahi* and *Nippon*

Times, following warnings to the Japanese press against publishing "inflammable" headlines and "needling" articles. In mid-August 1945, before any news of the aftereffects had been made public, a Gallup poll revealed that 85 percent of Americans approved of "using the new atomic bomb on Japanese cities" (see Document 93). It was not that the pursuit of victory made use of every weapon acceptable to the public. Two months earlier, only 40 percent favored using poison gas (outlawed after the First World War) against the Japanese. Those who so readily endorsed dropping the bomb made their judgment, like everyone else, without knowing what the effects would be.

Initially, as historian Paul Boyer has shown in *By the Bomb's Early Light: American Thought and Culture at the Dawn of the Atomic Age* (1986), Americans greeted the atomic bomb with a confused mixture of gratitude and foreboding. But according to journalist Hanson Baldwin, it had also "unleashed a Frankenstein monster" capable of killing its creators. It was regarded as more than a weapon—more, even, than a scientific breakthrough. From the start, the atomic bomb was also depicted as a demigod, literally endowing mankind with Olympian might.

Less than a week after the surrender of Japan, the editors of *Life* magazine pronounced fission a major step in subduing nature. Atomic energy was, to this generation, what fire had been to the ancients. The world should rejoice that "Prometheus, the subtle artificer and friend of man, is still an American citizen." On the other hand, *Life* editors reminded readers that the vaporization of Hiroshima contained a terrifying insight: "No limits are set to our Promethean ingenuity, provided that we remember that we are not Jove." Two years later, sobering anxieties turned such cautious enthusiasm into skepticism. A public opinion poll conducted in October 1947 found that only 55 percent of Americans (down from 69 percent in 1945) considered the development of the atomic bomb "a good thing." Thirty-eight percent (more than double the number two years earlier) believed it was "a bad thing."

However ambivalent Americans might have been about the atomic bomb, their culture absorbed and diffused the results with remarkable speed. Within a month of Hiroshima, one magazine ran the photograph of a bosomy Hollywood starlet who had been dubbed "The Anatomic Bomb." Bartenders at the Washington Press Club served up an "Atomic Cocktail" (a greenish concoction of Pernod and gin); department stores ran "atomic sales"; and advertisers promised "atomic results." An imaginative manufacturer gathered glasslike stones from sand fused by the test at Alamogordo and marketed them as costume jewelry, unaware of the danger of radioactivity.

As the postwar world unfolded, the ambivalence so characteristic of the early years continued to mark American—and international— thinking about atomic weaponry. Gregg Herken's *Counsels of War* (1985), which traces the deliberations over nuclear strategy since Hiroshima, concludes that all the major elements of later engagements with nuclear-arms policy were present at the creation: visions of a nuclear holocaust; desperate demands to reach an international agreement; naive faith in the power of expertise; the urge to rely on bigger and bigger bombs to maintain security. The questions raised during the Manhattan Project and immediately after Hiroshima and Nagasaki also remain at the heart of historical inquiry: Were the atomic bomb and its progeny instruments of peace or of war? Could an international agreement to control its development and use have been framed earlier? Did the atomic bomb even end the Second World War? This historical debate, like the debate over nuclear-arms policy, is yet another legacy of the Manhattan Project.

TOP SECRET

WAR DEPARTMENT
WASHINGTON

17 August 1945.

The Secretary of War,
War Department,
Washington, D. C.

Dear Mr. Secretary:

The Interim Committee has asked us to report in some detail on
the scope and program of future work in the field of atomic energy.
One important phase of this work is the development of weapons; and
since this is the problem which has dominated our war time activities,
it is natural that in this field our ideas should be most definite
and clear, and that we should be most confident of answering adequately the questions put to us by the committee. In examining these
questions we have, however, come on certain quite general conclusions,
whose implications for national policy would seem to be both more
immediate and more profound than those of the detailed technical recommendations to be submitted. We, therefore, think it appropriate to
present them to you at this time.

1. We are convinced that weapons quantitatively and qualitatively
far more effective than now available will result from further work on
those problems. This conviction is motivated not alone by analogy
with past developments, but by specific projects to improve and multiply
the existing weapons, and by the quite favorable technical prospects of
the realization of the super bomb.

2. We have been unable to devise or propose effective military
countermeasures for atomic weapons. Although we realize that future
work may reveal possibilities at present obscure to us, it is our firm
opinion that no military countermeasures will be found which will be
adequately effective in preventing the delivery of atomic weapons.

The detailed technical report in preparation will document these
conclusions, but hardly alter them.

3. We are not only unable to outline a program that would assure
to this nation for the next decades hegemony in the field of atomic
weapons; we are equally unable to insure that such hegemony, if

TOP SECRET

TOP SECRET

achieved, could protect us from the most terrible destruction.

4. The development, in the years to come, of more effective atomic weapons, would appear to be a most natural element in any national policy of maintaining our military forces at great strength; nevertheless we have grave doubts that this further development can contribute essentially or permanently to the prevention of war. We believe that the safety of this nation - as opposed to its ability to inflict damage on an enemy power - cannot lie wholly or even primarily in its scientific or technical prowess. It can be based only on making future wars impossible. It is our unanimous and urgent recommendation to you that, despite the present incomplete exploitation of technical possibilities in this field, all steps be taken, all necessary international arrangements be made, to this one end.

5. We should be most happy to have you bring these views to the attention of other members of the Government, or of the American people, should you wish to do so.

Very sincerely,

J R Oppenheimer
For the Panel

TOP SECRET

18 August 1945

MEMORANDUM FOR THE RECORD:

I showed the attached letter[1] and memorandum to Secretary Byrnes and emphasized that the subject matter in Paragraph 1B was a matter which would probably require early consideration and decision by the Administration, especially in view of the Oppenheimer letter addressed to Secretary Stimson and dated August 1y which he read. He was so interested in it that he asked me to leave a copy with him; this I did. Secretary Byrnes was definitely of the opinion that it would be difficult to do anything on the international level at the present time and that in his opinion we should continue the Manhattan Project with full force, at least until Congress has acted on the proposed Bill. He also said that we should continue our efforts and negotiations in behalf of the Combined Development Trust. In his opinion the whole situation justifies and requires a continuation of all our efforts on all fronts to keep ahead of the race. For that reason, he said that he would ask the President to sign a memorandum which Mr. Marbury and General Groves are to prepare requesting Mr. Snyder, Director of Mobilization, formally to approve a continuation of all necessary expenditure by the Manhattan Disctrict or by the Combined Development Trust.

Secretary Byrnes felt so strongly about all of this that he requested me to tell Dr. Oppenheimer for the time being his proposal about an international agreement was not practical and that he and the rest of the gang should pursue their work full force. I told Secretary Byrnes that I understood from Dr. Oppenheimer the scientists prefer not to do that (superbomb)[2] unless ordered or directed to do so by the Government on the grounds of national policy. I thought, however, work in the Manhattan District could proceed the way he wants in improving present techniques without raising the question of the "super" at least until after Congress has acted on our proposed Bill.

GEORGE L. HARRISON

[1]See Document 89.
[2]The hydrogen bomb, employing the power of nuclear fusion and immensely more powerful than the fission bombs that destroyed Hiroshima and Nagasaki.

AUGUST 22
JAPAN

Interviewing Date 7/27–8/1/45
Survey #352-K   Question #6

How should we treat the Japanese people after the war?

Control strictly, punish war criminals	53%
Treat fairly, start reeducating them	33
Treat with extreme harshness	14
Miscellaneous	3
No opinion	7
	110%

(Note: table adds to more than 100% because some persons suggested more than one treatment.)

AUGUST 25
POSTWAR PROBLEMS

Special Survey

Britons were asked: What do you think will be the chief postwar problem?

Housing	54%
Employment	13
Preparing for return of troops ..	4
Other	29

French citizens were asked: What do you think will be the chief postwar problem?

Food	38%
Internal politics	14
Collaborationists	11
Cost of living	8
Other	29

Americans were asked: What do you think will be the chief postwar problem?

Jobs	20%
Avoiding a depression	16
Permanent peace	15
Strikes	10
Other	39

AUGUST 26
WEAPONS AND JAPAN

Interviewing Date 8/10–15/45
Survey #353-K   Question #8c

Do you approve or disapprove of using the new atomic bomb on Japanese cities?

Approve	85%
Disapprove	10
No opinion	5

When this vote is broken down there is hardly any difference of opinion by sex, age, or education.

Interviewing Date 6/14–19/45
Survey #349-K   Question #3a

Would you favor or oppose using poison gas against the Japanese if doing so would reduce the number of American soldiers who are killed and wounded?

Favor	40%
Oppose	49
No opinion	11

A majority of young people favor the use of poison gas, while persons 50 years and older are substantially opposed to the idea. Men oppose the idea of using gas to a greater extent than women, and college-trained people are more opposed than people with no more than an elementary school education.

TOP SECRET

MEMORANDUM of Telephone conversation between General Groves and Lt. Col. Rea, Oak Ridge Hospital, 9:00 a.m., 25 August 1945.

G: " . . .   which fatally burned 30,000 victims during the first two weeks following its explosion."

R: Ultra-violet - is that the word?

G: Yes.

R: That's kind of crazy.

G: Of course, it's crazy - a doctor like me can tell that. "The death toll at Hiroshima and at Nagasaki, the other Japanese city blasted atomically, is still rising, the broadcast said. Radio Tokyo described Hiroshima as a city of death. 90% of its houses, in which 250,000 had lived, were instantly crushed." I don't understand the 250,000 because it had a much bigger population a number of years ago before the war started, and it was a military city. "Now it is peopled by ghost parade, the living doomed to die of radioactivity burns."

R: Let me interrupt you here a minute. I would say this: I think it's good propaganda. The thing is these people got good and burned - good thermal burns.

G: That's the feeling I have. Let me go on here and give you the rest of the picture. "So painful are these injuries that sufferers plead: 'Please kill me,' the broadcast said. No one can ever completely recover."

R: This has been in our paper, too, last night.

G: Then it goes on: "Radioactivity caused by the fission of the uranium used in atomic bombs is taking a toll of mounting deaths and causing reconstruction workers in Hiroshima to suffer various sicknesses and ill health."

R: I would say this: You yourself, as far as radioactivity is concerned, it isn't anything immediate, it's a prolonged thing. I think what these people have, they just got a good thermal burn, that's what it is. A lot of these people, first of all, they don't notice it much. You may get burned and you may have a little redness, but in a couple of days you may have a big blister or a sloughing of the skin, and I think that is what these people have had.

G: That is brought out a little later on. Now it says here: "A special news correspondent of the Japs said that three days after the bomb fell, there were 30,000 dead, and two weeks later the death toll had mounted to 80,000 and is continuing to rise." One thing is they are finding the bodies.

TOP SECRET

TOP SECRET

R: They are getting the delayed action of the burn. For instance, at the Coconut Grove, they didn't all die at once, you know - they were dying for a month afterward.

G: Now then, he says - this is the thing I wanted to ask you about particularly - "an examination of soldiers working on reconstruction projects one week after the bombing showed that their white corpuscles had diminished by half and a severe deficiency of red corpuscles."

R: I read that, too - I think there's something hookum about that.

G: Would they both go down?

R: They may, yes - they may, but that's awfully quick, pretty terrifically quick. Of course, it depends - - - - - but I wonder if you aren't getting a good dose of propaganda.

G: Of course, we are getting a good dose of propaganda, due to the idiotic performance of the scientists and another one who is also on the project, and the newspapers and the radio wanting news.

R: Of course, those Jap scientists over there aren't so dumb either and they are making a play on this, too. They evidently know what the possibility is. Personally, I discounted an awful lot of it, as it's too early, and in the second place, I think that a lot of these deaths they are getting are just delayed thermal burns.

G: You see what we are faced with. Matthias is having trouble holding his people out there.

R: Do you want me to get you some real straight dope on this, just how it affects them, and call you back in just a bit?

G: That's true - that's what I want. Did you also see anything about the Geiger counter? It says that the fact that the uranium had permeated into the ground has been easily ascertained by using a Geiger counter and it has been disclosed that the uranium used in the atomic bomb is harmful to human bodies. Then it talks about this, which is just the thing that we thought -- The majority of injured persons received burns from powerful ultra-violet rays and those within a two-kilometer radius from the center received burns two or three times, which, I suppose, is second or third degree. Those within three to four kilometers received burns to the extent that their skin is burned bright red, but if these burns are caused by ultra-violet, they hardly felt the heat at that time. Later, however, blisters formed resulting in dropsy.

R: That's why I say it's got to be a thermal burn.

G: Then they talk about the burned portions of the bodies are infected from the inside.

R: Well, of course, any burn is potentially an infected wound. We treat any burn as an infected wound. I think you had better get the anti-propagandists out.

TOP SECRET

---

[1]The Coconut Grove, a Boston nightclub, was the scene of a terrible fire in November 1942 that killed over 400 people.

TOP SECRET

G: Of course you are, because the whole damage has been done by our own people, there is nothing we can do except sit tight. The reason I am telling you is because we can't get hold of Ferry and because I might be asked at any time and I would like to be able to answer. Did you see about the Army men who had received burns on reconstruction? "Examination of 33 servicemen, of whom 10 had received burns in reconstruction projects, one week after the bombing took place, showed those with burns had 3150 white corpuscles and others, who were apparently healthy, had 3600, compared to the ordinary healthy person who has 7,000 to 8,000." This is a drastic decrease. Comes over from Tokyo. On the other hand, servicemen with burns had only 3,000,000 red corpuscles and others apparently healthy had just a little bit more when compared to 4,500,000 to 5,000,000 in the ordinary healthy person." What is that measured by?

R: You go by cubic millimeters. I would say this right off the bat - Anybody with burns, the red count goes down after a while, and the white count may go down, too, just from an ordinary burn. I can't get too excited about that.

G: We are not bothered a bit, excepting for - what they are trying to do is create sympathy. The sad part of it all is that an American started them off.

R: Let me look it up and I'll give you some straight dope on it.

G: This is the kind of thing that hurts us -- "The Japanese, who were reported today by Tokyo radio, to have died mysteriously a few days after the atomic bomb blast, probably were the victims of a phenomenon which is well known in the great radiation laboratories of America." That, of course, is what does us the damage.

R: I would say this: You will have to get some big-wig to put a counterstatement in the paper.

TOP SECRET

TOP SECRET

MEMRANDUM of Telephone conversation between General Groves and Lt. Col. Rea, Oak Ridge Hospital, 10:30 a.m., 25 August 1945:

G: .... with respect to the crater only, on the ground that nothing outside the crater had any effect at any time.

R: I tell you another one that I talked to Dr. Wensel about. He said that one person who could give some very good information, and who would be a little outside the inner circle, was L. F. Curtis. You know, he was down at Clinton Labs at one time, and is with the Bureau of Standards now. He knows more about radiation effects probably than anybody, and I think his number there is Ordway 4040. Of course, we do know this - I can't tell you much over the phone - we do know what some of these effects are, and it depends on the dose, etc. Undoubtedly, when you read this in here - we know, for instance, that radiation does not cause the burn immediately, it's later on, now the heat and the radiation going together, but the immediate effects they have are undoubtedly burns. No question at all about that. I notice, too, in the paper about that white count going down and the red count, but after all it's a very poorly-controlled experiment when you don't know those people's white counts specifically were beforehand. Some normal people have a 4,000 white count.

G: Is there any difference between Japanese blood and others?

R: As far as I can make out, no. About the same (I looked it up). It seems to be pretty standard. The way they print up the remark in this paper - it says: The broadcast, perhaps intended to arouse sympathy, also declared that persons in the area, as much as a week later, became ill, but did not state specifically that any of these persons died. Of course, you know, with rabbits, in those experiments, where they give them about 800 roentgens after about a week or so, it usually happens for some long prolonged time afterward.

G: They couldn't have possibly got 800 roentgens here, could they?

R: Well, it's a little unusual. You saw that report from Warren on the test? Well, they have a lot of stuff in that, you know. I think we had better get the OWI back and counteract some of this.

G: I think that, if nothing happens, it should just be ignored.

R: To tell you the truth, I don't think many people know the difference between a 2,000 white count and a 50,000 white count. I think the way it is written here, at the end of the article - AP release - "the radioactivity causes loss of appetite, etc." Ours is a very general article - I'm sure these things must be just good old thermal burns.

G: From what I've heard about how much food they get in Japan, I don't think they'd lose their appetite, do you?

R: I don't blame them.

TOP SECRET

TOP SECRET

R: Do you have the report from Col. Warren in here on the New Mexico tests?

G: Yes.

R: Listing of the blisters, of course, they mention here (some of the words
    are left out according to our report here, with words missing right here)
    they say what I told you about the kilometers, this reference might mean
    second or third degree burns - I think they give it away right there -
    what they're referring to.

G: Yes, I think so. When was that report of Warren's written?

R: On first test in May.

G: We got that one.

R: Then there is a written one by Frisdall.

G: We have it.

R: Myself, I'd just ignore this - we thought something was going to happen -
    the thermal burn was the main thing.

TOP SECRET

September 11, 1945.

Dear Mr. President:

In handing you today my memorandum about our relations
with Russia in respect to the atomic bomb, I am not unmindful of
the fact that when in Potsdam I talked with you about the question
whether we could be safe in sharing the atomic bomb with Russia
while she was still a police state and before she put into effect
provisions assuring personal rights of liberty to the individual
citizen.

I still recognize the difficulty and am still convinced
~~of the importance~~ of the ultimate importance of a change in Russian
attitude toward individual liberty but I have come to the conclusion that it would not be possible to use our possession of
the atomic bomb as a direct lever to produce the change. I have
become convinced that any demand by us for an internal change
in Russia as a condition of sharing in the atomic weapon would
be so resented that it would make the objective we have in view
less probable.

I believe that the change in attitude toward the individual in Russia will come slowly and gradually and I am satisfied
that we should not delay our approach to Russia in the matter of the
atomic bomb until that process has been completed. My reasons
are set forth in the memorandum I am handing you today. Furthermore, I believe that this long process of change in Russia is
more likely to be expedited by the closer relationship in the

-2-

matter of the atomic bomb which I suggest and the trust and
confidence that I believe would be inspired by the method of
approach which I have outlined.

Faithfully yours,

HENRY L. STIMSON

Secretary of War.

The President,

The White House.

11 September 1945

MEMORANDUM FOR THE PRESIDENT:

       Subject: Proposed Action for Control of Atomic Bombs

      The advent of the atomic bomb has stimulated great military
and probably even greater political interest throughout the civilized
world. In a world atmosphere already extremely sensitive to power,
the introduction of this weapon has profoundly affected political
considerations in all sections of the globe.

      In many quarters it has been interpreted as a substantial
offset to the growth of Russian influence on the continent. We can
be certain that the Soviet government has sensed this tendency and
the temptation will be strong for the Soviet political and military
leaders to acquire this weapon in the shortest possible time.
Britain in effect already has the status of a partner with us in the
development of this weapon. Accordingly, unless the Soviets are volun-
tarily invited into the partnership upon a basis of cooperation and
trust, we are going to maintain the Anglo-Saxon bloc over against the
Soviet in the possession of this weapon. Such a condition will almost certainly stimulate feverish activity on the part of the Soviet
toward the development of this bomb in what will in effect be a secret
armament race of a rather desperate character. There is evidence to
indicate that such activity may have already commenced.

If we feel, as I assume we must, that civilization demands
that some day we shall arrive at a satisfactory international arrangement respecting the control of this new force, the question then is
how long we can afford to enjoy our momentary superiority in the hope
of achieving our immediate peace council objectives.

Whether Russia gets control of the necessary secrets of
production in a minimum of say four years or a maximum of twenty years
is not nearly as important to the world and civilization as to make
sure that when they do get it they are willing and cooperative partners among the peace loving nations of the world. It is true that if
we approach them now, as I would propose, we may be gambling on their
good faith and risk their getting into production of bombs a little
sooner than they would otherwise.

To put the matter concisely, I consider the problem of our
satisfactory relations with Russia as not merely connected with but
as virtually dominated by the problem of the atomic bomb. Except
for the problem of the control of that bomb, those relations, while
vitally important, might not be immediately pressing. The establishment of relations of mutual confidence between her and us could afford
to await the slow progress of time. But with the discovery of the
bomb, they became immediately emergent. Those relations may be perhaps irretrievably embittered by the way in which we approach the
solution of the bomb with Russia. For if we fail to approach them

-2-

now and merely continue to negotiate with them, having this weapon rather ostentatiously on our hip, their suspicions and their distrust of our purposes and motives will increase. It will inspire them to greater efforts in an all out effort to solve the problem. If the solution is achieved in that spirit, it is much less likely that we will ever get the kind of covenant we may desperately need in the future. This risk is, I believe, greater than the other, inasmuch as our objective must be to get the best kind of international bargain we can -- one that has some chance of being kept and saving civilization not for five or for twenty years, but forever.

The chief lesson I have learned in a long life is that the only way you can make a man trustworthy is to trust him; and the surest way to make him untrustworthy is to distrust him and show your distrust.

If the atomic bomb were merely another though more devastating military weapon to be assimilated into our pattern of international relations, it would be one thing. We could then follow the old custom of secrecy and nationalistic military superiority relying on international caution to prescribe the future use of the weapon as we did with gas. But I think the bomb instead constitutes merely a first step in a new control by man over the forces of nature too revolutionary and dangerous to fit into the old concepts. I think it really caps the climax of the race between man's growing technical

-3-

power for destructiveness and his psychological power of self-
control and group control -- his moral power. If so, our method
of approach to the Russians is a question of the most vital importance in the evolution of human progress.

Since the crux of the problem is Russia, any contemplated
action leading to the control of this weapon should be primarily
directed _to_ Russia. It is my judgment that the Soviet would be more
apt to respond sincerely to a dirct and forthright approach made by
the United States on this subject than would be the case if the approach were made as a part of a general international scheme, or if
the approach were made after a succession of express or implied
threats or near threats in our peace negotiations.

My idea of an approach to the Soviets would be a direct
proposal after discussion with the British that we would be prepared in effect to enter an arrangement with the Russians, the
general purpose of which would be to control and limit the use of
the atomic bomb as an instrument of war and so far as possible to
direct and encourage the development of atomic power for peaceful
and humanitarian purposes. Such an approach might more specifically
lead to the proposal that we would stop work on the further improvement in, or manufacture of, the bomb as a military weapon, provided
the Russians and the British would agree to do likewise. It might
also provide that we would be willing to impound what bombs we now

-4-

have in the United States provided the Russians and the British would agree with us that in no event will they or we use a bomb as an instrument of war unless all three Governments agree to that use. We might also consider including in the arrangement a covenant with the U.K. and the Soviets providing for the exchange of benefits of future developments whereby atomic energy may be applied on a mutually satisfactory basis for commercial or humanitarian purposes.

I would make such an approach just as soon as our immediate political considerations make it appropriate.

I emphasize perhaps beyond all other considerations the importance of taking this action with Russia as a proposal of the United States - backed by Great Britain - but peculiarly the proposal of the United States. Action of any international group of nations, including many small nations who have not demonstrated their potential power or responsibility in this war would not, in my opinion, be taken seriously by the Soviets. The loose debates which would surround such proposal, if put before a conference of nations, would provoke but scant favor from the Soviet. As I say, I think this is the most important point in the program.

After the nations which have won this war have agreed to it, there will be ample time to introduce France and China into the covenants and finally to incorporate the agreement into the scheme of the United Nations. The use of this bomb has been accepted by

-5-

the world as the result of the initiative and productive capacity
of the United States, and think this factor is a most potent
lever toward having our proposals accepted by the Soviets, whereas
I am most skeptical of obtaining any tangible results by way of any
international debate. I urge this method as the most realistic
means of accomplishing this vitally important step in the history
of the world.

                                        HENRY L. STIMSON
                                        Secretary of War.

-6-

JAPAN'S STRUGGLE TO END THE WAR

The Hiroshima and Nagasaki atomic bombs did not defeat Japan, nor by the testimony of the enemy leaders who ended the war did they persuade Japan to accept unconditional surrender. The Emperor, the Lord Privy Seal, the Prime Minister, the Foreign Minister, and the Navy Minister had decided as early as May of 1945 that the war should be ended even if it meant acceptance of defeat on allied terms. The War Minister and the two chiefs of staff opposed unconditional surrender. The impact of the Hiroshima attack was to bring further urgency and lubrication to the machinery of achieving peace, primarily by contributing to a situation which permitted the Prime Minister to bring the Emperor overtly and directly into a position where his decision for immediate acceptance of the Potsdam Declaration could be used to override the remaining objectors. Thus, although the atomic bombs changed no votes of the Supreme War Direction Council concerning the Potsdam terms, they did foreshorten the war and expedite the peace.

Events and testimony which support these conclusions are blue-printed from the chronology established in the first sections of this report:

(a) The mission of the Suzuki government, appointed 7 April 1945, was to make peace. An appearance of negotiating for terms less onerous than unconditional surrender was maintained in order to contain the military and bureaucratic elements still determined on a final Bushido defense, and perhaps even more importantly to obtain freedom to create peace with a minimum of personal danger and internal obstruction. It seems clear however that in extremis the peacemakers would have peace, and peace on any terms. This was the gist of advice given to Hirohito by the Jushin in February, the declared conclusion of Kido in April, the underlying reason for Koiso's fall in April, the specific injunction of the Emperor to Suzuki on becoming premier which was known to all members of his cabinet.

(b) A series of conferences of the Supreme War Direction Council before Hirohito on the subject of continuing or terminating the war began on 8 June and continued through 14 August. At the 8 June meeting the war situation was reviewed. On 20 June the Emperor, supported by the Premier, Foreign Minister, and Navy Minister, declared for peace; the Army Minister and the two chiefs of staff did not concur. On 10 July the Emperor again urged haste in the moves to mediate through Russia, but Potsdam intervened. While the Government still awaited a Russian answer, the Hiroshima bomb was dropped on 6 August.

(c) Consideration of the Potsdam terms within the Supreme War Direction Council revealed the same three-to-three cleavage which first appeared at the Imperial conference on 20 June. On the morning of 9 August Premier Suzuki and Hirohito decided at once to accept the Potsdam terms; meetings and moves thereafter were designed to legalize the decision and prepare the Imperial rescript. At the conclusive Imperial conference, on the night of 9–10 August, the Supreme War Direction Council still split three-to-three. It was necessary for the Emperor finally to repeat his desire for acceptance of the Potsdam terms.

(d) Indubitably the Hiroshima bomb and the rumor derived from interrogation of an American prisoner (B-29 pilot) who stated that an atom bomb attack on Tokyo was scheduled for 12 August introduced urgency in the minds of the Government and magnified the pressure behind its moves to end the war.

7. The sequence of events just recited also defines the effect of Russia's entry into the Pacific war on 8 August 1945. Coming 2 days after the Hiroshima bomb, the move neither defeated Japan nor materially hastened the acceptance of surrender nor changed the votes of the Supreme War Direction Council. Nego-

tiation for Russia to intercede began the forepart of May 1945 in both Tokyo and Moscow. Konoye, the intended emissary to the Soviets, stated to the Survey that while ostensibly he was to negotiate, he received direct and secret instructions from the Emperor to secure peace at any price, notwithstanding its severity. Sakomizu, the chief cabinet secretary, alleged that while awaiting the Russian answer on mediation, Suzuki and Togo decided that were it negative direct overtures would be made to the United States. Efforts toward peace through the Russians, forestalled by the imminent departure of Stalin and Molotov for Potsdam, were answered by the Red Army's advance into Manchuria. The Kwantung army, already weakened by diversion of its units and logistics to bolster island defenses in the South and written off for the defense of Japan proper, faced inescapable defeat.

There is little point in attempting more precisely to impute Japan's unconditional surrender to any one of the numerous causes which jointly and cumulatively were responsible for Japan's disaster. Concerning the absoluteness of her defeat there can be no doubt. The time lapse between military impotence and political acceptance of the inevitable might have been shorter had the political structure of Japan permitted a more rapid and decisive determination of national policies. It seems clear, however, that air supremacy and its later exploitation over Japan proper was the major factor which determined the timing of Japan's surrender and obviated any need for invasion.

Based on a detailed investigation of all the facts and supported by the testimony of the surviving Japanese leaders involved, it is the Survey's opinion that certainly prior to 31 December 1945, and in all probability prior to 1 November 1945, Japan would have surrendered even if the atomic bombs had not been dropped, even if Russia had not entered the war, and even if no invasion had been planned or contemplated.

'Thank God for the atom bomb.'

Many years ago in New York I saw on the side of a bus a whiskey ad which I've remembered all this time, for it's been for me a model of the brief poem. Indeed, I've come upon few short poems subsequently that evinced more genuine poetic talent. The ad consisted of two lines of "free verse," thus:

> In life, experience is the great teacher. In Scotch, Teacher's is the great experience.

For present purposes we can jettison the second line (licking our lips ruefully as it disappears), leaving the first to encapsulate a principle whose banality suggests that it enshrines a most useful truth. I bring up the matter this August, the 30th anniversary of the A-bombing of Hiroshima and Nagasaki, to focus on something suggested by the long debate about the ethics, if any, of that affair: namely, the importance of experience, sheer vulgar experience, in influencing, if not determining, one's views about the first use of the bomb. And the experience I'm talking about is that of having come to grips, face to face, with an enemy who designs your death. The experience is common to those in the infantry and the Marines and even the line Navy, to those, in short, who fought the Second World War mindful always that their mission was, as they were repeatedly told, "to close with the enemy and destroy him." I think there's something to be learned about that war, as well as about the tendency of historical memory unwittingly to resolve ambiguity, by considering some of the ways testimonies emanating from experience complicate attitudes about the cruel ending of that cruel war.

"What did you do in the Great War, Daddy?" The recruiting poster deserves ridicule and contempt, of course, but its question is embarrassingly relevant here. The problem is one that touches on the matter of social class in America. Most of those with firsthand experience of the war at its worst were relatively inarticulate and have remained silent. Few of those destined to be destroyed if the main islands had had to be invaded went on to become our most eloquent men of letters or our most impressive ethical theorists or professors of history or international jurists. The testimony of experience has come largely from rough diamonds like James Jones and William Manchester, who experienced the war in the infantry and the Marine Corps. Both would agree with the point, if not perhaps the tone, of a remark about Hiroshima made by a naval officer menaced by the kamikazes off Okinawa: "Those were the best burned women and children I ever saw." Anticipating objection from the inexperienced, Jones, in his book *WWII*, is careful to precede his chapter on Hiroshima with one detailing the plans already in motion for the infantry assaults on the home islands of Kyushu, scheduled for November 1945, and ultimately Honshu. The forthcoming invasion of Kyushu, he notes, "was well into its collecting and stockpiling stages before the war ended." (The island of Saipan was designated a main ammunition and supply base for the invasion, and if you visit it today you can see some of the assembled stuff still sitting there.) "The assault troops were chosen and already in training," Jones reminds us, and he illuminates the situation by the light of experience:

> What it must have been like to some old-timer buck sergeant or staff sergeant who had been through Guadalcanal or Bouganville or the Philippines, to stand on some beach and watch this huge war machine beginning to stir and move all around him and know that he very likely had survived this far only to fall dead on the dirt of Japan's home islands, hardly bears thinking about.

On the other hand, John Kenneth Galbraith is persuaded that the Japanese would have surrendered by November without an invasion. He thinks the atom bombs were not decisive in bringing about the surrender and he implies that their use was unjustified. What did he do in the war? He was in the Office of Price Administration in Washington, and then he was director of the United States Strategic Bombing Survey. He was 37 in 1945, and I don't demand that he experience having his ass shot off. I just note that he didn't. In saying this I'm aware of its offensive implications *ad hominem*. But here I think that approach justified. What's at stake in an infantry assault is so entirely unthinkable to those without experience of one, even if they possess very wide-ranging imaginations and sympathies, that experience is crucial in this case.

A similar remoteness from experience, as well as a similar rationalistic abstraction, seems to lie behind the reaction of an anonymous reviewer of William Manchester's *Goodbye Darkness: A Memoir of the Pacific War* for the *New York Review of Books*. First of all the reviewer dislikes Manchester's calling the enemy Nips and Japs, but what really shakes him (her?) is this passage:

> After Biak the enemy withdrew to deep caverns. Rooting them out became a bloody business which reached its ultimate horrors in the last months of the war. You think of the lives which would have been lost in an invasion of Japan's home islands—a staggering number of Americans but millions more of Japanese—and you thank God for the atomic bomb.

Thank God for the atomic bomb. From this, "one recoils," says the reviewer. One does, doesn't one?

In an interesting exchange last year in the *New York Review of Books*, Joseph Alsop and David Joravsky set forth the by now familiar arguments on both sides of the debate. You'll be able to guess which sides they chose once you know that Alsop experienced capture by the Japanese at Hong Kong in 1942 and that Joravsky made no mortal contact with the Japanese; a young soldier, he was on his way to the Pacific when the war ended. The editors of the *New York Review* have given their debate the tendentious title "Was the Hiroshima Bomb Necessary?"—surely an unanswerable question (unlike "Was It Effective?") and one suggesting the intellectual difficulties involved in imposing *ex post facto* a rational ethics on this event. Alsop focuses on the power and fanaticism of War Minister Anami, who insisted that Japan fight to the bitter end, defending the main islands with the same means and tenacity with which it had defended Iwo and Okinawa. He concludes: "Japanese surrender could never have been obtained, at any rate without the honor-satisfying bloodbath envisioned by . . . Anami, if the hideous destruction of Hiroshima and Nagasaki had not finally galvanized the peace advocates into tearing up the entire Japanese book of rules." The Japanese planned to deploy the undefeated bulk of their ground forces, over two million men, plus 10,000 kamikaze planes, in a suicidal defense. The fact, says Alsop, makes it absurd to "hold the common view, by now hardly challenged by anyone, that the decision to drop the two bombs on Japan was wicked in itself, and that President Truman and all others who joined in making or who [like Oppenheimer] assented to this decision shared in the wickedness." And in explanation of "the two bombs" Alsop adds: "The true, climactic, and successful effort of the Japanese peace advocates . . . did not begin in deadly earnest until *after* the second bomb had destroyed Nagasaki. The Nagasaki bomb was thus the trigger to all the developments that led to peace."

Joravsky, now a professor of history at Northwestern, argues on the other hand that those who decided to use the bomb on cities betray defects of "reason and self-restraint." It all needn't have happened, he asserts, "if the US government had been willing to take a few more days and to be a bit more thoughtful in opening the age of nuclear warfare." But of course in its view it wasn't doing that: that's a historian's tidy hindsight. The government was ending the war conclusively, as well as irrationally remembering Pearl Harbor with a vengeance. It didn't know then what everyone knows now about leukemia and carcinoma and birth defects. History, as Eliot's "Gerontion" notes,

> . . . has many cunning passages, contrived corridors
> And issues, deceives with whispering ambitions,
> Guides us by vanities. . . .
> Think
> Neither fear nor courage saves us.
>   Unnatural vices
> Are fathered by our heroism. Virtues
> Are forced upon us by our impudent crimes.

Understanding the past means feeling its pressure on your pulses and that's harder than Javorsky thinks.

The Alsop-Javorsky debate, which can be seen as reducing finally to a collision between experience and theory, was conducted with a certain civilized respect for evidence. Not so the way the new scurrilous agitprop *New Statesman* conceives those favoring the bomb and those opposing. They are, on the one hand, says Bruce Page, "the imperialist class-forces acting through Harry Truman," and, on the other, those representing "the humane, democratic virtues"—in short, "fascists" opposed to "populists." But ironically the bomb saved the lives not of any imperialists but only of the low and humble, the quintessentially democratic huddled masses—the conscripted enlisted men manning the fated invasion divisions. Bruce Page was nine years old when the war ended. For a man of that experience, phrases like "imperialist class-forces" come easily, and the issues look perfectly clear.

He's not the only one to have forgotten, if he ever knew, the savagery of the Pacific war. The dramatic postwar Japanese success at hustling and merchandising and tourism has (happily, in many ways) effaced for most people important elements of the assault context in which Hiroshima should be viewed. It is easy to forget what Japan was like before it was first destroyed and then humiliated, tamed, and constitutionalized by the West. "Implacable, treacherous, barbaric"— those were Admiral Halsey's characterizations of the enemy, and at the time few facing the Japanese would deny that they fit to a T. One remembers the captured American airmen locked for years in packing-crates, the prisoners decapitated, the gleeful use of bayonets on civilians. The degree to which Americans register shock and extraordinary shame about the Hiroshima bomb correlates closely with lack of information about the war.

And the savagery was not just on one side. There was much sadism and brutality—undeniably racist—on ours. No Marine was fully persuaded of his manly adequacy who didn't have a well-washed Japanese skull to caress and who didn't have a go at treating surrendering Japs as rifle targets. Herman Wouk remembers it correctly while analyzing Ensign Keith in *The Caine Mutuiny*: "Like most of the naval executioners of Kwajalein, he seemed to regard the enemy as a species of animal pest." And the enemy felt the same way about us: "From the grim and desperate taciturnity with which the Japanese died, they seemed on their side to believe they were contending with an invasion of large armed ants." Hiroshima seems to follow in natural sequence: "This obliviousness on both sides to the fact that the opponents were human beings may perhaps be cited as the key to the many massacres of the Pacific war." Since the Japanese resisted so madly, let's pour gasoline into their emplacements and light it and shoot the people afire who try to get out. Why not? Why not blow them all up? Why not, indeed, drop a new kind of big bomb on them? Why allow one more American high school kid to see his intestines blown out of his body and spread before him in the dirt while he screams when we can end the whole thing just like that?

On Okinawa, only weeks before Hiroshima, 123,000 Japanese and Americans *killed* each other. "Just awful" was the comment not of some pacifist but of MacArthur. One million American casualties was his estimate of the cost of the forthcoming invasion. And that invasion was not just a hypothetical threat, as some theorists have argued. It was genuinely in train, as I know because I was to be in it. When the bomb ended the war I was in the 45th Infantry Division, which had been through the European war to the degree that it had needed to be reconstituted two or three times. We were in a staging area near Reims, ready to be shipped across the United States for final preparation in the Philippines. My division was to take part in the invasion of Honshu in March 1946. (The earlier invasion of Kyushu was to be carried out by 700,000 infantry already in the Pacific.) I was a 21-year-old second lieutenant leading a rifle platoon. Although still officially in one piece, in the German war I had already been wounded in the leg and back severely enough to be adjudged, after the war, 40 percent disabled. But even if my legs buckled whenever I jumped out of the back of the truck, my condition was held to be satisfactory for whatever lay ahead. When the bombs dropped and news began to circulate that "Operation Olympic" would not, after all, take place, that we would not be obliged to run up the beaches near Tokyo assault-firing while being mortared and shelled, for all the fake manliness of our facades we cried with relief and joy. We were going to live. We were going to grow up to adulthood after all. When the *Enola Gay* dropped its package, "There were cheers," says John Toland, "over the intercom; it meant the end of the war."

Those who cried and cheered are very different from high-minded, guilt-ridden GIs we're told about by the late J. Glenn Gray in *The Warriors* (1959). During the war in Europe Gray was an interrogator in the Counter Intelligence Corps, and in that capacity he underwent the war at division level. After the war he became a professor of philosophy at Colorado College (never, I've thought, the venue of very much reality) and a distinguished editor of Heidegger. There's no doubt that Gray's outlook on everything was noble and elevated. But *The Warriors*, his meditation on modern soldiering, gives every sign of remoteness from experience. Division headquarters is miles behind the places where the soldiers experience terror and madness and relieve these pressures by sadism. "When the news of the atomic bombing of Hiroshima and Nagasaki came," Gray asks us to believe, "many an American soldier felt shocked and ashamed." But why, we ask? Because we'd bombed civilians? We'd been doing that for years and, besides the two bombs, wiped out 10,000 Japanese troops, not now often mentioned, John Hersey's kindly physicians and Jesuit priests being more touching. Were Gray's soldiers shocked and ashamed because we'd obliterated whole towns? We'd done that plenty of times. If at division headquarters some felt shocked and ashamed, down in the rifle companies none did, although Gray says they did:

> The combat soldier knew better than did Americans at home what those bombs meant in suffering and injustice. The man of conscience realized intuitively that the vast majority of Japanese in both cities were no more, if no less, guilty of the war than were his own parents, sisters, or brothers.

I find this canting nonsense: the purpose of dropping the bombs was not to "punish" people but to stop the war. To intensify the shame he insists we feel, Gray seems willing to fiddle the facts. The Hiroshima bomb, he says, was dropped "without any warning." But actually, two days before, 720,000 leaflets were dropped on the city urging everyone to get out and indicating that the place was going to be obliterated. Of course few left.

Experience whispers that the pity is not that we used the bomb to end the Japanese war but that it wasn't ready earlier to end the German one. If only it could have been rushed into production faster and dropped at the right moment on the Reich chancellery or Berchtesgaden or Hitler's military headquarters in East Prussia or—Wagnerian *coup de théâtre*—at Rommel's phony state funeral, most of the Nazi hierarchy could have been pulverized immediately, saving not just the embarrassment of the Nuremburg trials but the lives of about four million Jews, Poles, Slavs, gypsies, and other "subhumans," not to mention the lives and limbs of millions of Allied and Axis soldiers. If the bomb could have been ready even as late as July 1944, it could have reinforced the Von Stauffenberg plot and ended the war then and there. If the bomb had only been ready in time, the men of my infantry platoon would not have been killed and maimed.

All this is not to deny that like the Russian revolution, the atomic bombing of Japan was a vast historical tragedy, and every passing year magnifies the dilemma into which it has thrown the contemporary world. As with the Russian revolution there are two sides—that's why it's a tragedy rather than a disaster—and unless we are simple-mindedly cruel, like Bruce Page, we need to be painfully aware of both at once. To observe that from the viewpoint of the war's victims-to-be the bomb was precisely the right thing to drop is to purchase no immunity from horror. See, for example, the new book *Unforgettable Fire: Pictures Drawn by Atomic Bomb Survivors*, issued by the Japan Broadcasting Corporation and distributed here by Pantheon Books. It presents a number of amateur colored-pencil, pastel, and water-color depictions of the scene of the Hiroshima bombing made by the middle-aged and elderly survivors for a peace exhibition in 1975. In addition to the heartrending pictures the book offers brief moments of memoir, not for the weak-stomached:

> While taking my severely wounded wife out to the riverbank . . . , I was horrified indeed at the sight of a stark naked man standing in the rain with his eyeball in his palm. He looked to be in great pain but there was nothing that I could do for him. I wonder what became of him. Even today, I vividly remember the sight. It was simply miserable.

The drawings and paintings, whose often childish style makes them doubly touching, are of skin hanging down, breasts torn off, people bleeding and burning, dying mothers nursing dead babies. A bloody woman holds a bloody child in the ruins of a house, and the artist remembers her calling, "Please help this child! Someone, please help this child. Please help! Someone, please." As Samuel Johnson said of the smothering of the innocent Desdemona in another tragedy, "It is not to be endured." Nor, we should notice, is an infantryman's account of having his arm blown off in the Arno Valley in Italy in 1944:

> I wanted to die and die fast. I wanted to forget this miserable world. I cursed the war, I cursed the people who were responsible for it, I cursed God for putting me here . . . to suffer for something I never did or knew anything about. For this was hell, and I never imagined anything or anyone could suffer so bitterly. I screamed and cursed. Why? Why? What have I done to deserve this? But no answer came. I yelled for medics, because subconsciously I wanted to live. I tried to apply my

right hand over my bleeding stump, but I didn't have the strength to hold it. I looked to the left of me and saw the bloody mess that was once my left arm; its fingers and palm were turned upward, like a flower looking to the sun for its strength.

The future scholar-critic of rhetoric who writes *The History of Canting in the Twentieth Century* will find much to study in the utterances of those who dilate on the wickedness of the bomb-droppers. He will realize that such utterance can perform for the speaker a valuable double function. First, it can display the fineness of his moral weave. And second, by implication it can also inform the audience that during the war he was not socially so unfortunate as to find himself at the cutting edge of the ground forces, where he might have had to compromise the pure clarity of his moral vision by the experience of weighing his own life against other people's. Down there, which is where the other people were in the war, is the place where coarse self-interest is the rule. When the young soldier with the wild eyes comes at you firing, do you shoot him in the foot, hoping he'll be hurt badly enough to drop or mis-aim the gun with which he is going to kill you, or do you shoot him in the chest and make certain he stops being your mortal enemy? It would be stupid to expect soldiers to be very sensitive humanitarians ("Moderation in war is imbecility"—Admiral of the Fleet Lord Fisher); actually, only the barest decencies can be expected of them. They didn't start the war, except in the terrible sense hinted in Frederic Manning's observation based on his experience in the Great War: "War is waged by men; not by beasts, or by gods. It is a peculiarly human activity. To call it a crime against mankind is to miss at least half its significance; it is also the punishment of a crime." Knowing that fact by experience, soldiers have every motive for wanting a war stopped, by any means.

The predictable stupidity, parochialism, and greed in the postwar international mismanagement of the whole nuclear problem should not tempt us to mis-imagine the circumstances of the bomb's first "use." Nor should our well-justified fears and suspicions occasioned by the capture of the nuclear business by the mendacious classes (cf. Three Mile Island) tempt us to infer retrospectively extraordinary corruption, cruelty, and swinishness in those who decided to drop the bomb. Times change, Harry Truman was not a fascist, but a democrat. He was as close to a real egalitarian as we've seen in high office for a very long time. He is the only president in my lifetime who ever had the experience of commanding a small unit of ground troops obliged to kill people. He knew better than his subsequent critics what he was doing. The past, which as always did not know the future, acted in ways that ask to be imagined before they are condemned. Or even before they are simplified.

Appendix

1. The War Against Germany in the West, 1942-1945

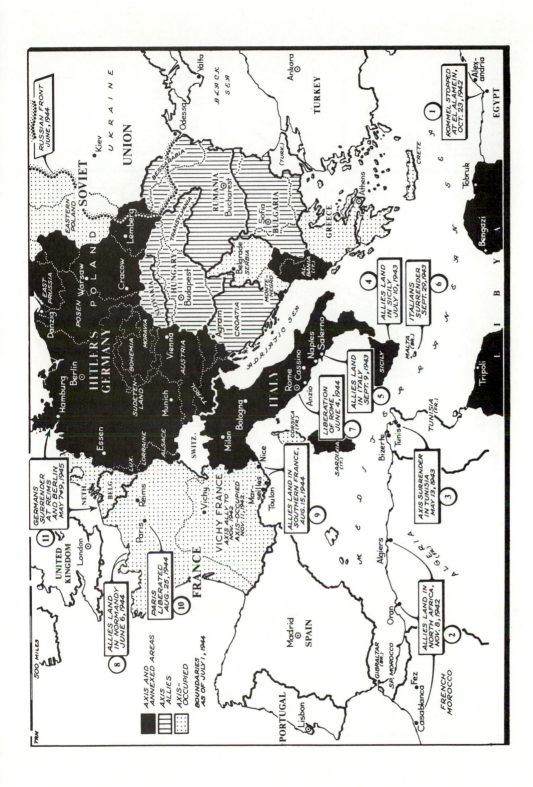

Source: Gaddis Smith, *American Diplomacy During the Second World War* (New York: Wiley, 1965), p. 23. Used with permission.

2. Japan: Conqueror and Conquered, 1931-1945

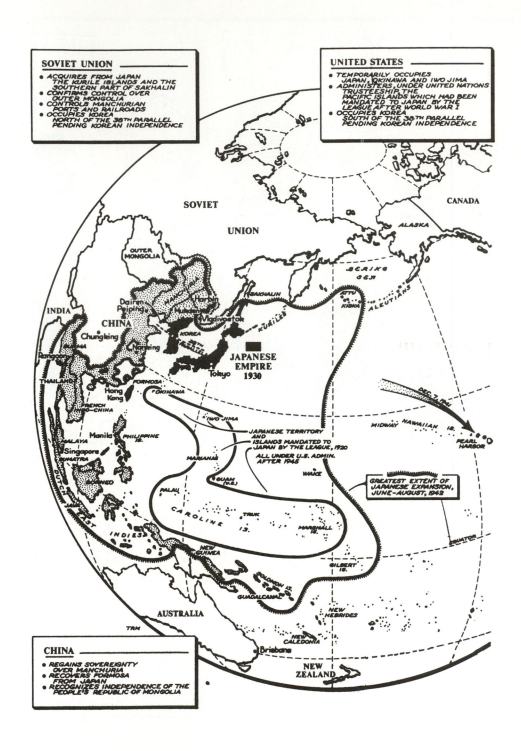

SOVIET UNION
- ACQUIRES FROM JAPAN THE KURILE ISLANDS AND THE SOUTHERN PART OF SAKHALIN
- CONFIRMS CONTROL OVER OUTER MONGOLIA
- CONTROLS MANCHURIAN PORTS AND RAILROADS
- OCCUPIES KOREA NORTH OF THE 38TH PARALLEL PENDING KOREAN INDEPENDENCE

UNITED STATES
- TEMPORARILY OCCUPIES JAPAN, OKINAWA AND IWO JIMA
- ADMINISTERS, UNDER UNITED NATIONS TRUSTEESHIP, THE PACIFIC ISLANDS WHICH HAD BEEN MANDATED TO JAPAN BY THE LEAGUE AFTER WORLD WAR I
- OCCUPIES KOREA SOUTH OF THE 38TH PARALLEL PENDING KOREAN INDEPENDENCE

CHINA
- REGAINS SOVEREIGNTY OVER MANCHURIA
- RECOVERS FORMOSA FROM JAPAN
- RECOGNIZES INDEPENDENCE OF THE PEOPLE'S REPUBLIC OF MONGOLIA

JAPANESE EMPIRE 1930

JAPANESE TERRITORY AND ISLANDS MANDATED TO JAPAN BY THE LEAGUE, 1920 ALL UNDER U.S. ADMIN. AFTER 1945

GREATEST EXTENT OF JAPANESE EXPANSION, JUNE-AUGUST, 1942

Source: Gaddis Smith, *American Diplomacy During the Second World War* (New York: Wiley, 1965), p. 159. Used with permission.

3. The Final Stages of the War in the Pacific

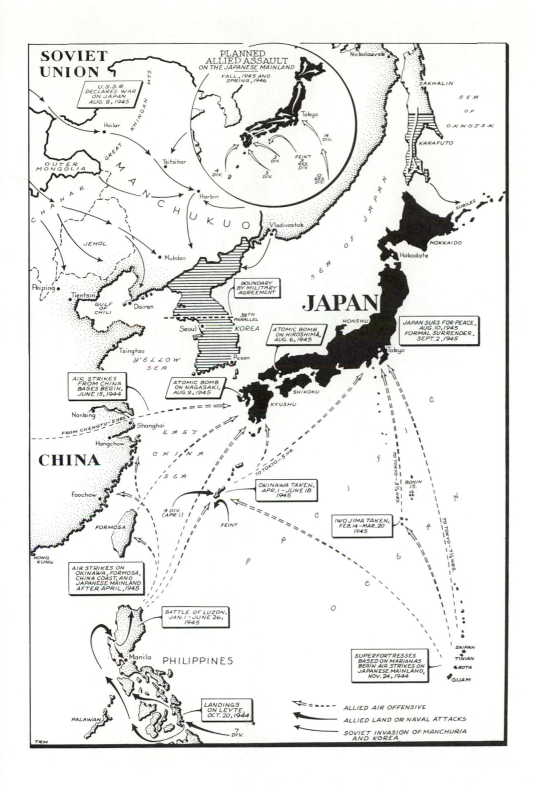

Source: Frank Freidel et al., *American History*, 2d ed. (New York: Knopf, 1966), p. 838. Used with permission.

4. Hiroshima at Bombing Time (with key)

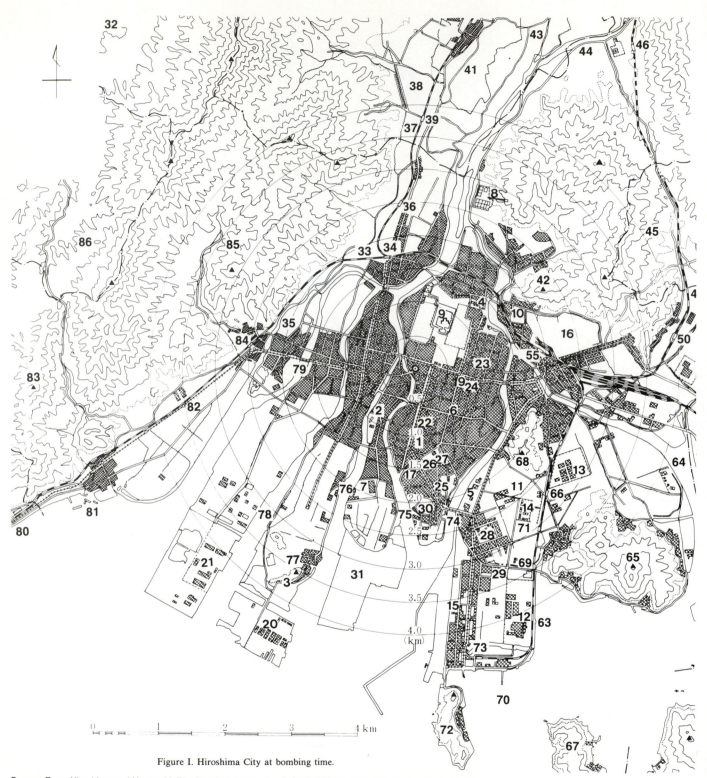

Figure I. Hiroshima City at bombing time.

Source: From *Hiroshima and Nagasaki: The Physical, Medical, and Social Effects of the Atomic Bombings*, by The Committee for the Compilation of Materials on Damage Caused by the Atomic Bombs in Hiroshima and Nagasaki. Translated by Eisei Ishikawa and David L. Swain. Copyright © 1981 by Hiroshima City and Nagasaki City. Reprinted by permission of Basic Books, Inc., Publishers, New York.

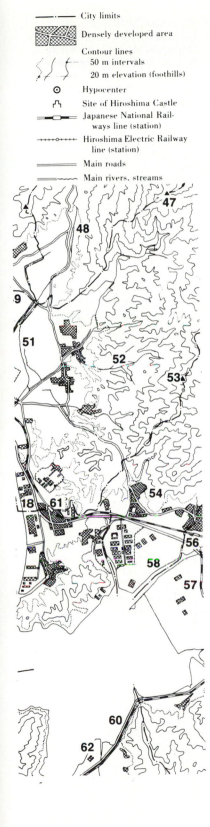

Legend:

- City limits
- Densely developed area
- Contour lines
  - 50 m intervals
  - 20 m elevation (foothills)
- ☉ Hypocenter
- Site of Hiroshima Castle
- Japanese National Railways line (station)
- Hiroshima Electric Railway line (station)
- Main roads
- Main rivers, streams

1. Hiroshima City Office
2. Hiroshima Prefectural Office
3. Hiroshima District Meteorological Observatory
4. Hiroshima Communications Bureau
5. Hiroshima District Monopoly Bureau
6. Hiroshima District Court/Court of Appeal
7. Hiroshima Prison
8. Hiroshima Municipal Filtration Plant
9. Chūgoku Regional Military Headquarters
10. Second Army Headquarters
11. Army Marine Communications Regiment
12. Army Marine Training Division
13. Hiroshima Army Ordnance Supply Depot
14. Hiroshima Army Clothing Depot
15. Hiroshima Army Provisions Depot
16. Eastern Drill Ground
17. Hiroshima Red Cross Hospital
18. Tōyō Kōgyō Co., Ltd.
19. Fukuya Department Store
20. Mitsubishi Heavy Industries Hiroshima Shipyard
21. Mitsubishi Heavy Industries Hiroshima Machine Tool Works
22. Chūgoku Power Distribution Company
23. Hiroshima Central Broadcasting Station (NHK-Hiroshima)
24. Chūgoku Shinbun News Publishing Company
25. Hiroshima Electric Railway Company
26. Hiroshima University of Literature and Science
27. Hiroshima Higher Normal School
28. Hiroshima Higher School
29. Hiroshima Prefectural Women's College
30. Hiroshima Technical College
31. Army Air Field
32. Numata Town
33. Sanyō Main Line
34. Yokogawa Station
35. Yamate River
36. Mitaki Station
37. Kabe Railway Line
38. Gion Town
39. Aki-Nagatsuki Station
40. Shimo-Gion Station
41. Yasu River
42. Mt. Futaba
43. Furu River
44. Ota River
45. Nakayama Village
46. Hesaka Station
47. Mt. Takao
48. Nukushina Village
49. Geibi Railway Line
50. Yaga Station
51. Nukushina River
52. Fuchū Town
53. Mt. Chausu
54. Funakoshi Town
55. Hiroshima Station
56. Kaitaichi Station
57. Kaitaichi Town
58. Seno River
59. Yano Town
60. Kure Railway Line
61. Mukainada Station
62. Saka Town
63. Ujina Railway Line
64. Enkō River
65. Mt. Ogon
66. Kami-Ōkō Station
67. Kanawajima Island
68. Hijiyama Hill
69. Tanna Station
70. Ujina Port
71. Shimo-Ōkō Station
72. Ujina Island
73. Ujina Station
74. Kyōbashi River
75. Motoyasu River
76. Honkawa River
77. Eba Hill
78. Tenma River
79. Fukushima River
80. Inokuchi Village
81. Kusatsu Harbor
82. Miyajima Streetcar Line
83. Mt. Onigajō
84. Koi Station
85. Mt. Chausu
86. Ishiuchi Village

5. Nagasaki at Bombing Time (with key)

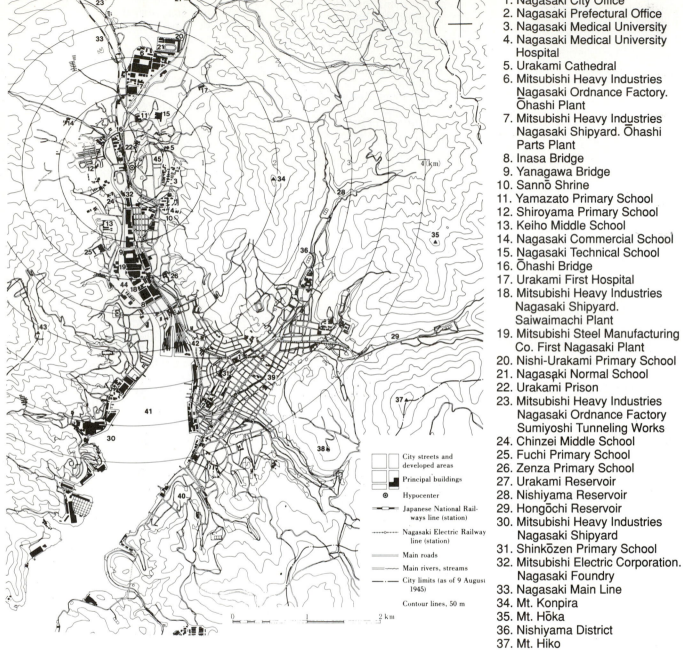

1. Nagasaki City Office
2. Nagasaki Prefectural Office
3. Nagasaki Medical University
4. Nagasaki Medical University Hospital
5. Urakami Cathedral
6. Mitsubishi Heavy Industries Nagasaki Ordnance Factory. Ōhashi Plant
7. Mitsubishi Heavy Industries Nagasaki Shipyard. Ōhashi Parts Plant
8. Inasa Bridge
9. Yanagawa Bridge
10. Sannō Shrine
11. Yamazato Primary School
12. Shiroyama Primary School
13. Keiho Middle School
14. Nagasaki Commercial School
15. Nagasaki Technical School
16. Ōhashi Bridge
17. Urakami First Hospital
18. Mitsubishi Heavy Industries Nagasaki Shipyard. Saiwaimachi Plant
19. Mitsubishi Steel Manufacturing Co. First Nagasaki Plant
20. Nishi-Urakami Primary School
21. Nagasaki Normal School
22. Urakami Prison
23. Mitsubishi Heavy Industries Nagasaki Ordnance Factory Sumiyoshi Tunneling Works
24. Chinzei Middle School
25. Fuchi Primary School
26. Zenza Primary School
27. Urakami Reservoir
28. Nishiyama Reservoir
29. Hongōchi Reservoir
30. Mitsubishi Heavy Industries Nagasaki Shipyard
31. Shinkōzen Primary School
32. Mitsubishi Electric Corporation. Nagasaki Foundry
33. Nagasaki Main Line
34. Mt. Konpira
35. Mt. Hōka
36. Nishiyama District
37. Mt. Hiko
38. Mt. Atago
39. Nakashima River
40. Ōura District
41. Nagasaki Port
42. Nagasaki Station
43. Mt. Inasa
44. Urakami River
45. Urakami District

Source: From *Hiroshima and Nagasaki: The Physical, Medical, and Social Effects of the Atomic Bombings,* by The Committee for the Compilation of Materials on Damage Caused by the Atomic Bombs in Hiroshima and Nagasaki. Translated by Eisei Ishikawa and David L. Swain. Copyright © 1981 by Hiroshima City and Nagasaki City. Reprinted by permission of Basic Books, Inc., Publishers, New York.

6. Bombed and Related Areas Affected by the Atomic Bombing of Hiroshima

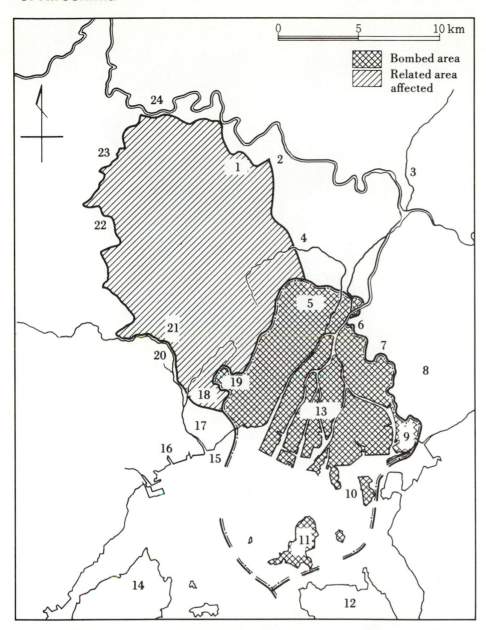

Bombed and related areas affected by the atomic bombing of Hiroshima (Hiroshima Shiyakusho, A-bomb Survivors Measures Department).

1. Kuchi
2. Kegi
3. Kabe Town
4. Chōrakuji
5. Gion Town
6. Hesaka Village
7. Nakayama Village
8. Fuchū Town

9. Mukainada
10. Kanawajima Island
11. Ninoshima Island
12. Etajima Island
13. Hiroshima City
14. Itsukushima Island
15. Yahata River
16. Itsukaichi Town

17. Inokuchi Village
18. Toshimatsu
19. Yamada
20. Nakagō
21. Uokiri
22. Ege
23. Yanagare
24. Usa

Source: From *Hiroshima and Nagasaki: The Physical, Medical, and Social Effects of the Atomic Bombings*, by The Committee for the Compilation of Materials on Damage Caused by the Atomic Bombs in Hiroshima and Nagasaki. Translated by Eisei Ishikawa and David L. Swain. Copyright © 1981 by Hiroshima City and Nagasaki City. Reprinted by permission of Basic Books, Inc., Publishers, New York.

7. Bombed and Related Areas Affected by the Atomic Bombing of Nagasaki

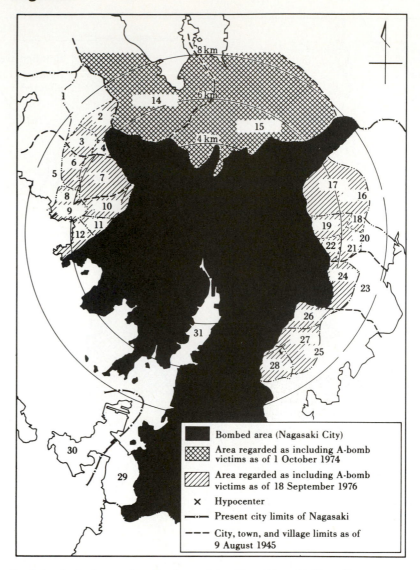

Bombed area (Nagasaki City)

Area regarded as including A-bomb victims as of 1 October 1974

Area regarded as including A-bomb victims as of 18 September 1976

× Hypocenter

—·— Present city limits of Nagasaki

——— City, town, and village limits as of 9 August 1945

Bombed and related areas affected by the atomic bombing of Nagasaki (Nagasaki Shiyakusho, A-bomb Survivors Measures Department 1978, p. 21).

Place names*
1. Mie Village
2. Tōnokoba
3. Tsumenouchi
4. Shiraga
5. Shikimi Village
6. Makino
7. Koba
8. Mukai
9. Teguma

10. Kamiura
11. Nakaura
12. Kakidomari
13. Fukuda Village
14. Togitsu Village
15. Nagayo Village
16. Yagami Village
17. Utsutsugawa
18. Satsumajiro
19. Tanokōchi

20. Tanaka
21. Nakao
22. Yahazu
23. Himi Village
24. Kawachi
25. Mogi Town
26. Tadewara
27. Koba
28. Tagami
29. Fukahori Village
30. Kōyagi Village
31. Nagasaki Port

*Place names are those in use as of August 9, 1945.

Source: From *Hiroshima and Nagasaki: The Physical, Medical, and Social Effects of the Atomic Bombings*, by The Committee for the Compilation of Materials on Damage Caused by the Atomic Bombs in Hiroshima and Nagasaki. Translated by Eisei Ishikawa and David L. Swain. Copyright © 1981 by Hiroshima City and Nagasaki City. Reprinted by permission of Basic Books, Inc., Publishers, New York.

Selective Bibliography of Secondary Literature

Alperovitz, Gar. *Atomic Diplomacy: Hiroshima and Potsdam*, rev. ed. (New York: Penguin, 1985).

Barker, Rodney, *The Hiroshima Maidens* (New York: Viking, 1985).

Bernstein, Barton (ed.). *The Atomic Bomb: The Critical Issues* (Boston: Little, Brown, 1976).

Boyer, Paul. *By the Bomb's Early Light: American Thought and Culture at the Dawn of the Atomic Age* (New York: Pantheon, 1986).

Butow, R. J. C. *Japan's Decision to Surrender* (Stanford, Calif.: Stanford, 1954).

Committee for the Compilation of Materials on the Damage Caused by the Atomic Bombs in Hiroshima and Nagasaki. *Hiroshima and Nagasaki: The Physical, Medical, and Social Effects of the Atomic Bombings* (New York: Basic Books, 1981).

Dallek, Robert. *Franklin D. Roosevelt and American Foreign Policy, 1932–1945* (New York: Oxford, 1979).

Davis, Nuel P. *Lawrence and Oppenheimer* (New York: Simon and Schuster, 1968).

Feis, Herbert. *The Atomic Bomb and the End of World War II*, rev. ed. (Princeton, N.J.: Princeton, 1966).

_____. *Between War and Peace: The Potsdam Conference*, rev. ed. (Westport, Conn.: Greenwood, 1983).

Gowing, Margaret. *Britain and Atomic Energy, 1939–1945* (New York: St. Martin's, 1964).

Groueff, Stephane. *Manhattan Project: The Untold Story of the Making of the Atomic Bomb* (Boston: Little, Brown, 1967).

Herken, Gregg. *Counsels of War* (New York: Knopf, 1985).

_____. *The Winning Weapon: The Atomic Bomb in the Cold War, 1945–1950* (Santa Rosa, Calif.: Vintage, 1981).

Hersey, John. *Hiroshima, with a New Postscript* (New York: Knopf, 1985).

Hewlett, Richard G., and Oscar E. Anderson. *A History of the Atomic Energy Commission, 1939/1946*, vol. I, *The New World* (University Park, Penn.: University of Pennsylvania Press, 1962).

Iriye, Akira. *Power and Culture: The Japanese-American War, 1941–1945* (Cambridge, Mass.: Harvard, 1982).

Irving, David. *The German Atomic Bomb* (New York: Simon and Schuster, 1968).

Jungk, Robert. *Brighter Than a Thousand Suns: A Personal History of the Atomic Scientists* (New York: HarBrace J., 1970).

Kurzman, Dan. *The Day of the Bomb: Countdown to Hiroshima* (New York: McGraw-Hill, 1985).

Lifton, Robert J. *Life in Death: The Survivors of Hiroshima* (New York: Random House, 1967).

Lytle, Mark H. "The Decision to Drop the Atomic Bomb," in James W. Davidson and Mark H. Lytle, *After the Fact: The Art of Historical Detection*, 2d ed. (New York: Knopf, 1986).

Mee, Charles L., Jr. *Meeting at Potsdam* (New York: M Evans, 1975).

Morton, Louis. "The Decision to Use the Atomic Bomb," in Kent Roberts Greenfield (ed.), *Command Decisions*, (Washington: U.S. Army, 1960).

Osada, Arata. *Children of the A-Bomb* (New York: Putnam, 1963).

Oughterson, Ashley W., and Shields Warren. *Medical Effects of the Atomic Bomb in Japan* (New York: McGraw-Hill, 1956).

Pacific War Research Society Staff. *Japan's Longest Day* (New York: Ballantine, 1972).

Publishing Committee for Children of Hiroshima. *Children of Hiroshima* (Boston: Oelgeschlager, 1981).

Radosh, Ronald, and Joyce Milton. *The Rosenberg File: A Search for the Truth* (New York: Random, 1984).

Rhodes, Richard. *The Making of the Atomic Bomb* (New York: Simon and Schuster, 1987).

Rose, Lisle A. *The Coming of the American Age, 1945–1946*, vol. 1, *Dubious Victory, the United States and the End of World War II* (Kent, Ohio: Kent State, 1973).

Rosenblatt, Roger. *Witness: The World Since Hiroshima* (Boston: Little, Brown, 1985).

Sherwin, Martin J. *A World Destroyed: The Atomic Bomb and the Grand Alliance* (New York: Random, 1977).

Smith, Alice Kimball. *A Peril and a Hope: The Scientists' Movement in America, 1945–1947*, rev. ed. (Boston: MIT, 1971).

Spector, Ronald H. *Eagle Against the Sun: The American War with Japan* (New York: Random, 1985).

Toland, John. *Rising Sun: The Decline and Fall of the Japanese Empire: 1936–1945* (New York: Random, 1970).

Wyden, Peter. *Day One: Before Hiroshima and After* (New York: S&S, 1984).

Questions

Part 1

Document(s)

1   **1.** Why did the renowned physicist Albert Einstein recommend the construction of an atomic bomb?

2   **2.** What action did President Roosevelt take?

3   **3.** Why do you suppose that it took nearly three years to get the project off the ground? (Consider what other matters between 1939 and 1942 might have required attention from the Roosevelt administration, and consider, as well, possible doubts about the feasibility of the project.)

3   **4.** What sorts of firms and institutions were brought into the project, and how do they reflect an emerging "military-industrial complex"?

4   **5.** To whom did Roosevelt delegate the project, and why was he concerned with secrecy?

5   **6.** According to Winston Churchill, what agreement had he reached with Roosevelt over cooperation on the bomb project? Should we trust his memory?

7   **7.** How did J. Robert Oppenheimer become involved in the project? Why was Los Alamos chosen as a suitable site for the primary laboratory? What was the nature of the security arrangements, and how did they affect those working there? How might security procedures hamper scientific work?

8   **8.** On what grounds was information to be exchanged between the British and Americans? Among Americans themselves? Why? Why did the British object to this procedure?

9   **9.** According to Churchill, why did Roosevelt decide to share information?

10 and   **10.** Harry Truman, as chairman of a special Senate committee
18–20   investigating war contracts, was responsible for examining many government expenditures during the war. How did Secretary Stimson respond to Truman's inquiries regarding the bomb-project plant at Pasco, Washington? In your view, should Truman have been informed of the nature of the project?

12–14   **11.** What agreement did the British and Americans finally come to concerning cooperation on the project? What do their arguments reveal about the supposed harmony of the Anglo-American wartime alliance? Why were the British worried about Russia, at the time an ally in the fight against Germany?

15–16   **12.** What was the nature of the labor problems at Berkeley? Why were they considered dangerous, and how were they resolved? What does that resolution indicate about the rights and power of labor during war?

17   **13.** Why were leaders in the House of Representatives finally informed of the project (consider where appropriations bills must originate), and what was their reaction?

21–22   **14.** Why was the antitrust suit against Dupont and the Imperial Chemical Company suspended? What does that action suggest about the effect of the war on government relations with industry?

23   **15.** What was the Declaration of Trust, and how did it help to improve relations between Great Britain and the United States?

Part 2

Document(s)

24–25 and 27   **1.** Why, according to Frankfurter, were the Russians bound to learn about the project? Why does Frankfurter's "Danish friend" (Niels Bohr) consider it important to make an official disclosure immediately to the Russians? What is Roosevelt's reaction to Bohr? Why might the United States want to keep knowledge of the project from its Russian allies during the war?

26   **2.** Why did Roosevelt and Churchill reject informing the "world" of work on the bomb (recall that Bohr had only mentioned informing the Russians)? What do they conclude about using the bomb against Japan? About continued British-American cooperation on Tube Alloys?

28–29   **3.** What were Roosevelt's thoughts, as communicated to Bush, on using the bomb against Japan? What were Roosevelt's hopes for an Anglo-American atomic alliance after the war?

30   **4.** What did Conant and Bush conclude about the future international handling of atomic bombs? Why did they come to that conclusion? (Consider especially their estimate of when other nations might begin to prepare bombs.)

31   **5.** What was Stimson's position on informing the Russians as of December 1944, on the eve of Roosevelt's summit at Yalta with Stalin and Churchill? What did Roosevelt think?

33   **6.** Why was James F. Byrnes concerned about the cost of the project?

35	**7.** Why did Churchill insist on secrecy, even with respect to allies such as France and Russia?
14,23,26, 28–29	**8.** By the time of Roosevelt's death in mid-April 1945, what, if anything, had he decided about the following issues: (1) wartime and postwar atomic cooperation with the British? with the Russians? and (2) use of the bomb against Japan? To what courses of action had he *officially* committed the United States in these matters?

Part 3

Document(s)

37–38	**1.** How did the new President, Harry Truman, learn about the atomic-bomb project? Why was Stimson so concerned about future control of the weapon? What will the select committee consider?
39	**2.** What were the primary targets as recommended by the Target Committee in May 1945? What factors did the committee take into account?
40	**3.** Why did Stimson refer to the bomb as his "master card" at the upcoming summit of Truman, Churchill, and Stalin at Potsdam, Germany? (Note his remark about "quid pro quo" in Document 31.)
41	**4.** According to Stimson's opening statement, what issues was the Interim Committee supposed to examine? With reference to problems of international control (which are discussed in Parts 5, 6, and 7), why did scientists A. H. Compton and J. Robert Oppenheimer favor sharing American knowledge of the bomb? Why were civilian and military leaders such as James Byrnes, George Marshall, and Henry Stimson skeptical about sharing knowledge with the Russians? What does such an attitude suggest about the Russian-American wartime alliance and the possibilities for general cooperation between the two nations after the war?
41	**5.** What did the Interim Committee decide about using the bomb against Japan? Did the committee give "mature consideration" (see Document 26) at this first meeting to *whether* to drop the bomb on Japan, or was this a foregone conclusion?
41	**6.** Why was the Scientific Panel called in?
43	**7.** According to A. H. Compton, when did the issue of a warning to Japan in the form of a demonstration of the bomb arise? What was the reaction? Why did the Scientific Panel reject this course?

44   **8.** At the June 1, 1945, meeting of the Interim Committee, how was the decision to use the bomb against Japan made? Was there any discussion or dissent? What did the Interim Committee conclude in this matter?

45   **9.** During Stimson's meeting with Truman on June 6, 1945, what conclusion did they reach about informing Russia? What "quid pro quos" might they seek at the July meeting of the Big Three (Truman, Stalin, and Churchill) to be held at Potsdam? Why was this meeting postponed by Truman?

47   **10.** What problems did the policy of "unconditional surrender" pose? Why did Stimson seek to avoid using that phrase?

Part 4

Document(s)
48–49   **1.** What was the nature of the "Political and Social Problems" identified by members of the Chicago "Metallurgical Laboratory"? According to Compton, what considerations were *not* mentioned in the Franck Report? Why consider them important?

49   **2.** What was the purpose of the Franck Report? In Franck's view, what were the dangers presented by atomic weapons? What were the prospects for an agreement over such weapons, and how would dropping the bomb on Japan without a demonstration endanger those prospects? Why did Franck and his colleagues urge consideration of long-range policy rather than current military necessity?

51   **3.** What were the conclusions of the Scientific Advisory Panel, and why did Oppenheimer and his colleagues reject the Franck approach?

52–53   **4.** When was the invasion of the Japanese home islands, beginning with Kyushu, to take place? What were the projected casualties for the first thirty days of fighting on this first of four Japanese islands? What was the projected military effect of Russian entry into the war against Japan?

54   **5.** What did the Interim Committee recommend on June 21, 1945, regarding informing the Russians of the bomb and using the weapon against Japan?

56   **6.** What did Under Secretary of the Navy Ralph A. Bard recommend with respect to the use of the bomb against Japan? How did his position differ from that of the Interim Committee?

58   **7.** What was the position of Secretary Stimson as to the invasion and occupation of Japan? What sort of warning did he contemplate giving Japan? In his scenario, what role would the bomb play? Did he intend to offer the Japanese any reassurances that in your view violated the Allied policy of *unconditional* surrender?

59   **8.** How, finally, did Truman, with Stimson's advice, decide to tell the Russians about the bomb?

62   **9.** What did Leo Szilard and other dissenting scientists ask in their petition to the President? Does their view conform to the Franck Report (Document 49)?

61   **10.** What was the view of the scientists polled by Farrington Daniels? What do you think was meant by "a military demonstration in Japan"?

63   **11.** What did the Combined Intelligence Committee conclude about probable Japanese political and military strategies? How might their conclusion about "intermittent peace feelers" affect Allied responses to those feelers? What did the committee conclude about Japanese fear of losing the institution of the Emperor?

Part 5

Document(s)

67   **1.** Why did Stimson believe that mid-July 1945 was the proper moment to commence warnings to Japan? From his memo to Truman, what can you conclude about the nature of those warnings? What was Stimson's attitude toward Russian participation in the occupation of Japan after the war? Why was Stimson concerned about the Russians?

68   **2.** Note the ironic way in which Groves describes the successful testing of the bomb, and note Farrell's reference to the test as a "birth." What were the reactions of Groves and his colleagues? What, in Groves's view, remained to be done?

69   **3.** While in Germany at the Potsdam summit, Stimson discusses with his two aides, Harvey Bundy and John McCloy, relations with the Russians. What, in his opinion, was the primary problem with the Russian system? How was the development of the atomic bomb bringing the problem "to a focus"?

70   **4.** While President Truman and his advisers were conferring with the Allies in Potsdam, Germany, the Interim Committee continued to meet. What did the Interim Committee con-

clude about postwar management of atomic energy at its July 19 meeting? What themes and procedures from the wartime administration of the Manhattan Project will continue into the postwar period?

71   **5.** How did Truman react to Groves's report (delivered by Stimson) of the successful test of the atomic bomb? What effect did that news seem to have on Truman during the Potsdam negotiations? Why might the successful test have fortified Truman in dealing with the Russians?

72   **6.** In Stimson's opinion, what was the basic problem of the future and from what did it arise? How would the bomb ("X") play a role in solving this problem? How and why had Stimson's thinking about the effect on the Russians of offering to share the bomb changed from his earlier views (see Documents 31 and 45)?

73   **7.** How did the United States respond to Russian demands for new territory during the Potsdam summit? How did the atomic bomb influence that response? Why were the Americans no longer as interested as they had been earlier in having the Russians enter the war against Japan? Why was Stimson interested in allowing the Japanese to retain the institution of the Emperor, even though it would violate the Allied policy of unconditional surrender? Did Truman agree —and why? Why was Kyoto dropped from the target list? What does that suggest about American projections for the shape of the postwar world?

74   **8.** The Potsdam Declaration represented Allied terms of surrender. What were those terms? Was there any mention of the Emperor and his fate? Of the atomic bomb? Why?

75   **9.** According to Secretary of the Navy James Forrestal, why was Secretary of State James Byrnes "anxious to get the Japanese affair over with"?

Part 6

Document(s)

76   **1.** At Potsdam, according to Truman's Memoirs, how did he inform Stalin of the atomic bomb? (Was it ever mentioned by name?) What was Stalin's reaction? Why didn't Truman offer his Russian allies more information? By when did Truman expect the defeat of Japan to be accomplished through invasion of the home islands? At what cost in American lives? Did Truman offer any explanation for not having included any reference to retaining the Emperor in the Pots-

dam Declaration? Why did Truman order the bombs to be dropped? Were there other reasons than those he offers?

78   **2.** What effects did the Hiroshima bombing have on those who survived?

80   **3.** When did the Soviet Union declare war on Japan? Do you think the bombing of Hiroshima influenced the timing of the declaration, even though it came three months after the end of hostilities in Europe (in other words, just about the time the Russians had promised at the Yalta conference to enter the Asian war)?

82–83   **4.** What effect did the dropping of the atomic bombs have on thinking about the future size of the Army? According to Stimon's memorandum for the press, why were the bombs dropped?

85   **5.** What was the initial Japanese response to the bombing of Hiroshima, as transmitted through the Swiss Legation on August 11, 1945? Is the comparison to the use of poison gas valid? Why might it have taken the Japanese so long to condemn the bombing? (Consider here the problems of communication and reconnaissance in a city devastated by an atomic attack and in a nation reeling from conventional bombings of other cities.)

87   **6.** What were the Japanese terms for their surrender? How did the American Secretary of State respond, particularly to Japanese demands for retention of the Emperor? By making the authority of the Emperor subject to the Supreme Commander of the Allied powers, didn't the Allies implicitly accept retention of the Emperor? Why did Secretary of State Byrnes agree to this demand, violating thus the policy of unconditional surrender?

Part 7

Document(s)

89   **1.** What was Oppenheimer's assessment of future prospects for the development of even more powerful atomic weapons? How optimistic was he over prospects for peace based on weapons alone? Do you agree with his evaluation?

90   **2.** According to George L. Harrison, what was the opinion of newly appointed Secretary of State Byrnes regarding continued development of atomic weapons? Why do you think Byrnes rejected the idea of an international agreement? (Consider Byrnes's past attitudes, especially toward the Russians.)

91   **3.** How do you account for the results of the public opinion polls reprinted here, especially regarding attitudes on the use of the atomic bomb and the use of poison gas?

92   **4.** Why was General Groves concerned about reports from Tokyo of severe burns afflicting many victims of the atomic bombings? Why did he conclude that these were thermal rather than radiation burns and that Japanese authorities were engaging in propaganda? What did this telephone conversation suggest about American foreknowledge of the effects of atomic bombing?

93   **5.** What was Stimson's attitude toward sharing atomic secrets with the Russians? Trace the changes in his attitude, and explain why he came to the position he took in September 1945? In what ways does this new point of view resemble the arguments made by dissenting scientists in Part 4?

94   **6.** According to the U.S. Strategic Bombing Survey, what effect did the atomic bombs have on the Japanese decision to surrender? What effect did the Russian declaration of war have? On what information are these conclusions made? What do the Survey's observations suggest about the difficulties facing a nation when it attempts to "declare" peace? In view of such considerations, should the United States have dropped any atomic bombs, only one, or both? Was there any reason not to drop the bombs *at the time the decision was made*?

95   **7.** What does Paul Fussell conclude about the bombing of Hiroshima? Nagasaki? Why does he reach the conclusion he has? Do you agree? If so, why?